For Mary

with much love,
Celia
October 1990

A NATION OF PROVINCIALS

A Nation of Provincials

The German Idea of Heimat

CELIA APPLEGATE

UNIVERSITY OF CALIFORNIA PRESS

Berkeley   Los Angeles   Oxford

University of California Press
Berkeley and Los Angeles, California
University of California Press, Ltd.
Oxford, England
© 1990 by
The Regents of the University of California

Library of Congress Cataloging-in-Publication Data
Applegate, Celia.
  A nation of provincials : the German idea of Heimat / Celia Applegate.
    p.   cm.
  Includes bibliographical references.
  ISBN 0-520-06394-5 (alk. paper)
    1. Ethnicity—Germany (West)—Palatinate.   2. Ethnology—Germany
(West)—Palatinate.   3. Palatinate (Germany)—Ethnic relations.
I. Title.   II. Title: Heimat.
DD801.P448A67   1990
943'.435004—dc20   89-20522
                                                          CIP

Printed in the United States of America
1   2   3   4   5   6   7   8   9

To the memory of my grandparents
Earl and Lena Applegate
John and Virginia Strait

Contents

Preface

Consciousness of national belonging is one of the most striking and least understood of modern phenomena. The modern nation asserts its legitimacy in many ways, but most strikingly in the willingness of its members to believe in it, to identify with it, and even to die for it. Our continuing fascination with national character—our own and that of others—further attests not so much to the reality of the nation as to our seemingly unbreakable attachment to the national category. Yet a disjunction persists between national claims and national realities, between the enormity of the influence of the national idea in the world today and the arbitrariness of national identities themselves. In the study that follows, I explore the implications of one aspect of that disjunction: the capacity of borders themselves to take on cultural meaning that transcends their political or economic purposes.

The nation in question is Germany. The border in question is one Germany shares with France. The people in question lived in one small corner of the nation, in the midst of almost continuous disputes over the location and the significance of the border. Their capacity nevertheless to shape and to maintain a coherent national identity that incorporated the peculiarities of their local experience is the precise subject of this study. I base this study on what people said and did about their collective identity: form clubs, write books, speeches, and poems, take journeys around their province, and investigate its past. I take into account the political interests expressed, as well as the social and political changes reflected in such activities. But the people's identity itself remains my primary concern throughout.

Although the peculiarities of the Germans, especially in their incarnation as Pfälzers, necessarily claim our attention here, the theme I seek to illuminate transcends the shifting borders of any one nation. That theme is the struggle of people continually to renew the communities they have formed, not just at the level of political arrangements, but at the level of symbolic depictions as well. In this study, the focus for an examination of such community renewal is the concept of *Heimat*, home or homeland, the evolution of which I follow through a century and a half of profound change in the pragmatic bases of one community, the Rhenish Pfalz. Heimat came to express a "feeling of belonging together" (in German, the *Zusammengehörigkeitsgefühl*), whether across class, confessional, or gender lines, or across the lines that divided the province from the nation surrounding it. In the end, Heimat teaches us as much about the durability of the communitarian impulse as about the multiplicity, and the tenuousness, of its forms.

I would like to thank the institutions and foundations that have supported this work in its successive stages. Fellowships from the Beinecke Memorial Foundation and the Stanford University Graduate School of Arts and Sciences supported me at several stages in the United States. A Fulbright-Hays Doctoral Fellowship and additional support granted by the Social Science Research Council and the American Council of Learned Societies made possible my research in the Federal Republic of Germany. A Charlotte W. Newcombe Fellowship granted by the Woodrow Wilson National Fellowship Foundation supported the first stage of writing. Along the way, the Gertrude M. Slaughter Fellowship of Bryn Mawr College and supplementary grants from the David M. Harris and Weter funds of Stanford University have also assisted me. To the trustees and administrators of these various awards I am deeply grateful.

The staffs of the Pfälzische Landesbibliothek and the Pfälzische Landesarchiv in Speyer and of the Bayerische Hauptstaatsarchiv in Munich helped me in West Germany. Professor Karl Otmar Freiherr von Aretin and the staff at the Institut für Europäische Geschichte in Mainz offered me the resources of their library and their knowledge. Professor Konrad Fuchs at the Universität Mainz kindly lent his assistance at several stages during my stay in Germany; two of his students, Hannes and Waltraud Ziegler, introduced me to some of the finer pleasures of the Pfälzer landscape.

I owe my first and greatest thanks to my mentors at Stanford University, Paul Robinson and James Sheehan. David Blackbourn, Mack Walker, Carl Degler, Bruce Schulman, Nelly Hoyt, Klemens von Klemperer, Lee Wandel, and Larry Winnie have also been generous with their wisdom and encouragement. I am grateful to all those involved with the book at the University of California Press for having seen it safely through to publication. My parents, James and Joan Applegate, have nourished my aspirations and

my interests through their own. Stewart Weaver is responsible for many pronouns having proper antecedents and many nouns having proper pronouns,
for many a well-constructed parallelism and many a felicitous turn of phrase,
and, above all, for many a word never making it into the final draft. It seems
almost ungrateful to construct an inelegant sentence in his praise, but, after
all, stylistic correction was the least of his contributions.

ONE

Heimat
and German Identity

This is a study of how a geographical border shaped the lives and loyalties of a group of modern Germans. The border winds along the Rhine River south from Worms almost to Karlsruhe, veers west through the low mountains of Alsace, edges around the Saarland and French Lorraine, then circles east across the southern edge of the old Prussian Rhineland to meet the river again. With the exception of the Rhine, there is no obvious topographical logic to the border, and the innocent traveler could easily pass from Mainz, outside the border, to Speyer, inside it, without noticing any change in the nature of the landscape, the cultivation of the land, or, least of all, the character of the people. Yet in the course of the nineteenth century the border, created as a minor addendum to the territorial settlements of 1815, acquired a cultural resonance that, at least for Germans, gave the journey between these two similar Rhenish cities an entirely new meaning. By 1871 the German traveler would have passed across the border into a place he recognized as the Pfalz and to people he called Pfälzers.[1]

By 1871, the Pfalz represented a definite place on the map of Germany, and its people held an increasingly articulated sense of their own distinctiveness, to which a growing collection of local literature and local associations attested. Their self-conscious regional identity began in the mid–nineteenth century, flourished at the turn of the century, and survived, taking on new purposes and meanings, in the wars, occupations, and political upheavals of

---

1. This study uses the terms *Pfalz* and *Pfälzer* throughout rather than the cumbersome though perhaps more familiar English translations *Palatinate* and *Palatine*.

1

The Rhenish Pfalz in the nineteenth century (hollow squares indicate castles).
Inset: Germany in 1871.

the twentieth century. The historical significance of such doggedly narrow loyalties remains, however, obscure. The persistence of Pfälzer identity—or, for that matter, Bavarian, Saxon, Berliner, or Pomeranian identity—long after the achievement of German nationhood is a fact more likely to find its way into travel than scholarly literature; it bespeaks quaintness rather than conflict, nostalgic backwardness rather than modernity. It is possibly charming and certainly irrelevant. Yet the growth and survival of Pfälzer consciousness raise a number of intriguing questions about the nature of what is often dismissingly called provincialism and, by extension, about the nature of nationalism and national identity, which provincialism is assumed to oppose. For the case of the loyal Pfälzers has at its heart the much-discussed case of Germanness itself: where it came from, what constituted it, what held it together, what were its consequences. In the course of taking on the smaller case, this study is intended to illuminate the larger one, even if not, Holmes-like, providing any unexpected solutions.

In measuring the historical significance of persistent regional identities in Germany, one must note from the outset that those who held on to such identities were, with a few exceptions, not conscious of doing or being anything remarkable. They understood their regionally directed activities, if they thought about them at all, as a private enjoyment, comparable to a hobby, and as a public service—a civic-minded contribution to the health of the community. They wrote small historical articles; they collected objects, customs, and words; they organized local festivals and staged local celebrations; they marked out nature trails, picked up litter, and raised observation towers on the tops of mountains. Ranging from the practical to the sentimental and taking in a bewildering array of ephemera along the way, these efforts nevertheless constituted a single body of activity and knowledge for most Germans. Pulling these efforts together and bestowing on them both coherence and purpose was the word *Heimat*. In its simplest sense, *Heimat* means home or homeland; in the context of these activities, it referred above all to the Pfalz. The Pfalz was the homeland; the Pfalz was Heimat. Out of *Heimatliebe*, the Pfälzer undertook *Heimatpflege* and thought *Heimatgedanken*. During his life, he might call himself a *Heimatkundler* or simply a *Heimatler*, and after his death his obituary would praise him for having truly loved his Heimat.[2]

---

2. As a rule, these German words have no direct counterparts in English, which is precisely why they make a subject for historical study. *Heimatliebe* is, of course, love for one's homeland. *Heimatpflege* is a term with medical and civic connotations that refers to any and all activities that "care for" the Heimat: it harks back to the *Stadtpfleger*, a leading political position in the early modern constitutions of independent German cities. A *Heimatkundler* or a *Heimatler* was someone who engaged in activities that promoted the Heimat, either investigating its history, preserving its folklore, or boasting of its natural beauties. Finally, the use of the masculine *he* is in this case mostly conventional: many Heimat activists, though by no means the majority, were women.

But to conclude that the "meaning" of all these activities and attitudes is to be found in the "meaning" of Heimat would be far too simple. For the term *Heimat* carries a burden of reference and implication that is not adequately conveyed by the translation homeland or hometown. For almost two centuries, Heimat has been at the center of a German moral—and by extension political—discourse about place, belonging, and identity. Unfortunately, the very ordinariness of the contexts in which the word crops up has obscured the range and richness of what Heimat can tell us about the "peculiarities of German history."

Rescued from archaic German in the late eighteenth century, the word gathered political and emotional resonance in scattered legal reforms and popular literary invention of the Biedermeier period. In the second half of the nineteenth century, Heimat identified the diverse and mostly local efforts (like those of the Pfälzers) to appreciate provincial cultures and, simultaneously, to celebrate German nationhood. During the war, it served the Germans in the same way that the term *home front* served the English. By the 1920s and 1930s, a profoundly incompatible group of republican activists, conservative nationalists, and German racialists competed for control of Heimat. But their struggle over Heimat did not end (as did, for example, the struggle over the term *Gemeinschaft*) with Nazi seizure and irreversible corruption. Instead, in both East and West Germany, the general cultural discussion about Heimat has continued since the fall of the Third Reich.[3] Heimat has played a major role in the state-sponsored efforts to reestablish German society on a new but firm moral basis, particularly in the realm of civic and political education. The question of a legal "right" to a Heimat has also been at the center of discussions and accusations between the Federal Republic and the postwar states of the Soviet bloc. On the level of popular culture, Heimat has been the theme of so many films, novels, sentimental songs, and earnest radio and television talk shows (and, most recently, an immensely popular television series) that it would be impossible to imagine postwar German culture, particularly of a certain milieu, without it.[4]

The term *Heimat*, one could argue, has entered into so many different discussions in such diverse areas of German society that it would be a great mistake to search for a solitary meaning, a single truth beyond all the white noise. And yet the ubiquity of the term and the deep emotionality of its appeal have proven irresistible temptations to interpreters in search of an essence for which Heimat is the expression. Their results have not always been enlightening. In a Hessen radio discussion in 1970, for instance,

3. Günther Lange's *Heimat—Realität und Aufgabe. Zur marxistischen Auffassung des Heimatbegriffs* (Berlin, 1973) provides an East German Marxist perspective on the discussion in both East and West Germany.

4. One out of every five films made in the Bundesrepublik between 1947 and 1960 was a Heimat film. See the study by Willi Höfig, *Der deutsche Heimatfilm 1947–1960* (Stuttgart, 1973).

Heinrich Böll, Günther Grass, and Norbert Blüm, among others, debated whether Heimat referred to "something lost" and "only available to the memory" or to any place where one was settled and familiar. The discussion ended, not untypically, with Blüm defending the environmental and housing policies of the Christian Democratic Union (CDU) against the attacks of both Böll and Grass.[5]

The scholars have been, if anything, less enlightening than the writers and politicians. Sociologists and social psychologists have explained Heimat as a basic human need, comparable to eating or sleeping, "to be known, to be recognized, and to be accepted."[6] They have asked the literal question "What is Heimat?" and have answered, with a confusing series of examples and exceptions, that Heimat is where one is born, where one receives an education, comes to consciousness of selfhood, adjusts oneself to family and society, or constructs a "social entity."[7] Political scientists have also spoken of Heimat in terms of natural human tendencies, in particular tendencies to form political allegiances, whether on the local or the national level.[8] But to discuss Heimat as the human condition is to illuminate that condition, not the term itself. Ina-Maria Greverus, herself a leading proponent of the idea of Heimat as an expression of "territorial man," notes that books about Heimat usually resort to discussions of Heimat *and* or *as* something else: Heimat and speech, Heimat and nation; Heimat as family, as community, as tradition, as natural surroundings. Heimat, she suggests, represents a synthesis "which perhaps only the poets can grasp."[9]

What poets know and what scholars often forget is that words themselves are slippery, infinitely malleable, capable of saying many things. Instead of generating more definitions for a word that has collected so many, this study will investigate the history of the word itself, which in the case of Heimat

5. Alexander Mitscherlich and Gert Kalow, eds., *Hauptworte-Hauptsachen. Zwei Gespräche: Heimat, Nation* (Munich, 1971), pp. 14–20. Blüm is today the CDU minister of labor; then he was only a member of the CDU leadership when Helmut Kohl seemed far from the chancellorship.

6. Wilhelm Brepohl, "Heimat und Heimatgesinnung als soziologische Begriffe und Wirklichkeiten," in *Das Recht auf die Heimat. Vorträge, Thesen, Kritik*, ed. Kurt Rabl (Munich, 1965), p. 48; the German words are *kennen, erkennen*, and *anerkennen*. See also Wilhelm Brepohl, "Die Heimat als Beziehungsfeld: Entwurf einer soziologischen Theorie der Heimat," *Soziale Welt* 4 (1952–53): 12–22; Heiner Treinen, "Symbolische Ortsbezogenheit: Eine soziologische Untersuchung zum Heimatproblem," *Kölner Zeitschrift für Soziologie und Sozialpsychologie* 17 (1965): 73–97, 254–97; Ina-Maria Greverus, *Der Territoriale Mensch. Ein literatur-anthropologisches Versuch zum Heimatphänomen* (Frankfurt, 1972); and Ina-Maria Greverus, *Auf der Suche nach Heimat* (Munich, 1979).

7. Brepohl, "Heimat und Heimatgesinnung," p. 43; and Klaus Weigelt, "Heimat—Der Ort personaler Identitätsfindung und sozio-politischer Orientierung," in *Heimat und Nation. Zur Geschichte und Identität der Deutschen*, ed. Klaus Weigelt (Mainz, 1984), p. 15.

8. See the contributions to Weigelt, *Heimat und Nation*; and Werner Weidenfeld, *Die Identität der Deutschen* (Munich, 1984).

9. Greverus, *Territoriale Mensch*, p. 31.

means the history of a certain way of talking and thinking about German society and Germanness. Heimat has the resonance of what Raymond Williams called a "key word."[10] Comparable to his words *industry, democracy, class, art,* and, above all, *culture, Heimat* came into its current usage at a certain juncture in German history and has remained in both an everyday and a more formally argumentative vocabulary ever since. Out of the interplay between change and constancy in its meaning there emerges what Williams called a map to wider changes in the society and to broader movements of opinion. Heimat suggests a long-standing though not always explicit debate in German society about the proper relation between the locality and the nation, the particular and the general, the many and the one.

The significance of Heimat, then, lies not only within the borders of the Pfalz and within the self-regard of the Pfälzers, although those overlapping realms of experience will have pride of place in the chapters that follow. Heimat's claim to the status of a key word in German history goes beyond the particularities of regionality and the generalities of nationality to rest finally on what both region and nation have in common: the effort, for better or for worse, to maintain "community" against the economic, political, and cultural forces that would scatter it. To put the problem in such a way is immediately to suggest the relevance of the celebrated distinction between *Gesellschaft* and *Gemeinschaft,* posited by Ferdinand Tönnies at just about the time when Heimat enthusiasm was at its peak. As Tönnies eventually came to assert, these two terms identified not two stages in a unilinear and dichotomizing historical development, in which all historical actors became either modernizers or reactionaries, but rather two poles between which all forms of human association could fluctuate.[11] Similarly, the adventures and misadventures of the idea of Heimat over the past century and a half of German history reveal at the very least the profoundly uneven course that "modernization" has taken, and possibly the inappropriateness of the concept altogether. The ironies that have characterized one culture's experience of modernity will thus form a subtext of the story that follows. The Pfälzers' effort to maintain the commonality invoked by the idea of Heimat can tell us much about both the dangers and the value of a communalist vision of the good life.

10. Raymond Williams, *Culture and Society: 1780–1950* (New York, 1966), p. xi; see also his *Keywords,* rev. ed. (Oxford, 1983). Heimat is not included in the closest thing in German to Williams's *Keywords,* the *Geschichtliche Grundbegriffe,* ed. Otto Brunner, Werner Conze, and Reinhart Koselleck (Stuttgart, 1972).

11. See especially W. J. Cahnmann's introduction to *Ferdinand Tönnies: A New Evaluation,* ed. W. J. Cahnmann (Leiden, 1973); and Dan S. White, "Tönnies Revisited: Community in Imperial Germany," paper delivered at the Conference of the New York State Association of European Historians, Niagara University, September 1989.

The word *Heimat* has ancient German roots, according to Jacob and Wilhelm Grimm, and has been identifiably present in various German dialects since the fifteenth century.[12] But as late as the eighteenth century the small elite of writers and publicists who were the self-appointed representatives of the German language used the word infrequently and certainly without particular significance. As part of a broad effort in the 1780s to restore ancient and neglected words to the language, early Romantic writers recommended the adoption of *Heimat* and began to incorporate it into their vocabulary. One, Karl Phillip Moritz, wrote that this "venerable expression" joined with the word *Vaterland* to suggest an image of "homey tranquillity and happiness . . . which is contained in the lovely sound of the German word *heim*."[13]

Several features of this rebirth of a word are noteworthy for the light they shed on Heimat's role in subsequent German history. The first thing one notes is that the actors in this linguistic drama were people of a particular sort. They were writers preoccupied with the idea of the German language as the expression of the German people and as the promise of a German nation. Their German language was not that in everyday use in the small towns and the countryside. Rather, it was a language conscious of its audience, a public language for the growing body of Germans who identified with change, who looked to the future, and who for the most part pictured the future in terms of a single nation and state.

The second and closely related feature of this rebirth is its timing. *Heimat* reentered the language at a moment when the political structure of the German states was disintegrating. "In the beginning was Napoleon," wrote Thomas Nipperdey in his history of nineteenth-century Germany, and so it was also for the idea of Heimat.[14] Under the influence of the overwhelming fact of Napoleonic power, the delicate stasis which the Holy Roman Empire had maintained among the many political constitutions of central Europe dissolved. Particularly the larger states were left to find a way to deal not only with Napoleon but also with the baffling diversity of their own internal structures. The ensuing confrontation between the reforming, centralizing, rationalizing representatives of a so-called General Estate and the community-bound people of the hometowns is the proper context in which to understand the evolution of the term *Heimat*.[15] *Heimat* took on much of its modern connotation in the General Estate's attempt to understand and to reshape the German locality. In common with words like *Nation, Staat, Volk,*

12. Jakob Grimm and Wilhelm Grimm, *Deutsches Wörterbuch*, vol. 4, pt. 2 (Leipzig, 1877), pp. 864–66.

13. Friedrich Maurer and Friedrich Stroh, *Deutsche Wortgeschichte*, vol. 2 (Berlin, 1959), p. 294.

14. Thomas Nipperdey, *Deutsche Geschichte 1800–1866. Bürgerwelt und starker Staat* (Munich, 1983), p. 11.

15. This discussion draws on the political sociology Mack Walker developed in *German Home Towns: Community, State, and General Estate, 1648–1871* (Ithaca, N.Y., 1971).

and *Vaterland*, whose historicity is well recognized, *Heimat* participated in the development over the next fifty years of the vocabulary of German public, bourgeois life.[16]

To be sure, Heimat does not seem to be about this public sphere, this *Öffentlichkeit* of liberal hopes. It brings to mind instead the restricted and secure society of a childhood memory; the very word would seem to emanate from, as well as refer to, the society of the hometown burgher, the unabashedly local German. But *Heimat* is not, I think, a word like *Eigentum*, which described a quality of place and identity genuinely characteristic of the home-townsmen.[17] It represents the modern imagining and, consequently, re-making of the hometown, not the hometown's own deeply rooted historical reality. It is a term that dwelt in one world, that of the self-conscious centralizers, modernizers, and nationalists of the General Estate, while evoking another. The Heimat of Moritz and others like him was an invention and a mythology—nostalgic and sentimental, but also potentially useful.

A mixture of practicality and sentimentality became the distinguishing feature of Heimat and characterized even the first tentative treatments of the Heimat theme in the early nineteenth century. A few examples will make this clear. The *Heimatrecht* (law of domicile) of the 1820s formed part of an administrative effort to make the definition of citizenship uniform and all-inclusive. In Bavaria, where these liberal statutes passed in 1825 along with new regulations on civil marriage, inheritance settlements, and trade free-doms, Heimat bespoke a right to dwell in a place and "invoke its aid in case of impoverishment"; moreover, any Bavarian subject could under these laws "stay and work in any Bavarian town he liked, provided he stayed within the law and supported himself."[18]

This use of the term *Heimat* represented more than a "novel breadth" to an essentially old term.[19] The Bavarian administrators were substituting a new principle of state citizenship for the old practice of community control over who belonged and who did not. That so familiar and innocuous a term as *Heimatrecht* should have embodied this principle reveals an important moment, not just in the confrontation between bureaucrats and hometownsmen, but in the discussion within the progressive bureaucracy on the role of localities in a greater state. Heimat represented a thoroughly flexible concept by which the state could reproduce itself at the local level of civic experience characteristic of most people's lives. Heimat, claimed a Bavarian administrator in his presentation of the new Heimatrecht to the Landtag, was "the

16. For a discussion of the historical aspect of some of these terms, see James J. Sheehan, *German Liberalism in the Nineteenth Century* (Chicago, 1978), part 1.

17. Walker, *German Home Towns*, pp. 2–3.

18. Ibid., p. 296.

19. Ibid.

cradle of complex and beautiful relations and sensibilities from which the sense of cooperation for common ends develops . . . [the] nursery of civic virtues and order, whose foundation and whose cultivation shall be regulated by this law."[20]

Such a Heimat was not the genuine hometown, in which the idea of civic virtue had been wholly inner-directed, implying little about service to a greater state. The genuine hometown, moreover, was regulated by anything but law, if we take law to mean, as this speaker does, a codified and written body of statutes. The Heimat of these 1825 statutes was an administrative fiction, whose essential modernity became over the next century more and more obscured by the deceptive antiquity of the word and perhaps more importantly by the demise of the real hometown. Rotteck's *Staatslexikon* of 1839, inventory of the liberal program, mentioned the old rights of communities as the original Heimatrecht but then proceeded to identify contemporary Heimatrecht not with hometown autonomy at all, but rather with state administrative laws like those of 1825 in Bavaria.[21] To be sure, uses of the term were often ambiguous and contradictory. But the trend favored the state, not the hometown, and the fate of Heimat, the seat of "civic virtue and order," was bound up with the state.

In the literature of the mid–nineteenth century, the Heimat theme expressed similar contradictions. The Heimat of numerous novels and poems about the countryside and village life was an idyll of local communities, close family harmony, and a domesticated, friendly nature.[22] In the works of writers like Auerbach and Immermann, Gotthelf and Storm, Heimat stood in opposition to the city; it was the seat of folk customs and speech, the place where the old ways were remembered and preserved. And yet in several important respects this Heimat was not the hometown, the sealed, exclusively local society that was still present on the German political landscape; these writers' Heimat was instead a nostalgic construction that reproduced the localness of hometown life without preserving its qualities of isolation and independence. This Heimat contrasted to a *Fremde* or *Ferne* of late romantic adventurers in strange lands. It was the place to which one finally returned: the homeland.[23]

20. Emil Riedel, *Commentar zum bayerischen Gesetze über Heimat, Verehelichung und Aufenthalt vom 16 April 1868* (Nördlingen, 1868), p. 26; cited in ibid.

21. Carl von Rotteck and Carl Welcker, *Staats-Lexikon oder Enzyklopädie der Staatswissenschaften*, vol. 7 (Altona, 1839), p. 665.

22. Erika Jenny, "Die Heimatkunstbewegung" (diss., Universität Basel, 1934), pp. 13–15; Leonore Dieck, "Die literargeschichtliche Stellung der Heimatkunst" (diss., Universität München, 1938), p. 10. See also Norbert Mecklenburg, *Erzählte Provinz. Regionalismus und Moderne im Roman* (Königstein/Taunus, 1982); and Greverus, *Territoriale Mensch*.

23. Maurer and Stroh, *Wortgeschichte* 2:392; Helmut Schelsky, "Heimat und Fremde: Die Flüchtlingsfamilie," *Kölner Zeitschrift Für Soziologie und Sozialpsychologie* 3 (1950–51): 163.

Writers like Auerbach and Gotthelf tried, furthermore, to use the "individual stories" and "differentiated natures" of the localities to illuminate what was true of Germans and Germanness in general.[24] Even as they depicted the villages, their subject was Germany—and perhaps just as important, their audience was German, or at least considered itself so. The reading public made Auerbach a phenomenal success.[25] To speak of a reading public is to speak, however tentatively, of newspaper subscriptions, publishing and bookselling businesses, voluntary associations, and other phenomena of an emergent bourgeois public society.[26] And although the contours of that bourgeois world would change dramatically in the last half of the nineteenth century and in the twentieth, the idea of Heimat would change with it, surviving long after the real hometown had ceased to have any place in the constitution of the German nation.

In both law and literature, then, the utility of Heimat lay in its capacity to obscure any chasms between small local worlds and the larger ones to which the locality belonged. The Heimatrecht theorizers denied the political chasm; the Romantic writers of village tales denied the emotional one. The Heimat they described, legislated, or memorialized was a creation, not less invented for being tinged with nostalgia for a past that never was or, if it was, bore little relation to their Heimat. Like most "traditions" of dubious antiquity, the modern idea of the Heimat originated in a period of rapid social transformation.[27] It tried to make sensible at least small pieces of that changing society, brushing them with a false patina of fixedness and familiarity. Those who created and promoted Heimat, consciously or not, were suggesting a basic affinity between the new, abstract political units and one's home,

24. Jenny, "Heimatkunstbewegung," p. 19.

25. Dieck, "Literargeschichtliche Stellung der Heimatkunst," p. 10; Jenny, "Heimatkunstbewegung," pp. 14–15.

26. For perspectives on the reading public and its relation to bourgeois society, see Sheehan, *German Liberalism*; David Blackbourn, "The Discreet Charm of the Bourgeoisie: Reappraising German History in the Nineteenth Century," in David Blackbourn and Geoff Eley, *The Peculiarities of German History* (New York, 1984); Rainer S. Elkar, *Junges Deutschland in polemischen Zeitalter. Das schleswig-holsteinische Bildungsbürgertum in der ersten Hälfte des 19. Jahrhunderts* (Düsseldorf, 1979), esp. chaps. 1 and 3; and Günter Wiegelmann, ed., *Kultureller Wandel im 19. Jahrhundert* (Göttingen, 1973), esp. introductory essays by Rudolf Braun and Hermann Bausinger. The by-now classic text on the emergence of the "public" is Jürgen Habermas's *Strukturwandel der Öffentlichkeit* (Neuwied, 1962), although Habermas's public sphere of rational discourse is already impinged upon and undermined by the emergence of a mass public.

27. See Eric Hobsbawm and Terence Ranger, eds., *The Invention of Tradition* (Cambridge, 1983), especially the introduction by Eric Hobsbawm. Heimat ideas fall into Hobsbawm's first and most common variety of invented traditions, "those establishing or symbolizing social cohesion or the membership in groups, real or artificial communities" (p. 9). See also several of the essays in Hermann Bausinger and Konrad Köstlin, eds., *Heimat und Identität. Probleme regionaler Kultur* (Neumünster, 1980).

thus endowing an entity like Germany with the emotional accessibility of a world known to one's own five senses.

In reality, of course, Heimat's nostalgic evocation of a closed and close-knit community reflected its replacement by these larger and less personal forms of political and territorial belonging. Heimat's depiction of the small town as a "cradle" of the greater political unity both eased the transition and defined an entirely new, more malleable kind of localness. The idea of Heimat potentially embraced all of Germany, from its individual parts to its newly constituted whole. It offered Germans a way to reconcile a heritage of localized political traditions with the ideal of a single, transcendent national-ity. Heimat was both the beloved local places and the beloved nation; it was a comfortably flexible and inclusive homeland, embracing all localities alike.

Nevertheless, the usefulness of a word like *Heimat* becomes fully apparent only when one considers the requirements for national integration after the formal unification of Germany under Prussian leadership in 1871. That Heimat—with its dubious historicity and remarkable imprecision—should speak at all to the problem of German nationhood needs some explanation. Recent wisdom has for the most part turned away from such cultural phe-nomena, suggesting that German nationhood was less the final stage of the unfolding and maturing of an idea, as Friedrich Meinecke magisterially revealed it, than the creation of measurable processes of economic trans-formation and administrative, educational, and political communication.[28] Nationalism, by extension, was not the natural expression of a deep cultural communion but the psychological reflection of real social and economic bonds. The growth of nationalism represented another victory of base over superstructure: increasingly complex networks of social interchange in a given territory produced a revolution in the minds of men and women. Feel-ings of belonging together in a nation thus followed from the actual ex-perience of being together—in trade, in educational institutions, in the imaginary world created by the supralocal press.[29]

The value of this anti-idealist perspective for illuminating the social his-tory of German nationalism is clearly great. From its beginnings within a core group of supporters to its diffusion throughout wide circles of the

28. See, e.g., Robert Berdahl, "New Thoughts on German Nationalism," *American Historical Review* 77 (1972): 65–80; Eric Hobsbawm, "Some Reflections on Nationalism," in *Imagination and Precision in the Social Sciences*, ed. T. J. Nossiter, S. Rokkan, and A. H. Hanson (London, 1972), pp. 385–406; and Geoff Eley, "Nationalism and Social History," *Social History* 6 (1981): 83–107. The theoretical innovator in this approach was Karl Deutsch in his *Nationalism and Social Com-munication* (Cambridge, Mass., 1966). Two of the most important efforts to apply Deutsch's ideas, though neither deals with Germany, are Eugen Weber, *Peasants into Frenchmen: The Mod-ernization of Rural France, 1870–1914* (Stanford, 1976); and Miroslav Hroch, *Social Preconditions of National Revival in Europe*, trans. Ben Fowkes (Cambridge, 1985).

29. For fascinating speculation on the importance of this last factor, see Benedict Anderson, *Imagined Communities: Reflections on the Origin and Spread of Nationalism* (London, 1983).

bourgeoisie, German national consciousness could not have spread without networks of railroads and rivers, printing presses and postal offices, academic halls, associational meeting rooms, and army training posts. By 1871, local communities had at least lost their physical and political isolation. And although the new Reich was an administrative monstrosity, haphazardly combining elements of federalism and central control in an imperfect reflection of the diversity of inner-German relations, it made the presumptive nationness of Germany into a tangible reality. It was responsible, moreover, for the further assertion of the national presence through national schooling, national military service, national currency, and, not least of all, national monuments.[30]

Ironically, the problem with the anti-idealist perspective is that it has paid scant attention to the feeling of national belonging itself, concentrating instead on the forces that produced it. As a consequence, it still requires us to make a grand leap of assumption from the workings of "social communication" to the existence, and persistence, of national identity. By linking national feeling to the forward march of modern social forms, the anti-idealism of modernization theory obscures the phenomenological difference between an individual's material existence and an individual's interpretation of that existence. Calling oneself a German may, in other words, have nothing to do with how often one reads a particular newspaper; calling oneself a German may not preclude hanging on to any number of other self-interpretations. The trouble with seeing national consciousness as a necessary concomitant of political and economic modernization is that one comes to believe that a certain rationality and progressivism ought to characterize national feeling—and when they do not, one blames the nationalists for their barbarism. Perhaps more important, one becomes dulled to the tremendous flexibility and ambiguity of the national idea itself. The unique characteristics of a national identity—its peculiar capacity to create a general identity that is nevertheless exclusive, its recently coined antiquity, its philosophical superficiality—all remain inexplicable without a serious effort at the interpretation of culture.[31] If, as seems to be the case in most European countries, national belonging had become the dominant type of social and cultural identification by the late nineteenth century, we need to find out why and how it appealed to so many, under such diverse circumstances. We need to understand how national belonging was fit into a structure of social and cultural identities, some of which already existed and some of which evolved alongside the new nationalism.

The idea of Heimat can provide some answers to these questions. The

30. Thomas Nipperdey, "Nationalidee und Nationaldenkmal in Deutschland im 19. Jahrhundert," *Historische Zeitschrift* 206 (1968): 529–85.

31. These are Benedict Anderson's suggestions for what makes nationalism so peculiar as ideology; see *Imagined Communities*, pp. 14–15.

presence of such a word as *Heimat* in the German language of nationhood is not, as some have mistakenly thought, a sign of malaise in the German political culture—whether the malaise be characterized as the political submissiveness of privatism or the antimodern philistinism of particularism.[32] The Heimat consciousness and Heimat institutions that developed over the course of the nineteenth century were characterized neither by withdrawal from public affairs nor by resistance to membership in larger political communities. Rather, the increasing, widening uses of Heimat, especially after 1871, reveal how the idea of the nation settled into people's minds. The evolution of Heimat as a concept followed the shifting hierarchies of belonging, from hometown to territorial state to nation. In many German regions, the revived interest in local history, customs, and dialects and the proliferation of songs and lyrical writings on the qualities of the locale—all of which came under the rubric of *Heimatbestrebungen*, or Heimat endeavors—created a new mythology about the region's contribution to German nationhood. Many revived or newly invented festivals further provided opportunities to celebrate publicly the nation and the region together.[33] Identification with the nation did not, in other words, require that all peasants, hometownsmen, and other unregenerate localists shed themselves of their premodern burden of provincial culture. Nationalism could embrace their smaller worlds; Germanness could encompass their diversity.

National integration, to return to where this discussion began, thus presents itself not simply as a problem of power and regulation but, as Theodor Schieder has put it, as a "question of consciousness."[34] For the incomplete nation of 1871, the invented traditions of the Heimat bridged the gap between national aspiration and provincial reality. These efforts might be called federalist, in the sense that Heimat enthusiasts celebrated German diversity. They supported national cohesion without necessarily showing any enthusiasm for its symbols or for its agents, Prussia and the national government.[35] Nor was such enthusiasm for Prussian culture required of Germans: Bismarck himself was opposed to what he saw as French-style (hence un-German) centralization, preferring to "absorb . . . German indi-

32. These interpretive tendencies, characteristic especially of works that seek to explore the German "mind," are evident throughout Hermann Glaser's *The Cultural Roots of National Socialism (Spiesser-Ideologie)*, trans. Ernest Menze (Austin, Tex., 1978); in the first three chapters of George Mosse's *The Crisis of German Ideology: Intellectual Origins of the Third Reich* (New York, 1964); and in the introduction to Fritz Stern's *The Politics of Cultural Despair* (Berkeley and Los Angeles, 1961).

33. For a study of how local festivals and folksongs were adapted to the new Swiss federal state of the nineteenth century, see Rudolf Braun, *Sozialer und kultureller Wandel in einem ländlichen Industriegebiet im 19. und 20. Jahrhundert* (Erlenbach/Zürich, 1965), esp. chap. 6.

34. Theodor Schieder, *Das deutsche Kaiserreich von 1871 als Nationalstaat* (Cologne, 1961), p. 9.

35. Thomas Nipperdey's "Nationalidee und Nationaldenkmal" mentions some regional differences in the building of Bismarck towers; that discussion might profitably be expanded.

vidualities without nullifying them."[36] Federalism and regionalism have long been recognized as important though distinct concepts in understanding the particular nature of the German national state.[37] It should then come as no surprise to learn that regional allegiances continued to play an important role in the national feeling of Germans and that regional and national loyalties could be compatible and mutually reinforcing.[38] Finally, the postunification career of Heimat can cast light on what Mack Walker once described as the German conundrum: how to have a nation that would be like a hometown.[39] For Walker, this conundrum, this quest for a true *Volksgemeinschaft* (popular or national community), lay at the heart of the German problem; after 1871, nostalgia for a hometown community that had never really existed made philistines out of ordinary folk and reactionaries out of intellectuals. Nazism, with its overheated rhetoric of national community, was the terrible but unsurprising fulfillment of this fatal nostalgia.

But the conundrum is perhaps better appreciated as the desire to have *both* community and nation, not the latter masquerading as the former. This certainly is what Theodor Fontane, a Brandenburger, seemed to be saying in 1853: "Now let me again breathe freely / The air of the Fatherland. . . / He in his deepest heart is true / Who loves his Heimat as do you"; or Christian Mehlis, a Pfälzer, in 1877: "Love for the Fatherland is rooted in the love and knowledge of the Heimat"; or Christian Frank, a Bavarian, in 1927: "In the Heimat lies the unity of the Germans"; and Georg Schnath, a Saxon, in 1958: "A good friend to his Heimat will always be a good citizen of the state."[40]

36. Cited in Hans A. Schmitt, "From Sovereign States to Prussian Provinces: Hanover and Hesse-Nassau, 1866–1871," *Journal of Modern History* 57 (March 1985): 41; see also pp. 55–56.

37. See especially Karl Möckl, "Föderalismus und Regionalismus im Europa des 19. and 20. Jahrhunderts," in *Von der freien Gemeinde zum föderalistischen Europa* (Berlin, 1983), pp. 529–49; Heinz Gollwitzer, "Die politische Landschaft in der deutschen Geschichte des 19./20. Jahrhunderts: Eine Skizze zum deutschen Regionalismus," *Zeitschrift für bayerische Landesgeschichte* 27 (1964): 523–52; Karl-Georg Faber, "Was ist eine Geschichtslandschaft?" in *Geschichtliche Landeskunde: Festschrift für Ludwig Petry* (Wiesbaden, 1968), pp. 1–28; and Dietrich Gerhard, "Regionalismus und ständisches Wesen als ein Grundthema europäischer Geschichte," *Historische Zeitschrift* 174 (1952): 307–37.

38. Jürgen Habermas, in his introduction to *Observations on "The Spiritual Situation of the Age,"* trans. Andrew Buchwalter (Cambridge, Mass., 1984), wrote that "given the background of German history, the concept of the nation preserves ties to regionally rooted folk cultures more strongly than is the case with older nation-states, even more so than in Italy" (p. 17). Eric Hobsbawm, speculating on the nature of nations, asserted that large nations could accept local differences and that there was no irreconcilability between "micro and macro cultures" ("What Are Nations?" lecture, 10 October 1985, Stanford University).

39. Walker, *German Home Towns*, pp. 425–29.

40. Theodor Fontane, *Gedichte*, 17th ed. (Stuttgart, 1912); Christian Mehlis, *Fahrten durch die Pfalz. Historische Landschaftsbilder* (Augsburg, 1877), p. 2; Frank quoted by Otto Riedner, "Vorwort" to Karl von Manz, Alois Mitterweiser, and Hans Zeiss, eds., *Heimatarbeit und Heimatforschung. Festgabe für Christian Frank zum 60. Geburtstag* (Munich, 1927), p. 7; Georg Schnath, *Heimat und Staat. Betrachtungen eines Niedersachsen* (Hannover, 1958), p. 28.

Beyond the sentimental conventionality of these expressions lies a persistent belief that the abstraction of the nation must be experienced through one's common appreciation of a locality, a Heimat. This belief could take an explicitly political turn, as we shall see in the ideal of local citizenship promoted by Weimar republicans. Or it could remain in the realm of consensual invocation, as we shall see in one region's civic rituals.

But the very persistence of Heimat feeling should not mislead us into finding a single trajectory along which German history has traveled inexorably on to the final tragedy. What the long-standing concern with locality and integration—the communal conundrum—conceals is the real fragmentation in the German national experience between 1870 and 1955. Within this fragmented political culture, *Heimat* has been a term not of conflict but of attempted consensus. The chapters that follow examine its invocation over the course of almost a century of severe challenges to a particular region's social stability and political identity. The concern here is with what one scholar has called the "conscious appropriation" of past customs for present purposes and another has characterized as the "active reproduction" of certain values and traditions "through a succession of new conjunctures between the 1870s and 1930s."[41] As an organizing ideology for people quietly seeking a haven from the uncertainties of modern life, Heimat was at the heart of both these processes.

In the Rhenish Pfalz, the interplay between invention and tradition, between nation and locality, was particularly lively. The Pfalz existed on the periphery of its nation and suffered the minor indignities that such a position entails. But the Pfalz has never been isolated from dramatic change. Its sense of regional identity was a product of the upheavals of the nineteenth and twentieth centuries, not a testimony to its detachment from them. Lying as it does between France and Germany, the Pfalz experienced as major quakes what might have passed as tremors in other parts of Germany. French revolutionary and Napoleonic rule first created the political boundaries of the Pfalz, then radically altered social and political life within them. Although the question of a lingering affinity between the French and the Pfälzers would exercise many subsequent generations of local historians, Pfälzers did seem to welcome French reforms at the time, and they held on to them tenaciously under successive forms of rule.[42]

In 1816, the Pfalz came to the Kingdom of Bavaria by way of a treaty

41. Gottfried Korff, "Folklorismus und Regionalismus: Eine Skizze zum Problem des kulturellen Kompensation ökonomischer Rückständigkeit," in Bausinger and Köstlin, *Heimat und Identität*, p. 40; and Geoff Eley, "What Produces Fascism—Preindustrial Traditions or a Crisis of a Capitalist State?" *Politics and Society* 12 (1983): 63.

42. Partly because of its experience under the French, Heinz Gollwitzer calls the Pfalz a "classic case" of *politische Landschaftsbildung*, or the political formation of a region, grouping it with Upper Swabia and Franconia ("Die politische Landschaft," p. 533). His notion of *Landschaftsbildung* is interestingly close to Hobsbawm's invented traditions. Gollwitzer writes, "Con-

between Bavaria and Austria. For the Bavarians, this suspiciously Francophilic fragment of territory, physically separated from Bavaria by the Kingdom of Baden, was not a satisfactory substitute for the cities of Frankfurt, Mainz, and Saarbrücken, which had been their real desire; neither were the Pfälzers, for their part, pleased at the prospect of rule by Catholic Bavaria. The next sixty years of often stormy relations between the territory and its ruling state were crucial in giving substance and contour to Pfälzer local feeling and to the Pfälzer version of German nationalism. At issue throughout this time was the form that national identity would take: would it be mediated by loyalty to the Bavarian state, or did true Germanness demand the overcoming of all such interventions? That question, which corresponded roughly to the political debate between *großdeutsch* and *kleindeutsch* ("big German" and Prussian-dominated "small German") visions of national integration, was further complicated by the confessionally divided character of the Pfalz and by repeated outbursts of political radicalism in the region. As a result, the Pfalz suffered from a split personality in the middle decades of the nineteenth century. On the one hand, a considerable proportion of the local elite supported Bavaria's efforts at state building, participating, for instance, in a local historical establishment friendly to the dynasticism of the Wittelsbachs. On the other hand, democratic and pro-Prussian sentiment, overlapping with the Protestant elite, resisted assimilation into Bavaria and Bavarian-sponsored nationalism.

A compromise was finally forged on the eve of unification. Its political basis was the ascendancy in both Bavaria and the Pfalz of the National Liberal party, with its amalgam of kleindeutsch visions of unification and a mostly Protestant liberalism; and its strength lay in the domination of a political style, that of the *Honoratioren*, or local notables. With one eye on the nation, the source of their pride, and the other on the locality, the source of their distinction, these worthy gentlemen embodied the dual nature of Heimat consciousness. The formal honoring of the Heimat, which really began in the 1870s, was their work and reflected both their pride and their privilege. Its chief institutional expression was the Historical Association of the Pfalz (Historischer Verein der Pfalz), refounded in 1869 for the promotion of *Heimatgeschichte*, the history of the Heimat. From the beginning the society's membership included the political, religious, and economic leaders of the Pfalz. In a province with no dominant city, no aristocratic circles, and a comparatively undeveloped associational life, the Historical Association held the premier position in regional cultural affairs. It was the patron of museum

---

sciousness of tradition reveals itself to us—as paradoxical as this may sound—upon closer consideration as particularly flexible and changeable" (p. 531). What was decisive in the Pfalz, he asserts, was "the thorough inculcation of Enlightened opinion among the population—the liberal and democratic mentality taken from the West" (p. 536).

collections, the sponsor of lecture series, the preserver of monuments, and the promoter and publisher of historical, archeological, and ethnographic research. From 1870 to 1890, its monopoly over the evidence of a Pfälzer past corresponded to its domination of the civic associations of the Pfälzer present.

But the Honoratioren political style was not robust. It eventually gave way, in the Pfalz as in the rest of Germany, to a politics of large, national parties directed, even at the local level, toward mass constituencies. Local associational life, once the preserve of the local worthies, was inundated with new clubs, new participants, new interests. The staid ceremonial speeches that had been the forum for the patriotism of the local worthies now competed for public attention with extravagant parades, mass outings in the forests, and other equally undignified civic rituals. By the turn of the century, Heimat patronage had become the Heimat movement. Local patriotism, instead of slowly fading into insignificance with its former sponsors, was flourishing as never before. In a political culture with no satisfactory national symbology, the Heimat movement provided occasions to express one's sense of national as well as local belonging and to celebrate, however superficially, a community of common purpose.

Despite their recent origins, those rituals proved their worth in the difficult years of wartime and occupation that, following close on the heyday of the Heimat, tested the strength of national loyalties in the Pfalz. The 1920s in particular were marked by a series of crises, from revolutions to separatist putsches, that undermined the legitimacy of Bavarian rule and threatened to disassociate the Pfalz from Germany itself. In the face of disintegrating forces from outside and within, the Pfälzer Heimat clubs turned their energies to an aggressive assertion of the Germanness of the Pfalz. Their Heimat was both besieged and inviolate, vulnerable and eternal. The image had been effective in wartime and proved equally so in the unhappy years of the Republic. At the same time, Heimat promotion increasingly fell under the supervision of state agencies. Both the Bavarian and German governments poured resources into Heimat associations in the 1920s, continuing a practice that had begun informally during the war. On the surface, Heimat promotion was still the domain of voluntary associations; in reality, however, it had become a branch of official German propaganda.

Yet the Heimat activities of the Weimar Republic were a more complicated and interesting phenomenon than such a description would suggest. An important group of republican activists hoped that the medium of the Heimat—its clubs, its publications, its festivities—might serve the cause of democracy as effectively as it was serving the cause of German patriotism. Drawing on a mixture of political traditions, from Stein's ideal of communal self-administration to the democratic liberalism of the Pfälzers' own Hambach Festival, the Heimat republicans tried to infuse local patriotism with the spirit of self-rule and responsible citizenship. In the context of the occupation, their efforts could not succeed. The republicans were thwarted by pro-Bavarian cultural conservatives on the one hand and by the increasingly noisy radical nationalists on the other. A "school for political violence," the French occupation unwittingly aided the rise of National Socialism in the Pfalz. By 1930, when the French finally withdrew, the quiet voices of the Heimat republicans had become almost inaudible.

Whatever independence from the state the idea and institutions of Heimat still had by the end of the French occupation, they lost after 1933. Nazi rule intensified the nationalism of Heimat sentiment and destroyed the autonomy of local associational life. In the writings of the Nazi ideologues of the 1930s, Heimat became simply one more term among many that revolved around the central themes of race, blood, and German destiny. Stripped of its provincial particularities, Heimat ceased to mean much of anything. Its survival in the Nazi period is testimony to little more than the Nazi capacity to make use of the materials at hand. At least in the Pfalz, its contribution to the Nazi appeal was negligible before 1933 and irrelevant afterward. By the final years of the war, Heimat activities had ceased altogether. If indeed Heimat loyalties lived on, they did so covertly and, unlike during the First World War, in resistance to the war itself.

For all these reasons, Heimat emerged from the Nazi experience as though unsullied. The rebirth of Heimat in the postwar era bore an odd resemblance to its emergence in the tentative first years of the General Estate. Once again Heimat suggested a new way to think about localness and Germanness together; once again it contributed to a process of creating a new German identity. But since 1945 Heimat has expressed a far more ambivalent attitude toward nations and their power. Its supporters have mostly subscribed to the interpretation of Nazism as centralized power gone mad; they have recommended Heimat as an antidote not to Germanness as such but to excessive Germanness. In 1946, for instance, a local almanac writer in the Pfalz felt that the most important project of the day was to restore "Heimat thinking" to "healthy channels": "The Pfälzers must learn again to feel themselves as Pfälzers."[43] The major consequence of this attitude was an attempt to restore Heimat associational activities to the center of local civic life, the position they had held at the turn of the century.

More recently still, the filmmaker Edgar Reitz made Heimat the title and theme of a long treatment of life in the twentieth century for the inhabitants of a small German village. Reitz's *Heimat* appeared on German television over nine weeks in 1984, gathering an enormous popular audience as well as considerable attention in academic and political circles. Reitz has been criticized (often by Americans) for consigning Nazism in general and Nazi

43. Hans Reetz, ed., *Pfälzerland: Illustrierter Familien-Kalender* (Landau/Pfalz, 1946).

atrocities in particular to the periphery of his characters' lives.[44] But this criticism surely misses the point—not because it fails to understand the reality of small-town isolation but because it fails to understand the non-literal, the symbolic importance of Heimat itself. *Heimat* has never been a word about real social forces or real political situations. Instead it has been a myth about the possibility of a community in the face of fragmentation and alienation. In the postwar era, Heimat has meant forgiving, and also a measure of forgetting. Right up to the present, it has focused public attention on the meaning of tradition and locality for the nation itself. The survival and transformation of Heimat reveal to us the struggle to create a national identity out of the diverse materials of a provincially rooted society.

44. For a sampling of the critical reaction, see the special issue of *New German Critique*, no. 36 (Fall 1985), esp. the articles by Miriam Hansen ("Dossier on *Heimat*," pp. 3–24) and Michael E. Geisler ("'Heimat' and the German Left: The Anamnesis of a Trauma," pp. 25–66); Timothy Garten Ash, "The Life of Death," *New York Review of Books* 32 (19 December 1985): 26–29; and Kenneth D. Barkin, "Modern Germany: A Twisted Vision," *Dissent* (Spring 1987): 252–55. See also Anton Kaes, *From Hitler to Heimat: The Return of History as Film* (Cambridge, Mass., 1989), esp. pp. 163–92.

TWO

Taming
the Revolution

Although the Rhenish Pfalz began to acquire its "consciousness of community" or *Gemeinschaftsbewußtsein*, as one local scholar described it, only in the
first decades of the nineteenth century, already by the end of the century
Pfälzer consciousness had become a condition of life as "natural" as the
landscape itself.[1] On the face of it, this late but thoroughgoing realization of
local character should come as no surprise. Before the nineteenth century,
the region consisted of forty-four different political units, most of them mere
fragments of states centered elsewhere. There was, in other words, no community of which one could be conscious. Then in the two decades following
1815 the region became a single territory, acquiring a form and locus of
political rule; its own religious administration, Protestant and Catholic; economic rights and obligations; and, not least important, a name. Also by the
1830s the region had an established middle class, several newspapers, a modest but thriving associational life, and many ties, educational, economic, and
political, to other parts of Germany. All these factors made possible the rapid
spread of both local and national feeling; by midcentury in the Pfalz one can
find evidence of both. It would seem, then, to have been an easy step, or at
most several easy steps, from the birth of the political unit to the establishment of the felt community—in the case of the Pfalz, from the setting of its

1. Rudolf Schreiber, "Grundlagen der Entstehung eines Gemeinschaftsbewußtseins der
Pfälzer im 19. Jahrhundert," in *Die Raumbeziehungen der Pfalz in Geschichte und Gegenwart. Nieder-
schrift über die Verhandlungen der Arbeitsgemeinschaft für westdeutsche Landes- und Volksforschung in
Kaiserslautern 6–9. X. 1954* (Bonn, 1954), p. 35.

borders by Bavaria in 1816 to the recognition of its communal reality by its inhabitants over the course of the next half-century.

But the "consciousness of community" in the Pfalz was a far more contested phenomenon than that simple sequence of events suggests. A distinctive Pfälzer identity evolved not linearly, from infancy to maturity, but dialectically, from radicalism and volatility to a conciliatory stability in the Heimat associations of the 1880s. Its final form represented a delicate balance among the Pfalz's Rhenish heritage, its Bavarian governance, and its overwhelmingly German orientation. The traditions, the celebrations, the literature, folklore, and history writing that together gave substance to Pfälzer identity can each be traced to some conjuncture in the nineteenth century when they were first revived, discovered, invented, or promoted. Each helped to temper Pfälzer radicalism. Each helped to tame the revolutionary influence, first of French egalitarianism, then of Rhenish democratic liberalism, and finally of nationalism itself.

Pfälzer identity, as it took shape in the nineteenth century, did not wholly lack some genuine infusion from a prerevolutionary past. The existence of an "old Pfalz" mentality cannot be decisively proven because of the difficulty of distinguishing between the influence of the past itself and that of local historians, eagerly searching for a lost feudality. Nevertheless, it seems likely that at least two elements of the old regime contributed to the nature of "Pfälzerness," even after the thorough transformation of local society under French rule.[2] The first was the religious heritage of the region; the second, closely related, its history of emigration. In the sixteenth and seventeenth centuries, aggressively Calvinist princes had made the region a refuge for religious exiles and later a battleground for religious conflict.[3] The influence of their Protestantism was still felt in the nineteenth century, when Pfälzer Protestants rejected the state Lutheranism (as well as, of course, the Catholicism) of Bavaria. Also significant was the effect of the massive emigrations from the Pfalz, which began by the early eighteenth century, at least partly in response to the devastation wrought by a century of religious wars, and continued to the end of the nineteenth century. The people from the area informally called the "Pfalz" were so numerous among the travelers both at points of departure and arrival that *Pfälzer* became a generic term for Ger-

---

2. Schreiber would claim more: he sees a generalized consciousness both of being "subjects of the Kurpfalz" and of constituting "a community of distress," a *Notgemeinschaft*; both these forms of *Gemeinschaftsbewußtsein* extended beyond the nineteenth-century borders of the Pfalz to other regions previously under Kurpfalz rule (ibid., p. 36).

3. Hermann Schreibmüller, "Der Begriff Pfalz im Wandel der Jahrhunderte," *Mannheimer Generalanzeiger*, 13 November 1920; more recently, Claus-Peter Clasen, *The Palatinate in European History, 1559–1660* (Oxford, 1963), on the role of the Calvinist princes in the religious strife in Central Europe.

man emigrants, even before the "Pfalz" in its modern sense existed.[4] Emigration shaped Pfälzer identity in ironic ways: not only were some of the most self-conscious regionalists those struggling to preserve local customs and ties in strange lands, but the phenomenon of emigration also heightened awareness of local roots for those who stayed behind. By the late nineteenth century, almost every family could claim relatives in foreign lands. The extent of Pfälzer emigration fed local pride also, for it was said to be evidence of Pfälzer initiative and independence.

The ironies of a local identity that derives from a shared experience of disintegration and distress (the *Notgemeinschaft*, to use the German term) are compounded when one considers the overwhelming importance of a foreign power—the French—in shaping this particular version of Germanness. For the experience of French rule was undoubtedly the opening act in the prolonged drama of the Pfalz's identity crisis. Its transformative effects were felt only gradually: in the first year or so after the arrival in 1792 of the French revolutionary armies, local people probably saw their presence only as one more chapter in a depressingly familiar story of invasion and exploitation. After the military crisis of 1793, the French used the Rhineland as a source of much-needed income for the impoverished government in Paris. The looting and pillaging of an irregularly supplied army merely added to the burden of government levies and taxes on local inhabitants.[5] The first glimmerings of a new order came only in 1797, when the Paris government created four new departments in the Rhineland. One of them, the Département Mont-Tonnerre, embraced most of the later Pfalz and areas to its north around Mainz. Within its borders, legal reforms established an independent judiciary, as well as a "clear and comprehensible set of rights" for all citizens. New civil and criminal law codes abolished the restrictive powers of guilds, the legal existence of the aristocracy, and the old town constitutions. The Catholic church lost both its privileges and its property; church and state

4. At first paradoxical, that fact can probably be explained by the authorities' need for a short designation for place of origin: *Pfalz* is easier to write than the dozens of names and titles that would have been required to specify the exact political identity of a village or town. Daniel Häberle noted in his 1909 book on the subject of Pfälzer emigration that arrival records in Philadelphia show anomalous entries, such as "Pfälzer from Holstein," that indicate the confusion between Pfälzer and German (*Auswanderung und Koloniegründung der Pfälzer im 18. Jahrhundert* [Kaiserslautern, 1909], pp. v–vi). See also Fritz Trautz, *Die Pfalz am Rhein in der deutschen Geschichte* (Neustadt, 1959), p. 25; Karl Scherer, ed., *Pfälzer-Palatines. Beiträge zur pfälzischen Ein- und Auswanderung* (Kaiserslautern, 1981); Albert Pfeiffer, "Die Pfalz," MSS, 8 June 1947, Pfälzisches Landesarchiv Speyer (hereafter cited as PLAS) C 1382; Karl Kollnig, *Wandlungen im Bevölkerungsbild des pfälzischen Oberrheingebietes* (Heidelberg, 1952).

5. T.C.W. Blanning, *The French Revolution in Germany: Occupation and Resistance in the Rhineland, 1792–1802* (Oxford, 1983), esp. chap. 7; Max Braubach, "Vom Westfälischen Frieden bis zum Wiener Kongress (1648–1815)," in *Rheinische Geschichte*, ed. Franz Petri and Georg Droege,

were separated.[6] In 1804, in an act that had enduring consequences for the structure of property ownership in the region, the French sold the former aristocratic and ecclesiastical lands to the highest bidder. Unlike in Baden, where the aristocracy survived and took over the bulk of church lands, the bourgeoisie bought most of this land in the Pfalz. The number of property holders doubled in some communities. Taken together, the effect of the sales and of partible inheritance (another French legacy) turned the Pfalz into a region of small landholders, with freehold as the absolute rule.[7]

By 1814, the French had pushed the Pfalz not so much toward an independent identity as toward a "community of consciousness" with the Rhineland as a whole. The "Rhenish institutions," as they came to be called, represented the height of progress, the most radical political transformation of the time.[8] Other German states, however much reformed, had achieved only partial emancipation from the feudal past.[9] Less demonstrable but more important to travel writers and other contemporary observers were the consequences of French rule on the personality of the people. Whether they liked it or hated it, most observers found a spirit of liveliness (insolence), of matter-of-factness (heartless materialism), of equality (except as regards to money), and of flexibility (spiritual shallowness) to be characteristic of Pfälzers and Rhinelanders as a whole. But that such distinctiveness should receive the additional encouragement of political sovereignty was the wish only of Jacobins and other troublemakers. The victorious powers of 1815 adamantly opposed the formation of a single Rhenish state. The left-Rhenish lands were instead divided among a number of sovereign powers, with the bulk of the former Département Mont-Tonnerre going to the Bavarian state in 1816.

French reforms had created the possibility of Pfälzer distinctiveness; Bavarian political hegemony made it a reality. Within the Bavarian state, the Pfalz was a complete anomaly. The two regions had little, if anything, in

vol. 2 (Düsseldorf, 1976), p. 334; see also the polemical but carefully researched account by Max Springer, *Die Franzosenherrschaft in der Pfalz 1792-1814* (Stuttgart, 1926).

6. Elisabeth Fehrenbach, "Die Einführung des französischen Rechts in der Pfalz und in Baden," in *Strukturwandel im pfälzischen Raum von Ancien Régime bis zum Vormärz*, ed. Friedrich Ludwig Wagner (Speyer, 1982); Wolfgang Hans Stein, *Untertan-Citoyen-Staatsbürger. Die Auswirkungen der Französischen Revolution auf den rheinisch-pfälzischen Raum* (Koblenz, 1981), p. 107; Braubach, "Vom Westfälischen Frieden," p. 335; Blanning, *The French Revolution in Germany*, p. 138.

7. Wolfgang Hans Stein, "Französische Zeit," in *Geschichte des Landes Rheinland-Pfalz*, ed. Franz-Josef Heyen (Freiburg, 1981), p. 101; Erich Hehr, "Karte der Strukturverschiebungen im Grundbesitz der Gemeinde Klingenmünster 1750-1842," in Wagner, *Strukturwandel im pfälzischen Raum*, pp. 119-20; Max Spindler, ed., *Handbuch der bayerischen Geschichte*, vol. 4, part 2 (Munich, 1975), p. 773.

8. Karl-Georg Faber, "Die rheinischen Institutionen," in *Hambacher Gespräche 1962* (Wiesbaden, 1964), pp. 20-40.

9. Nipperdey, *Deutsche Geschichte*, pp. 74-78.

common in matters of religion, custom, dialect, or even geography. Bavaria's social and economic structure remained essentially unaltered throughout the years when Pfälzer society was revolutionized. State-sponsored reform had somewhat changed political-constitutional arrangements in Bavaria, though in this case also the Pfalz had gone much further.[10] Adding to the social, political, and sheer geographical distance between the two regions was Bavaria's resentment at the settlement by which it had acquired the Pfalz. The Bavarian dynasty of the Wittelsbachs, indulging dreams of becoming the third great power in Central Europe, equal to Prussia and Austria, had wanted much more; disappointed, various Wittelsbachs schemed throughout the century to trade the Pfalz for other, more prestigious territory elsewhere. Soberer officials feared the region's disruptive potential. Only a few ardent reformers, admirers of Rhenish institutions and Rhenish prosperity under the French, actively welcomed the new territory.[11]

These reformers, by lobbying for the survival of the Rhenish institutions, assured the Pfalz of its future identity. As a result of their influence, the Bavarian government chose to annex the region not as a regular district but as a client state, an arrangement that left the area's civil structure intact.[12] When the leading reformer, Montgelas, fell from power in 1817, the region lost some of its special privileges. It became the "Rhenish district," subject to regular central administration. Yet even in the conservative reaction against the Montgelas era, its Rhenish institutions—and presumably the Rhenish personality—survived.[13] The Bavarian state, however, made no further moves toward reform, so the new Rhine district remained isolated in its civil constitution from the state that in every other way ruled over it.

For the new "Rhenish Bavarians," the Bavarian state represented a standing insult to their independent-mindedness, as well as a potentially

---

10. Ibid., p. 79; Walter Demel, *Der Bayerische Staatsabsolutismus 1806/08–1817. Staats- und gesellschaftspolitische Motivationen und Hintergründe der Reformära in der ersten Phase des Königreichs Bayerns* (Munich, 1983).

11. Kurt Baumann, "Bayern und die oberrheinischen Territorialfragen vom Wiener Kongress bis zum Ausgang des Ersten Weltkrieges," in *Die Raumbeziehungen der Pfalz*, pp. 32–35; Kurt Baumann, "Kronprinz Ludwig von Bayern, und die Oberrheinlande 1809–1819," in *Abhandlungen zur saarpfälzischen Landes- und Volksforschung*, vol. 1 (1937), p. 157; Kurt Baumann, "Probleme der pfälzischen Geschichte im 19. Jahrhundert," *Mitteilungen des Historischen Vereins der Pfalz* 51 (1953): 242–43; Albert Becker, *Die Wiedererstehung der Pfalz. Zur Erinnerung an die Begründung der bayerischen Herrschaft auf dem linken Rheinufer . . .*, Beiträge zur Heimatkunde der Pfalz, 5 (Kaiserslautern, 1916), pp. 65–66.

12. Heiner Haan, ed., *Hauptstaat–Nebenstaat. Briefe und Akten zum Anschluß der Pfalz an Bayern, 1815/1817* (Koblenz, 1977), pp. 30–33.

13. Heiner Haan, "Die Stellung der Pfalz in der bayerischen Verfassung von 1818," in *Land und Reich, Stamm und Nation. Probleme und Perspektiven bayerischer Geschichte*, ed. Andreas Kraus, vol. 2 (Munich, 1984), p. 458. See also Max Spindler, "Die Pfalz in ihrem Verhältnis zum bayerischen Staat in der ersten Hälfte des 19. Jahrhunderts," in *Festgabe für seine königliche Hoheit Kronprinz Rupprecht von Bayern* (Munich, 1953).

dangerous threat to their positions in society. Any effort by Bavaria to rein-
state even a few of the ground rights and estate privileges of the old regime
would have entailed loss of property and prestige for both prominent and
ordinary citizen alike.[14] And even though that threat was not realized, the
relationship remained fraught with discomforts and injustices. Pfälzer Protestants, who comprised over half of the region's inhabitants, never felt
comfortable within the Catholic state of Bavaria, despite having the independence of administering their own regional church.[15] Exacerbating the
Pfälzers' sense that they lacked any influence in the Bavarian state was the
actual underrepresentation of the district as a whole in both the upper and
lower houses of the Bavarian Landtag. Bavaria still clung to the old practice
of representation by *Stand* or estate, of which the Pfalz no longer had any,
neither aristocracy nor clergy nor university professors. Of the General
Estate the Pfalz had plenty, but this body's theoretical universality was little
acknowledged in Bavarian parliamentary practice.[16]

Making the whole situation unbearable, finally, was the consistent insen-
sitivity of the Bavarian state to the economic interests of its Rhine district.
The year 1816 was a "hunger year," a period of crop failures and food
shortages.[17] The loss of the French market and sudden commercial isolation of the region from its immediate trading partners to the north and east
drove many local industries into bankruptcy.[18] Unwilling to put aside their
jealousy of Baden for the sake of Pfälzer commerce, the Bavarians refused to
negotiate toll reductions.[19] Even the Zollverein (Customs Union) of 1834
brought no relief to the Pfalz. Its economy entered into a state of backwardness relative to the rest of the Rhineland. People clung to tiny plots of land
because commercial ventures did not pay, or else, as in the eighteenth century, they emigrated.[20] According to one contemporary observer, Bavaria
had simply "left the Pfalz to choke in its own fat."[21]

14. Winfried Dotzauer, "Kontinuität und Wandel in den Führungsschichten des pfälzischen Raumes," in Wagner, *Strukturwandel im pfälzischen Raum*.

15. The exact figures in 1825 were 56.9 percent Protestant, 29.8 percent Catholic, and 3.4
percent Mennonite, Anabaptist, and Jew; see Willi Alter, "Die Bevölkerung der Pfalz," in *Pfalzatlas*, ed. Willi Alter (Speyer, 1963–81), 1:180, 190. The scattered geographical distribution of
the confessions is shown in Wolfgang Eger, "Die Konfessionsverteilung im Jahre 1825," in ibid.,
pp. 245–51.

16. Haan, *Hauptstaat–Nebenstaat*, p. 378.

17. Theodor Zink and Ludwig Mang, *Das Wirtschaftsleben der Pfalz in Vergangenheit und Gegenwart* (Munich, 1913), p. 107.

18. Hermann Schreibmüller, *Bayern und Pfalz* (Kaiserslautern, 1916), pp. 23–24.

19. Baumann, "Probleme," pp. 248–49.

20. See especially Mack Walker, *Germany and the Emigration* (Cambridge, Mass., 1964); and
Albert Zink, "Die pfälzische Auswanderung des 19. Jahrhunderts im Lichte des pfälzischen
Wirtschaftslebens," *Pfälzer Heimat* (hereafter cited as *PH*) 5 (1954): 56–60.

21. Albert Becker, *Wiedererstehung der Pfalz*, p. 34.

Pfälzer identity, a shared consciousness of singleness and distinctiveness among the inhabitants of the Rhenish district, began rapidly to take shape under the pressure of such economic grievances against the Bavarian state. In the Bavarian Landtag, Pfälzer deputies formed a markedly left-wing block.[22] The logic of their opposition to Bavarian policies led them, moreover, to an increasing enthusiasm for the idea of German nationhood. An economically unified nation, like that envisioned by Friedrich List, offered the obvious solution to the Pfalz's trade problems. Nor were Pfälzer leaders ignorant of what it was like to belong to a great nation. The era of Napoleonic rule, accompanied by war and taxes though it had been, had brought great prosperity to the left-Rhenish lands. It had also left its traces in popular memory: organizations of Napoleon's Rhenish veterans, the "Napoleon stones" that stood in many Rhenish cemeteries, folk legends and songs, all attested to a lingering affection for those days of glory.[23] The continual need to defend their Rhenish-French institutions united the Pfälzers in the Bavarian parliament as much as did their opposition to Bavarian economic policy. Faced with trade barriers and a state officialdom far more imposing than those of the old regime, Pfälzer leaders and ordinary citizens alike looked back to the Napoleonic Empire for inspiration and turned toward the German nation for redress.

Sympathy for French liberalism did not, in other words, preclude the presence of German nationalism as an equally essential part of the Pfalz's growing "consciousness of community."[24] Indeed, their German nationalism was if anything the more strident for their laboring under the chronic suspicion of Francophilia. But it was also undeniably radical, whether thanks to the French or not. Rhinelanders as a whole had not been much affected by the currents of patriotic awakening in the era of Prussian reform; consequently their national enthusiasm tended to be less oriented toward the state.[25] The people, understood romantically and intuitively, would accomplish national unification for themselves.[26] The state, at least in its Bavarian form, was seen not as the vessel but as the enemy of unification—oppressive, particularistic, and backward. Bavaria was, as Veit Valentin described it, the "classic state" of antinational reaction, "too small to be itself the flagship of

22. Schreibmüller, *Bayern und Pfalz*, p. 24.

23. Walther Klein, *Der Napoleonkult in der Pfalz* (Munich, 1934); Albert Becker, *Wiedererstehung der Pfalz*, p. 35; "Westpfälzer Napoleons-Veteranen," *Pfälzisches Museum–Pfälzische Heimatkunde* (hereafter cited as *PM–PH*) (1928): 48.

24. Baumann, "Probleme," pp. 246–47.

25. Nipperdey, *Deutsche Geschichte*, pp. 29–30.

26. Kurt Baumann, "Ludwig Roediger aus Neunkirchen am Potzberg, ein Vorkämpfer der Burschenschaft, 1798–1866," *PH* 2 (1951): 115. Baumann sees the change in the tone of regional grievance as a generational phenomenon. Young men like Roediger had absorbed the romantic nationalism of Fichte and Jahn at the universities and applied them to the problems of their "Heimat."

national unity" but "large enough to pose a serious obstacle" to its supporters.[27] And, as Thomas Nipperdey has suggested, if people could no longer be Rhinelanders, then they wanted to be Germans, not Prussians or Bavarians.[28]

The Pfälzers made their first open bid for such status in 1832. The Hambach Festival, the first and possibly the only large political demonstration of the liberal German bourgeoisie, expressed currents of economic grievance and popular radicalism in the region. It brought together a miscellaneous collection of over twenty thousand students, liberal activists, and local farmers and townspeople for two days of speeches in an old castle ruin outside the wine center of Neustadt-an-der-Haardt.[29] Amid the calls for German unity, the denunciations of French aggression, and the proclamations of support for Polish nationalists there could also be heard a specifically Pfälzer demand for an autonomous government, separate from that of Bavaria. The significance of Hambach for early-nineteenth-century German liberalism surely transcended its local importance.[30] Nevertheless, for the Pfalz the mass gathering demonstrated the extent to which anti-Bavarianism, indeed Pfälzer identity altogether, had crystallized into German nationalism. In 1832 regional consciousness had emerged as political in form, radical in style, and national in object.

Between the Hambach Festival in 1832 and the Frankfurt Parliament in 1848, these tendencies became only more marked.[31] All eleven of the Pfälzer representatives to the Frankfurt Parliament belonged to the left; all voted for a German constitution and against the election of the king of Prussia as emperor. Bavaria of course refused to recognize the constitution and, together with Prussia, put down the revolutionary uprisings of the following year. But again, as at Hambach, opposition to Bavarian policies and support for German unity were two sides of one coin. The national cause embraced both romantic ideals and pragmatic calculations. If some participated only out of idealism, others only out of economic grievance, the combination was nonetheless powerful, and the nationalist stamp it impressed on regional politics and regional identity nonetheless marked. As Carl Schurz, the

27. Veit Valentin, *Geschichte der deutschen Revolution von 1848–1849*, vol. 2 (Berlin, 1931), p. 565.

28. Nipperdey, "Der deutsche Föderalismus zwischen 1815 und 1866 im Rückblick," in Kraus, *Land und Reich, Stamm und Nation*, p. 7.

29. For a fuller account of the Hambacher Fest, see Veit Valentin, *Das Hambacher Nationalfest* (Berlin, 1932); and the recent facsimile reprint of Wilhelm Herzberg's *Das Hambacher Fest* (1908; reprint Darmstadt, 1982).

30. Wolfgang Schieder, "Der rheinpfälzische Liberalismus von 1832 als politische Protestbewegung," in *Vom Staat des Ancien Régimes zum modernen Parteienstaat. Festschrift für Theodor Schieder*, ed. Helmut Berding et al. (Munich, 1978), pp. 169–95.

31. Baumann, "Probleme," p. 258.

German-American progressive, put it, "it is understood by the Pfälzers themselves that if the king of Bavaria does not want to be German, then the Pfalz must cease to be Bavarian.[32]

Making its inconspicuous debut in the midst of all this political turmoil was the name *Pfalz* itself. This part of the southern Rhineland had been the "Pfalz" for centuries of popular usage, though the informal application of the term had never completely coincided with the formal political boundaries of, say, the Kurpfalz. When Bavaria acquired the land, it simply followed its own practice and named it after a river: "Rhine District," like "Isar District," was a designation of administrative convenience. But in 1837, in an act resonant of the Biedermeier turning-away from bureaucratic enlightenment, the government chose to rename all the districts after their *Stamm*, or tribe. The Isar District became Oberbayern (Upper Bavaria); the Rhine District became the Pfalz. In the region itself, the name was adopted "with an alacrity and enthusiasm granted to no other Munich directive: now for the first time it was possible to speak of oneself."[33] From the point of view of the Pfälzers, then, the name strengthened their distinct political consciousness by giving legitimacy to their fully felt but only half-articulated sense of separateness. As for their German nationalism, the name with all its historical resonance represented a direct claim, unmediated by Bavaria, to participation in the cultural nation.

But the politics of the name included not just how the Pfälzers used it but what the Bavarians had intended by it. For the prestige-hungry Wittelsbachs, the term *Pfalz* brought to mind visions of Mannheim and Heidelberg, not Pirmasens and Kaiserslautern. The renaming revealed, in a minor way, their persistent desire to acquire more territory on the Upper Rhine, particularly at the expense of Baden, which, to their minds, had usurped the title to the Kurpfälzer inheritance. More generally, the name had an attractively conservative, dynastic ring to it in Bavarian ears. Renaming the Rhine district formed part of a broader effort to defeat Pfälzer radicalism by promoting a rival regional identity. Embedded within a variety of cultural projects, historical, literary, and folkloric, the "Pfalz" referred not to a land of liberal and democratic radicalism, but to a land of picturesque castle ruins and charming folkways. Between the failure of the Frankfurt Parliament and the crowning of a German emperor at Versailles, Pfälzer identity did lose most of its radical flavor. What it did not lose, however, was its nationalism.

The second stage, then, in the emergence of Pfälzer identity fell in the years of political repression and conservative nation-building after 1848. German

32. Carl Schurz, *Vormärz in Deutschland*, reprint ed. Herbert Pönicke (Munich, 1948).
33. R. Schreiber, "Grundlagen," p. 40.

national identity and Pfälzer local identity had never been entirely separate propositions in the Pfalz; after 1848, their interdependence became even clearer as the emphasis in both shifted from protest to integration. Localness, like nationness, became less and less a condition of grievances and unfulfilled desires. Neither of politics nor yet completely above it, the meaning of "Pfälzerness" changed in step with political expectations in the region, while at the same time gaining new extrapolitical content. Both trends worked against Pfälzer radicalism. A political rapprochement between the Pfalz and Bavaria, based on Bavaria's reluctant acquiescence in the Pfalz's now-tame German nationalism, conditioned a broadly cultural transformation of local identity. The Pfalz would never assimilate fully into Bavaria, but neither would it torment the larger state with its insolence and rebellion.

The simplest explanation for the shifting import of Pfälzer identity was the waning of popular radicalism in the region. Bavaria's suppression of associations and the press in the wake of the 1849 rebellions effectively destroyed any independent public life in the Pfalz. The liberal, democratic leaders were all in exile or jail, and no other political faction had as yet coalesced.[34] Economic misery throughout the midcentury years led this time to political passivity. Overpopulation placed unbearable pressure on food supplies and land, and an agricultural depression that included the all-important wine trade continued well into the 1850s.[35] In 1846, ten thousand people emigrated from the Pfalz; in 1849, fourteen thousand; in 1852, nineteen thousand; and in 1855, twenty-two thousand.[36] The overall population of the region sank from 600,000 to 575,000 between 1848 and 1855, and the number of registered poor doubled.[37] In the 1850s, the Pfalz could claim a quarter of Bavaria's vagrants and beggars and a seventh of its suicides.[38]

When political and economic life together began to revive in the 1860s, neither much resembled what they had been in the 1830s and 1840s. In the first place, the economy began to industrialize. The chemical, paper, and machine industries established themselves in the 1860s along the Rhine and in the less fertile western parts of the region; railroad building began in the late 1850s. Although their contribution to the region's productivity would

34. Karl-Georg Faber, "Die südlichen Rheinlande," in Petri and Droege, *Rheinische Geschichte* 2:412.

35. Joachim Kermann, "Die Industrialisierung der Pfalz im 19. Jahrhundert," in *Pfälzische Landeskunde. Beiträge zu Geographie, Biologie, Volkskunde und Geschichte*, ed. Michael Geiger, Günter Preuß, and Karl-Heinz Rothenberger (Landau/Pfalz, 1981), 2:280–85; Zink, "Pfälzische Auswanderung," p. 57.

36. These are rounded figures; the exact ones may be found in Zink, "Pfälzische Auswanderung," p. 57.

37. Schreibmüller, *Bayern und Pfalz*, p. 50.

38. Ibid., p. 52.

not equal that of agriculture until 1882, the new industries nevertheless heralded the arrival of a new political economy, less dependent on small producers with radical political inclinations.[39] Those inclinations had in any case been broken in the 1850s. Despite the efforts of democrats like Georg Friedrich Kolb with his People's party, the political activity of the petty bourgeoisie did not revive until the 1880s, and then its radicalism was not of the left.[40]

What emerged in the 1860s to fill the political void was a new, elitist, and decidedly Prussian variety of liberalism, one having little in common with the großdeutsch and democratic liberalism traditional to the region. The Deidesheimer circle of pro-Prussian liberals was led by the so-called *Flaschenbaronen* (Bottle Barons), a group of wealthy bourgeois landowners and vintners; it also included high-ranking officials of the state and even a few industrialists.[41] In 1863 these Pfälzers participated in the founding of the kleindeutsch Bavarian Progressive party in Nuremberg; in 1866 they formed an "Association for the Protection of German Interests on the Left Bank of the Rhine," which incited local fears of another Napoleonic invasion; and in 1867, in the Bavarian Landtag, they called for immediate union with Prussia.[42] In 1868 Deidesheimer National Liberals won all the Pfälzer seats in the German Zollparlament (Customs Parliament). A year later they won all but one of the district's seats in the Bavarian Landtag.[43] The Franco-Prussian War, fought on the borders of the Pfalz, only reinforced the popularity of the National Liberals, who then helped Bismarck maneuver Bavaria into ratifying his treaty.[44] Finally, at the first Reichstag election of 1871, Pfälzer National Liberals won all the local seats, establishing an absolute monopoly on political representation that they held until 1898.

What had happened by 1871 was not just a conservative turn in the Pfalz but a more liberal turn in Bavaria. Bavarian Progressives and Pfälzer National Liberals cooperated closely. Bavaria acquired some of the legal arrangements that had distinguished the Pfalz, and the Pfalz lost a few of its

39. Kermann, "Industrialisierung," p. 280; Erich Schneider, "Die Anfänge der sozialistischen Arbeiterbewegung in der Rheinpfalz, 1864–1899: Ein Beitrag der süddeutschen Parteiengeschichte" (diss., Universität Mainz, 1956), p. 4; Ernst Otto Bräunche, *Parteien und Reichstagwahlen in der Rheinpfalz von der Reichsgründung 1871 bis zum Ausbruch des Ersten Weltkrieges 1914* (Speyer, 1982), p. 29.

40. On Kolb, a lifelong hater of Prussia, see Theodor Schieder, *Die kleindeutsche Partei in Bayern in den Kämpfen um die nationale Einheit 1863–1871* (Munich, 1936), pp. 25ff.; and Schneider, p. 16.

41. Schneider, "Anfänge der sozialistischen Arbeiterbewegung," p. 27.

42. Ibid., p. 15.

43. For a complete account of that crucial election, see Ludwig Allmann, "Die Wahlbewegung zum Ersten Deutschen Zollparlament in der Rheinpfalz" (diss., Universität Strassburg, 1913).

44. Baumann, "Probleme," p. 267.

administrative peculiarities.[45] Anti-Bavarian sentiments in the Pfalz and anti-Pfälzer sentiments in Bavaria became exceptional. Most important, Bavaria at least superficially dropped its resistance to national unification, thus accepting a position that had long defined Pfälzer exceptionalism. Pfälzer politicians could with justification claim the outcome of 1870–71 as confirmation of the old political wisdom that in 1816 "Bavaria had surrendered to the Pfalz."[46]

But the political pacification of the Pfalz can form only part of an explanation for the marked shift in emphasis in how Pfälzers described themselves or celebrated their Pfälzerness. In the first half of the nineteenth century, both self-description and celebration attested to an essentially political sense of identity: the Pfalz was understood above all as a political entity; hence, to be a Pfälzer implied a political attitude—that of radicalism—more than a cultural, religious, or even plainly geographical sensibility. But as the intensity of the Pfalz's political exceptionalism waned, the importance of those other factors in local identity grew—with the connivance of the Bavarian state and the now-hegemonic National Liberals. Beginning roughly in the 1850s, the region underwent a cultural awakening, which took the form of a new fascination with local history, local folklore, and the landscape. This politically inspired renaissance of Pfälzerness decisively reoriented the region away from France, toward full inclusion in German culture.

The Pfalz's turn toward a cultural identity also brings us in contact with the phenomenon of Heimat for the first time in the region's development. The Pfalz, after all, had no need for such Heimat legislation as eased many a Bavarian town's adjustment to state rule.[47] All the old legal structures had abruptly ceased to exist at the beginning of the century, and the Pfalz's inhabitants had made a rapid acquaintance with the modern nation in its most dynamic and assertive form. Thus the usefulness of the idea of Heimat did not initially lie in the area of political education, where the Pfalz could for years claim a sophistication unusual for so small a region. The cultivation of the Heimat became instead a way to assert the Germanness of the Pfalz in the realm of culture. Like the strident nationalism of Pfälzer radicals and conservatives, expressions of Heimat love implicitly countered the widespread suspicion that Pfälzers were a little too fond of their French institutions, and hence not quite German. Indeed, throughout its history the Pfalz's cultivation of the Heimat might well have taken as its motto the words of Pfälzer Deputy Schmitt to the Frankfurt National Parliament in 1848: "We are Germans through and through, as much so as any inhabitant of a prov-

45. Faber, "Die südlichen Rheinlande," pp. 414–15.

46. Wilhelm Heinrich Riehl, Die Pfälzer. Ein rheinisches Volksbild (1857; rev. ed. Neustadt/ Pfalz 1973), p. 235.

47. See Chapter 1, pp. 8–9; Walker, German Home Towns, p. 254.

ince in the middle of Germany or on the Baltic Sea. We respect France, but we do not wish to be a part of it. We speak German; we have true German feeling."[48]

Two early works of "Heimat discovery" from the 1830s suggest the subjects and strategies that later writers would also adopt. The first was a guide to the Pfalz's geography prepared by the secondary school teacher Christian Grünewald and published in 1833. His *Beschreibung der Rheinbaiern* (Description of Rhenish Bavaria) represented in its modest way the worldview of the General Estate, even as it centered on a single province. Drawing on the pioneering geographies of Carl Ritter and Wilhelm Harnisch, Grünewald depicted the region in terms that encouraged both comparison and generalization. Drawing on the pedagogical theory of Pestalozzi, he advocated actual physical contact with the land he descibed. He prepared a student for the big world by a thorough acquaintance with a small one: "He [the student] will not only get to know the conditions of his Heimat, and all that they offer to our contemplation and consciousness, but he will also retain a measuring stick with which to judge properly other places and other phenomena."[49] Grünewald's method asserted that the locality could be understood and indeed experienced as the beginning of all knowledge, not as its exclusion; that belief informed all later works of *Heimatkunde*, or Heimat studies.

His work attempted, moreover, to classify the geography of the Pfalz, as though its borders had a geographical, not just a political, rationale. Although it was not Grünewald's own intention, study of the region's geography over the next seventy years would give a scientific solidity to the vaguer assertions of regional distinctiveness. In the words of Grünewald's most important successor in the field of Pfälzer geography, Daniel Häberle, "the being of the Pfälzer is to a certain extent the expression of the nature of the land itself."[50] And if geography created personality, it followed that without a Pfälzer geography there could be no Pfälzer personality. Hence the study of the land, which began with Christian Grünewald, made possible an infinite elaboration on the theme of the people's distinctiveness. Moreover, if the Pfalz could be said to consist of two, or possibly three, basic geographical divisons, then perhaps the undeniably various nature of local people—a problem for the integrity of the single term *Pfälzer*—followed such a scheme also. Vorderpfalz and Hinterpfalz (literally, the Pfalz-in-front and the Pfalz-behind), or the Rhine Basin, the Haardt Mountains (at the dividing line be-

48. Quoted in Baumann, "Probleme," p. 246.

49. Kurt Reh, "Christian Grünewald: Beschreibung von Rheinbaiern," in *Die Pfalz auf der Suche nach sich selbst. Über bedeutsame Pfalzbeschreibungen der letzten 150 Jahre*, ed. Carl Heupel (Landau/Pfalz, 1983), p. 41.

50. Daniel Häberle, "Pfälzer Land und Volk," in *Die Pfalz am Rhein. Ein Heimatbuch*, ed. Daniel Häberle, Albert Becker, and Theodor Zink (Berlin, 1924), p. 28.

tween "vorder" and "hinter" Pfalz), and, beyond them, the Westrich—these
physical divisons formed an image of the Pfalz that appealed to all who
sought to describe the region's individuality. One writer might distinguish,
albeit tongue-in-cheek, between the "alluvial Pfälzers" of the Rhine plain,
the "bedrock Pfälzers" of the Haardt, the "sandstone Pfälzers" of the wooded
and mountainous areas, and the "coal Pfälzers" of the Saar corner.[51]
Another would contrast the lively and sunny character of the Rhine Valley
dwellers with the dour reticence of the westerners. All were in some sense
beneficiaries of the most basic insight of Grünewald: that the Pfalz had its
own geography.

But all that was in the future. In his own time, Grünewald was too much
of a liberal nationalist and a rationalist to be acceptable to the Bavarian
school authorities, and although his teaching was evidently highly regarded
and imitated locally, he never received state recognition.[52] The opposite was
true of the romantic pastor Friedrich Blaul, whose deeply conservative depiction of the Pfalz, first published in 1838, was little read or regarded by his
Pfälzer contemporaries but fit right into the schemes of Bavarian cultural
architects a few decades later. Blaul's *Träume und Schäume vom Rhein* (which
can be inelegantly rendered as "Dreams and Froth of the Rhine"), written
when Blaul was twenty-nine, took the form of an old man's account of his
travels in the Pfalz, where he found as much to criticize as to admire. Later
billed by a Heimat enthusiast of 1867 as "one of the loveliest pieces of tourist
literature ever," the book combined already-tired romantic clichés about the
landscape with politically loaded longings for the good old days before the
French arrived.[53] The Pfälzers themselves had many traits of personality and
political behavior that this observer greatly regretted, in particular their
apparently total lack of spirituality. But instead of attributing their unfortu-
nate behavior to political grievance or ideological belief, Blaul trivialized
Pfälzer radicalism by attributing it to their Stamm, or tribal tendencies.
"Pfälzers tend to be complainers by nature" was the Blaul line of argument,
and although the complainers themselves showed no sign of appreciating this
analysis in the 1830s or 1840s, others seized on it enthusiastically in the next
two decades. Blaul's work was at that time "discovered"; in 1882 it was
reprinted to great fanfare in the Heimat periodicals.[54] Its particular style of
sentimentalizing the land and trivializing the people became characteristic of
much, though by no means all, of Heimat writing. More important, the book
represented a subtle kind of propaganda in its implication that Pfälzers
could, if they would just pay more attention to their folk and feudal heritage,

51. Riehl, *Die Pfälzer*, p. 30.
52. Reh, "Christian Grünewald," p. 37.
53. See the excellent analysis of Blaul's work by Wolfgang Diehl in Heupel, *Die Pfalz auf der Suche nach sich selbst*, pp. 58–80.
54. Ibid., pp. 77–79.

be other than they were. Blaul's was a strategy for explaining away their radicalism to the Pfälzers themselves, and whatever the failings of the book itself, it established an important precedent.

The writer who really grasped the political possibilities of an awakened folklorism and a personalized geography, both for the Pfalz and for Germany, was the so-called father of German *Volkskunde* (folklore studies or, grandly, anthropology), Wilhelm Heinrich Riehl. Trained originally in theology, Riehl's interests had turned quickly to the study of contemporary German society, which he pursued as a journalist, novelist, and independent scholar, outside the usual structure of academic disciplines. Before he arrived in Bavaria in 1854 to serve King Max II, he had already produced an astonishing 670 articles on music, theater, art, social policy, political theory, agricultural history, folklore, and contemporary politics.[55] His outstanding accomplishment, however, was the three-volume *Naturgeschichte des deutschen Volks* (Natural History of the German People), in which he laid out his own scheme for classifying and describing German society and culture.[56] Even though his thought derived much from others—Dahlmann, the brothers Grimm, Vischer, and Arndt, among others—Riehl's work had a grittiness and unpretentious sharpness of observation that brought him a wide audience. His opposition to cities, to industrial society, to France, all grew out of his objection to uniformity in social life. His favorite metaphor was a rainbow, and in the infinitely various shadings of customs, landscapes, and personalities that characterized traditional life Riehl found the essence and the vitality of Germany.

For all his conservative distaste for modern society, however, Riehl had something of the social planner in him—and this, one suspects, is what Max II of Bavaria found so attractive. Riehl was invited to Munich by Max ostensibly to develop a governmental press bureau, but he seems instead to have taken over a pet project of the king, an "Ethnography of Bavaria," then languishing under a surfeit of material and a severe shortage of coherence.[57] Under Riehl's direction, the project became a complete "statistical, historical, topographical, and ethnographic description" of the "land and people of Bavaria."[58] In Riehl's *Bavaria*, moreover, the contours of folkloric varia-

55. Dennis McCort, *Perspectives on Music in German Fiction: The Music Fiction of Wilhelm Heinrich Riehl* (Frankfurt and Bern, 1974), p. 11.

56. The finest account of the work in English is still that of George Eliot, whose article "The Natural History of German Life: Wilhelm Heinrich Riehl" (in *The Essays of George Eliot*, ed. Nathan Sheppard [New York, 1883]) is also the culmination of her work as an essayist.

57. Victor von Geramb, *Wilhelm Heinrich Riehl. Leben und Wirken 1823–1897* (Salzburg, 1954), p. 238; Antonie Hornig, "Wilhelm Heinrich Riehl und König Max II von Bayern" (diss., Universität München, 1938), pp. 17, 47.

58. From the draft proposals in the royal archives, cited in Hornig, "Riehl und König Max," p. 49.

tion followed the borders of modern Bavarian political districts, a design that reflected something more than convenience. In a memorandum to Max's cabinet in 1856, Riehl explained that "the most important requirement for a reasonable administration of the land...is for all authorities to possess knowledge of the land and its people—everything that promotes this knowledge is a victory for the whole state."[59] Folklore could serve the state because it, more than any other discipline, revealed the German social essence. Riehl suggested that the king establish an "ethnographic cabinet" and expand university lectures on German customs and rural life, in addition to completing the volumes of *Bavaria*. In Riehl's opinion—which King Max seemed to share—the foundation of the best state lay not in uniformity of law (in contrast to the French example) but in flexibility of administration. Such government would take into account the individual characteristics of the people—or, to use Riehl's more expressive term, the *Volkseigentümlichkeit*.[60]

Riehl's involvement with the troublesome character of the Pfälzers emerged from this confluence of ethnography and government. In 1854, shortly after coming to Munich, he began research for an ethnographic study of the region, which he published in 1857 as *Die Pfälzer: Ein rheinisches Volksbild* (The Pfälzer: a Portrait of Rhenish People). The Pfalz, he wrote, displayed "more clearly than almost any other land" the "motto" of middle Germany: "Diversity without unity."[61] It belonged to what in his *Naturgeschichte* he had called the "individualized country."[62] Riehl thought, moreover, that the Pfalz was the German province that "pulled together in the narrowest of spaces all the contradictions of the German nationality [*Volkstum*], as well as the German landscape"; it was "a sampler of German nature, piecemeal, changeable, and unified only by its character of perplexing manifoldness."[63] The book itself consisted of a journey from the earth to the spirit, from topography and farming to religion, pausing for food and politics along the way. Its organization reflected his belief that ethnography reiterated topography, that the land formed the people.[64] His dissection of the Pfälzer people thus depended more than he might have admitted on the geographical work of Christian Grünewald.[65]

59. "Vorschläge zur Förderung der socialen [*sic*] und staatswissenschaftlichen Studien," reprinted in ibid., pp. 121–24.

60. Ibid., p. 121.

61. Riehl, *Die Pfälzer*, p. 15.

62. Wilhelm Heinrich Riehl, *Land und Leute*, vol. 2 of *Naturgeschichte des deutschen Volkes* (Stuttgart, 1853), pp. 75–204.

63. "Eine Musterkarte deutscher Natur, zerstückt, wechselvoll, und nur in dem Charakter verwirrender Mannigfaltigkeit einheitlich" (Riehl, *Die Pfälzer*, p. 29).

64. These are most clearly set out in *Land und Leute*, published just a few years before Riehl set out on his Pfälzer research. See also Hannes Ginzel, "Der Raumgedanke in der Volkskunde unter Berücksichtigung Wilhelm Heinrich Riehls" (diss, Universität Würzburg, 1971).

65. On the existence of that influence, see Reh, "Christian Grünewald," p. 44.

In the introduction to *Die Pfälzer*, Riehl suggested that his method amounted to no more than observation and conversation and that his theoretical guide was common sense.[66] As a child, he had sat at his Pfälzer grandfather's feet listening to the stories of the old man's childhood; as a student, he had wandered through the countryside acquainting himself with the simple people and their ways; as ethnographer to King Max, he spent several months walking from village to village and speaking with the local people.[67] As for why he wrote the book, Riehl acknowledged only intellectual and sentimental motives.[68] *Die Pfälzer* could stand as a case study of the individualized country, demonstrating the very connections between land, human nature, and social arrangements that Riehl had recently explained in *Land und Leute* (Land and People), the first volume of his *Naturgeschichte*.[69]

But *Die Pfälzer* could stand equally well as a case study in Riehl's politics of ethnography and administration. The book represented an attempt to understand the Pfalz in its troublesome relation to Bavaria and thereby to change it.[70] It was a document directed both at Bavarian officialdom and at the Pfälzers themselves, in the first instance to inform, in the second, to persuade and ultimately to convert. In the fall of 1854 and spring of 1855, Riehl had spent about four months in the Pfalz itself, walking (as he said in his introduction) from town to town during the crucial agricultural seasons, but also speaking extensively with Bavarian officials in the communities and in the district presidium. In the months between his field trips, he read the historical and geographical literature on the region. He came to two sets of conclusions, one published in the book itself and the other privately conveyed to King Max in a progress report late in 1854.[71] Both sets of conclusions centered on the distinctive character of the Pfälzer people, but the moral signs reversed themselves in the process of publication. In his report to the king of Bavaria, Riehl had hardly a charitable word to say for the Pfälzers.

---

66. Riehl, *Die Pfälzer*, foreword.

67. Ibid. See also Wolf von Gropper, "Wilhelm Heinrich Riehl: Ein Gedenkblatt zum 50. Todestage," *Pfälzer Bote: Volks- und Heimatkalender 1948* (Neustadt/Haardt, 1947), p. 72; and Walter Plümacher, "Der große Wanderer durch unsere Heimat: W. H. Riehl und die Pfälzer," *Pfälzische Heimatblätter* 1 (15 October 1952): 1.

68. The intellectual and sentimental justifications were accepted by later Heimat writers. See Albert Becker's review of the new 1907 edition of the book, in *Pfälzerwald* (hereafter cited as *PW*) 1 (15 December 1907): 191; and Karl Gruber, "W. H. Riehl und August Becker schreiben über die Pfalz," *Kurpfalz* (April 1953): 16.

69. See, e.g., Riehl, *Die Pfälzer*, pp. 15, 31, 33, 211.

70. The Pfälzer historian Kurt Baumann, whose insights are penetrating but often hidden in obscure local journals, suggested the possibility of such an interpretation in his review of Victor von Geramb's biography of Riehl; see *PH* 7 (February, 1956): 77.

71. Hornig, "Riehl und König Max," happened to reprint the entire report in her appendix, though she made little of it in her text; see pp. 115–21, "Gutachten über die Pfälzer," from the Geheime Hausarchiv.

Their distinctive character was a curse, which had caused them between 1832 and 1849 practically to destroy the internal peace of Bavaria. To be sure, the Pfälzer was not entirely to blame for his bad behavior. A heritage of political fragmentation added to a contemporary experience of land division, industrialization, easy credit, and massive emigration had undermined the people's natural integrity. Above all, Riehl blamed the French interregnum for destroying the "genuine kernel" of folk life in the region. "The chief assignment of the Bavarian government should be," he concluded, "to tear the Pfälzers away from this false and destructive singularity [*Sonderthümelei*]."[72]

The report suggested ways in which firm administration could accomplish this task. What the Pfalz lacked was a "concentration both inward and outward, which it will find only in the closest relation to the Bavarian state."[73] Riehl criticized earlier Bavarian disengagement from the region. The Bavarian government had allowed too many French laws to stand and had devolved too much authority on Pfälzer officials, who of course did all they could to retain their disgraceful "Sonderthümelei." What the region needed was a "strong regiment, a serious enforcement of law, and the authority of public power."[74] The Pfälzer was potentially loyal, but his loyalty was passive and easily lost. Pfälzers harbored, moreover, an irrational hatred of Bavarians; the presence of intelligent and efficient Bavarian administrators, Riehl thought, would cure them of it.[75]

In *Die Pfälzer*, Riehl professed far more affection for the people than he had in his report to King Max. He used the book to reveal that "true kernel" of folk life which political and social disruption had all but destroyed. His treatise on Pfälzer life consequently centered on landscape and tribe, not much on history, and hardly at all on the legacy of the French. Riehl's analysis of the Pfälzer character both in the book and in the report was informed by a distinction between his terms, *Eigenthümelei* and *Sonderthümelei*. The *Eigentum* of the Pfälzers was their heritage of genuine folk customs and beliefs, the true expression of a people, their "ownness" (the literal meaning of *Eigentum*) and essence. *Sondertum*, a term of opprobrium in the report, was the collective curse of the French on a German folk group, distinctiveness without deeper justification, an aberration. The report, concerned as it was with governmental policy, concentrated on the disease—Sondertum. *Die Pfälzer*, in contrast, was really about a people's Eigentum. To save this quality from the aberrant influences of modernity and political liberalism was the foundation of all Riehl's social politics.

72. Ibid., pp. 116, 119.
73. Ibid., p. 116.
74. Ibid., p. 117.
75. Ibid.

The propagandistic task at the heart of *Die Pfälzer* reveals itself most clearly in Riehl's attempt to sanitize and disarm Pfälzer Sondertum, for which in the book he adopted the polite term *Selbstbewußtsein*, or "self-consciousness." He admitted both the strength of "self-consciousness" and the role that Napoleonic power and French institutions had played in its formation.[76] But he then asked, could politics alone account for such a deeply held and sure sense of identity? He answered, not surprisingly, no, that in fact "landscape, upbringing, customs and morals, and communal life" were the essence not simply of Pfälzer identity but of a "strong and proud... Bavarian-Pfälzer" identity. The region's distinctive modern institutions were simply the "putty" that held all else together.[77] In case the metaphor confused anyone, he became more explicit a few pages later: "With mistrust our forefathers took on the French laws; with love they have held fast to them. But in the process, they have transformed them and Germanized them.... Practically unnoticed," their German sensibility and morality "raised a hundred objections to these same conditions that their rational convictions tried to maintain."[78]

The message of the book was "Pfälzers, you know yourselves not." All that they believed to be their distinction and its manifestations—liberality, Hambach—was at best the wayward counsel of a superficial rationality. If, as Riehl told King Max in his report, the Pfälzer wanted to be a Pfälzer and not a Bavarian, then the social politician and the ethnographer must redefine what "Pfälzer" meant. In his book, Riehl attempted to disengage regional distinctiveness from the French Revolution, from sixty years of recent political and economic experience, from politics in its entirety.

Riehl's Pfälzer ethnography was a far more ambitious and deliberate undertaking than Blaul's Rhenish dreaming had been. One initial reaction to the book, from the very class of people that could be expected to read it and take it to heart, suggested that his message was received. In 1858, a Dean Scholler wrote to a friend that "no one has ever seen so deeply into our hearts.... He has opened the hidden springs out of which the natural strength of our lives flows; with a hundred... witnesses, he has explained the inner purpose of our essence."[79] Certainly the Pfälzer historical, ethnographical, and geographical clubs that developed in the following decades took up Riehl's ideas with enthusiasm. His rediscovery—or invention—of Pfälzer folk life lay at the heart of the "Pfalz" volume of *Bavaria*, which finally appeared in 1868. That book, under Riehl's general editorship, collected,

76. Riehl, *Die Pfälzer*, pp. 234, 243.

77. Ibid., p. 234.

78. Ibid., p. 253.

79. Letter from *Dekan* Scholler to unknown correspondent, Johannisruhe, 9 March 1858; printed in *PW* I (15 December 1907): 190.

catalogued, and described all lingering traces of the "true kernel" of Pfälzer life.[80] August Becker's book *Die Pfalz und die Pfälzer* extended Riehl's interpretation into the realm of popular travel literature, ultimately reaching a broader range of people than Riehl's more analytical work.

Riehl's efforts at conversion also gave new vigor to a long-standing but far less intellectually compelling attempt to transform Pfälzer consciousness through a reinterpretation of Pfälzer history. Riehl himself had proposed in his memorandum of 1854 that the Bavarian government further promote the association of the Bavarian king with the defunct office of *Pfalzgraf* (usually translated as Count Palatine), a ploy against unruly provinces reminiscent of the English creation of a Prince of Wales. The government had in fact attempted to cultivate such Bavarian "state consciousness" since the 1820s, with dubious success.[81] Its key was the invention of a dynastic and historical tradition that could embrace not just the Bavarian heartland but all the Swabians, Franconians, and Pfälzers on its edges as well. In 1827, King Ludwig of Bavaria had announced that thenceforth "the animation of the national spirit, the study of the history of the Fatherland, and the spread of the discipline" of history and historical preservation would be official state policy.[82] Local authorities, in cooperation with "friends of History and Art," were to begin at once to preserve the past, not omitting regular reports to the Ministry of the Interior and occasional historical gifts to the Bavarian Academy of Science.

At one level, the new policy had posed no problem for the Bavarian administrators of the Pfalz, which did have plenty of historical remains to be collected, particularly of the Roman era. In 1827, a new Historical Association of the Pfalz came into being, gathering together some forty men with a "love for history and antiquity."[83] By 1839, the presidium of the district had recruited over five hundred men of appropriate "education and station" to join the association.[84] The fledgling group belonged to what one historian has identified as a second phase of association building in Germany, in which associations took a conservative turn away from their initial Jacobinism, re-

80. Ludwig Schandein et al., *Rheinpfalz*, in *Bavaria. Landes und Volkskunde des Königreichs Bayern*, ed. Wilhelm Heinrich Riehl (Munich, 1860–68).

81. On Bavarian state-building in general, see Werner K. Blessing, *Staat und Kirche in der Gesellschaft. Institutionelle Autorität und mentaler Wandel* (Göttingen, 1982), passim; see also Christa Stache, *Bürgerlicher Liberalismus und katholischer Konservatismus in Bayern, 1867–1871* (Frankfurt, 1981), p. 70.

82. Kabinettsbefehl, 29 May 1827, cited by Albert Becker, *Hundert Jahre Pfälzer Geschichtsforschung, 1827–1927* (Speyer, 1927), p. 5; on Ludwig, see also Kurt Baumann, "Ludwig I," in *Deutscher Westen—Deutsches Reich. Saarpfälzische Lebensbilder*, ed. Karl von Raumer and Kurt Baumann (Kaiserslautern, 1938), vol. 1.

83. Historicher Verein der Pfalz (hereafter cited as HVP), "Rechenschaftsbericht vom Jahre 1834–1842," PLAS, T1.

84. Ibid.

publicanism, and radical nationalism.[85] By their nature associations continued to attract and measure men by activity and talent rather than by
birth, but particulary the historical associations increasingly affiliated themselves with the Enlightenment of rationalism and the state.[86] King Ludwig
had intended from the start that the new Historical Association be a "conservative element," to balance the radical associational tendencies so deeply
rooted in the Pfalz, and consequently he discouraged large increases in
membership.[87] The association's members were not in any case rebellious
types; they included high civil servants, jurists, and professors, priests and
councillors, Bavarians and Pfälzers, but not the freelance journalists and
small-town lawyers so prominent at Hambach and Frankfurt.[88]

The encouragement of love for the Wittelsbachs did, however, pose a
problem for the new Historical Association of the Pfalz. By 1816 the Wittelsbach connection, tenuous and unevenly distributed across the region as it
had been, was twenty years in the past and vastly overshadowed by the
Napoleonic phenomenon. The Bavarian dynasty never developed any popular following in the Pfalz, and by the time the two regions had drawn closer
together politically, Wittelsbachism was everywhere losing ground to the
charisma of Bismarck and his Reich.[89] Nevertheless, the Historical Association did try to represent the Wittelsbach's claims on the loyalties of Pfälzers.
Its charter called for the integration of local history into "history in general,"
in order to "animate . . . the attachment to the settings and customs of the
Heimat and to the princely house which is part of our inheritance."[90] The
idea that the Kurpfalz was the historical predecessor to the contemporary
Rhine District received some publicity. King Ludwig even went so far as to
build himself a vacation estate in what he dubbed the "land of his fathers."
After the region's renaming in 1838, the Historical Association began to refer
to the Wittelsbach monarch exclusively as "His Royal Pfalzgraf."[91] Perhaps
most important, the mere existence of the association, however meager its

85. Hermann Heimpel, "Geschichtsvereine einst und jetzt," *Geschichtswissenschaft und
Vereinswesen im 19. Jahrhundert*, ed. Hermann Heimpel (Göttingen, 1972), p. 48.
86. Ibid., p. 50. See also Thomas Nipperdey, "Verein als soziale Struktur in Deutschland
im späten 18. und frühen 19. Jahrhundert," in *Gesellschaft, Kultur, Theorie. Gesammelte Aufsätze zur
neueren Geschichte* (Göttingen, 1976).
87. Hermann Heimpel, "Über Organisationsformen historischer Forschung in Deutschland," *Historische Zeitschrift* 189 (1959): 207.
88. HVP, "Verzeichnis der Vereins-Mitgliedern" (1847), PLAS, T1.
89. Werner K. Blessing, "The Cult of the Monarchy, Political Loyalty, and the Workers'
Movement in Imperial Germany," *Journal of Contemporary History* 13 (1978): 365–66.
90. From section 1 of "Statuten des Vereins," in the HVP "Rechenschaftsbericht" (1839–
42), Landesarchiv Speyer, T1.
91. HVP, "Rechenschaftsbericht von Juli 1842 bis November 1846," Landesarchiv Speyer,
T1.

production of scholarly works, preempted the propagation of alternate historical views. The Hambach Festival had demonstrated the symbolic power and the practical convenience of castle ruins for popular assemblies. After the foundation of the Historical Association, a repetition of that regrettable affair was rendered unlikely, if not impossible, for all castle ruins now came under the "protection" of a staunchly conservative and pro-Bavarian preservationism.[92] Hambach itself was "given" to then Prince Max in 1839, in an act of supposedly spontaneous affection on the part of his loyal Pfälzer subjects.

Riehl himself was probably no more successful than the Historical Association had been in making Pfälzers love the Wittelsbachs, but by 1869 dynasticism had ceased to be an issue. The educated, politically active bourgeoisie had settled into a more or less comfortable compromise with the Bavarian state, the capstone of which was the unification of Germany in 1871. The resolution of political differences between the Pfalz and Bavaria, reinforced by the discovery of a distinctive Pfälzer history, folk life, and geography, cleared the way for new cultural institutions to flourish. In January 1869, on the eve of war and unification, the new administrative president of the Pfalz, Sigmund von Pfeufer, announced the refounding of the old Historical Association, which had dispersed in the 1850s. Pfeufer himself was an outspoken member of the kleindeutsch faction in Bavaria; his appointment to the Pfalz represented the willingness of Bavaria to accommodate its western province.[93] The Historical Association inevitably reflected this state of affairs between the Pfalz and Bavaria. For the first time, its membership included both the local bourgeoisie and Bavarian officials. Its first-secretary was Riehl's associate in the writing of the Pfälzer volume in *Bavaria*, the folklorist Ludwig Schandein. For the next thirty years, the Historical Association and the National Liberal party reigned jointly over the cultural and political life of the province, sharing members and a common understanding of the Pfalz in both Bavaria and Germany as a whole. Their ascendancy represented a unique cohesion of Bavarian, Pfälzer, and German patriotism. The combination would never again be so stable.

What made this fusion of local, state, and national loyalties possible was the remarkable cohesion of the Honoratioren, a largely bourgeois elite whose essence was local but whose dreams had long been national. The worldview of these notables began at home and ended up at large in the national sphere, where it stopped, venturing into cosmopolitanism or imperialism only excep-

---

92. Heimpel, "Geschichtsvereine einst und jetzt," p. 52. The point may seem trivial, but symbolism carries extra importance when power itself is in short supply, as it was for the popular movement.

93. Werner Schineller, *Die Regierungs-Präsidenten der Pfalz* (Neustadt/Pfalz, 1980), p. 53.

tionally. This particular journey of the imagination, reiterated in Honoratioren politics as well as in social and cultural life, gave German identity its
enduringly provincial character and gave provincial identities, like those of
the Pfälzers, their unmistakable Germanness. The Honoratioren thus hold at
least one key to understanding the way that Germans came together after
1871. Indispensable though war and diplomatic brilliance were in giving
Germany its nationhood, they tell us much less about the nature of national
consciousness than do these mental paths leading outward from every German province and hometown. Not bellicosity but provincialism was the hallmark of Honoratioren nationalism, and through their influence in the first
years of national unity it impressed itself on popular apprehension of the
nation as well.

   This localist worldview—or perhaps more accurately, "nationview"—
can be seen most clearly in the conduct of politics. The new national political
scene took shape after 1871 without benefit of long-standing national traditions or men of truly national experience.[94] Its leading figures, the first public
men of a united Germany, were for the most part the local notables, and
what they had to offer was their common experience of Germany's provincial
diversity. *Honoratiorenpolitik* (notable politics), more a political style than a
program, was a politics of both social privilege and provincial influence. The
political power of the Honoratioren grew out of the coalescing of the many
separate powers derived from local wealth or local bureaucratic office. It
reproduced itself through circles of friendship, influence, and association
among the locally prominent.[95] Even the elite status of the Honoratioren,
though it relied on commonly recognized standards of *Bildung und Besitz* (cultivation and property), had greater resonance in the locality than in the
nation.[96]

   The National Liberals, who considered themselves the standard-bearers
of unification, illustrate more clearly than any other political group this balance between local prestige and national ambition.[97] Even at the level of
national organization, the National Liberal party was essentially a collection
of distinct regional groups. At the cost of coherence, the national party
leader, Heinrich von Marquandsen, decided in 1870 to retain the "fluid
boundaries" that enabled the party nominally to represent such presumably
various constituencies. He argued, in words reminiscent of Riehl's social

   94. Sheehan, *German Liberalism*, p. 128.
   95. See the discussion by Geoff Eley in *Reshaping the German Right: Radical Nationalism and
Political Change after Bismarck* (New Haven, 1980), p. 20.
   96. Klaus Vondung, "Zur Lage der Gebildeten in der wilhelminischen Zeit," in *Das wilhelminische Bildungsbürgertum. Zur Sozialgeschichte seiner Ideen*, ed. Klaus Vondung (Göttingen, 1976),
p. 25.
   97. Dan S. White, *The Splintered Party: National Liberalism in Hessen and the Reich, 1867–1918*
(Cambridge, Mass., 1976), esp. pp. 1–10.

politics, that "our deference to local diversity and to liberalism as a whole remains most important and forbids a more rigorous centralization."[98] In the Pfalz, where National Liberals owned and ran most of the regional newspapers, controlled the region's district council, and provided most of its mayors, as well as all its representatives to the Reichstag and Bavarian Landtag, sympathy with von Marquandsen's national strategy did not preclude centralized and efficient control of regional politics.[99] The Pfälzer National Liberals were also socially homogeneous: all wealthy and all privileged in both educational and professional terms.[100]

But the Honoratioren brought more to national politics than decentralized parties rooted in carefully maintained provincial strongholds. They also brought the legacy of German associationalism, or *Vereinswesen*, for a long time the most important constituent of a German public sphere. To be a notable meant to belong to any number of voluntary associations, whether political, religious, professional, or simply avocational. The notables' associations were, moreover, testimony to a liberal tradition turned nationalist, then conservative. Voluntary associations had first flourished in Germany in the late eighteenth century as gathering places for the self-consciously enlightened. Free in their outward form from the constraints of station and rank, they created a space for a kind of inward freedom also: the freedom to speculate, to question, to speak of the common good, to consider oneself a member of the party of humanity and a representative of the general interests of mankind.[101] As voluntary associations became both more widespread and socially inclusive, they also became more specific in their goals, often dedicated to a particular aspect of agricultural improvement or a particular group of the needy poor. The voluntary associations of the nineteenth century came to represent, as one historian has put it, the "mastery of life through the medium of association."[102]

Voluntary associations were also closely allied to political liberalism and the nationalist movement, but after midcentury reaction and repression brought most under governmental ban. When they began to reappear in the 1860s, the majority had shed the legacy of enlightenment, of radicalism, and

98. Cited in Thomas Nipperdey, *Die Organisation der deutschen Parteien vor 1918* (Düsseldorf, 1961), p. 111.

99. Bräunche, *Parteien und Reichstagswahlen*, pp. 5, 42–43, 54ff.

100. Schneider, "Anfänge der sozialistischen Arbeiterbewegung," p. 86.

101. See especially Nipperdey, "Verein als soziale Struktur"; Otto Dann, "Die Anfänge politischer Vereinsbildung in Deutschland," in *Soziale Bewegung und politische Verfassung*, ed. U. Engelhardt, Volker Sellin, and Horst Stuke (Stuttgart, 1976); Werner Conze, "Der Verein als Lebensform des 19. Jahrhunderts," *Die Innere Mission: Zeitschrift des Werkes Innere Mission und Hilfswerk der Evangelischen Kirche in Deutschland* 50 (1960): 226–34; Heinz Schmitt, *Das Vereinswesen der Stadt Weinheim an der Bergstraße* (Weinheim, 1963), p. 8.

102. Braun, *Sozialer und Kultureller Wandel*, p. 17.

of reform, hanging on only to their philanthropic and cultural guises and to their commitment to action by the few for the many.[103] When those few had been a beleaguered minority—like the enlightened bourgeoisie of the old regime—their altruism had potentially revolutionary consequences; but when the few became the representatives of privilege itself, the Honoratioren of an increasingly mass society, the political coloration of voluntary associations was bound to change. Thus by the 1870s most voluntary associations tended to reproduce the social hierarchies that already existed, rather than to challenge the very notion of hierarchy. Associations provided the local notables with opportunities for the acquisition and exercise of influence; in their meetings people met, talked, disputed, planned, exchanged news, or simply showed themselves to one another.

The Pfälzer notables, for instance, saw one another at the political meetings of the National Liberal's regional association in Neustadt, at the regional Chamber of Commerce in Ludwigshafen, at associations of the United Protestant Church or Catholic associations in Speyer, and in countless other smaller associations in every town of the region. After 1869 they gathered also at the monthly meeting of the Historical Association of the Pfalz in Speyer. Beyond simply providing another forum for the enjoyment of exclusivity, the Historical Association created and in its activities promulgated a regional historical tradition that legitimated both their regional rootedness and their national aspirations. Just as Honoratiorenpolitik preserved and built on the essential political integrity of the locality, so the Historical Association preserved the region's cultural integrity and maintained it, invented or not, as the surest constituent of German nationhood.

The renewal of the Historical Association of the Pfalz in 1869 under the patronage of the Honoratioren marked a third stage in the emergence of Pfälzer identity. In it, the Honoratioren played the role of the consolidators, the builders of institutions and the founders of journals, both of which, for better or for worse, gave an official voice to provincial distinctiveness. The new association was the first of these group efforts and for a long time the most successful. It immediately exceeded the expectations of its founders.[104] Within a few months of the public announcement of its reopening about six hundred people had joined, among whom could be counted the most important political, administrative, and religious leaders of the region. Led by the administrative president of the region himself, it quickly became a focus of elite society in the Pfalz and the leading guardian of regional culture in all its forms. The founders hoped that the association could bring recognition to a

103. In 1869, for instance, Bavaria granted *Rechtsfähigkeit*, or legal standing, only to associations "pursuing idealistic goals"; see Wolfgang Meyer, "Das Vereinswesen der Stadt Nürnberg im 19. Jahrhundert" (diss., Universität Würzburg, 1970), pp. 14, 30.
104. Albert Becker, *Hundert Jahre Pfälzer Geschichtsforschung*, p. 139.

region that had been "the continuous site of far-reaching and momentous historical events . . . from the earliest stirrings of German culture to the present" and yet still suffered under the opprobrium of its closeness to France.[105] The Historical Association would prove to Pfälzers and Germans alike the region's importance to the nation.

The statutes of the Historical Association, approved on April 3, stated its purpose to be "the research of native [*einheimisch*] history and the preservation and collection of its monuments amd remains."[106] The property of the association would devolve on the Pfälzer district government in the case of dissolution—an unusual provision for voluntary associations in general but standard for historical ones, whose quasi-official status corresponded to their public role as guardians of the region's past. Other paragraphs made provision for open membership, dues, leadership, regular meetings, and local representatives to oversee historical business in each of the region's towns.[107]

This administrative structure, unremarkable in every way, nevertheless had important affinities with the structure and operation of notable politics. First of all, the association's system of indirect voting reproduced the electoral procedures both of the local National Liberal party and of the Bavarian Landtag. The actual directors (or candidates or deputies) received their mandate from an ever-narrowing circle of electors. Indirect voting assured the influence of an elite at the expense of the active participation of ordinary members. Elections were held only to confirm decisions already made; they brought no surprises and contained little drama. For most offices the candidate went unopposed: neither intrigue nor dispute was permitted to disturb the operation of local affairs.

Since the 1830s, the position of chairman was held by whoever happened to be the Bavarian-appointed district president in the Pfalz. It was an arrangement as deferential as it was calculated, as inflexible as it was informal. The association received the benefits of official sponsorship, and the president multiplied his informal ties to local business and political leaders, who in turn joined in great numbers, at least in part because of his presence and patronage.[108] On the symbolic level, Bavaria emphasized its commitment to the Pfalz by allowing its highest official to participate in matters of purely voluntary and local interest; the Pfalz in return put its very history at Bavaria's command. In this elitist setting, where harmony and unity were to

105. "Einladung zur Betheiligung an einem historischen Vereine der Pfalz" (January 1869), Pfälzische Landesbibliothek Speyer (hereafter cited as PLBS).

106. They were modelled on those of a Swabian historical club. Becker, *Hundert Jahre*, p. 143.

107. "Satzungen des historischen Vereines der Pfalz," *Mitteilungen des Historischen Vereins der Pfalz* (hereafter cited as *MHVP*) 1 (1870): 24–27.

108. Or so speculated First-Secretary Ludwig Schandein, and his observation seems reasonable; Schandein is cited in Albert Becker, *Hundert Jahre*, p. 139.

everyone's advantage, the giving and receiving of benefits were circular and continuous. The Historical Association provided such a setting, and the ex officio participation of the district president ensured its survival. The ordinary membership to the Historical Association also reflected the distribution of power, wealth, and education in the region. High officials, clerics, educators, businessmen, minor bureaucrats, and other professionals each accounted for about 15 percent of the total membership of 586, but the distribution of the groups across the Pfalz varied widely, its pattern revealing the differentiated local structures of the notables.[109] Doctors, lawyers, tax collectors, parsons, and teachers were to be found in every town, but military officers came only from Landau, engineers from Ludwigshafen, iron magnates from the corner by the Saar, and wine magnates from the Rhine hills. Speyer, capital of the province, offered the most glittering array of titles, from the heads of the Protestant general synod and the Catholic diocese to a large assortment of *Regierungsdirektoren, Regierungsräte, Gymnasialprofessoren*, and *Konsistorialräte*. The association also boasted fifteen mayors, a replication at the municipal level of the district president's leadership at the regional level. Thus, although theoretically anyone could join, the association maintained a clear social exclusivity.[110] Perhaps a certain level of education was required of members to comprehend, if not to appreciate, the esoteric nature of the group's historical activities, and the dues and letter of application could have been an obstacle to some. But probably the process of exclusion operated less directly. Membership in the Historical Association was not, after all, so much an avenue to prominence and prestige as a symbol of having attained them. The association recognized those who had no need of its recognition, and the rewards for joining were intangible.

Certainly a club of this sort derived its coherence as much from its membership as from what it actually did. Indeed, the records of its regular meetings, undeniably dull affairs, would lead one to think that the only plausible explanation for the association's existence was its provision of a dignified forum for self-congratulation.[111] But that would not do justice to the genuine enthusiasm the association's members had for local history, or to the public

---

109. The calculations are rough: out of 586, high government officials and mayors accounted for 89 members, or 15 percent; minor bureaucrats, 115, or 19 percent; teachers of all levels, 80, or 14 percent; businessmen, including bankers, factory owners, and large estate owners, 105, or 18 percent; clerics, both Catholic and Protestant, 95, or 16 percent; and professionals, including doctors, lawyers, and engineers, 77, or 13 percent. In addition, the Verein included 16 men of independent means and 9 military officers. Only one woman belonged to the Verein; she was a landowner. See "Verzeichniss der Mitglieder," *MHVP* 1 (1870): 27–41.

110. Letters requesting membership in the association, PLAS, T1, no. 14.

111. See the "Jahresberichte" of the Historische Verein in *MHVP* 2, 3, 5, 6, 7, 9 (1871, 1872, 1875, 1877, 1878, 1880); and Protokollbücher, 1869–99, PLAS, T1, no. 4.

significance they attributed to pursuit of that history. Both the enthusiasm and the civic-mindedness are evident in the activity closest to the hearts of association members: the collection, excavation, and restoration of artifacts from the past. In the latter half of the nineteenth century, excavations were the playgrounds of eager amateurs. To see the past embedded within nature heightened its appeal, and digging things up—particularly Roman things— became the rage of the educated bourgeoisie.[112] In the decades of *Kulturkampf* (Bismarck's anti-Catholic campaign), moreover, ancient coins and vessels served as the holy relics of enlightened Catholics and Protestants, both groups eager to distance themselves from the irrational excesses of popular religion. Outings to excavate and restore the past were like pilgrimages— collective rituals of which the Historical Association, divided between Protestants and Catholics, stood in symbolic need.

The Historical Association was able to organize much hitherto random excavation and direct it toward public ends. It sponsored its own archeological digs and its own restorations of ruined castles and abbeys. It brought in experts from Munich and Heidelberg to assist in excavation and restoration and organized the financial and physical support of local groups, in return for later public access to the findings.[113] Yet lack of funds prevented the association from undertaking all it would have liked. In 1872, for instance, the association, in consultation with the Bavarian government, decided to abandon its efforts to restore the old and new castles of Wolfstein, neither of which could claim architectural or historical distinction. Association and state contented themselves, however, with a "true likeness in oil or a photographic image."[114]

That the association should have settled for a painting in lieu of an actual restoration gives us a clue to the particular mentality of these gatherers of the past. The painting of "Alt und Neu Wolfstein" was more accessible than the castles themselves, which were hidden in a remote corner of the Pfalz, far from Speyer, far from the Rhine, far, indeed, from most places where Pfälzer notables tended to congregate. The painting, unlike the castles, could be moved to Speyer, where its testimony to the Pfälzer past could be properly absorbed and appreciated. Later generations of Heimatkundlers would extend their reach into the forests, but the Honoratioren historians were most

---

112. Arnold Esch, "Limesforschung und Geschichtsvereine: Romanismus und Germanismus, Dilettantismus und Facharchäologie in der Bodenforschung des 19. Jahrhunderts," in Heimpel, *Geschichtswissenschaft und Vereinswesen*, p. 163.

113. Occasionally complaints were raised against the historical clubs of Germany for being academically sloppy and isolated from real scholars; see, e.g., Gustav Bossert, *Die Historische Vereine vor dem Tribunal der Wissenschaft* (Berlin, 1883). Innovators they were not, but the scholarly respectability of their work has been generally acknowledged.

114. "Jahresbericht," *MHVP* 3 (1872): 147.

interested in small objects that could be put in museums: a painting of a castle was better than the castle itself; an actual piece of the castle—if one could justify such removal—was best of all.

Indeed, for all their talk of restoration and preservation, what the association members really devoted themselves to was acquisition.[115] In 1869, the same awakening of interest in regional history that produced the Historical Association sparked a renewed interest in an old and dusty collection of Roman artifacts that had sat in a shed by the Speyer cathedral since the 1830s.[116] The city of Speyer and the Pfälzer district council voted to establish a district museum to house the pieces; the city also contributed some of its own historical objects, to which were added the private collections of several founding members of the association.[117] A museum commission, representing city, state, and Historical Association, shared in the administration.[118]

The museum gave the association a decidedly public face. Housed in rooms at the *Gymnasium* (university-preparatory secondary school), where it would be available "to any man and at any time," the museum's collection seemed to its founders to be a gift to the "friends of patriotic history" and an honor to the "whole Fatherland."[119] With a taxonomic enthusiasm, they urged people to contribute inscribed stones, sculptures, altarpieces, Germanic and Roman tombs, vases, weapons, jewelry, coins, holy vessels, furniture, carpets, carved work, ornamental glass, portraits of historically significant people, books with miniatures, family trees and patents with heraldic drawings, guild emblems, documents, seals, and artistic depictions—of all sorts and from all eras—of festivals, battles, costumes, cities, public places, castles, palaces, churches, and ordinary houses. To those possessed of the acquisitive urge, the Pfalz was a treasure house tantalizingly full of lost and hidden objects. Ludwig Schandein, the association's secretary, encouraged

115. The budgets of the association from 1869 through 1880 show that the largest single expenditure each year was "Anschaffungen für die Sammlungen und die Bibliothek." Other expenses came from mailing costs, servants' wages, and, above all, the costs of publishing the journal. But more than half the overall outlay of money throughout that decade was for acquisitions—an average of 555 florins per year, or 52 percent of annual expenditure. In contrast, the association spent only 200 florins on restoration during the whole decade. See "Auszüge aus der Rechnung des historischen Vereines," *MHVP* 1–9 (1870–80).

116. The artifacts had been left to the old HVP by a departing Bavarian administrator and amateur archeologist, Joseph von Stichaner. For a more cheerful account of the museum's beginnings, see Albert Becker, *Hundert Jahre*, pp. 87–93; and Ludwig Schandein, "Kurze Geschichte des Historischen Vereines der Pfalz," *MHVP* 1 (1870): 129–30.

117. Albert Becker, *Hundert Jahre*, p. 147.

118. Karl Schultz, "Wesen und Wandel des pfälzischen Landesmuseum," *PH* 11 (1960): 116ff.

119. "Die Verwaltung des historischen Museums der Pfalz in Speier an die Freunde der vaterländischen Geschichte" (January 1870), PLBS.

members to search the fields and attics of local people (with, of course, their consent and help). The various subdistrict representatives of the association were sent out to urge private collectors to give up their treasures to the public museum in Speyer.[120] Association leaders persuaded city guilds to contribute their records, seals, historical tools, and whatever else might be deemed significant. The ongoing construction of the railroad in the Pfalz also proved a source of booty: early negotiations with the railroad authorities in Ludwigshafen brought the association a large and miscellaneous collection of old objects turned up by the railroad builders since the 1840s.[121] And when in 1869 a piece of meteor fell near the Pfälzer village of Krähenberg, an association representative was quickly at the scene of the excitement to buy it for the museum.[122] Piece by piece, the association brought the Pfälzer past to Speyer and put it on display, labeled, categorized, and open to the public. The vision was comprehensive and powerful: if it could retrieve a rock from the heavens and call it a piece of Pfälzer history, little else could remain alien for long.

In fact, what soon strikes one about the historical activities of the club is the remarkable absence of attention to conventional standards of historical "greatness." At a time when the self-proclaimed national historians were demonstrating a slavish devotion to questions of state power and prestige, these localists ran around the countryside in pursuit of the most trivial bits of everyday life in the past. Not only the museum but the club's annual journal as well was filled as much with information about local building and dress, local festivities and religious practices, and local folk customs as with testimonials to dead princes and bygone wars.[123] Even the occasional accounts of wars dwelt far more on the disturbance of local life and the destruction of property than on the valor of kings and nobles.[124] In an article in 1877, Christian Mehlis, teacher and association member, wrote that "each object, even the smallest, is a stone in a great building that mankind has alternately constructed and destroyed for thousands of years."[125]

Pfälzer historians preferred this kind of broadly defined *Kulturgeschichte*

120. "Jahresbericht, 1869/70," *MHVP* 2 (1871): 127ff.
121. "Kurze Geschichte," *MHVP* 1 (1870): 19.
122. Ibid.; and Albert Becker, *Hundert Jahre*, p. 147.
123. See, e.g., Philipp Schneider, "Die Mähtergerechtigkeit und das Mähterbuch von Mussbach," *MHVP*, Festgabe (1874): 11ff.; or the regular reports by Ludwig Schandein on *Weistümer*: "Weisthum von Hagenbach, c. 1480," *MHVP*, Festgabe (1874), or "Weisthum von Neuhofen, 1534," *MHVP* 7 (1878).
124. See, e.g., C. Weiss, "Der Kriegsschäden, welchen die freie Reichstadt Speier im XVII und XVIII Jahrhundert durch die Franzosen erlitten hat, nachgewiesen aus Urkunden der Speier Stadtarchiv," *MHVP* 2 (1871): 37ff.; or the same author's "Das Rechnungswesen der freien Reichstadt Speier im Mittelalter," *MHVP* 5 (1875): 27ff.
125. Dr. C. Mehlis, "Die praehistorische Funde der Pfalz," *MHVP* 6 (1877): x.

(history of cultures) at least in part because of the nature of the available evidence. The important archival collections of the more prominent local rulers lay outside the Pfalz in Heidelberg, Karlsruhe, Munich, Darmstadt, and Vienna. The only past for which records remained belonged to minor lords or to ordinary burghers and peasants. So perhaps the past political fragmentation of the Pfalz led the association to follow the intellectual model of the brothers Grimm rather than that of Heinrich von Treitschke.[126] But the association's tendency to find its past not in tales of glory but in the land itself was also a conscious choice, for which Wilhelm Heinrich Riehl was indirectly responsible. He turned its attention away from political history to the Eigentum and everyday experience of the people. Schandein, a dialect poet who gave intellectual leadership to the association in its first decade, had studied with Riehl, under whose direction he wrote large portions of the "Pfalz" volume in the ethnographic blockbuster *Bavaria*.[127] Christian Mehlis, too, had heard Riehl lecture, and he brought to his concern with prehistoric archeology a Riehlian mission to uncover the true essence of the people. The prehistoric past, thought Mehlis, contained the key to the "customs and morals" of man and revealed his "essential claims [*Eigenthums-rechte*] to state, law, religion, art, and science."[128] "Know thyself," admonished Mehlis, in attributing to the remnants of prehistory the same revelatory power that Riehl saw in folk life in general.

Most important, folk life, not politics, was what gave the Pfalz its most profound connection to the German essence. Ludwig Schandein's favorite project in these early years of the history club drew together folklore and history, the locality and the nation. Beginning in his first yearly report, he encouraged association members, especially teachers and parsons, to take on the writing of their town's or village's history. "Our goal," he wrote in 1870, "is to make possible in the future a comprehensive history of the Pfalz . . . A historical association should not concern itself only with the . . . history that is over and done with: it should also concern itself with history coming into being. We [are] the witnesses of the present."[129] Schandein wanted the village chroniclers to record everything that happened in their village, from weather to religion, paying particular attention to the events of the war then in progress. Each chronicle was to have been preceded, moreover, by as full

126. In fact, the association's interest in the collection and publication of *Weistümer* stemmed in part from Jakob Grimm's work on them, in which he used Pfälzer examples; see Ludwig Schandein, "Ganerbenweisthum von Hanhofen," *MHVP* 2 (1871): 21.

127. The admiration was evidently mutual: Riehl cited Schandein in *Die Pfälzer* as one of three great dialect poets in the region; see *Die Pfälzer*, p. 226. For Schandein's work on the "Pfalz" volume, see Ernst Christmann, "Ludwig Schandein als Volkskundeforscher," *PH* 14 (1963): 78–79; see also above, pp. 34–35.

128. Mehlis, "Die praehistorische Funde," p. 2.

129. Ludwig Schandein, "Zur Einführung von Ortschroniken," *MHVP* 1 (1870): 42.

an account of the village's past as could be reconstructed. "Out of these many particular histories," Schandein argued, "in which the stamp of the whole is mirrored in the locality, emerges the history of the district, the region, the province, the whole land."[130] To develop a "historical sensibility" in people of the present, one had to begin with "the narrow Heimat." This historical sensibility in turn was "the teacher of the future: the love of the Fatherland is rooted in the love of Heimat."[131]

With such projects and such intellectual models, the Historical Association bestowed order on the random avocational pursuits of the local bourgeoisie and coherence on a chaotic collection of artifacts with dubious claim to the adjective *Pfälzer*. The Pfalz patently lacked a regional tradition to give substance to its regional identity, and without a regional tradition the achievements of its notable citizens suffered an intangible loss of dignity. What was the Pfalz, and who were the Pfälzers? One needed only to visit the museum to find a preliminary answer to the question—an answer pieced together from many artifacts of many pasts. It mattered less that the artifact was Roman or late medieval than that it had been found in the province and attested to past human settlement there. The museum made an argument for the historical existence of the Pfalz that also reinforced the region's contemporary existence, recent and arbitrary though its borders may have been. Walking through the rooms of the museum, a local notable could feel his position of influence securely rooted in ancient stones. Moreover, in his collecting and excavating, he had conquered that elusive past and brought it to Speyer, where its glories might shine to brighten his own.

The act of making whole a fragmented past must also have resonated for contemporaries with the politically parallel creation of national unity. The Heimatgeschichte practiced by Schandein and others revealed the connections that bound merely local artifacts and facts to a German national history. So too, on an institutional level, did the formal ties the club maintained with other regional history clubs and with the Gesamtverein der deutschen Geschichts- und Altertumsvereine (General Association of German Historical and Antiquarian Associations), founded "in order to bring the spirit of

---

130. Ibid., pp. 44–45.
131. Ibid., p. 48. Schandein envisioned these local chronicles filling the district archive, but apart from a few pieces published in the club's journal, there is little evidence that any were written. See, e.g., A. Stauber, "Kloster und Dorf Lamprecht," *MHVP* 9 (1880): 50–228, which not only discusses the social organization of the cloister but also includes a respectable social history of the village, with accounts of property relations, legal arrangements, the Wallonians and their cloth industry, economic matters, population change, church, schools, and conflicts between the Kurpfalz and the bishopric as they affected the village. See also Hermann Zapf, "Über die Zeit der Entstehung von Pirmasens: Eine geschichtliche, sprachliche und topographische Untersuchung, zugleich Beitrag zur ältesten westricher Landesgeschichte," *MHVP* 11 (1883): 99–144.

common German history to the various provincial and territorial efforts."[132] In 1874, the national group held its annual convention in Speyer, a public celebration of the confluence of region and nation in the pursuit of Heimatgeschichte.[133] The nationalism of such groups was rooted in the region; their purpose, the interweaving of all German histories. Regions—regional politics, culture, society—gave substance to the nation, and in the first years of unification both the parts and the whole that they constituted claimed their victory over the fragmentation of the past.

Although the Historical Association was the chief beneficiary of the civic activism of the Pfälzer notables, thus the chief guardian of Pfälzer identity, it was not the only collective effort to celebrate local distinctiveness in the first decades after unification. An expansive interest in local culture, history, monuments, and nature characterized local society in general, and hence a number of heterogeneous groups and individuals in particular. Other Heimat activists may not have had the comprehensive reach or the scholarly weight of the Historical Association, but they do tell us about tensions within Pfälzer society that affected the definition and celebration of Pfälzerness itself. Local identity, even though purged of radicalism and Francophilia, was not immune to a variety of interpretations. No matter how uncontroversial the Historical Association may have considered its keeping of the Pfälzer flame, there were others who objected either to its history or to its social exclusivity. Lines of geography, of class, of religion, and of politics all left subtle but recognizable marks on the emerging consciousness of a Pfälzer community.[134]

Of these, the most important for the period in which Pfälzer identity was consolidated were the confessional differences. The precise effect on Pfälzer identity of religious conflict—between a bare majority of Protestants and a substantial Catholic minority—is hard to pin down, since associational

---

132. Cited in Albert Becker, *Hundert Jahre*, p. 151. For a listing of all the local historical journals to which the Verein subscribed, see "Katalog der Bibliothek," *MHVP*, Festgabe (1874): 41–80; see also George Biundo, "Entwicklung und Stand der pfälzischen Heimatforschung," *MHVP* 51 (1953): 10–11.

133. See the accounts in Albert Becker, *Hundert Jahre*, pp. 151–52; *Speierer Anzeiger*, no. 223 (24 September 1874); *Unterhaltungsblatt zum Speierer Anzeiger*, no. 110 (24 September 1874); *Speierer Beobachter*, no. 225 (26 September 1874).

134. The notables themselves were not a homogeneous group. Roger Chickering argues for a diversity of context—i.e., the notables of a villages versus the notables of a major city—and a diversity of social background, marking out particularly the "new men" of the late nineteenth century, who achieved a higher academic education than had their parents, at a time, moreover, of enormous increases in the ranks of the professions, technical services, and secondary education. See his *We Men Who Feel Most German* (Boston, 1984), pp. 111–13; see also Vondung, "Zur Lage der Gebildeten," pp. 26–27.

records acknowledged it only by silences and omissions, never by overt signs of hostility. Nevertheless, the official version of Pfälzer patriotism that took hold after unification had a distinctly Protestant bias. The Pfälzer bourgeoisie was a largely Protestant group and, to the extent that political and social characteristics coincided, largely liberal. At least in the eyes of conservative Catholics (whether the Pfälzer clergy or the Bavarian administration), liberalism, Protestantism, and the bourgeoisie had an unholy affinity for one another in the Pfalz. And since those who had longest and loudest proclaimed their loyalty to the Pfalz were precisely these liberal bourgeois Protestants, Catholic leaders kept their distance from local patriotism even in its toned-down form. Their own parishioners were mostly poor, often agricultural laborers rather than landowners, workers rather than store-keepers, rural people rather than town dwellers. They had not been active in the years of political agitation; their religious leaders had thus been free to support the conservative, monarchical cause without much popular Catholic resistance.[135]

The decade of the 1850s was a high point for established Catholicism in the Pfalz, which was able to strengthen the church organization and church attendance with the support of a sympathetic Bavarian administration. However, the 1860s and above all the 1870s were marked by the confluence of a number of crises, all of which tended further to distance the Catholic establishment from the celebratory expressions of Pfälzer identity. In the first place, Pfälzer patriotism, under the patronage of the National Liberal notables, became increasingly tied to the Prussian-led nationalist movement in the 1860s. The Bavarian administration itself came under the control of liberals like Johann Lutz who were unsympathetic to Catholic independence. Kleindeutsch nationalism was already wreaking havoc among the German Catholics, placing them in the impossible position of having to choose between Rome and Germany at a time when Rome itself was demanding their absolute obedience. And unlike the Rhineland to the north of the Pfalz, where Catholicism and local patriotism could together make common cause against Prussia, the Pfalz, having found itself in resistance to a Catholic state, now asserted sympathy for a militantly Protestant one. Catholic alienation from official Pfälzerism became only more marked in the decade of Kulturkampf. To be sure, the liberal campaign against the political and cultural influence of Rome was, as one historian put it, only a cold war in Bavarian territories, one that rarely reached the extent or pitch of the Prussian campaign. Nevertheless, on issues of schooling and state influence it became hot enough, particularly in the Pfalz. There the clergy lacked the support of majority opinion in the Landtag and among the populace that protected it in

135. Ludwig Stamer, *Kirchengeschichte der Pfalz*, vol. 4 (Speyer, 1964), pp. 150–57, 196–97.

old Bavaria. In the course of the conflict in the Pfalz, the bishopric of Speyer stood empty for much of the 1870s because a candidate acceptable to both church and state could not be found, and the one Catholic Gymnasium in the region was forced to abandon its confessional character.[136]

The Catholic notables in the Pfalz played an equivocal role throughout these uncomfortable years. Many, including the man who briefly filled the Speyer bishopric in the early 1870s, participated in local affairs alongside their political opponents. The Historical Association, headed by the Bavarian, Protestant, and National Liberal von Pfeufer, attracted Catholic membership, even while it pursued a strenuously nonconfessional history and implicitly supported the teaching of such history in nonconfessional schools.[137] Indeed, the Catholic Honoratioren, a small minority among their social and professional equals, seemed for the most part to have pursued an assimilationist course, even to the extent of sympathizing with the "old Catholic" movement against the tightening orthodoxy of Pope Pius IX.[138]

One voice among the Catholic notability stands out both for its resistance to such assimilation and for its representation of a love for the Pfalz that did not hang on the Deidesheim-Berlin axis. For decades the only publication in the region dedicated to Heimat literature, *Palatina* was a belletristic supplement to the Catholic *Pfälzer Zeitung*, edited by the conservative politican Lukas Jäger and later by his son Eugen.[139] Both were outspokenly anti-Prussian. Eugen supported the federalist case for a decentralized empire and, in 1878, made the paper an official organ of the Catholic Center party.[140] He attempted, moreover, to raise the intellectual and aesthetic level of the *Pfälzer Zeitung* and *Palatina*, in order to win a readership of educated Catholics who might be diverted from their assimilationalist course.

Accordingly, *Palatina*'s editor in the 1870s, Eduard Geib, tried to make the magazine a "clean and noble" undertaking that "no one would be ashamed or embarrassed to read . . . no father, no mother, would have cause to put it aside for fear it fall into the hands of a daughter or a son."[141] Like the nationally circulated *Gartenlaube*, *Palatina* was a paper with modest literary— but high moral—pretensions. Indeed, while the *Gartenlaube* sought to appeal to tastes and aspirations held in common by German middle-class society,

---

136. Ibid., pp. 260–76.

137. The issue of history teaching was central to the controversy over the Speyer *Gymnasium*; see ibid., p. 264.

138. Their position was distinctly in the minority among the Pfälzer Catholics, both clergy and laity, who stuck loyally to the pope; see Stamer, *Kirchengeschichte*, pp. 235–48.

139. Lorenz Wingerter, *Geschichte der "Palatina"* (Speyer, 1926), pp. 6–12; Bräunche, *Parteien und Reichstagswahlen*, p. 113.

140. Wingerter, *Geschichte der "Palatina,"* p. 47.

141. "Einführung," *Palatina* (1859).

Palatina took up the complementary provincial task of emphasizing the national in local life, literature, and folklore, of promoting "Fatherland thoughts"—in short, of "enlivening and deepening the feeling for Heimat" among Pfälzers.[142]

But in common with its parent newspaper, *Palatina* also had a vision of the Pfalz and its place in Germany different from that of the Historical Association and its patrons among the National Liberals. The journal's editors held firmly to the ideal of a greater Germany, to their respect for Austria, and to their support for Catholicism.[143] For instance, a group of poems by the Pfälzer Johannes Hüll, reviewed in *Palatina* in 1875, spoke out against the materialism and soullessness of contemporary German nationalism. According to the reviewer, the strongest proof of nationalism's philistinism was the "so-called Kulturkampf, which is really a struggle *against* culture, *for* social revolution and the destruction of German folk life."[144] In the end, *Palatina* suffered from its failure to attract prominent local sponsors from the ranks of the wealthy Protestants and hence never became the local literary counterpart to the Historical Association. Nevertheless, its survival well into the 1920s attested to the existence of a Catholic minority in quiet dissent from the reigning institutions of local culture.

The politics of unification and national consolidation made allies out of unlikely combinations of forces; in the Pfalz, it brought together conservative political Catholicism with democratic liberalism and social democracy, in common cause against the reign of the National Liberals. Although the overtly political alliance of these groups did not emerge until the 1890s, when they cooperated to defeat National Liberal candidates in a few Pfälzer districts, as early as the 1870s the grounds for agreement, at least between the großdeutsch Catholics and Democrats, were clear enough to make the Pfälzer novelist and Democrat August Becker a frequent contributor to *Palatina*. Becker himself tried in the 1870s to establish a literary journal in the region but ran up against the same lack of sympathy among the Honoratioren that ultimately lessened the influence of *Palatina* as well.

Becker had been born in the Pfalz but had lived in Munich most of his creative life, whence he looked back on the Pfalz with more affection than he had felt while actually there. Indeed, this perpetual émigré devoted his entire literary output to the people and places of the Pfalz, becoming the region's favorite Heimat novelist and, with the publication of *Die Pfalz und die Pfälzer*

---

142. Wingerter, *Geschichte der "Palatina,"* p. 15.

143. See, e.g., H. A. Schaufert, "Es gibt nichts Neues unter der Sonne," *Palatina* (1860): 91–92, 95–96, 103–4—essentially a call for German cultural diversity and political union with Austria.

144. Eduard Geib, "*Wächterrufe*: Neue Gedichte von Johannes Hüll," *Palatina* (1874): 151.

in 1858, its best known folklorist also.[145] More thorough in his examination of local culture than Riehl had been in *Die Pfälzer*, Becker also admired the democratic spirit of the Pfälzers more than had the monarchist Riehl—so much more, in fact, that the Bavarian establishment that had welcomed Riehl's work ignored Becker's. When Becker did finally decide to return to the region in 1868, he staked his fortunes on a literary journal, despite the Pfälzers' notorious indifference to the benefits of poetry for the better appreciation of life.[146]

His faith in the eventual openness of Pfälzers to his plans was based on his faith in the essential goodness of the folk character, which was in turn the basis of his democratic politics. "All it would take," he confided to his son, "would be to offer the people something better out of their own house and yard, field and forest [than has up until now been available]: for the peasants, to depict their doings and desires engagingly, in an entertaining, descriptive, and instructive fashion, with humor and earnestness, lively and intelligible, and most of all, without learned pedantry.[147] His offering was to be a low-priced weekly paper called *Die Heimat*. He went so far as to draw up the outline for a first issue and in 1878 sent it out to friends and potential patrons in the Pfalz. But despite his great enthusiasm ("traveling and working in the Pfalz would be my life," he wrote to a friend, "and one could make little more claim to happiness in life!"), the project failed to gain the support of the district president, Paul von Braun, and other high officials, whose patronage Becker's friends in the Pfalz thought to be crucial.[148] "I see that he is also president in matters of taste, in the realm of ideas and intellectual undertakings!" wrote Becker, maddened that his potential supporters followed the judgment of the "all-prevailing" von Braun. "So it stands in the free-thinking, enlightened Pfalz!"[149] When friends tried nevertheless to per-

145. According to most accounts, Becker wrote the work as an entry for a royal contest for the best study of a Bavarian folk group, supposedly "won" by W. H. Riehl with his *Die Pfälzer*. The actual existence of this contest remains dubious and may have been no more than a public way of rewarding Riehl for a study he had been working on for years and of which King Max was fully informed. Becker's work more probably was commissioned as a travel guide. See Oskar Bischoff, introduction to the new edition of Becker's *Die Pfalz und die Pfälzer* (Landau/Pfalz, 1983), p. x.

146. He often complained bitterly, for example, of the lack of appreciation his own works received there—a past neglect for which time has certainly made up. See Oskar Bischoff, "August Beckers Leben und Schaffen," in the 1983 edition of *Die Pfalz und die Pfälzer*, p. xxi; A. Schmitt, "August Beckers Leben und Werke," *Pfälzisches Museum. Monatsschrift für heimatliche Literatur und Kunst, Geschichte und Volkskunde* (hereafter cited as *PM*) 19 (1902).

147. Karl August Becker, "August Beckers 'Heimat' blieb Projekt. Stehen wir heute vor den gleichen Schwierigkeiten?" *Pfalz und Pfälzer: Monatshefte für Kultur, Heimatpflege und Unterhaltung* (hereafter cited as *PP*) 1 (April 1950): 2.

148. Ibid.
149. Ibid.

suade him to move to the Pfalz, he replied: "My homesickness is not so great that I would take on the role of toady."

As Becker's final remarks reveal, the challenge implicit in the Heimat-literary efforts of both himself and *Palatina* was not so much to the politics of the National Liberals or to the religion of the Protestants as simply to the influence of the Honoratioren over all matters of local importance. Religious and political differences certainly informed that challenge, but in the case of Heimat activities they were less important than the mere fact of a narrow elite's unwillingness to give broader play to the expressions of local patriotism. After the passions of unification died down, the question became one of who was to have charge of the Pfälzer identity: under whose auspices its castles would be visited, its mountains climbed, its ruins excavated, its history investigated, its forests and villages extolled. Patronage, not ideology, was at stake.

In 1880, the paths to local cultural success still led through, if not to, the Protestant notables, the Bavarian state, and the Historical Association of the Pfalz. But the claims of the Historical Association and the notables to represent something that transcended the bounds of both their essential regionality and their social exclusivity would be undermined in the next decades of unrelenting popularization of the Heimat theme. It in turn followed on the heels of social, economic, and political changes that seriously weakened the traditional political practices of the notables. By 1880 the notables' position was questioned not just by the claims of the petty bourgeois and working classes but by the very existence of political conflict. Their unity was always more social than political, and in the last decades of the nineteenth century conflict over economic issues led to the attenuation of notables' power and prestige, particularly on the level of national politics but also regionally.[150]

The Historical Association bore an ambiguous relation to the political and economic changes the Pfalz underwent after 1870. On the one hand, its removal from any explicitly political realm protected it from specifically political disruptions. But on the other, it still represented the triumph of a particular vision of Pfälzer identity, stripped of its revolutionary origins and tamed into assimilation with a nonliberal, nondemocratic, and certainly non-revolutionary national state. In fact, its articulation of local and national identity was too closely bound to the prestige of its members and to the legacy of Pfälzer pacification to protect it from either challenge or change. Although the association continued to promote the history of the Pfalz and even began to broaden its audience beyond the highly educated and prop-

150. Blackbourn, "Discreet Charm of the Bourgeoisie," p. 261.

ertied notables, its monopoly over regional traditions was no longer absolute. Its position may have remained dominant and its academic preeminence uncontested, but these other associations, other publications, and other people all contributed to a transformation, one that would reach its climax in the two decades before the war, of the once-guarded landscape of Heimat.

THREE

The Heimat Movement

In 1916, while the distant boom of German shells exploding at Verdun was heard in the classrooms of Kaiserslautern, the local teacher and historian Hermann Schreibmüller reflected on the rebirth of local consciousness that had taken place in the Pfalz over the past twenty-five years: "All that embodies the nature of the people was carefully protected or newly revived: people sang the old songs of the *Volk*; the old costumes, dances, and customs . . . were brought back to life, and outside in the forests everything was re-animated, the historic festivals of the people filled with fresh life."[1] Taken together, these manifestations of Pfälzer *Heimatsinn*, or feeling for Heimat, amounted to a cultural phenomenon extensive enough to be called a movement; indeed, in the retrospective glance of Schreibmüller there was little question but that his subject was the "Heimat movement." Building on local traditions new and old, this movement devised new forms of celebrating the locality, and it involved unprecedented numbers of provincial people in the effort. It transformed people's conceptions of nature, of folklore, of history, and of localness—or Heimat—itself. By the fall of 1914 the celebrating had to end, but for the many thousands who had been drawn into the Heimat movement, their new Heimat sensibilities survived as the most intimate expression of their national loyalties.

The Heimat movement came together in the decades preceding the First World War amid significant changes in the economic and political landscape of the Pfalz, and it in turn affected cultural and natural landscapes, making

---

1. Schreibmüller, *Bayern und Pfalz*, p. 62.

them conform to the current needs of Pfälzers. It was above all else a popular movement. Its associations claimed not hundreds but thousands of members; its journals boasted not of their erudition but of their circulation; and its most characteristic events were not ceremonial dinners but large public festivals and parades. In content also, the Heimat movement promoted a characterization of the German Pfälzer that relied on common folksiness. Pfälzer identity, the theme on which the Heimat movement devised so many variations, thus continued, as it had from its beginnings, to denote a "consciousness of community" attuned more to changes in that community than to the eternal call of a folk character. Advancing industrialization, commercialization, and urbanization all left their marks on the Pfälzer sense of community, as a fragmented but undoubtedly more dynamic society broke open the cramped consensus of Honoratioren hegemony.

By 1882, industry had begun to overtake agriculture in its share of the regional product in the Pfalz. Agriculture continued in importance, but its decline was hurried along by the small size of most businesses, their reliance on intensive labor, and their slowness to adopt new technologies.[2] In the 1890s, a number of crises overtook formerly prosperous sectors of local agriculture: wine production fell victim to vine diseases; tobacco and grain production suffered from foreign competition.[3] Politically, agricultural decline in the region pushed the small producer toward the Agrarian League (Bund der Landwirte), a movement that marked the first sign of crisis in the National Liberal party. Meanwhile, poor Catholic farmers in the southern Pfalz were mobilizing for the first time under the auspices of the Center party. Both political tendencies suggested the inability of the party of the Honoratioren to come to grips with economic change in the region.

The rise of population in the region as a whole, and in its cities in particular, was another challenge to which the established party proved unequal. Between 1871 and 1914 the population of the Pfalz nearly doubled, despite ongoing emigration, with the growth of the eight largest cities in the region accounting for over half of that total rise.[4] These cities, not the declining small towns, would provide the mass support for the turn-of-the-century Heimat movement. They also were home to a new Pfälzer working class and, along with it, an increasingly powerful Social Democratic movement, which

2. Zink and Mang, *Wirtschaftsleben*, pp. 126–27.

3. In the region around Neustadt, the center of the Pfälzer wine industry, the volume of wine produced dropped 45 percent in one decade—from 214,287 hectoliters in 1890 to 100,240 in 1898 (Bräunche, *Parteien und Reichstagswahlen*, p. 33), and the number of independent tobacco growers in the Pfalz declined from nearly 20,000 in 1880 to a little under 7,000 in 1900 (ibid., p. 34). See also Zink and Mang, *Wirtschaftsleben*, pp. 132, 149.

4. Between 1871 and 1905, the population grew from 624,619 to 885,833; see Theodor Zink, *Deutsche Geschichte auf heimatkundlicher Grundlage* (Kaiserslautern, 1909), 1:302; Willi Alter, "Die Bevölkerung der Pfalz," in Alter, *Pfalzatlas* 1:188; Zink and Mang, *Wirtschaftsleben*, p. 279.

spread to the Pfalz from Baden in the 1860s and 1870s, won its first major electoral victory in 1898, and by 1912 had become the single largest party in the region, with a full third of the popular vote.[5] The industrial proletariat that voted for Social Democrat candidates grew not only in the region's few cities, but also in small towns and semirural areas, according to the decentralized and diverse nature of Pfälzer industrialization.[6] This diffusion probably attenuated the social dislocation usually associated with industrialization. In any case, neither the industrial workers nor a new middle class of office workers fit easily into the old electoral strategies of the National Liberals. By 1900 the party found itself in search of an organization, a program, and, most desperately, a constituency.[7]

The problem faced by Pfälzer National Liberalism after 1890 was common to all parties that had relied on the shared secrets of Honoratiorenpolitik. In the Pfalz as in the rest of Germany, voters began to express in their electoral choices not ties of patronage but religious, economic, or ethnic identities.[8] The Pfälzer National Liberals tried to adjust to the new situation, but for every alliance they managed to forge with the Agrarian League there was a counteralliance between Catholics and Social Democrats. And when the agrarian strategy of the party fell apart in 1904, efforts by Young Liberals to create a stronger, more centralized party structure, one responsive to public opinion and ideologically coherent, met with resistance from an old guard, who disliked the idea of entering the political mass market.[9]

Like it or not, though, the nature of the political scene had changed since

5. Schneider, "Anfänge der sozialistischen Arbeiterbewegung," pp. 120–22, 149, 165–66, 182–189; see also Erich Schneider, "Franz Josef Ehrhardt," in *Pfälzer Lebensbilder*, ed. Kurt Baumann (Speyer, 1964), 1:273–319; Wolfgang Hartwich, "Die Ergebnisse der Reichstags- und Bundestagswahlen von 1890 bis 1969," in Alter, *Pfalzatlas* 2:665.

6. By Frank Tipton's scale of regional differentiation, the Pfalz lagged behind much of the Rhineland in its industrialization but was close to the national average throughout the latter half of the nineteenth century; see his *Regional Variations in the Economic Development of Germany During the Nineteenth Century* (Middletown, Conn., 1976), pp. 3–17, 200. See also Schneider, "Anfänge der sozialistischen Arbeiterbewegung," p. 20; Bräunche, *Parteien und Reichstagswahlen*, p. 35; Zink and Mang, *Wirtschaftsleben*, pp. 226, 230–31; Kermann, "Industrialisierung der Pfalz," pp. 280–304.

7. Dan White sees this problem of representation as central to the National Liberal party as a whole; see his *Splintered Party*, p. 3. On the rising proportion of office workers as compared to the self-employed, see Zink and Mang, *Wirtschaftsleben*, p. 227. For definitions of the so-called new Mittelstand, see Vondung, "Zur Lage der Gebildeten," pp. 30–31; and Geoff Eley, "The Wilhelmine Right: How It Changed," in *Society and Politics in Wilhelmine Germany*, ed. Richard Evans (London, 1978), p. 118.

8. Stanley Suval, *Electoral Politics in Wilhelmine Germany* (Chapel Hill, N.C., 1985), p. 8.

9. Bräunche, *Parteien und Reichstagswahlen*, pp. 83–85; Nipperdey, *Organisation der deutschen Parteien*, pp. 97–101. For the Young Liberals, "ideological coherence" meant a renewed insistence on the dangers of political Catholicism and a revival of the *Kulturkampf* spirit within the National Liberal party (Bräunche, *Parteien und Reichstagswahlen*, pp. 109–115).

unification. Elections, voters, campaigns, slogans, and rallies all came to play a much greater part in public life. The days when candidates could be chosen and, to all intents and purposes, elected during a cozy evening of wine and conversation at the estates of the Bottle Barons were past. Such influential circles of acquaintance still existed, but they no longer constituted the main forum of politics. Indeed, not just political life but associational life of all kinds expanded enormously in the late 1880s and 1890s.[10] Societies of all sizes, classes, and purposes proliferated, as both the working class and the new middle class of industry and commerce caught the associational mania. Women, too, were more involved in associational life at the turn of the century, not just in their own clubs but in some of the older, predominantly male organizations as well.[11]

The Heimat movement accounted for part of this expansion and democratization of public life in the Pfalz around the turn of the century, in effect rescuing German localism from the collapsing edifice of the localist political culture of the Honoratioren. Nevertheless, how and why the Heimat movement participated in trends toward urban living, industrial employment, and consumerism is not at first obvious. It celebrated local diversity simultaneous with the consolidation of central rule and the development of a genuinely national culture. It gloried in nature at a time when the city was changing the landscape, in ruins when new buildings were springing up everywhere, in handicrafts when factory work predominated. The Heimat movement reflected the reality of centralization, urbanization, and industrialization by reacting against each one of them. But even that is too simple a characterization of its contemporaneity, for its undoubted nostalgia for older ways of life and smaller communities could go hand in hand with an enthusiastic receptivity to present glories, to big, vital cities, to technological wonders, and, most of all, to national prestige. What appears to the historian as inconsistency—indeed, incoherence—was to the participants themselves simply patriotism. Whatever could be called "Pfälzer," whatever could reveal "Pfälzerness," whatever could enhance the Pfälzer reputation in Germany as a whole, was of interest to the Heimat movement. And if such solipsism seems somewhat childish, one should consider that the real enemies against which the Heimat movement struggled were homogeneity and anonymity. Insofar as one had to embrace them both to love modernity, Heimat enthusiasts were indeed antimodernists. But ambivalence would be a more accurate description of their stance, for while Heimat enthusiasts were

10. In Nuremberg, for instance, the number of registered associations—which did not even begin to account for all the informal *Kränzchen, Stammtische,* and the like—doubled each decade, growing from 445 in 1880 to almost 2,000 by the turn of the century; see Meyer, "Vereinswesen," p. 265.

11. Ibid., pp. 69, 259–61.

essentially content with their times, they were also determined—whether through nature, folk life, or history—to assert their own identity.

The Pfälzers of the Heimat movement set out the reclaim the nature of their region with the zeal and high-mindedness of their contemporaries the Arctic explorers. A small botanical and zoological association known as Pollichia had been in existence since 1847, investigating and classifying the local flora and fauna; yet the celebration of nature characteristic of the Heimat movement owed more to sentiment than to science. In a late flowering of romantic sensibilities, Pfälzers found in nature enduring testimony to Pfälzer distinctiveness. And happily for those wishing more than spiritual sustenance, they found in nature the basis for a new Pfälzer prosperity as well. The promotion of tourism would become an essential part of localist efforts to take over nature in the name of the Pfalz. Tourism and romanticism combined to make the out-of-doors into a public space, equally infused with local patriotism and national pride.

The pathbreakers in the naturalization of Heimat and the commercialization of nature were groups of civic promoters called *Verschönerungsvereine*, or beautification societies. Although the activities of such societies, which usually concentrated on restoring historic ruins or marking paths from ruin to town, had something in common with the interests of the Historical Association, the beautifiers tended to regard castles as decorations on the landscape.[12] By fixing up the local ruin, they hoped to enhance the reputation of their particular town, strengthen its civic pride, and improve its appearance and recreational offerings. They also intended their activities to translate more or less directly into money for local businesses, particularly in areas of declining economic prosperity.[13]

According to one (albeit partisan) estimate, fifty-two Pfälzer beautification societies were founded between 1872 and 1900, mostly in small towns; by 1898 they had managed to spend nearly 26,000 marks on path markings, maps, parklands, and castle maintenance.[14] In 1891, the beautification societies made a combined effort to articulate what it was they were trying to

12. They often named themselves after their local ruin or natural attraction. Thus the Trifels Verein of Annweiler was named for the imperial castles, and the Drachenfels Club of Bad Dürkheim was named for striking local rock formations.

13. Bad Dürkheim, for instance, lay in the heart of the wine-producing district of the Vorderpfalz and had been a thriving center for the spa trade until lingering resentments over the Franco-Prussian War arrested the flow of French tourists and patients (Zink and Mang, *Wirtschaftsleben*, p. 217). The founders of its Drachenfels Club hoped to stimulate local pleasure in the surrounding sights and attract visitors from outside the Pfalz. See August Wilde, "60-jähriges Jubiläum des Drachenfelsclub," *Die Pfalz am Rhein: Touristen-Zeitung* 16 (June 1933): 285.

14. Christian Mehlis, *Touristische Erfahrungen in Rheinlande* (Mannheim, 1900), p. 23; review of the book in *PM* 17 (1900): 62–63, 20–23; Christian Mehlis, *Von den Burgen der Pfalz* (Freiburg, 1902), pp. 97–100. Neither Ludwigshafen nor Speyer had such clubs.

do. The result, the so-called Landstuhler Theses, was hailed by its creators as the embodiment of a new "touristic principle."[15] More than just a guide for the "systematic" development of local tourism, the "touristic principle" required of those who professed it an attachment to patriotic ideals. The beautification movement, according to Christian Mehlis, its self-appointed spokesman, was inseparable from the nationalist movement; hence, what could be more proper than to "beautify" nature by building a Moltke Tower and a Bismarck Tower atop the region's highest mountain?[16] For Mehlis the revisionist, the Hambach Festival of 1832 had been "the first identifiable work of beautification of a Pfälzer castle": not only had the participants tidied up the place in preparation for the demonstration, but, most important, they had dedicated themselves to the cause of "a unified Germany, proud and free"—a dream finally fulfilled in 1871.[17]

Mehlis also called the beautification movement a popular movement, "pushed forward from above and below, by princes and poets, by crown and people."[18] Although wrong about the princes, whose support existed only in his wishful thinking, Mehlis was in one sense right about the people.[19] Beautification had embodied the impulse to make local nature accessible and attractive to the public at large, and although initiated by small-town grandees, its popularity inevitably spread downward on the social scale as more

15. Mehlis, *Touristische Erfahrungen*, p. 22.

16. Mehlis claimed this was one of the first Bismarck Towers in all Germany (ibid., p. 20). It was also said to be possible to see Sedan from the top of the mountain on a clear day, a rare enough occurrence that the assertion may never have been tested.

17. Ibid., p. 90. For Mehlis, ludicrously, Hambach was important not as the site of protests against Bavaria but as the expression of the long-standing interest of Maximilian I and his son Ludwig I in castles, an interest that continued after the Hambach "festivities" ended (p. 88).

18. Ibid., p. 89.

19. Mehlis was a uniquely colorful (which is to say disreputable) figure amongst the conventionally proper cheerleaders of Heimat patriotism. A poem written in 1910 by Paul Münch, a comic writer in the local dialect, gives a hint at the nature of his dubious reputation, referring to Mehlis's discovery of Noah's Ark in the Pfalz (Paul Münch, "For die Inweihung vum historisch Museum," *PW* 10, Sondernummer 2 [Spring 1910]: 85):

> Die Arche Noah is noch do,
> Nadeerlich alt und ganz verbo',
> Am Dummerschberg vor Jahre schun
> Hat se de Mehlis ufgefunn,
> Un so e Mann, der weess geweiss
> Ob das die Arch Noah is . . . .

Lukas Grünenwald, prominent Pfälzer scholar, purportedly said that Mehlis had undertaken the excavations "for himself" and predicted, sarcastically, "that he would brilliantly answer back to every criticism and test." A recent assessment grants him credit for having made Roman ruins and artifacts popular, "if often with inadequate expertise, doubtful methods, and meager means" (*100 Jahre Museum*, Festgabe of the *MHVP* [1969], pp. xviii, xix). Mehlis fell afoul of Bavaria in the 1920s, when he seems to have consorted with the French occupiers in a mild sort of way.

people took advantage of the new paths and promenades in the landscape. An important step in that process of popularization came in 1900, when the beautification societies of the Pfalz worked with a newspaper editor in Zweibrücken, Eugen Croissant, to establish a periodical called *Der Pfälzerwald* (The Pfälzer Forest). A "Weekly Journal for Tourists, Bicyclists, and Travelers in the Pfalz and Its Surroundings," the paper appeared during the summer months as a free supplement to the local daily newspaper. Under the heading "What We Want," editor Croissant outlined a program to transform the collective image of the region: "Our glorious Rheinpfalz, with its vine-garlanded Haardt, its refreshing forests, its lovely valleys and castle-crested heights, deserves far more attention and recognition . . . than has heretofore been its portion. . . . The Pfälzers themselves know their own Pfalz too little, and the charms of its landscape are for the most part still unknown to outsiders." The beautification societies, with the aid of the "propagandistic tool" of the newspaper, would spread the name and enhance the beauties of "our glorious Pfälzerland."[20]

But the societies themselves did not end up carrying on the task so confidently proclaimed by Croissant. After 1900 they faded into insignificance, in part the victims of population shifts that took people away from the small towns and into the region's few cities.[21] Ludwigshafen was by 1900 the largest of these, having grown from nothing in 1844 to a population of eighty-five thousand in 1881 on the strength of the phenomenally expansive chemical industry.[22] There in November 1902, a group of successful business-men—railroad employees, chemists, bank tellers, and city administrators—announced by public advertisement in the city newspaper their intention to form a hiking and convivial club. On November 27, the founding assembly took place in a large city restaurant, with one hundred people in attendance.[23] Statutes were drawn up, officers elected, a name chosen, and within a month the new Pfälzerwald Verein (Pfälzer Forest Association) had already enrolled three hundred members—as many as all the beautification societies combined could claim.

The Pfälzerwald Verein would become the Pfalz's Heimat association par

20. "Was wir wollen," *PW* 1 (4 May 1900): 2.

21. Total membership probably never reached much more than 340 (*PW* 1 [28 September 1900]: 3). Another reason for their decline was that the societies lost their hold on castle ruins, which in 1907 came under the care of the Konservatorium der Kunstdenkmale und Altertümer Bayern, an official organization of the Bavarian government. See Wolfgang Maria Schmid, *Anleitung zur Denkmalpflege im Königreich Bayern* (Munich, 1897), pp. 14–15; and "Denkmalpflege in Bayern: Sitzung in München," *PM* 24 (1907).

22. Because of its rapid growth after 1871 the economic historians of the Pfalz, Zink and Mang, called it an "American-style city" (*Wirtschaftsleben*, 255–57). See also Bräunche, *Parteien und Reichstagswahlen*, pp. 35–36; Schneider, "Anfänge der sozialistischen Arbeiterbewegung," p. 21; Zink and Mang, *Wirtschaftsleben*, p. 240.

23. "Ersten Jahresbericht des Pfälzerwald Vereins," *PW* 5 (8 February 1904): 2–3.

excellence, taking over the projects and the propaganda of the small-town beautifiers.[24] Its original statement of purpose pledged its members not only to the promotion of practical programs like hiking, conservation, and tourist advertising but, more ambiguously and ambitiously, to the cultivation of "Heimat sensibilities" as well.[25] From organizing day-trippers to "serving the Pfalz," from a *Wanderklub* to a *Heimatverein*, the Pfälzerwald Verein had evolved within its first month into an association with an explicitly moral and communal mission, aimed particularly at city dwellers. Cities, declared a club founder at the first general meeting, provided the opportunity for work, education, and human contact, but unfortunately they also caused "nervousness" and lung diseases. The speaker, railroad clerk Alber Grimmeisen, believed that "there live[d] in every human heart, consciously or unconsciously, a joy in the beauties and eternal freshness of nature"; such joy drove people out into "God's garden" to "seek rest and recovery away from the pressures of daily work."[26]

The appeal of this combination of civic and outdoor activity proved immediate and widespread. By the end of 1903 the Pfälzerwald Verein had two thousand members, over half of whom were from Ludwigshafen and Mannheim.[27] By the end of 1904 there were three thousand members in sixteen chapters; a decade later, nearly seventeen thousand in over one hundred thirty chapters, not just in Pfälzer towns, but in many German cities, and even in Paris, New York, and San Francisco.[28] By far the largest Heimat association in the region, it was also one of the largest associations of any kind in the Pfalz, and certainly the largest specifically Pfälzer organization.[29] As its chairman, *Oberforstrat* Karl Albrecht von Ritter, observed in 1906, the Pfälzerwald Verein, like the city of Ludwigshafen itself, had grown with unprecedented speed to unimagined proportions.[30]

Membership in the Verein required neither education, social position, nor wealth, but simply the desire to do one's walking and traveling in the company of others and to devote some of one's time to community affairs. The

24. Whereas I use the English term for the more generic "Historischer Verein," for the Pfälzerwald Verein I retain the German title in order to preserve the aura of the "Pfälzerwald" itself.

25. "Die Pflege des Heimatsinnes": see Heinrich Grass, "25 Jahre Pfälzerwald Verein: Gründungsgeschichte," *Wanderbuch des Pfälzerwald Vereins* (hereafter cited as *Wanderbuch*) (1928): 40.

26. *PW* 5 (8 February 1904): 1.

27. There were also chapters in Kaiserslautern, Bergzabern, Landau, Neustadt, Kirchheimbolanden, Edenkoben, Bad Dürkheim, and Grünstadt (ibid., p. 3).

28. "Zusammenschluß der auswärtigen Pfälzer," *Des Pfälzers Heimat in Wort und Bild: Ein Heimatblatt für Ausland* 1 (1910): 33.

29. The Volksverein für Katholische Deutschland, for instance, had by 1913 more members in the Pfalz, but it was a national organization, not one specifically devoted to the Pfalz.

30. Report of the steering committee of the Pfälzerwald Verein, *PW* 7 (15 June 1906): 127. An *Oberforstrat* was a high-ranking official in the Bavarian forest administration.

great majority of the membership came from the petty bourgeoisie, particularly the new white-collar workers of the cities, although some factory workers became involved through their employers.[31] While the Verein actively recruited women, its enthusiasm for their participation in its activities did not extend to electing any to positions of even minor authority.[32] Catholics, Protestants, and Jews all seem to have been represented. Among the founders, for instance, were a Catholic priest, a Protestant clerk, and a Jewish businessman.

To some extent, then, the Verein's egalitarian claim to exist for all Pfälzers, regardless of rank, confession, or sex, was justified.[33] The inspirational but casual "Wald-Heil" with which members greeted one another consciously echoed the "Gut-Heil" of Friedrich Ludwig Jahn's gymnastic movement. Members were known as *Wäldler* or *Wäldlerinnen*, and nicknames abounded in reports of Verein hikes and committee meetings. At the large celebrations of the Verein, strangers could even use the familiar *Du* with one another. On the face of it, the Pfälzerwald Verein offered a real alternative to the formality and status-consciousness of organizations like the Historical Association.

Nevertheless, the Verein managed to give rank its due. The Honoratioren retained a certain priority in the association, even if its large size and petty-bourgeois membership contrasted sharply with smaller, more exclusive clubs. Its central leadership showed the persistence of the deferential arrangements that no longer characterized its local organizations.[34] The first chairman, Anton Fasig, was a *Geheimer Kommerzienrat*, a title of honor granted by the government to particularly prominent businessmen. After Fasig retired, the position devolved on the top forestry official in the regional government, a practice that paralleled the Historical Association's honoring of the district president with its chairmanship.[35] Notables contributed in

31. In particular, the Badische Anilin und Soda Fabrik (BASF) contributed both money and members to the Verein. Workers who were members of the Social Democratic party tended to have their own Social Democratic hiking organizations. See Vernon Lidtke, *The Alternative Culture* (New York, 1986), pp. 64–65.

32. In the words of the secretary of the Verein, "It is most gratifying that our members, above all the ladies, whom we see today in nearly every calling and can admire on every playing field, also honor the efforts of the Pfälzerwald Verein by their high participation" ("Vereinsnachrichten," *PW* 10 [1 April 1900]: 40).

33. See, e.g., the encomium on its twenty-fifth birthday, which emphasized particularly its classlessness, its quality of being a true "Volksverein," in "25 Jahre Pfälzerwald Verein," *PM–PH* 45/24 (1928): 49.

34. See the listing of the steering committee and chairmen of the local chapters, in the *Wanderbuch* (1907): 1–2. In the local chapters, about half the chairmen were of the educated upper middle class (*Bildungsbürgertum*) and half from the lower middle class.

35. L. Hartmann, "Der Pfälzer und das Wandern," in *Pfalz-Bayerischer Heimgarten 1919– 1920*, ed. Bayerischer Landesverein für Heimatschutz (Munich, 1919), p. 96; "Karl Albrecht von Ritter: 50-jährige Dienst Jubiläum," *PW* 8 (15 February 1907): 11.

traditionally paternalistic ways to the Verein, lending their names and patronage to its activities.[36] Academics, like the geologist Daniel Häberle and the philologist Albert Becker, found in the Pfälzerwald Verein a broad and deferential audience for their work and more recognition than strictly academic circles had to offer them.

But deference always mixed with equality in the constitution and social norms of the Pfälzerwald Verein. Most voluntary associations in Germany had a more or less homogeneous social composition: in a town of moderate size, it would not have been uncommon to have many different singing groups, for instance, each with members from distinctly different social backgrounds.[37] Yet throughout the Pfalz there was really only one hiking club, and as a consequence its members came from a wide range of social classes. Moreover, those of higher social rank who participated in the Pfälzerwald Verein were in fact adapting themselves to a new kind of association, one with its own, more democratic standards. As in politics, where even the National Liberals came to accept some degree of large-scale organization and broad voter participation, so too in civic and cultural affairs democratic standards began to prevail. Becker and Häberle, the scholars in the crowd, served ultimately as popularizers of ethnography, geography, and history. Similarly, Heinrich Kohl, the wealthy art patron, affected the dress of a simple outdoorsman in all his official photographs for the publications of the Verein. Most important, however, the activities to which the Verein was pledged, including the cultivation of Heimat sensibilities, all had an essentially inclusive, popular character. They reached out to draw people into the Pfälzerwald circle and win them over to its concerns. Where the Historical Association of the Pfalz had been content to preserve, the Pfälzerwald Verein wanted to convert. Activism contrasted to academic reserve, thousands of members to hundreds.

Even though the Pfälzerwald Verein soon expanded into the realms of history and folklore, it derived its name and its sense of purpose from nature—specifically, Pfälzer nature. The chief activity of the Verein always remained its sponsorship of hikes, and the monthly club-sponsored *Ausflug*, members agreed, was the key to the Verein's unity and progress.[38] Club hikes would begin at a prearranged hour at the train station and, once in the countryside, follow paths laid out by foresters or (better for fine views) by the local beautification societies, with which the Pfälzerwald Verein cooperated

36. For instance, Verein founder Heinrich Kohl was a patron of local artists both through the Verein and outside of it; see obituary of Kohl, *Wanderbuch* (1937): 6–7.

37. Meyer, "Vereinswesen," p. 259.

38. Report of the steering committee. *PW* 7 (15 February 1906): 14; schedules of walks, held even in the months of January and February, and reports on the weather conditions that prevailed on any given day were reported in *Der Pfälzerwald* each month.

in path marking, bench making, tower building, and nature conserving.[39] Yet by far the most important contribution of the Pfälzerwald Verein was in filling the paths, the benches, the towers, and the nature with people. The Ludwigshafen chapter alone sent out eighteen hundred people to the Pfälzerwald in 1906, and nearly two thousand in 1907.[40] In the larger towns, the average number of participants on each monthly outing was about one hundred fifty; the smaller chapters could mobilize about fifty.[41] New members were recruited on these occasions, and old members were rewarded for outstanding records of participation with gold medals or an official Pfälzerwald Verein walking stick. (Again, these marks of distinction were both an imitation of and an egalitarian alternative to the awards and titles that marked one's position in society as a whole.) In 1908, the Verein extended its activities to school expeditions, combining pedagogy with the deep breathing of fresh air.[42] The school hikes "awakened and maintained the feeling for Heimat among schoolchildren," while at the same time securing the loyalties of a future generation for the Verein itself.[43]

The event that soon became the Verein's chief reason for being began as an "expedition," albeit a glorified one. The first so-called *Gesamtausflug*, or joint excursion, was held in 1906 in the south Pfälzer town of Bad Bergzabern. Over three thousand Wäldlers gathered on a Sunday, wandered around the town and into the surrounding hills, listened to speeches in the town square, ate, drank, and went back home.[44] The event was repeated every year until the war, with increasing numbers of participants.[45] Town councils vied for the honor—and profitability—of hosting the extravaganza, and the Verein used it to increase its own reputation and membership.[46]

Certainly the leaders of the Pfälzerwald Verein found the explanation for the rapid growth and widespread popularity of their organization in the

39. Report of the steering committee, *PW* 5 (8 February 1904): 3; "Wegebezeichnung im Pfälzerwald und Ausschuß für Wegebezeichnung," *Wald-Heil! Mitteilungen der Pfälzerwald-Vereins der Ortsgruppe Ludwigshafen-Mannheim* (hereafter cited as *WH*), no. 32 (1919): 6.

40. Report in *PW* 7 (15 December 1906): 230; *PW* 8 (15 December 1907): 189.

41. *PW* 7 (15 February 1906): 14.

42. In 1910, the Ludwigshafen chapter proudly led the first ever *Mädchenwanderung*, an expedition of four hundred schoolgirls to Heidelberg; before that time, school hikes had involved only boys. See *PW* 11 (1 August 1910): 134.

43. Report of the main hiking committee *PW* 9 (15 April, 1908): 53 and 10 (15 July 1909): 113. For a complete account of the school expeditions, see L. Hartmann, "Jugendwandern," *Wanderbuch* (1928): 53–59.

44. An account of the first Gesamtausflug may be found in *PW* 7 (15 May 1906): 93–95.

45. The largest, in 1911, took place in Bad Dürkheim with over twelve thousand in attendance.

46. In 1906, a debate over whether to hold the event in Edenkoben or Zweibrücken was decided in favor of the latter, despite vigorous lobbying by Edenkoben businessmen, because Heinrich Kohl thought that the Verein needed to expand into the Westrich. See the report of the main hiking committee in *PW* 7 (15 November 1906): 224.

special relationship to nature that such extravaganzas exemplified. Albert Grimmeisen, the first secretary of the association, believed that the great popularity of *Wandersport* revealed every man's "joy in hiking in God's free nature" as well as a "healthy reaction of the spirit [*Gemüt*] against the victorious drive of intellect and technology."[47] As the poet laureate and cofounder of the Verein, Fritz Claus, pronounced: "Hundreds of times have we felt the great importance of our beautiful Pfälzer Forest for the soul, the heart, and the spirit [*Geist, Herz und Gemüt*]."[48] The programs of the Pfälzerwald Verein, wrote Grimmeisen, "correspond to the wishes and tendencies of our times."[49] They brought the city dweller out of workplace and cramped apartment into the open air; they offered rest and recovery from the prevailing nervousness and strain of urban living.[50]

And yet, one would by no means do justice to the "timeliness" of the Pfälzerwald Verein if one viewed it simply as a romantic flight from the city into nature, an anti-urban, antitechnological, and anti-intellectual reaction against the modern world. Certainly a dissatisfaction with machines, cities, and factories, as well as with the routines of urban life, found expression in the Pfälzerwald Verein, but it was the dissatisfaction of people who desired to leave the cities once in a while, not abandon them altogether. Although the fact of the association's largely urban membership might be interpretable as a sign of deep resistance to urbanization in the Pfalz—and Germany—it more likely represented the particular needs of city dwellers for a recreational outlet compatible with their jobs and their way of life. The rise of the Pfälzerwald Verein is inconceivable without the existence both of the weekend and of leisure, definitions of time that emerged only in contrast to the working week and working time.[51] The Verein organized the weekend for those who had one. In an important sense, then, it represented an urban, not an anti-urban, phenomenon. Even its poets were engineers, and its single greatest patron was the largest business in the region.[52]

Moreover, the approach of the Verein to the out-of-doors revealed far more careful planning than romantic fancy. Grimmeisen himself attributed the association's success as much to the "systematic and well-planned hikes"

47. Report of the general convention, *PW* 8 (15 February 1907): 10.
48. Speech at a Gesamtausflug *PW* 8 (15 May 1907): 83.
49. Report of the general convention *PW* 8 (15 February 1907): 10.
50. *Wanderbuch* (1928): 26.
51. For a treatment of these issues in Germany, see Gerhard Huch, ed., *Sozialgeschichte der Freizeit: Untersuchungen zum Wandel der Alltagskultur in Deutschland* (Wuppertal, 1980). The focus of most of these essays is the regulation of workers' lives through recreational activity that took them out of the beer halls and into atmospheres more amenable to moral edification as well as social control (like the exercise hall).
52. BASF gave 100 marks yearly to the Verein; see biographical notices of H. Kiefer, railroad engineer and Heimat poet, in *PM-PH* 46/25 (1929): 58–59; and of Karl Räder in *WH*, no. 30 (1919): 7.

and "goal-oriented organization" as to man's deep longing for nature.[53] Train schedules were printed weekly during the summer months in the journal *Der Pfälzerwald*. Every expedition was mapped out and even rehearsed ahead of time; weather forecasts were consulted, and maps and "hygienic tips" distributed.[54] People were also instructed on how to behave in the out-of-doors. Whatever they might write about man's instinctual understanding of nature, the Verein's organizers assumed his ignorance. They cautioned hikers not to litter and not to carve their names in trees, under penalty of public humiliation in the pages of *Der Pfälzerwald*. Nor should hikers break off branches, pick flowers, or otherwise disturb nature's own order. Walkers "with even the least claim to education" should indeed condemn any behavior showing "such a great lack of any feeling for order."[55]

The Pfälzerwald Verein also made important contributions to the organization and regulation of nature itself, which for all the forbearance of litterers was not entirely tidy. The ongoing construction of paths was the most important step toward conquering nature's contrariness. Benches, markers, and handrails further eased the transition from city to forest. Between 1903 and the war, the Pfälzerwald Verein and the beautification societies undertook several cartographic projects. These maps assured travelers that they would be as at home on the paths of the forest as on the city streets. When in 1913 the Bavarian government decided to begin a comprehensive remeasurement of the region, the Pfälzerwald Verein greeted the news with happy cries.[56] Without the paths and the maps to guide the visitor to grottos, gulches, and mountaintops, wrote Lorenz Wappes, Verein chairman and ranking Pfälzer forestry official, the forests might just as well not exist.[57]

Wappes's observation, sensible though it seems, must be read as a reflection of an essentially urban attitude toward the out-of-doors. Villagers and peasants had, after all, managed for centuries without the maps of the Pfälzerwald Verein or its hygienic hints. The Wäldlers were very far from being peasants, however they may have clothed themselves on festive occasions, and their nature was that of the tourist, not the farmer. From such a perspective, romantic effusions about God's garden were wholly compatible with the careful study of local train schedules. Indeed, what Grimmeisen referred to as the "timeliness" of the Pfälzerwald Verein derived not only from its compatibility with the routines, schedules, and mentalities of modern Germans but also from its self-created place within the structure of Pfälzer commerce.

53. Report of the general convention, *PW* 8 (15 February 1907): 10.

54. These tips included advice on what clothing to wear to avoid toothaches and earaches, catarrh, rheumatism, lung disease, and other likely (as well as unlikely) maladies that might result from hiking; see Fritz Hetz, "Hygienische Winke für Wanderer," *PW* 9 (10 May 1908).

55. *PW* 7 (15 April 1906): 67; *PW* 9 (15 August 1905): 144.

56. *PW* 10 (1 July 1909): 105.

57. *Wanderbuch* (1928): 122.

From the beginning, the Verein's founders imagined for it a role in the development of tourism, an economic activity that in their opinion had been sadly neglected in the Pfalz. Their Main Committee on Commerce endeavored to attract tourists by placing advertisements for the Pfalz in newspapers all over Germany, printing picture postcards, and distributing travel brochures at tourist conventions.[58] Committee meetings were taken up with questions of how to get the railroad directors to institute Sunday trains and tourist rates, or how to make Pfälzer hotels more elegant.[59] Members were urged to invite cousins and colleagues to favorite Pfälzer haunts and to complain loudly about bad service in restaurants.

The extent of the Verein's success in stimulating tourism is difficult to gauge. The largest clientele for the hotels of the Pfalz was local, especially weekend visitors from Ludwigshafen and Mannheim. Tourist traffic to the local spas had never been the same since the Franco-Prussian War, and, one suspects, a Bad Gleisweiler or Bad Dürkheim would have had difficulty competing with a Bad Homburg, Marienbad, or Baden-Baden as these glamorous spots became accessible even to the burgher of moderate means.[60] Nevertheless, the Pfälzerwald Verein, with a thoroughly modern complacency, had faith in the efficacy of a little advertising. The Pfalz, after all, had wine, and the Pfälzerwald Verein (despite its name) worked with vintner organizations to spread the reputation of this wine throughout Germany: "We value wine as the leading product of our blessed Heimat, and we are not ashamed to admit loudly that we love it."[61] A purely commercial tourist bureau in Neustadt cooperated with the Verein in a joint tourist committee for the entire Pfalz, and Verein chapters in both Munich and Berlin were another crucial link in the dissemination of touristic propaganda. In 1911, the Pfälzerwald Verein represented the region at the enormous International Travel and Tourism Exhibition in Berlin. The term *forester* was taking on a whole new meaning.

If commerce could become a concern of Pfälzer nature-lovers, so could science and even technology. Albert Becker wrote in 1914 that "we have long yearned for a new deepening of life, for an ennobling of our pleasures, for a return to nature, without having to give up the sources and forms of our education."[62] A poetic appreciation of nature did not, in other words, pre-

58. These courses of action were determined as early as the first meeting in December of 1903; see *Wanderbuch* (1928): 40.

59. See, e.g., *PW* 8 (15 February 1907): 20–21, on the Pfälzerwald Verein's set of standards for the restaurant trade, which included such recommendations as fresh fruit, cold butter, and clean linen.

60. S. L. Bensusan, *Some German Spas: A Holiday Record* (London, 1925).

61. *WH*, no. 18 (1919): 3.

62. Transcript of lecture, in Albert Becker, *Ziele und Aufgaben eines Heimatmuseums* (Kaiserslautern, 1914), p. 21.

clude a scientific one: indeed, the Verein magazine *Der Pfälzerwald* had as many articles on soil types and plant varieties as poems on the arrival of spring. Daniel Häberle, a professor of geology at Heidelberg University and an expert on the Pfalz, contributed regularly to Verein publications. His treatise *Die natürlichen Landschaften der Rheinpfalz* (The Natural Landscapes of the Rhenish Pfalz) was popular science at its local best; it was published, moreover, in the Pfälzerwald Verein's annual *Hiking Handbook*. Through its Committee on the Conservation of Nature, the Verein maintained an interest in up-to-date forestry methods.[63] In 1906, the Verein and the Bavarian forestry administration together assembled a display of the varieties of Pfälzer wood for the Bavarian Exhibition of Agriculture, Industry, Commerce, and Art in Nuremberg.[64] The Verein's building projects, finally, facilitated not only the admiration of nature but its exact measurement and study as well. Their most ambitious and highly touted scheme before the war was the construction of a weather station on the top of Kalmit Mountain.

Nor was the Pfälzerwald Verein alone in its simultaneously scientific and poetic representation of nature. The mixture characterized the treatment of nature in all Heimat textbooks, organizations, and periodicals and attested to both the comprehensiveness and the eclecticism of the Heimat synthesis. In Georg Baer's *Die Pfalz am Rhein: Pfälzische Heimatkunde*, for instance, a section on the geological, topographical, botanical, and zoological features of the region was interspersed with poetry on nature's beauties.[65] In Bavaria, *Heimatschutz*—Heimat protection, that most vague of terms comprising everything from natural conservation to cultural promotion—included mountain railway building and rural electrification.[66] Certainly the Heimat movement was romantic, but in its desire to find spiritual uplift in nature it did not reject science, technology, and rationality out of hand, but rather integrated them into its conception of the region.

The timetables, the rationality, and the business of the city shaped the Pfälzerwald Verein's discovery of nature, and to the city the Verein eventually came back, in a curious return trip of reconciliation and new appreciation.

63. Lorenz Wappes, for instance, was not only the leading advocate of "modern" forestry practices in the Pfalz but also the author of an article, "Die aesthetische Bedeutung des Waldes" (reprinted in Theodor Künkele et al., eds., *Festschrift zum 90. Geburtstag von Lorenz Wappes* [Munich, 1950]), that took a scientific approach to the preservation of the natural beauty of the forest.

64. "Der Pfälzerwald in der Bayerisches Jubiläums Landes-, Industrie-, Gewerbe-, und Kunstausstellung," *PW* 7 (15 May 1906): 93.

65. Georg Baer, *Die Pfalz am Rhein: Pfälzische Heimatkunde* (Nuremberg, 1915). The inclusion of technological advance in the history of the Heimat was evident in Theodor Zink's *Deutsche Geschichte auf heimatkundlicher Grundlage*, vol. 1.

66. "Der Deutsche Bund Heimatschutz und seine Landesvereine," in *Der deutsche Heimatschutz: Ein Rückblick und Ausblick*, ed. Gesellschaft der Freunde des deutschen Heimatschutzes (Munich, 1930), p. 200.

The homecoming took place gradually, but certainly by 1910 the city had become as much a part of the Pfälzer landscape as the vine-covered hills. In 1906, for instance, the Verein sponsored a citywide Parkfest in Ludwigshafen, which included a harbor tour of the industrial ports. In 1908, the annual business meeting in Ludwigshafen took the form of a festivity open to all members. Verein poet Eugen Croissant wrote an ode to the city, "Willkommen in Ludwigshafen," that could be sung to the popular melody "Strömt herbei, Ihr Völkerscharen":[67] "Not the sunny vineyard gardens," ran the lyrics, "but still with wondrous gifts."[68] In the same year, the annual extravaganza was held in Lambrecht, an unremarkable, indeed somewhat ugly, industrial town on the Rhine plain; the following year it moved to Kaiserslautern, the region's second industrial center, situated, as Verein flyers chose to describe it, in the "heart" of the Pfälzerwald. Verein-sponsored school outings also took industrial sites as their goal.[69] Factories and forests shared the landscape, and the Pfälzerwald Verein, with the Heimat movement, embraced them all.

The sentiment that proved so receptive, honoring city and forest alike, was patriotism, or love of the Heimat. That "the love of Heimat bore and brought forth the Pfälzerwald Verein" was a common refrain of Wäldlers, and nature in turn received credit for awakening, nourishing, and sustaining this Heimatliebe.[70] The natural attributes of the homeland inspired loyalty and pride; to appreciate nature was to feel the solemn joy of patriotism and to understand the deepest roots of local and national character.[71] At the first joint excursion of the Verein, one of the speakers asserted that although "Wanderlust and joy in mountain and valley are the soul of our Verein," it was "the love . . . of the beautiful land that stretches from the Rhine over the Wasgau and Haardt to the west" that gave "[our efforts] their special content." Indeed, the speaker concluded, "the Pfalz deserves to be and must become Germany's national park."[72]

Patriotism—for the Pfalz, Bavaria, and Germany—informed the building and preservation projects of the Verein and formed another avenue for the imposition of civic values on the out-of-doors. A striking rock formation

67. *PW* 9 (5 July 1908): cover page.
68. Ludwigshafen's rapid growth was also naturalized by comparison to the rising of a water nymph from the Rhine.
69. *Wanderbuch* (1928): 57.
70. "Die Liebe zur Heimat gebär dereinst den Pfälzerwald Verein"; see, e.g., yearly report, *WH*, no. 13 (1918): 4. See also the works of A. Schmidt, quoted in Georg Baer's *Die Pfalz am Rhein:* "Da draußen fließt der Born der Heimaterkenntnis, welcher die Heimatliebe nährt" (p. 1); or Fritz Claus, "Im Pfälzerwald": "in the outdoors . . . our senses and soul are awakened by our beautiful Pfälzer Heimat" (*PW* 1 [4 May 1900]: 2).
71. See, e.g., Hartmann, "Der Pfälzer und das Wandern"; and Wappes, "Aesthetische Bedeutung des Waldes," p. 25.
72. *PW* 7 (15 May 1906): 94.

would be designated a "natural monument."[73] Natural settings became as popular as town squares for civic memorials. The "Ritter stones" that marked paths in the forests were named after the forestry director and Verein leader and were intended as a public monument to one man's public service.[74] In 1907, the Pfälzerwald Verein, with the district president himself in attendance, held the dedication ceremony for its newly completed Luitpold Tower on the Weissenberg, in honor of the prince regent of Bavaria. Like the ubiquitous Bismarck Towers, the monument paid tribute to both man and nature: awesome natural beauty would be complemented by larger-than-life human accomplishment, and vice versa.[75]

The integration of the patriotic monument into the natural world complemented the appropriation of the natural world itself by the public realm of ceremony and celebration. The annual gatherings of the Pfälzerwald Verein publicly affirmed the local and national loyalties of the Wäldlers. The day's activities and speechmaking dwelt on the Pfälzer's love for nature and for Germany. A feature of the festivities that became traditional, the singing of the "Pfalzlied," also drew together nature, public ceremony, and collective identity. Written by a Prussian, set to music by a Frenchman, first sung by a Swede, and first published in Hesse, the Pfalzlied derived legitimacy as a regional anthem entirely from its adoption by the Pfälzerwald Verein, but it nevertheless served both Verein and region well.[76] The poem's speaker stands on a mountaintop with the Pfalz visible on all sides and is moved to deep love for this "speck of earth," its man made as well as its natural structures.[77] The singing of the song was usually followed in the ceremony by

---

73. Government attention to "natural monuments" did not satisfy the Pfälzerwald and Verschönerungs-Verein at the time, consisting as it did of the merest acknowledgment of the importance of natural conservation, without monetary support. See Palatinus (pseudonym, probably for Christian Mehlis), "Zur Pflege der Naturschönheiten in der Pfalz," *PW* 4 (15 August 1903).

74. *Wanderbuch* (1928): 123.

75. *PM* 30 (1913): 81; Fritz Claus, "Der Luitpoldturm im Pfälzerwald," *PW* 10 (15 October 1909): 152–53.

76. See Albert Becker, "Der Pfalzlied," *Der Pfälzer in Berlin: Mitteilungen des Pfälzerwald-Vereins, e.V. Ortsgruppe Berlin* (hereafter cited as *PB*) (1937): 74–75; and "Einiges über die Entstehung des Pfälzer Liedes von Eduard Jost," *WH*, no. 17 (1918): 6.

77. "Das Pfälzer Lied," by Eduard Jost:

> Am deutschen Strom, am grünen Rheine
> Ziehst du dich hin, O Pfälzer Land!
> Wie lächelst du im Frühlingsschmucke,
> Wie winkt des Stromes Silberband!
> Da steh ich auf des Berges Gipfel
> Und schau auf dich in süßer Ruh
> Und jubelnd ruft's aus meinem Herzen:
> O Pfälzer Land, wie schöne bist du!

the singing of the German national anthem in an affirmation of the compatibility of local and national identities.

School and government also promoted the kind of nature-oriented civics favored by the Pfälzerwald Verein. Heimatkunde, as it came increasingly to be adopted and taught in the lower schools, invariably began out-of-doors in order to establish children's relation to and proper feeling for their surroundings—a technique first promoted in the Pfalz by Christian Grünewald in the 1830s. A popular textbook writer of the early twentieth century wrote that "Heimatkunde must be imparted out in the open, with the lands and landscapes of the Heimat as the first object of attention. All else follows from that."[78] Ludwig Zimmer, another writer whose elementary school text appeared in 1905, began by describing the schoolyard and the points of the compass, then proceeded from the public buildings of the town directly into the fields and uncultivated land surrounding it.[79] Political and natural categories collapsed into each other; schoolchildren were to find their orientation in the world from both. The controlling metaphor of Pfälzer poetry, the *Gesichtskreis* or circle of vision that imaginatively comprised the entire Pfalz, also controlled the pattern of civic instruction.

Around the turn of the century, amateur *Heimatschutz* and *Naturschutz* (nature conservation), which included just about anything undertaken by the Pfälzerwald Verein, began to receive state approval and eventually state funds.[80] And although the connection of nature with patriotic feeling was undoubtedly a general stage in the development of all nineteenth-century nationalisms, the Pfälzerwald Verein, and the Pfälzer Heimat movement of which it was the chief representative, achieved an especially close symbiosis between the two. Unlike the neighboring clubs on which it was modeled— the Odenwald Verein and the Schwarzwald Verein—the Pfälzerwald Verein promoted an exact identification between the political region and the nature they glorified. At the meetings of the League of German Mountain and Hiking Clubs, the conventioneers came as members of their Alpine clubs rather than as Bavarians, but the Wäldlers were still Pfälzers.[81] The term *Pfälzerwald* itself attested to the primacy of political categories. Until the end of the nineteenth century, people knew of no one Pfälzerwald but of many different wooded areas, separately conceived and named.[82] Forestry officials and rail-

78. Baer, *Die Pfalz am Rhein*, p. 2.

79. Ludwig Zimmer, *Heimatkunde für die Schulen der Rheinpfalz* (Pirmasens, 1905).

80. Gustav von Kahr (state minister of the interior) to Albert Becker, 10 October 1909, on the ministry's support for the undertakings of the Pfälzerwald Verein, PLBS, Albert Becker Papers.

81. Report of the gathering of the Verband Deutscher Gebirgs- und Wandervereine in the Pfalz, *PW* 11 (15 August 1910), cover page.

82. There is no mention of the Pfälzerwald in the works of Riehl and August Becker in the 1850s.

road builders seem to have used the collective appellation occasionally in the second half of the century, but its adoption into everyday language was the work of the beautification societies and of the Pfälzerwald Verein itself.[83] The latter increasingly used it to refer to all unsettled, uncultivated land in the political region—a convenient and evocative shorthand for that which contrasted to what man had built and sown. The train, too, spread the name, for in 1906 the Pfälzer railroad company named a new fast locomotive the "Pfälzerwald," in recognition of the Verein's promotion of travel as much as of the trees themselves.[84]

The term *Pfälzerwald* soon lost its novelty, together with any lingering sense of artificiality. Its invention and promotion by foresters, entrepreneurs, Verein members, and railroad officials was emblematic of the role they had each played in reshaping the categories in which people conceived of nature. The existence of a single Pfälzerwald contributed in subtle ways to the integrity of the entity "Pfalz" altogether. Science followed sentiment and adopted the term in analysis and description of the land.[85] Indeed, the whole natural world gave the impression of having arranged itself in accordance with the borders of the homeland and the demands of patriotism.

The Pfälzer men and women of the late nineteenth and early twentieth century neither mystified nature nor deified it but rather remade it in their own urban-dwelling image. Their nature, filled with paths, huts, and castle ruins, constituted an alternative milieu that did not fundamentally challenge the necessity of cities or indeed their value. But the surge out from the cities into nature also represented a search for a source of collective identity not to be found in the urban environment. The movement was informed by the presumption that what all Pfälzers had in common was the land. Nature alone could be the appropriate symbol as well as source of Heimat feeling; love of nature, like love of Heimat, was not bound by social class or confession. Workers shared it with industrialists, old with young, uneducated with educated, Catholic with Protestant and Jew.

And though this vision of a social harmony following on a natural one remained the stuff of public rhetoric, the Heimat movement's appropriation of nature nevertheless represented an inclusive and tolerant impulse. Nature was to be neutral, above party and confessional strife.[86] Its popularity at the end of the century represented not so much an inability to deal with political

---

83. Daniel Häberle, *Der Pfälzerwald. Entstehung seines Namens, seine geographische Abgrenzung und die Geologie seines Gebietes* (Kaiserslautern, 1911), pp. 4–6; Georg Wagner, "Heißt es 'Pfälzerwald' oder 'Pfälzer Wald'? Ursprung, Bedeutung und Schreibung dieses geographischen Sammelnamens," *Pälzer Feierowend* 5 (1953).

84. *Wanderbuch* (1928): 41.

85. See Häberle's account of the name, whose novelty he explains then proceeds to use in his technical analyses (in *Der Pfälzerwald*).

86. See Lidtke, *Alternative Culture*, pp. 64–65, on workers and nature.

78 A NATION OF PROVINCIALS

conflict as a desire to exclude it from some areas of endeavor and to create a public environment that all could share. The forest, wrote Wappes, was an *Allgemeingut*, a commonly held treasure of the people.[87] Its preservation was everyone's duty; its enjoyment, everyone's right. Indeed, in its redefinition of nature and of man's relation to it, the Heimat movement in the Pfalz, and in particular the Pfälzerwald Verein, tentatively represented a concept of general citizenship in the region, at least in the sense of the rights and responsibilities of belonging.

The turn-of-the-century renewal of provincial culture in the Pfalz may have begun with the popular discovery of nature, but it soon led to a revival of folk custom, song, dance, and dress. One of the Heimat movement's protagonists, Albert Becker, later remembered the "ever-widening circle of interests" that were then "enclosed within the single word *Heimat*." The term "expanded on all sides," he wrote, "all the way to the Pfälzer countrymen of German ethnicity outside the Heimat borders on the other side of the ocean."[88] Indeed, the step from nature to folk life—and from there to the study of emigration—was a logical one. The same desires that led urban people to seek out nature drew them also to peasant and rural customs and to an interest in their preservation in strange environments, like the city or the foreign land. As filled with illusions in this context as in their approach to nature, as likely to transform the objects they admired, the members of Heimat associations found in "traditional" ways of life a simplicity and harmony they thought lacking in their own, another focus for their sociability, and another expression of their sense of collective identity.

In seeking a basis for Pfälzer identity within peasant life, the Heimat movement followed the example of Wilhelm Heinrich Riehl. In *Die Pfälzer*, Riehl had deliberately abandoned recent political definitions of the land and its inhabitants and dwelt instead on the insights into local character provided by styles of dwelling, eating, working, worshiping, and speaking.[89] Riehl believed, as did his many followers in the fields of Volkskunde and Kulturgeschichte, that the land shaped and limited character. Hence those who lived closest to the land, in the "pure natural life," were also the clearest representatives of the Pfälzer type. Informed by a romantic dichotomy between nature and civilization, the bourgeois people who participated in the associational life of Heimat tried to emphasize their own sense of "Pfälzerness" by a self-conscious imitation of those whose lives were, they thought, more essentially "Pfälzer" than their own. Through scholarly investigation and

87. *Wanderbuch* (1928): 125.
    88. Albert Becker, "Erinnerungen aus der Geschichte der Pfälzer Heimatbewegung," *PB* 19 (15 March 1939): 26.
    89. See Chapter 2.

popular festivity, they established folklore alongside nature as a defining, constitutive element of Pfälzer identity. The scholarly efforts of Pfälzers to establish their ethnographic identity began within the Historical Association of the Pfalz, thanks to secretary Ludwig Schandein's close connections to Riehl. Volkskunde was a young discipline, barely recognized within the universities and uncertain whether its loyalties were to philology, history, or physical science. Its intellectual predecessors were nevertheless highly respected, from Johann Gottfried Herder to Jakob Grimm, and by the 1890s it could claim representation in a number of scholarly institutions throughout Germany. After Schandein, August Becker, and Riehl, a number of amateur scholars and historians carried on Pfälzer folk studies, and in 1894 the founding in Würzburg of the Verein für bayerische Volkskunde und Mundartforschung (Association for Bavarian Folk Studies and Dialect Research) gave regional folk studies in Bavaria an academic home.[90]

Georg Heeger, a high school teacher who became one of the most prominent of the Pfälzer folklorists, had studied briefly with Oskar Brenner in Würzburg. Scholarly folk studies then consisted mainly of the systematic collecting of available evidence of peasant culture. Heeger initiated work on a dictionary of Pfälzer dialect and on a collection of Pfälzer folksongs— projects that contributed to the establishment of folklore as a field of scholarly study.[91] In 1908 Heeger's published collection of Pfälzer folksongs received wide attention and praise in the Pfalz for its "exact study of the people's soul." None but a Pfälzer, "intimately grown up with the thinking and feeling of his Heimat," could have written this work, wrote one reviewer.[92] Heeger himself believed that the study had afforded him "deep insight" into the Pfälzer people; he expressed his "joy" at discovering such "fullness of originality and strength" in the people, who had survived "storms . . . like no other land in the course of the centuries has endured."[93]

The efforts of others, like Albert Becker (no relation to August Becker), were prolific but piecemeal. The serious study of Pfälzer folk life in this period achieved no synthesis comparable to Riehl's of a quarter century earlier. The material did not prove amenable to the framework and the assumptions folklorists brought to it: the classic peasant was hard to find in the Pfalz,

90. For Pfälzer folk studies of the 1890s, see the characteristic articles by Ludwig Eid, "In Bürgers Haus und Hof im 1597: Ein Bild pfälzischer Kultur," *MHVP* 15 (1891): 41–80; and Lukas Grünenwald, "Ein Pfälzischer Bauernkalender: Beitrag zur Volkskunde der Hinterpfalz," *MHVP* 20 (1896): 181–237.

91. Ernst Christmann, "Georg Heeger," *PH* 7 (1956): 114–15. In 1913, the Bavarian Academy of Learning took over the dialect project (*PM* 30 [1913]: 41).

92. Theodor Zink, review of *Volkslieder aus der Rheinpfalz*, in *PM* 26 (1909): 28–29.

93. Georg Heeger and Wilhelm Wüst, *Volkslieder aus der Rheinpfalz, mit Singweisen* (Kaiserslautern, 1908), foreword.

having dwelt in towns and produced for markets for centuries or having left for America, taking his leather breeches with him. Pockets of superstition and ancient peasant festivity were few and far between. As Riehl put it, the French had driven out the ghosts and spirits.[94] The problem, by and large, was not that folk or popular culture did not exist, but that its scholars had an unreasonably narrow notion of what it in fact was. The research that proved most fruitful—the study of dialects and place-names—owed more to pure philology than to the neoromantic assumptions of its purveyors.

But what nature and history did not supply, man could always create. The turn-of-the-century revival of folklore demonstrated the inventiveness of the Pfälzers far more than either their investigative skills or their intrinsic folkiness. The liveliest of the branches of folklore was *Mundart*, or dialect, which in its forms of poetry, tale, dialogue, aphorism, essay, and even joke became the leading medium for a popular creation and celebration of folk identity. Dialect itself had always been present; the novelty was rather in a new consciousness of its existence and a new appreciation for its expressiveness. Dialect helped to "distinguish the Pfälzer *Eigenart* [originality or distinctive character] from the rest of the German population," wrote one proponent, railroad engineer and amateur dialect poet Emil Haas.[95] To use dialect in any context was to signal one's self-consciousness as a Pfälzer, particularly among those who could just as well speak educated high German. In contrast to standard German, dialect was the "most genuine [*ureigenst*] expression of a people's character." Its use, its proponents insisted, did not indicate an excess of regional feeling and a lack of national German feeling, but rather a general renewal of pride in the German language, in all its many forms. "Since Germany has become great and independent with the victory of 1870–71," wrote Haas in support of the value of dialect literature, "we hope some of this self-confidence will spread to the realm of speech, so that we can abandon our naive [*michelhaft*] prejudice in favor of foreign things and forever throw off the Frederican yoke of foreign words."[96] Germany's strength and distinction among nations was not its singleness but its diversity, and the cultivation of dialect, like the Heimat movement of which it was part, would attest to that truth.

Moreover, anyone could create within the medium of dialect; those who did were lauded not as the greatest writers of their time but as the truest representatives of the Pfalz and its people. Poets and writers in dialect, wrote Haas, "teach us to recognize, understand, and value the feeling and thinking

94. Riehl, *Die Pfälzer*, p. 51.

95. Emil Haas, "Die Pflege der Mundart und die Mundartabende in der Pfalz," part 3 in a series of articles by that name, *PM* 22 (1905): 97.

96. Haas, "Die Pflege der Mundart," part 1, *PM* 22 (1905): 5. There are interesting anti-Prussian overtones in this statement that may reflect anticentralist thinking as much as antipathy to Prussia as such.

of the people."[97] Daniel Kuhn, one of the most popular poets of this period, was praised for "deep insight into the being and character of the Pfälzer people."[98] Another, Lina Sommer, had a "generous love for the beautiful Pfälzer Heimat, its land, people, and soul [Wesen]."[99] In their own personalities, the poets represented the Pfalz: "A whole man!" was the description of one, "contemptuous of all superficiality and pretentiousness"; another had the "ready mother wit" of the Vorderpfälzers; another, their characteristic "lively intelligence, self-irony, Gallic prejudice for novelties, and love of company."[100] Paul Münch, the most celebrated dialect poet of his generation and author of a genuine Pfälzer bestseller, a collection of dialect poems called *Die pälzisch Weltgeschicht*, was the "embodied soul of our landscape": "Paul Münch was the Pfalz."[101]

Dialect poets tended to return the compliment to the land that had formed them, making the characteristics of the Pfalz and the foibles and fancies of the typical Pfälzer their leading themes. A comic and somewhat vulgar genre, dialect portraits depicted the Pfälzer as a loud, contentious, back-slapping, joke-telling, wine-guzzling, independent man, with a pure love for the land and the forests.[102] Münch indeed poked fun at the intrinsic self-centeredness of the genre, and of Heimat sentiment altogether, in his *Pälzisch Weltgeschicht*, which told the story of the world in a series of short comic poems, beginning with God's creation of Paradise—the Pfalz.

The commercial success of dialect publications and an increasing number of "dialect evenings" attested to popular enthusiasm for the genre. Sponsored by a local publisher and a local professor, the first "dialect evening" in the Pfalz was held in March 1903 in Kaiserslautern. Featuring a number of poets who read their works out loud "in friendly competition," it was so successful that many local clubs, in particular the Pfälzerwald Verein, adopted the entertainment themselves.[103] For the Verein, the cultivation of dialect followed logically from its role in the protection of the region's natural resources. Both endeavors sought to preserve the Eigenart or distinctive

97. Ibid., p. 4.

98. Review of Daniel Kuhn's "Aus der Hamet," *PM* 27 (1910): 190.

99. Paul Münch, on Sommer's "E Pälzer Blumenstraißel," *PM* 30 (1913): Beilage 3.

100. Haas, "Pflege der Mundart," part 2, *PM* 22 (1905): 20, on Karl Eduard Ney; obituary of Paul Gelbert, *PM–PH* 47/26 (1930): 98; Haas, "Pflege der Mundart," part 3, *PM* 22 (1905): 97, on Richard Müller.

101. Peter Luginsland, "In Memoriam Paul Münch," *PP* 2 (February 1951): 1; see also Albert Becker's review of the first edition of the *Weltgeschicht*, *PW* 10 (1 July 1909): 106.

102. See, e.g. Lina Sommer, "Pälzer Art," in *Heimatgrüße den Pfälzer Landsleuten ins Feld*, ed. Literarischer Verein der Pfalz (Speyer, 1916) (hereafter cited as *Heimatgrüße* [1916]); Fritz Claus, "Die Pälzer," in Baer, *Die Pfalz am Rhein*, p. 40; and Maximilian Pfeiffer, "Vom Handkäs," *PW* 11 (15 October 1910): p. 172.

103. Report on the Mundartabend of the Ludwigshafen chapter of the Pfälzerwald Verein, *PW* 11 (1 May 1910): 63.

character, of the region, whether in the form of its landscape or its people. After all, the originality of both was threatened, according to a Pfälzer Heimatler, by the same "highly developed modes of transportation" whose tendency was to make everything the same.[104]

In their desire to preserve the distinctiveness of Pfälzer ways in an increasingly homogeneous world, the activists of the Pfälzerwald Verein and related folklore groups became increasingly inventive. Without actually fabricating anything, they assembled under the rubric of Pfälzer folk culture a variety of simple styles of dress and dance, along with the songs and fables traditional to the various parts of the region. Some of this was genuine, some was not. But since the product—Pfälzer folklore—was not only greater but also more important than the sum of its parts, absolute authenticity was less critical than collective recognition. The Pfälzerwald Verein made itself both arbiter and sponsor of the revival. Its folkloric efforts had begun in 1906, mainly at the suggestion of Verein member Albert Becker, then teacher of philology at the Gymnasium in Ludwigshafen.[105] A new committee for Heimatpflege, or Heimat care, was set up, and resolved at its first meeting in 1907 to "awaken the interests of the general public for Pfälzer beliefs, customs, and speech."

Typical of all the Pfälzerwald Verein's undertakings, this foray into the field of ethnography revealed a capacity to adapt the raw material, be it forest or folksong, to consumable forms. The Pfälzerwald Verein packaged peasant culture for its members just as it had packaged nature. Take, for instance, the case of the traditional costume, or *Tracht*, of the Pfalz. Tracht, in its usual definition as the distinctive regional dress of the peasantry and smalltownsmen, had not existed within the geographical bounds of that nineteenth-century creation, the Pfalz, since the eighteenth century.[106] The area had experienced too much political and social upheaval to preserve styles of dress distinct from the rest of Germany, indeed of Europe. At the turn of the century a few remnants of peasant dress, still worn in villages to the north and west, were adopted by Tracht hobbyists from the towns and cities as a general Pfälzer Tracht.[107] Tracht—the meaning of which depended

104. Ibid. Note the irony here (one intrinsic to the undertakings of the Pfälzerwald Verein) that an organization so devoted to trains and the extension of train service should also be their critic. On the train as a threat to "local character," see also Wolfgang Schivelbusch, *The Railway Journey: The Industrialization of Time and Space in the 19th Century* (Berkeley and Los Angeles, 1986), pp. 38–42.

105. Report of the steering committee meeting of 10 June 1906, *PW* 7 (15 June 1906): 126; Becker, "Erinnerungen aus der Geschichte der Heimatbewegung," 18–19.

106. Riehl, *Die Pfälzer*, pp. 167–68; F. Gundelwein, "Pfälzer Volkstrachten," *PW* 11 (15 January 1910): 6–7.

107. Gundelwein, "Pfälzer Volkstrachten," p. 7. Otherwise a reliable observer, Gundelwein greeted this adaptation with pleasure.

to a large degree on the existence of its opposite, modern fashion—became the plaything of the big-city bourgeoisie, available in mail order catalogues and advertised in local magazines.[108] Men and women dressed up in their urban-manufactured peasant costumes and went to the newly invented festivities sponsored by the Pfälzerwald Verein or the Verein zur Hebung des Billigheimer Purzelmarktes (Association for the Revival of the Billigheim Purzelmarkt). In its more serious aspect, interest in Tracht, as in dialect, represented a concern for the preservation of regional distinctions in an increasingly monochromatic world. Georg Berthold, a historical association member, hoped that the "upper levels of society" would soon be of the opinion that this "patriotic clothing, that is, *Volkstracht*," was "the most genteel dress" and that the "modern fashions that reduce everything to sameness [were] an evil."[109]

The festivities of the Pfälzerwald Verein and other clubs fastened similarly on a version of rural song, dance, and custom. Here the purpose of folklore was to give substance and focus to celebrations of regional and national pride. The attempt of a local chapter of the Pfälzerwald Verein to celebrate midsummer in authentically traditional fashion resulted in a unique blend of pagan bonfires and brass bands, joined together by poems and songs to the Pfalz and its forests: "O Pfälzerland, wie schön bist du!"[110] In 1908, a "Pfälzer evening" sponsored by the Frankenthal chapter of the Verein für Fraueninteressen (Women's Club) began with a lecture by Georg Heeger on the importance of the word *Heimat*, with its evocation of the "poetry-filled past" of folksong and fairy tale. Women, Heeger urged, had an important role to play in the preservation of folklore, and through it of love for Heimat.[111] "Everywhere we see a return to the simple, the *volkstümlich* [folksy], and the natural," said Heeger. After he finished, members of this urban women's club, most unnaturally garbed in their "Pfälzer Tracht," paraded across the stage, followed by more men and women dressed as vintners. A few stand-up comedians told some "Pfälzer jokes," and finally, the chairwoman of the club, wife of a local judge, read a poem of her own composition

108. Cf. Palle Ove Christiansen, "Peasant Adaptation to Bourgeois Culture? Class Formation and Cultural Redefinition in the Danish Countryside," *Ethnologia Scandinavica* (1978): 128; cited in Hobsbawm, *Invention of Tradition*, p. 8. The author argues that the revival of traditional dress was a means for prosperous farmers to distinguish themselves from the poor agricultural day laborers and the urban dwellers. Theo Gantner sees the festive parades and Tracht displays in Switzerland as a "means of communication for the propagation of new economic consciousness as well as for the dissemination of the ideas of political aspirations"; see his "Brauchtumsvorführungen in Festumzügen des 19. Jahrhunderts," in Wiegelmann, *Kultureller Wandel*, p. 35.

109. "Zur Einweihung des historischen Museums der Pfalz," *PW* 11, Sondernummer 2 (Spring 1910): 70.

110. Account in *PW* 10 (15 July 1909): 109.

111. "Der Pfälzer Abend zu Frankenthal am 14 März 1908," *PM* 25 (1908): 84.

about her devotion to the nature and the people of the Pfalz, whom, she admitted with unintended candor, she did not fully understand.[112] The evening concluded with a display of Frankenthal porcelain—a genuine product of local culture, to be sure, but one whose origins lay in the eighteenth-century ducal court, not in the farmer's cottage. The whole evening, related the commentator, was "very pretty and arranged with taste."[113]

In German and foreign cities, the many clubs of Pfälzer *Landsleute*, or countrymen, further demonstrated the cohesive and symbolic force of an invented folklore. These so-called *Landsmannschaften* were characteristic of all German regional groups and attested in part to the extent of internal migration and urbanization that had taken place.[114] The Pfälzer Landsmannschaften were mostly founded in the first decade of the twentieth century. If not begun as such, most quickly became local chapters of the Pfälzerwald Verein.[115] Besides forwarding the Verein's efforts in tourism through their connections to large urban populations, the groups sponsored social evenings, in the course of which members would sing local songs, dress up in local costume, sample the wines of the Pfalz, and listen to readings in Pfälzer dialect.[116] Far away in both distance and culture from the folklore they celebrated, the groups used an urbanized folk culture as a pretext for socializing, for making important business connections, for establishing a civic profile,

112. "Ein Beitrag zur Heimatkunde," by Frau Justizrat Merckle:

> O daß ich dich so ganz verstehe
> Du Pfälzer Land, mein Heimat Land
> Wie Spätrot webt um deine Höhen
> Vergangenheit ihr flatternd Band.
> O daß ich dich so ganz verstehe
> Mein Pfälzer Volk, so froh und frei
> Du bliebst trotz aller Stürme Wehen
> Dir selbst im tiefsten Grund getreu. . . .

See *PM* 25 (1908): 85.

113. Ibid.

114. Zink and Mang (*Wirtschaftsleben*, pp. 279–80) observed that areas with industry and patterns of small property ownership held their population better than areas of large estates. The Pfalz lost 12.5 percent of its population between 1882 and 1910; the Rhineland, 7 percent; and Posen, 33 percent. These groups of displaced natives are similar to but not the same as the traditional student groups, also called *Landsmannschaften*.

115. The Verein Rheinpfälzer in Munich became a chapter of the Pfälzerwald Verein in 1910, with 113 members (*PW* 11 [15 August 1910]: 139); the Berlin group began as a local chapter and was soon the most important and politically significant Pfälzer Landsmannschaft (*PW* 11 [1 June 1910]: 107); there were also groups in Stuttgart, Cologne, Strasbourg, Würzburg, Saarbrücken, and Karlsruhe.

116. A contemporary Pfälzer periodical contained a series of photographs of these activities that illustrate the urbanity of the folksiness. Seated in formal parlors on Victorian horsehair sofas, a group of large, elaborately coiffed bourgeois women model Pfälzer Trachten. In another photograph, the men, sporting leather pants, hiking sticks, and hats, stand in front of a large white rowhouse with Ionian columns, wrought-iron fences, and heavy brickwork. See *Des Pfälzers Heimat in Wort und Bild* 1 (1910): 47–48.

and indeed for preserving their ties to the place—if not precisely the culture—of their origin. Perhaps, as Pfälzer writers from time to time suggested, the Pfälzer, being an emigrant and wanderer by nature and history, had a particular need for these clubs of countrymen and a special gift for forming them. "The Pfälzer spirit," wrote one who presumably had it, "everywhere unfolds itself in brotherly harmony and with an open, direct character"; both at home and abroad "a feeling of solidarity" has arisen.[117] Certainly, at the turn of the century those actually in the Pfalz developed a new interest in their fellow countrymen who had left for other parts of Germany and the world and in the preservation of Pfälzer identity among those emigrants. In 1909, Daniel Häberle dedicated his classic account of the Pfälzer emigration to "Pfälzers in the Heimat and in strange lands." His emigrants, who "to the present day in the midst of a foreign population preserved their essential [eigentümlich] character," implicitly affirmed the validity of that character.[118] Their exploits in the New World were widely recounted in the Pfalz, and, in an odd reversal, they became a source of identity for those who remained at home. Though perhaps a dubious source of pride, Pfälzers considered their own the premier land of German emigrants: as Häberle pointed out, for a period in the eighteenth century all German emigrants were known as "Pfälzers." Yet their enthusiasm for Pfälzer emigration rarely spread to contemporary movements of colonization and foreign adventurism.[119] The Pfälzer as such had not colonized Africa, and as far as the Heimat movement was concerned, the strongest affirmation of the Pfälzer character came from the prosperity of Pfälzer-Americans, not from German military predominance on the high seas.

For the hallmark of the Heimat movement, and of the cultivation of folklore within it, was its quality of referring all phenomena back to itself, back to the Pfalz. As a result, its participants tended to espouse a nationalism of which the most important determinants were internal: a nationalism defined by its constituent parts, not its opposing counterparts; by the regions within Germany, not the nations outside it. New colonial ventures and navies held little interest for those whose enthusiasms were all for the Heimat; nor did the aggressive, outward-turned nationalism of the Pan-German League, despite a superficially shared interest in German language and German folk culture in strange lands. The Heimat movement was above all concerned with the disappearance of distinctive regional cultures within Germany, and

117. Ibid.
118. Häberle, Auswanderung und Koloniegründung, p. 1. The occasion for the book was the two hundredth anniversary of the first mass emigration of Pfälzers to America in 1709.
119. An exception is Georg Berthold, who delivered a speech, "Über kolonialgeschichtliche Beziehungen Speyers," to the Deutsche Kolonialgesellschaft on the occasion of their visit to Speyer in 1907; see PM 24 (1907): 73ff.

all its efforts and energies went toward the preservation of that Eigenart. In contrast, the Pan-Germans and the Navalists were too fixated on national predominance and national unity above all else to pay much heed to the internal constitution of that nation; all they required was that it be strong enough.

Hence, although Heimat enthusiasts were certainly nationalists, their emphases and their projects were not identical with those of the militarists, imperialists, and centralizers, who in turn were suspicious of the potential for particularism within the Heimat movement.[120] The advocates of a navy or a colonial empire were, after all, the radicals, determined to break down the provincialism of Germans, the latecomers among the national peoples of Europe. The Heimat enthusiasts, in their belief in the Eigenart of Heimat as the key to both local and national identity, were articulating—in new contexts, to be sure—a more traditional conception of Germanness. A German was not a German without being a Pfälzer, a Bavarian, or a Silesian first. They were men who felt not only "most German," but most Pfälzer too.

Folklore, like nature, helped establish this dual identity by serving as a symbol for the diversity of cultures that existed within the German nation. The diversity of folk cultures was threatened by many of the same things that threatened the diversity of natural settings in Germany: mass technology and mass markets, centralized economies and governments, and social divisions and conflicts. In the face of a contemporary reality that was at once homogeneous and filled with contention, the cultivation of "folk identity" offered the promise of an egalitarian cooperation that would not suppress distinctiveness and particularity. From this perspective, the invented folk costume of the Pfalz was expressive of provincial solidarity across class and confessional divisions (though it perpetuated gender divisions to a striking degree); the folk costume parades and festivals, too, were celebrations of communalism itself. The very artificiality of the folk costume and of folklore revivalism at the turn of the century betrayed its essentially symbolic role in local society. To seek out evidence of folksiness—and to invent it where it did not actually exist—was to seek some common denominator, some cultural heritage available to all. Pfälzer folklore became the repository of a widespread longing, not for the bygone past as such, nor for the life of the farmer, peasant, or medieval artisan, but for the unalienated, undivided life. Germans in the Heimat movement thought they saw traces of such a life in the folksong and folktale; they demonstrated their belief in its realization in the modern world by wearing the Tracht, department store tags and all.

Thus, folk culture, like nature for the Heimat naturalists, became the

120. Geoff Eley, "Nationalist Pressure Groups in Germany," in *Nationalist and Racialist Movements in Britain and Germany Before 1914*, ed. Paul Kennedy and Anthony Nicholls (London, 1981), p. 59.

clearest embodiment of a "common good." Theodor Zink, praising Heeger's collection of folksongs, called the volume a "common treasure" that would bring "social reconciliation" to all Pfälzers: "for within it [the songbook] lies something that is or should be common to us all, the emotional life [Gemütsleben] of a people."[121] For Albert Becker, folklore addressed the "social question" directly. Its cultivation and study offered the possibility of bridging the gap that had grown up between the educated and the uneducated, the country folk and the city folk. For the "practical statesman and the bureaucrat whose goal is the reconciliation of socially divided levels of the people," folklore could be a "mediator." He suggested its efficacy also for theologians, doctors, jurists, and any educated person who needed to understand the peasant.[122]

For both Becker and Zink, the reconciling capacities of folklore were, ironically, embedded within the enlightening possibilities of education, both of the uneducated and of the already *gebildet*. They hoped, in Becker's words, to achieve their transformation of people's mentalities, to build new appreciation for the land and its people, "without having to give up the sources and the forms of our education."[123] The same hope informed the attempt to awaken a historical consciousness in the Pfalz during the period of the Heimat movement. The Pfälzer activists, who had taken up and recast first nature, then custom, dress, and song, now sought to reshape memory itself.

The third main category of local efforts gathered under the rubric of the Heimat movement was historical, in particular the genre of Heimatgeschichte, or Heimat history. A specifically Pfälzer history had already emerged under the general authorship of the Historical Association of the Pfalz, and the founding of fifteen smaller historical clubs between 1884 and 1914 reflected the spread of interest in the subject throughout the towns of the region. Indeed, after the 1890s the cultivation of historical consciousness took more popular forms, aimed at a broader audience than the Historical Association had ever desired. Along with nature and folkore, history too now contributed to the emergence of a popularly held local identity, attesting both to the distinctiveness of the Pfalz and to its participation in a broadly German culture. "On every side in the Pfälzer lands," wrote the editor of the region's popular historical journal in 1911, "the feeling for the remains of prehistory and for the history of the Heimat stirs and awakens."[124]

But the cultivation of history, unlike that of nature and folklore, generated

---

121. *PM* 26 (1909): 28–29.

122. "Volkskunde in der Pfalz," *PM* 20 (1903): 148–49.

123. Albert Becker, *Ziele und Aufgaben*, p. 21.

124. Friedrich Johann Hildenbrand, "Die Einweihung des Regino-Denkmals in Altrip," *PM* 28 (1911): 104.

a major tension within the Heimat movement. Historical studies had, after all, for many years been the territory of local elites. In contrast to the Historical Association, the tendency of the new organizations that made up the Heimat movement was toward mass participation, simplification, and popularization. Of little moment in and of themselves, the tensions within local historical studies and the Heimat movement in general reflected gradual loss of control by the Honoratioren over all aspects of provincial life. In their place, an increasingly diverse group of people began to take an active role, whether by voting or by joining associations, in shaping the public realm—its boundaries, its activities, and its collective identities.

The popularizers of Pfälzer history around the turn of the century built on the themes and forms of historical study already established in the Pfalz, adapting both to the requirements of mass consumption. The civic purposes of historical studies in the Historical Association had from the start been twofold: to establish local identity through the construction of a coherent historical past and to place that history and identity within the context of Germany, the Fatherland.[125] Both purposes had nevertheless remained incidental to the actual historical scholarship, confined to introductory and concluding paragraphs or to ceremonial speeches. Around the turn of the century, however, Heimat history coalesced into a set of complementary themes and subjects in which the contribution of the region's own past to the German national character determined the whole way in which history was conceived. As Theodor Zink explained in the introduction to his "stories and descriptions for school and home," *Deutsche Geschichte auf heimatkundlicher Grundlage* (German History on the Foundation of Heimat Studies): "Heimat history is only a piece of the great world history, but just as without world history there is no Heimat history, so is world history alone useless. . . . [In this work] German history will be depicted as it appears bound . . . to the Pfalz and Bavaria, and in that way will German history be all the more comprehensible and Heimat history all the more grand."[126]

Some subjects embodied the dual themes of nation and locality better than others. The favored historical figures of Heimat history displayed qualities not of greatness but of "Pfälzerness," in which "Germanness" was embedded. Liselotte von der Pfalz, trapped by marriage in the ritualized and rigid court life of Louis XIV, combined the frankness of Pfälzers with their sentimental love of home and country; moreover, she had been a victim, if an overfed one, of French iniquity. Franz von Sickingen, the evangelical knight of the sixteenth century, represented Pfälzer independent-mindedness and personal bravery. His skirmishes with Catholic princes were depicted as an

125. See Chapter 2.
126. Theodor Zink, *Deutsche Geschichte*, vol. 1, foreword.

early struggle against the enemies of German unity and strength.[127] The largely mythical figure of the "Jäger aus Kurpfalz" (Huntsman of the Kurpfalz), subject of a widely known German folksong, embodied the Pfälzers' love of nature and of country.[128] A variety of minor knights and brave peasants, Roman and Holy Roman emperors, and prominent emigrants also appeared in the literature and celebrations of Heimat history from time to time. The particular figure was in any case less important than his or her representative qualities: Liselotte, von Sickingen, and the Huntsman were legendary as well as real figures in the popular imagination.

Heimat history also lingered in the epoch of castle building, the period from the eleventh through the thirteenth centuries when the geographical area of the Pfalz was at the center of the Holy Roman Empire. The Speyer cathedral, the imperial castle of Trifels and its satellites, and the abbey of Limburg all symbolized the greatness of the old German empire and, by association, the importance of the Pfalz itself.[129] But the tale of national triumph was countered by the even more compelling tale of never-ending war, devastation, and disaster. The worthiness of the Pfalz followed also from its witness to the sufferings of Germany. Roman wars, barbarian invasions, medieval princely feuding, religious strife, and the ordeal of the Thirty Years' War—the Pfalz's survival of these horrors was eloquent testimony to the immortality of the national community itself. Their suffering at the hands of the French, from the Sun King to the emperor, gave further proof of the Pfälzers' embodiment of the greater German fate. Moreover, despite the efforts of the French to conquer and convert, the Pfälzers had remained steadfastly German. The French threat secured the no-longer-beleaguered Pfälzers' identification with their nation; indeed, had France not existed, the Pfälzer Heimat movement may well have had to invent it.

Yet despite the omnipresent French, Heimat historians rarely favored the recent past as a subject for their tales. The events and decisions that had really formed the Pfalz into the political entity it was made scant appearance in the record of the Heimat. The Hambach Festival was acknowledged only as a celebration of German national sentiment. As it had in Riehl's work, the influence of French law and constitutional practice was obscured. In place of

---

127. Ferdinand Lassalle, who had extensive contacts and experience in the Pfalz, wrote a historical play on the figure: an illustration, among other things, of Vernon Lidtke's assertion that regional patriotism was compatible with political radicalism (*Alternative Culture*, p. 92).

128. Pfälzers devoted much time to proving that the actual historical figure came from the Pfälzerwald, not some other forested region of Germany. See, e.g., Ernst Bilfinger, "Zur Geschichte des Jägers aus Kurpfalz," *PW* 8 (15 October 1907): 154–55.

129. Interestingly, the Trifels theme of German glory became much more prominent in Heimat literature and, not coincidentally, under the Nazis, who made a cult of the castle. See Chapter 7 below.

any account of the actual origins of the region, Pfälzer Heimat enthusiasts substituted a historical cult of the Bavarian house of Wittelsbach, whose contemporary rule was legitimated by the existence of dynastic links stretching back tenuously to the twelfth century. The recently fought war of 1870– 71 could also be assimilated into patriotic history, though not as the chroniclers of a triumphant Prusso-German destiny depicted it. For the Pfälzer Heimat historian, the war became yet another enactment of the French threat to the homeland, this time victoriously repulsed.[130] The Pfalz and the Rhineland, not Berlin, were at the center of such an understanding of German history, and while Pfälzers may have been willing to admit their marginality to some events of the German past, they would never concede their irrelevance to the struggle with France: in fact, many Pfälzers were inclined to credit the very achievement of the German nation to the Rhenish spirit of resistance to French influence.

But the popular medium in which Heimat-historical consciousness dwelt imposed constraints of its own on the provincial remembrance of things past. While monuments and memorials, the favored expression of historical consciousness in the beautification societies, could commemorate great figures, princely houses, and wars, they could stand less easily for political fragmentation or constitutional change. Beautification societies had emphasized castles and the past that these represented at least partly because castles were fine tourist attractions. Similarly, the history promoted by the Pfälzerwald Verein was restricted to the tales told by castle ruins, war memorials, and shrines to the Wittelsbachs. In June 1914, the Verein staged its most "historical" event: an enormous celebration of the Hambach Festival in the castle grounds themselves. The spirit of Hambach in its 1914 revival was one of *Heimatgefühl*, or Heimat sentiment. "A true people's festival" and a "celebration of our united German Fatherland," the commemoration involved all the costumes and props the Verein could assemble, more or less regardless of epoch. Social harmony, local patriotism, and national pride were the themes of the event, wine barrels, historical costume parades, and folk dancing their manifestation. Any resemblance to the revival's historical precursor remained purely coincidental.[131]

Even more revealing of the Pfälzerwald Verein's appreciation of the past

130. See, e.g., Emil Müller, *Die Pfalz im Jahre 1870*, reviewed in *PM* 24 (1907): 45 by Philipp Keiper, who wrote that the book would ignite in the younger generation the "fire of noble, self-sacrificing excitement for Germany's power and greatness, tied together with love for the narrow Heimat and interest in its history."

131. See Kurt Baumann, "Hambacher Erinnerungsfeiern: Das Hambacher Fest und die politische Tradition der Pfalz," *PH* 2 (1951): 54. Baumann quotes a contemporary, and ironic, commentary in the *Frankfurter Zeitung*: "Not as though one declared oneself in solidarity with ideas propagated back then or even with the means of their realization. No, we do not want to be 'revolutionaries,' but we can with confidence declare that whatever happened back then that was *not* just bombast, well, of that we may approve."

was the historical parade, or *Festzug*—an event that reached its zenith of popularity in the Second Empire, at least partly because it gave the bourgeoisie a suitably public but nonpolitical occasion to demonstrate its contribution to, as one historian put it, "the great house of the German national state."[132] These parades became an important feature of the yearly mass gatherings and involved elaborate costuming and parade floats. At festivities in Kaiserslautern in 1910, for instance, the Kurpfälzer Huntsman with his own hunting party led the parade, followed by a minstrel (a reminder of Richard Lion-Heart's brief stay in the Pfälzer castle of Trifels), several Pfälzer knights of uncertain epoch, and then the Kaiser himself, Friedrich Barbarossa, with consort Beatrice and pages. (Barbarossa had reputedly founded the town of Kaiserslautern on the spot where he liked to fish.) After the twelfth-century emperor came the sixteenth-century knight von Sickingen—also with his wife. The rest of the parade consisted of large groups of men and women dressed as artisans, old-time vintners, soldiers, and peasant maidens.[133]

Although chronologically chaotic, historical parades were not without rhyme and reason; their sense simply did not reside in a conventional historical narrative. Rather than telling the story of the Pfalz—which might have proved impossible—the parade strung together the most evocative and colorful moments from the region's past as a group portrait of Pfälzer identity. The position of the Huntsman at the front, literally blowing the Pfälzers' own horn, established the enduring presence of the forest and of nature at the center of Pfälzer identity. The luminaries who followed represented the historical importance of the region to Germany as a whole; the curious presence of their wives suggested the image of a Pfälzer family, in the best nineteenth-century bourgeois style. Despite the presence of the emperor at the center of the parade, the Wäldlers who participated, good townsfolk all, were not dressing up as nobility because they longed for the reinstatement of feudal arrangements, nor did they seem—in the spirit of the Rhenish *Karneval*, with which the parade shared obvious physical characteristics—to be turning upside down an otherwise oppressive social order to achieve a fleeting moment of power and self-expression.[134] On the contrary, the historical

132. Hermann Glaser, *Die Kultur der wilhelminischen Zeit. Topographie einer Epoche* (Frankfurt, 1984), pp. 215–16; see also Wolfgang Hartmann, *Der historische Festzug. Seine Entstehung und Entwicklung im 19. und 20. Jahrhundert* (Munich, 1976).

133. Full account with photographs may be found in *PW* 11 (1 July 1910): 109–12.

134. One is tempted to interpret these revelers along the lines suggested by Mikhail Bakhtin, wishing, perhaps, that something of the seductively attractive chaos of medieval society lingered in these annual extravaganzas. But the evidence of careful planning and highly regimented choreography does not support such an argument. Indeed, resemblances to the medieval Karneval were striking precisely because they were deliberate; the reasons for the well-planned imitation, not for the spontaneous expression of popular sociability, are what need to be explained.

parades were entirely affirmative occasions: affirmative of the prevailing social order, of the national past, and, most of all, of the historical integrity of
the Pfälzers themselves. The past they evoked was an idealized portrait of
the Pfälzer present, and the egalitarian mixing of kings, peasants, and guilds-
men, like the invented Tracht itself, symbolized a wished-for harmony
among all classes. By dressing up in the trappings of the old order, the home-
townsmen only emphasized the triumph of the new, not just over the landscape of the Pfalz, but over its unruly and disorganized past as well, now
contained within a festive celebration of the contemporary life of the
Pfälzer.[135]

Staging festivals, building monuments, and touring castles typified the
preference of the Pfälzerwald Verein for history as drama. Popular Heimat
history also took the form of Geschichtsblätter, or historical pages, that
appeared as supplements to many local newspapers. Between 1893 and the
war, twelve small newspapers in the Pfalz started their own historical pages,
which included short articles on local sites, local artifacts, or famous people
who had lived in the area. The editor of one such publication wrote in 1903
that "the desire for knowledge of the early history of our Heimat grows
among the people and will certainly have a good influence on mind and
temperament."[136] The Pfälzerwald Verein's own Pfälzerwald included short
articles on historical themes alongside its pieces on nature and folklore, and
in 1900 even the Historical Association took over sponsorship of a popular
periodical, Pfälzisches Museum—a decision that doubled association membership within a few years.[137]

Popular history in its printed form also encompassed textbooks and short
pamphlets on historical subjects, a genre of which the local masters were
Theodor Zink and Albert Becker. Zink, who by the time of his death in 1934
had written seventeen books and 532 articles on his Pfälzer Heimat, was a
teacher by profession, though his research, writing, and collecting become so
engrossing that in 1907 he took the position of city archivist in Kaiserslautern
in order to pursue them full time. Zink's most important work was the school
and home text Deutsche Geschichte auf heimatkundlicher Grundlage (German History on the Foundations of Heimat Studies), which provided an unbroken

---

135. In a more social-psychological vein, Glaser believes that "those who collected on the
festival fields . . . were actually costumed bourgeois citizens of the Machine Age, who sought to
overcome their anxiety about the way things are with the help of magically loaded images of the
way things were" (Kultur der wilhelminischen Zeit, p. 219).

136. From the Leininger Geschichtsblätter: review of local historical literature in PM 20 (1903):
62.

137. Report at the Mitglieder Versammlung, Historischer Verein der Pfalz, PM 30 (1913):
29. Its editor from 1903 to 1918, Friedrich Johann Hildenbrand, credited the paper's coverage of
archeological digs with keeping it financially "above water"—a testimonial to the popularity of
amateur excavations in the period (PM 35 [1918]).

narrative account of the Pfalz from the time of the Celts, through Julius Caesar, ending with Bismarck, Prince Regent Luitpold, and the railroad. "Our Heimat," he wrote, "looked different in the time of Julius Caesar than it does today"—but that it was the same Heimat throughout could not be doubted.[138] Zink assimilated all the many pasts of the region within the unifying idea of Heimat, and he used artifacts, folktales, and natural formations to demonstrate the existence of that past even in the present.[139] Becker was the master of the "George-Washington-slept-here" variety of local history. His popular series of short works, "Contributions to the Heimat Lore of the Pfalz," included, for instance, an account of Schiller's brief period of residence in the Pfalz; according to Becker, "even the tiny and insignificant gains high value when tied to the history of the greats."[140]

But for all the popularity of parades and pamphlets, the local museum— the *Heimatmuseum*—provided the fullest expression of the historical consciousness of the period. Local museums, with collections representing areas smaller than that of the Historical Association's museum in Speyer, spread throughout the region in the two decades before the war. The town of Bad Dürkheim had been precocious, founding its museum in 1872. By 1914, seven more Pfälzer towns had their own local museums, which meant that a region of only nine hundred thousand inhabitants and no major city could claim eleven museums—or more, if one counted the guild and natural history museums.[141]

The museums reflected a popular and inclusive conception of local culture that had much in common with the civic activism of the beautification societies and the Pfälzerwald Verein. The "modern museum," asserted Albert Becker in a 1914 lecture on the goals and tasks of a Heimat museum, should be a "people's school . . . open to every man": "our museums, for a long time places only of pure learning, have become places for the people's education"; further, "from creations of a private, aristocratic type, our museums today have become *volkstümlich*, democratic institutions."[142] The Heimat museum in Neustadt, for instance, was the project of the chamber of commerce, a minister, and a teacher, in conjunction, so said the town mayor in his dedicatory speech, "with the entire citizenry of our town."[143] Becker too, in his lecture on the foundation of a Heimat museum in Zweibrücken,

138. Zink, *Deutsche Geschichte*, p. 9.

139. Review of Zink's book by Albert Becker, *PM* 26 (1907): 152.

140. Albert Becker, *Schiller und die Pfalz*, Beiträge zur Heimatkunde der Pfalz, 1 (Ludwigshafen, 1907), foreword.

141. Friedrich Sprater, "Pfälzische Geschichtsvereine und Heimatmuseen," in *25 Jahre "Pfälzische Rundschau," Bedeutendste Zeitung der Pfalz*, ed. Pfälzische Rundschau (Ludwigshafen, 1924).

142. Albert Becker, *Ziele und Aufgaben*, pp. 3, 7, 10.

143. "Das Heimatmuseum für Neustadt a.d. Haardt und Umgebung," *PM* 32 (1915): 71.

called on the citizenry to contribute their time and artifacts to the project, out of a sense of public duty as well as civic pride.[144] The Heimat museum, he emphasized, would be "not a showpiece for the increase of tourism" but "for us, for our closest Heimat."[145]

Because they saw their museums as a means of popular education, local museum builders were guided by demands less of beauty than of pedagogy. Daylight through windows, thought to enhance one's powers of concentration, was preferred to electric light, and the "friendly, light, and wide" rooms were not to be so filled with objects as to bore the visitor.[146] Becker recommended a strong principle of organization to lead people through the museum. His own preference was to proceed in a Riehlian fashion from natural history to the cultural history of private life and then to economic and political (and here he included military and judicial) history.[147] The Neustadt museum had a strictly chronological organization that culminated in the Hambach Festival, a "local" event that gave Neustadt a claim to national prominence.[148]

More revealingly, Becker distinguished the new democratic Heimat museum from earlier aristocratic museums, insofar as Heimat museums sought neither high quality nor originality but representativeness in their collections: "here [in the Heimat museum] association and origin lend especial charm even to things of little value; even the least valuable items of our cultural heritage can fructify our being with ideal worth, just as our written speech gains ever new life from our Mundart."[149] The curators of Heimat museums, as a consequence, laid no particular stress on the genuine article: many museums contained as many casts and copies and even paintings of items as originals. Becker recommended plaster casts, not just because they were easier to maintain, but because they allowed a more complete collection of the past to be displayed—an obvious advantage for a pedagogical institution.[150] Truly superb pieces, he thought, should reside in the district museum, or even in the state or national museums in Munich and Nuremberg, where they would receive proper care and still redound to the credit of the Heimat.

Perhaps, too, the willingness of local Heimat museums to fill their rooms with copies reflected a growing belief—shared with the Pfälzerwald Verein—that the genuine article was to be found not in museums at all, but

144. Albert Becker, Ziele und Aufgaben, pp. 6–7, 36.
145. Ibid., p. 20.
146. Description of the Neustadt Heimatmuseum, PM 32 (1915); Becker, Ziele und Aufgaben, p. 24.
147. Becker, Ziele und Aufgaben, pp. 29–32.
148. "Das Heimatmuseum für Neustadt," PM 32 (1915).
149. Becker, Ziele und Aufgaben, p. 18.
150. Ibid., pp. 27–29.

rather out-of-doors. Through their mapmaking and path building, the Pfälzerwald Verein had physically opened up castle ruins and natural wonders to
the day-tripper; there was no longer any practical need to depend solely on
museums for one's acquaintance with the region as a whole. The intellectual
argument for the authenticity of things experienced in the open, in their original settings—an argument that can be encountered in every European
country in this period—seems to have followed from the new accessibility of
ruins and nature to the casual participant. For Albert Becker, what could be
left in its original setting, whether it be a stone carving or a native insect,
should be left there. Citing the rise of modern *Denkmalpflege*, or monument
preservation, he argued that "the time is past when one shows a piece the
greatest honor by uprooting it and sticking it—or burying it—in a
museum."[151] He urged instead the imaginative use of paintings and descriptions of the reality, which would supplement visits to actual sites.[152]

Supplementary to hiking expeditions, and secondary to regional and state
museums, the Heimat museum may not seem all that important, and yet,
with Becker leading the way, many Heimat activists of the period laid great
stress on the need for every town to have one. Heimat museums did something that no other museum, indeed no book, castle, or even pretty view,
could do, and that was depict the local genius "more clearly, more intensely
. . . than the reality itself." Large museums, moreover, lacked the "relation
with the soil" that Heimat museums cultivated above all else. The smaller
their area of representation, the "finer and more sympathetic" their portrait
of the Heimat would be and the better their "illumination" of "local color-
ing." Therein, believed Becker, lay the "charms, the justification, and the
assignments" of a Heimat museum."[153]

Therein lay the democratic and popular role of the Heimat museum as
well. The "little man," "for whom museums were too often windows to peer
through," could be led from the soil of Heimat to an appreciation of and even
pleasure in the highest offerings of culture.[154] Becker spoke approvingly of a
Social Democratic motion in the Saxon Landtag to make museum collections
more accessible, open in the evenings and welcoming to the working class.[155]
For Becker, the social-democratic impulse to include all classes in an appreciation of culture could be nowhere better answered than in local museums
that sought to educate the people and welcomed into German culture every

---

151. Ibid., p. 34.
152. Becker, not coincidentally, was an avid member of the Pfälzerwald Verein, active in all
its undertakings and for a short time editor of its magazine *Der Pfälzerwald*. The Neustadt
Heimatmuseum, among others, used numerous paintings in its displays (see description of the
museum, *PM* 32 [1915]).
153. Becker, *Ziele und Aufgaben*, p. 34, 17.
154. Ibid., pp. 7, 10.
155. Ibid., p. 8.

conceivable artifact of the past. Popularization, in other words, involved both form and content. The Heimat museum represented a setting for a new emphasis on comprehensive, folkloric history, whose starting point was not the king but the people, not the state but the land itself. Moreover, the Heimat museum encouraged a patriotic enthusiasm that began at the source, at the Heimat, and grew from there to include every man, "without regard to class or profession." In a society "ever more split by birth, rank, and profession," he concluded, "all classes of people can be reunited in the past that is common to us all."[156]

Even the Historical Association of the Pfalz, that bastion of Honoratioren power and patronage in the region, participated (haltingly, to be sure) in the popularization of the region's past and the development of new forms for the cultivation of history. A popular magazine, tours of historic sites for the general public, and joint meetings with the Pfälzerwald Verein were all tentative efforts to appeal to the historically uneducated.[157] The largest undertaking of the association, one that expressed both the increasingly public nature of its role and the persistence of its elite position, was the building of a new museum for the entire region. "The last great manifestation of the Heimat movement," as a Pfälzer historian of a later era put it, "before the dying out of the bourgeois spirit of patronage led to a life-or-death crisis in provincial culture," the new Historical Museum of the Pfalz was at the same time the least representative manifestation of that Heimat movement.[158] Certainly it affirmed the existence and the vitality of Pfälzer self-consciousness, but its planners meant also to secure their exclusive role as the guardians of that culture, a role called into question by the Pfälzerwald Verein as well as by local Heimat museums.[159] The new museum, then, was organized, built, and opened in a spirit as much of resistance to the tendencies of the Heimat movement as of participation in it.

The process began in 1898, when Georg Berthold, a government financial official of high rank, helped to establish an association to lobby state and "people" for a new building to house the Historical Association's modest public collection.[160] The group, which called itself the Verein Historisches Museum der Pfalz, already had 1,533 members by 1900; by 1903 it had raised some 300,000 marks, both from the government and from the region's

156. Ibid., pp. 35–36.

157. Historischer Verein der Pfalz, record of general convention (1906), PLAS, T1, no. 14; report of the monthly meeting, *PM* 28 (1911): 76; report in *PM* 30 (1913): 88.

158. Kurt Baumann, "Festveranstaltung zum Museumsjubiläum," *PH* 11 (1960): 113.

159. Becker, significantly, played no part in the building of the new museum, and was not even a member of the Historical Association until many years later.

160. "Denkschrift," *MHVP* (1899): 8, 17, 23; Karl Schultz, introduction to *100 Jahre Feier Historisches Museum der Pfalz* (special volume), *MHVP* 67 (1969): xxiii.

businesses and wealthy families.[161] The Museum Association also secured the contribution of several major historical collections from private owners. For the most part remnants of elite culture, these artifacts suited Berthold's ambition to build a "first-class" collection for the Pfalz, one that would make a "fine impression upon fine-minded people."[162] When in 1900 a prestigious group of scholars, commissioned by the Bavarian government, opened up the medieval emperors' crypt in the Speyer cathedral, Berthold seized the chance to acquire some of the project's findings—these "jewels of Germany," "the principal symbol of the strength of German unity"—for display in the future Historical Museum of the Pfalz.[163] He also managed to attract the patronage and the services of Gabriel von Seidl, official architect to the Bavarian government and designer of the Bavarian National Museum in Munich, who called it "the finest assignment of my life to build a museum for the Pfalz."[164] In 1905, after a keynote address by *Reichsrat* Franz von Buhl, one of the Pfalz's few men of title, the general assembly of the Historical Association of the Pfalz approved a budget of 585,000 marks, twice that projected half a decade earlier.

The new building's location in Speyer asserted unequivocally the centrality of regional historical consciousness to contemporary civic culture. Occupying a large plot of city land next to the classical Gymnasium, it stood across from the regional archives and the Protestant consistory of the Pfalz on one side, and the presidial building of the Bavarian regional government on the other. Its elaborate front façade faced across a city street to the emperors' cathedral itself. A ceremonial entrance, flanked by two large equestrian statues of Roman origin, reminded one poetically minded observer of "the forum of a city in a conquered province of the Roman world empire."[165] Atop the broad oaken doors stood another equestrian statue, the "Herald of

161. The Landrat, for example, contributed 100,000 marks per year to the project. See yearly reports of the Historical Association, *MHVP* 23 (1899): 286 and 25 (1901): 134–35; HVP miscellaneous records, PLAS, T1, no. 4.

162. The artifacts included the Roman Terra-Sigillata collection of *Kommerzienrat* Wilhelm Ludowici; the collection of Frankenthaler porcelain, from his brother August Ludowici; the historic clothing collection of the Bassermann-Jordans; as well as the major part of the collection for the wine museum, also from that family. Along with the group of artifacts from the cathedral crypt of the Holy Roman emperors, these constituted the main holdings of the museum. See Karl Schultz, "Wesen und Wandel des Pfälzischen Landesmuseum," *PH* 11 (1960): 117.

163. Yearly report, *MHVP* 26 (1903): 112.

164. Berthold, "Das Historische Museum der Pfalz," *PM* 25 (1908): 68; "Zum Museumsbau in Speyer," *PM* 21 (1904): 193.

165. Franz Jung, "Das Historische Museum in Speyer," *PM* 26 (1909). Another observer, Friedrich Johann Hildenbrand, considered that the statues "allowed one to recognize the importance of the building on first glance"; see "Der Neubau und die Sammlungen des Historischen Museums der Pfalz zur Zeit der Einweihung," *PM* 27 (1910): 74.

the Pfalz" (invented, not unearthed), with on either side of him the shields of Bavaria and the Kurpfalz. Two towers, in the style of the Heidelberg castle, were another pointed reminder of the Kurpfälzer heritage.[166] Fortresslike, the museum appeared as a formidable and literal guardian of Pfälzer culture, "ever victorious despite all storms."[167] For Pfälzer poets inspired by the occasion, it was a "secure place. . . a sign of the Pfälzer past and present and future," a "true place. . ./ What once lay upon billowing earth, / Among golden brilliance of the Rhenish treasure, / Now rests here for ever more, / The Heimat's treasures in secure port."[168] Altogether a mishmash of images and chronologies, the building's exterior was nevertheless a fair representation of the Pfalz itself: a few Roman remains and an indistinct medieval and princely heritage, all united in a distinctly nineteenth-century construction.

Within the two-storied building, a series of rooms around a central courtyard showed the "historical course of the development of culture on Pfälzer earth," each room replicating the period it depicted in a kind of fin-de-siècle fantasy about the region's past.[169] From prehistoric fossils and relics of the Stone and Bronze Ages to an imitation of the Baths of Caracalla, on to the severe Romanesque of the Speyer cathedral and the high Gothic vaulting of an imagined medieval Speyer, the progression ended upstairs in a series of "theme" rooms: for poor Liselotte, a reproduction of her prison—an elegant French salon; for the Pfälzer "people," the "Tracht Room," in which peasant and bourgeois dress were displayed; for the patriots, a room dedicated to the war of 1870–71; and so on, including even the meteor of 1869. Through the courtyard, past eighteenth-century statues of Fortuna, Bacchus, and a female figure dubbed "Palatina," and down into a series of low cellarlike rooms, a visitor would enter the wine museum—the first of its kind in Germany, as museum officials would have been quick to point out. Wine, that "noblest product of our sunny Pfalz," embodied the region's distinc-

166. "Das neue Historische Museum der Pfalz zur Zeit des Richtfestes im Juni 1908," *PM* 25 (1908): 67.

167. Albert Becker, "Dem Pfälzer Weinmuseum zum Gruß," *PW*, Sondernummer (Spring 1909).

168. E. Baer-Ritter, "Festgruß der Palatia zum 22. Mai 1910," *PW* Sondernummer 2 (Spring 1910): 70. Verses 2 and 3:

Es reckt der Türme ragende Warte
sich bis zum Rheine und kündet's laut
Seht hier, hier ist die treue Stätte
Die sich ein sehnendes Volk erbaut.
Wie einstmals lag auf wagendem Grunde
Im güld'nem Glanze des Rheines Hort
So ruh'n auch hier für alle Zeiten
Der Heimat Schätze in sicherm Port.

169. "Neue Museum der Pfalz," *PM* 25 (1908): 77.

tiveness.[170] And like Pfälzer character itself, wrote Friedrich Bassermann-Jordan, wine magnate and scholar, in an evocation of Schiller, the essence of wine had not changed in a thousand or more years: "As we hold the Roman glass in our hand, we think, and look, the sun of Homer, it smiles also on us!"[171]

In the festivities that accompanied the museum's opening in 1910, Pfälzer dignitaries and poets celebrated the institution as a symbol of Pfälzer identity, of national pride, of unity, of harmony, and of strength—in short, as the embodiment of the Heimat. Prince Rupprecht of Bavaria declared at the dedication on 22 May 1910: the museum "stands before us to awaken a feeling and a knowledge of the Heimat, to promote love for it, and to increase and maintain our memories of both glorious and miserable times."[172] District president von Neuffer asserted that the museum had been built "out of love for the Heimat and enthusiasm for its two-thousand-year development."[173] Albert Pfeiffer wrote in Der Pfälzerwald that love for the Heimat was the "tie that united all people," Heimat pride and Heimat loyalty its "finest flowers," and the Pfälzer museum the expression of the strength of that love, pride, and loyalty. Love for the Heimat, he continued, provided a "bridge between present and past," and the past lived on in the present through the museum: "We greet you, Life of the Past."[174] In a rewriting of the "Pfalzlied" into prose suitable to the celebration of the museum's opening, Franz Jung assumed the farseeing attitude of the singer/poet, whose view from the museum encompassed the whole Pfalz—across to the cathedral and to the Rhine, then, imaginatively, across all the comings and goings of centuries. "The past is alive," he concluded.[175] And so it was at the dedication ceremonies, when Prince Rupprecht was greeted by Palatina herself, the embodied spirit of the Pfalz, crowned in vine leaves and reciting a poem to the Pfalz, the Pfälzers, and their "beloved" Wittelsbachs.[176]

Yet for all the talk of the past, the museum stood most significantly as a symbol of the present and of its own constructive powers. As an assemblage of all the region's many and fragmented pasts, it was a massive, irrefutable

---

170. "Aufruf an alle Freunde des Pfälzers Wein," from Von Neuffer, Bassermann-Jordan, and Berthold, in PM 26 (1909): 49.

171. F. Bassermann-Jordan, "Das Weinmuseum der Pfalz," PW Sondernummer 1 (Spring 1909): 75.

172. PM 32 (1915): 62.

173. Ibid.

174. "Zum Geleit!" PW, Sondernummer 2 (Spring 1910).

175. Jung, "Das Historische Museum in Speyer," pp. 177–78.

176. Palatina was depicted by Fräulein Elisabeth Ferckel, her "Festgruß" written by Albert Kennel, head of the Gymnasium in Kaiserslautern. See Albert Pfeiffer, "Von der Einweihung des Historischen Museum der Pfalz," PW 11 (1 July 1910): 112–13.

demonstration of the reality of the Pfalz. Memory, as Prince Rupprecht himself said, was to be prompted, shaped, and indeed created. The Wittelsbachs and the Bavarian state were of course the beneficiaries of a past reconstituted to emphasize their centuries-old ties to the geographical area. Along with them came the recognition (reluctant?) of Catholicism. The emphasis on the Kurpfälzer theme served Protestants and ever-hungry Wittelsbachs equally, and even the Jews were tentatively drawn in through their contributions to the city and bishopric of Speyer: an ancient Jewish bath down the street from the new museum testified to this closeness, as well as to a distance continually reasserted.[177] Agriculture, commerce, and industry each received its due, as Georg Berthold pointed out to the wealthy businessmen and estate owners who were the museum's patrons. Wine, ceramics, and other artifacts "gave evidence," he wrote, "that for more than two thousand years industry and commerce have had a home here and have pulsated powerfully."[178] In short, the museum promoted a collective memory of unity, coherence, and continuity: a "two-thousand-year-development," in the words of von Neuffer; a single and ancient historical state, in the person of "Palatina."

Three years after being opened to the public, the museum had received seventy-five thousand visitors, mostly from the Pfalz itself.[179] The Museum Commission had instituted free tours for groups of schoolchildren from all over the Pfalz, and it maintained extensive open hours. The Museum Association issued an annual "Call to All Friends of Pfälzer Heimatkunde," which encouraged people to join the organization for a minimal fee and to contribute to the museum collections.[180] These gestures, taken together with the rhetoric of Heimat and Volk that accompanied the museum's opening, helped to establish its role as an educational institution for the whole Pfalz. As Georg Berthold wrote in *Pfälzisches Museum* at the time of the dedication, the Pfälzer visitor "will be able to say with pride of this museum on the German Rhine that what here we see united is rooted in the soil and represents the history of our region and people."[181]

And yet the new Historical Museum differed in significant ways from the ideal Heimat museum envisioned by Albert Becker. Its collections of fine furniture and delicate porcelain were hardly the stuff of Becker's folklore museum, with its plaster casts and paintings of (Pfälzer) insects. Moreover, despite the rhetoric of Pfälzer unity, despite the encouragement of all to visit and contribute, the museum's founders were intent on its being an institution

177. No references were made to the persecution of Jews in Speyer. The point is not that the museum's recognition was complete or even balanced, simply that such recognition of Jewish culture existed at all.

178. Yearly report of HVP, *MHVP* 24 (1900): 303.

179. Miscellaneous records of the Historische Museum, PLAS, T1, no. 4.

180. *PM* 22 (1910): 143; the call was also published in local newspapers.

181. Berthold, "Das Historische Museum der Pfalz," *PM* 25 (1908): 77.

above the participatory enthusiasms of the Heimat movement as a whole. In 1912, Georg Berthold wrote confidentially to the district president about the need to maintain the high quality of the collection, with its appeal to men of education and refinement.[182] He argued against allowing any members of the Museum Commission—a select board of overseers, separate from the Museum Association—to be elected by secret ballot from the Landrat or the general public: "The. . . organization will be competent and manageable only if the possibility of useful men being voted out or unwanted men being voted in is excluded." Our collections, he concluded, are "somewhat aristocratic and require therefore an administration that will not be reduced to vulgarity through slapdash measures and secret votes."[183] The dependence of the museum on wealthy donors and its correspondingly elitist governance were in sharp contrast to such local museums as Becker's in Zweibrücken, which survived on city and members' contributions. In 1912, the Museum Association raised over 74,000 marks in gifts and dues, of which 66,000 represented gifts from only twenty-eight donors, many of whom subsequently sat on the Museum Commission.[184] Indeed, the very arrangement of the museum rooms corresponded to donorship as much as to provenance or chronology: the Ludowici and Bassermann-Jordan collections received their own rooms, as did the Neumayer, the Joseph Stichaner, and the Heydenreich collections.

The enhancing of Honoratioren prestige was inherent in the entire museum project. Both the guardian of the Pfälzer past and the guarantor of the Pfälzer present, the museum suggested an ideal of social order and identity that was not only different from but also at odds with much of the rest of the Heimat movement. More hierarchic, more deferential to position and title, more exclusively devoted to the culture of elites both past and present, the Pfalz of the Historical Museum bore little resemblance to the Pfalz of the Pfälzerwald Verein or even of the local Heimat museum. Certainly all three shared a language—that of Heimat and one's devotion to it—but the common language did not preclude conflict over who could use it or how it was to be used.

If the Historical Museum showed the extent to which the old Honoratioren elite could still exclude popular participation from shaping the shibboleths of regional identity, the case of the Pfälzer flag illustrated the limits of

182. Georg Berthold, "Auszug aus der Denkschrift betreffend Historischen Museum der Pfalz, 1912" (14 March 1912), PLAS, T1, no. 4.

183. "Die Kreissammlung ist etwas aristokratisches und bedarf daher eine Verfassung, die nicht durch Schablone und geheime Wahlen geistlos wird" (Ibid).

184. These included wealthy individuals, Berthold himself among them, and banks and industries in the region. See Budget of the Verein Historisches Museum (1 January 1912–31 December 1912); and Minutes of Mitgliederversammlung, Verein Historisches Museum (6 July 1913), PLAS, T1, no. 4.

such power in the face of popular enthusiasm. In 1909, Dr. F. Heitz of Billigheim introduced to the Pfälzer public a flag based, he said, on the old
Kurpfälzer flag and newly designed by the local artist August Croissant.
Heitz, already a master of creative symbolism, was inspired to this new project by the wild success of Pfälzer Tracht, which he had introduced to the
public in 1906 at the first Billigheim Purzelmarkt. He wrote of the "powerful
movement coursing through the Pfälzer land . . . the reawakening of Pfälzer
fellow-feeling [*Volksempfinden*]. . . . Who does not know," he asked, rhetori-
cally, of all the "promotion and increasing appreciation" of Pfälzer folksong,
sayings and customs, Trachten and folk festivals, Pfälzer art, history, antiquity, handwork, the Pfälzer forest, and, not least of all, Pfälzer wine? And
yet, he lamented, we have no outward sign of our commonality: "We sing, 'I
am a Pfälzer, do you know my colors,' and most must answer, 'No, they are
totally strange and unknown to us!'" A flag to bedeck house and castle,
"symbol of our Heimat," would do just honor to members of this "old and
powerful tribe," the Pfälzers.[185]

The flag was endorsed by the ubiquitous Albert Becker in *Der Pfälzerwald*,
advertised in the general press, and rapidly adopted in the festivities of the
Pfälzerwald Verein. It was soon "joyfully waving in the Pfälzer breeze [note
that the winds themselves have loyalties] on every festive occasion . . . in
cities and villages, from castles and towers."[186] Unfortunately, neither the
Bavarian authorities nor their proxies in the Historical Association accepted
the banner. At a meeting in 1910, Albert Pfeiffer and Hans Oberseider (both
of the regional archives), Georg Berthold, and Friedrich Bassermann-Jordan
expressed concern about its authenticity, even while professing sympathy for
the lively Pfälzer sentiment that prompted its creation.[187] At their behest,
experts in both Munich and Karlsruhe objected to the heraldry and colors of
the new flag, and an expert in Heidelberg published a thorough refutation of
the flag's claims to authenticity. Both Croissant and Heitz responded in
print, the former arguing that heraldic rules were not binding on a modern
artist, the latter producing his own expert opinion, from Berlin, on the scholarly legitimacy of the design.[188] In 1915, the controversy still not resolved,
Albert Pfeiffer wrote in *Pfälzisches Museum* that "we stand now before the *fact*
that a new district flag has been introduced. . . . The question remains, are

185. "Des Pfälzers Fahne," *PW* 10 (1 July 1909): cover page.
186. *Des Pfälzers Heimat* 1 (1910): 24. A month after the publication of the announcement and
its endorsement, Becker received a letter from a man who had written a poem to the new Pfälzer
colors and hoped Becker could arrange to have it published or even set to music: "it will also
perhaps contribute to the awakening of Pfälzer fellow feeling." See August Vollmer to Albert
Becker, 31 August 1909, PLBS, Albert Becker Papers.
187. Report of meeting, *PM* 27 (1910): 60.
188. A summary of the controversy was published several years later by Albert Pfeiffer: "Die
Pfälzer Fahne," *PM* 34 (1917): 91–93.

there authentic regional arms or regional colors or a regional flag promulgated or approved by the competent authority? The answer is No!" The
new flag, he asserted, had neither "official nor historical legitimacy."[189]

The controversy did indeed have its roots in questions of legitimacy, but
ones to which historical accuracy in and of itself was incidental. Heitz's flag
was black and gold with a rampant red lion, a "provincial banner," he
argued, "that distinguished itself as sharply as possible from the white-blue
Bavarian flag."[190] This of course is precisely what bothered the Bavarian
authorities, and with them the Historical Association. The official statement
on the issue in the *Bayerische Reichsherold* asserted that no individual Bavarian
district should have its own colors, "because in the face of proliferating regional and city colors, the colors of Bavaria would be ever further pushed
into the background."[191] Pfeiffer and the Historical Association agreed, but
despite their efforts to discredit the flag, it continued to make its appearance
at festive occasions. In 1916, capitulating in the face of decided public preference, national emergency, and official distraction, Pfeiffer conceded that the
"new creation" was "certainly well suited to strengthen a feeling of togetherness and Heimat pride that will strengthen a more general national
courage."[192] A victory for Heitz? Or for the Pfälzerwald Verein? Perhaps,
but certainly a defeat for the Historical Association. The incident illustrated
the extent to which popular participation was shaping the symbols of regional identity and, conversely, the extent to which the Honoratioren could
no longer rule over regional culture as they had a few decades before.

In the end, the controversy over the Pfälzer flag petered out with the onset of
the war, and in that particular form the tensions within the Heimat movement never again made themselves felt. War, defeat, revolution, and occupation altered the issues that were at stake in celebrations of Pfälzer pride. In
the backward and filtered glance of Albert Becker in 1939, the Heimat movement before the war had been sincere and sometimes even practical, but
often "naive," "unconscious of itself," and "dreamy."[193] Although his words
reveal more about the highly charged and politicized atmosphere in which
Heimat activities survived in the 1920s and 1930s than about the period of
his remembrances, the contrast is nevertheless instructive. The Heimat
movement before the war was more inventive and creative than manipula-
tive, more genuinely inclusive than exclusive.

The particular strength of the Pfälzer movement at the turn of the century

189. "Die Pfälzer Fahne," *PM* 32 (1915): 54–55.
190. *PM* 34 (1917): 95.
191. Cited in *PM* 32 (1915): 55.
192. *PM* 33 (1916): 10–11.
193. "Erinnerungen aus der Geschichte der Pfälzer Heimatbewegung," *Der Pfälzer in Berlin*
19 (15 March 1939): 29.

was its embeddedness in the institutions and concerns of one locality—in short, its provincialism. As an essentially provincial movement, it had surprisingly little to do with the only "Heimat movements" recognized by the historical literature: the *Heimatkunst* (Heimat art) movement of Adolf Bartels and Friedrich Lienhard, the *Heimatschutz* (Heimat protection) movement of Ernst Rudorff and Paul Schultze-Naumburg, and Heinrich Sohnrey's Deutscher Verein für ländliche Wohlfahrts- und Heimatpflege (German Association for Agrarian Welfare and Heimat Care), all founded in the late 1890s and flourishing after 1900. Like those in the Pfalz, these national groups espoused a definition of Heimat that emphasized its roots in rural society, but otherwise their alienation from genuine provincialism was profound.[194] Sohnrey fought to improve rural living conditions in order to halt the so-called *Zug vom Lande* or flight from the countryside—something the Pfälzerwald Verein never even contemplated. Like Albert Becker, he saw the potential for social reconciliation in Heimatpflege, but unlike Becker and the Heimat movement that Becker represented, Sohnrey believed that such reconciliation required a return to old structures of social organization. His was a completely reactionary social program.[195] Bartels and Lienhard, whose work fluctuated between populist anti-Semitism and highbrow aestheticism, turned their attention to refuting the naturalist vision of society and promoting a romantic, rosy view of rural life in the pages of their periodicals and pamphlets.[196] Ernst Rudorff, an eccentric and extreme figure who originated the Bund Heimatschutz (League of Heimat Protection), shared with Bartels a virulent hatred for Berlin, with its cafés, litterateurs, and socialists, but also with its trains, travelers, technologies, and everything that seeped out from the city, polluting and destroying the pure life of the peasant.[197]

This obsessive hatred for Berlin, indeed for all big cities, did not, however, play the determining role in the evolution of the term *Heimat* that some have suggested it did.[198] Heimat did not suddenly emerge as a concept of cultural activism and organization in the 1890s, nor was its role in German society confined to reaction and opposition—even if one looks only at its few na-

---

194. See esp. Klaus Bergmann, *Agrarromantik und Großstadtfeindschaft* (Meisenheim am Glan, 1970), an insightful if tendentious account of these movements.

195. Ibid., p. 94.

196. Martin Greiner, "Heimatkunst," in *Real-lexikon der deutschen Literaturgeschichte*, ed. Klaus Kanzog et al., vol. 1 (Berlin, 1958), pp. 629–31; Jenny, "Die Heimatkunstbewegung"; Dieck, "Die literargeschichtliche Stellung der Heimatkunst."

197. Bergmann, *Agrarromantik*, p. 124.

198. Bergmann states unequivocally that all the neoromantic movements of renewal grew out of "Großstadtfeindschaft" (ibid. p. 87) and that discovery of the word *Heimat* came suddenly in the mid-1890s; it constituted, he belives, "the most important result" of cultural pessimism tied to "patriotic-conservative political pessimism" (p. 88).

tional manifestations. The Bund Heimatschutz, despite its association with the right-wing radical Rudorff, found all its support among the Honoratioren of the big cities, something that reflected as much the compatibility of its programs with bourgeois aspirations and self-consciousness as the inability of the German bourgeoisie "fully to identify with their own form of existence."[199] Rudorff's reactionary ideas had limited influence in the shaping of the league, whose work included the maintenance of monuments—national, "natural," and otherwise—the preservation of old buildings and picturesque ruins, and the cultivation of folk dress, custom, and art.[200] "Rationality" was to be reconciled with "feeling," and "intellect" with "emotion." "We do not have the foolish intention of trying to push back the extraordinary achievements of the present in practical matters," said Freiherr von Keckerinck-Borg at the opening of the Westphalian Commission for Heimatschutz in 1910; what they wanted, rather, was to achieve a "balance" between the "heartless exploitation of the Heimat earth and the demands of *Gemüt*."[201]

For although anti-urbanism, anti-Semitism, and antimodernism may have been reactions to some of the same transformations in German society that the Heimat movement attempted to shape and control, antimodernism and the Heimat movement were not the same thing, nor were the movements of Bartels, Sohnrey, and Rudorff as representative of attitudes toward Heimat and provincialism in Germany as they wished to claim. The influence of Bartels and his Heimatkunst movement was confined to northern and some of middle Germany; Sohnrey collected endorsements from groups as prestigious as the Verein für Sozialpolitik but had limited impact on the provinces whose cause he espoused; and the functions of the Bund Heimatschutz were limited to a kind of ceremonial supervision of work done in independently founded and organized provincial associations.[202] Those many local associations in turn reflected a diversity of programs, priorities, and origins that was not inimical but essential to the meaning of Heimat itself. The original charter of the Bund Heimatschutz declared its mission to be the protection "of the German Heimat in its naturally and historically developed diversity," and indeed the positive content of Heimat endeavors, no matter how various, was their concern for the preservation of distinctiveness and diversity, of *Eigenart* and *Vielgestaltigkeit*, within the overarching frame of the

199. Ibid., p. 82. The 120 members of the Deutsche Bund Heimatschutz, which was founded in 1904 in Dresden, were from the same social and educational background as members of local historical associations like that in the Pfalz. See "Der Deutsche Bund Heimatschutz," in Gesellschaft Heimatshutz, *Der deutsche Heimatschutz*, p. 187.

200. "Der Deutsche Bund Heimatschutz," in Gesellschaft Heimatschutz, *Der deutsche Heimatschutz*, pp. 187–204.

201. Ibid, p. 187.

202. Greiner, "Heimatkunst," p. 630; Bergmann, *Agrarromantik*, p. 89.

German nation.[203] Certainly, by the end of the century opposition to the
leveling, homogenizing, and centralizing forces of modernity came to be one
characteristic of Heimat endeavors and, with it, distrust of Berlin as the representative of the forces of centralization. The city as such, however, could be
and was both the seat of Heimat activities and a Heimat itself for its own
inhabitants, just as technology, particularly in the form of trains, was welcomed by the Heimat movement, and science utilized in its understanding of
the world.[204] Indeed, the original impulse, the informing and defining concept behind Heimat, was not antimodernism at all but belief in the importance of regional identity.

To the extent that propagandists like Sohnrey and Bartels subordinated
distinct regional identities to their own romantic and negatively shaped vision of the peasantry, they alienated themselves from the many regional
Heimat organizations, whose ties to national groups and to these self-
appointed national spokesmen tended in any case to be extremely loose. In
1906, an encounter between Albert Becker and Wilhelm Schubring, a representative of the Deutsche Verein für ländliche Wohlfahrts- und Heimatpflege, revealed the extent to which Sohnrey and his associates had failed to
grasp the point of local Heimat activities. Schubring asked Becker if he
would be interested in supplying them with a "selection of southwest German Heimat literature."[205] Becker agreed and soon received more specific
directions. Schubring wanted "no ties to political borders but only to tribal
units [Stammeseinheit]." He announced therefore that he was lumping the
Pfalz together with lower Saxony, Baden, and Alsace-Lorraine, and closed
with the coy remark, "Are you very shocked at this idea? I hope not!"[206]

Whether or not Becker was shocked, Schubring's idea undermined the
carefully constructed edifice of the Pfälzer Heimat movement, and, though
he was perhaps no more arbitrary in his categories of local identity, Schubring's notion that the Pfalz, Baden, Alsace, and Saxony could form one tribal
unit flew in the face of all Heimat assumptions of the preceding forty years.
Heimat, as a movement and as an object of civic organization, had represented the political unit's attempt to root itself firmly in local life while at the
same time claiming membership in the nation. The local civic context of
Heimat activities emerges from this perspective as not only the most impor-

203. "Der Deutsche Bund Heimatschutz," in Gesellschaft Heimatschutz, Der Deutsche
Heimatschutz, p. 188. See also Dieck: "To overcome [particularism] but to preserve the distinctiveness of the individual Heimat and indeed to bring together organically all of Germany was
for Germans a great concern at that time" ("Die literargeschichtliche Stellung der Heimatkunst," p. 13).
204. For instance, members of the Verein der Pfälzer in Berlin spoke of the city as the
"second Heimat."
205. W. Schubring to A. Becker, 10 October 1906, PLBS, Albert Becker Papers.
206. Schubring to Becker, 16 October 1906, PLBS, Albert Becker Papers.

tant context in which to understand the Heimat movement, but perhaps the only one. For the many Beckers, Bertholds, and Bassermann-Jordans of Germany, it mattered hardly at all that Lienhard, Bartels, Sohnrey, and Langbehn were singing the praises of provincial life in the abstract. What mattered was the Pfalz and, with the Pfalz, Germany in its entirety.

Moreover, that Heimat referred to a political unit—in this case, the Pfalz, and in the broader case, Germany—suggests its relevance not to an understanding of antimodernism in Germany but to the development and transformation of public life in the decades before the war. The conduct of politics in the narrow sense was changing with the rising importance of campaigns, the political press, large party organizations, and the mass electorate. Surrounding that arena of electoral politics was public life in general, defined by where and how people associated with one another and what assumptions and beliefs informed that association. As an increasing number of people participated in public life, its spaces and symbols acquired new significance and took on new forms. The Heimat movement formed part of the process of shaping a new public realm, a process also encompassing the Social Democratic culture, the culture of voluntary associations and nationalist pressure groups, and the national culture as such.

The particular contribution of the Heimat movement was to redefine the meaning of provincial culture at a time when national and international movements and classes were rendering it, if not moribund, then certainly of secondary importance. As civic education, Heimatkunde insisted on the priority of local belonging and local political and social units in constituting the first step to any larger categories of patriotism. As civic activism, Heimat promotion infused nature, "tradition," and history with a new patriotic significance and a new role of forming the stuff of local consciousness and local identity. And as a popular movement, the Heimat movement asserted the right of anyone to participate in the cultivation of a common tradition.

But if it succeeded in preserving the vitality of local culture, the Heimat movement did not succeed, as some of its members had hoped it would, in reconciling all classes and factions on the common ground of Heimat. To be sure, most seem to have participated in the public culture of Heimat—even the Social Democrats approved of local loyalty and began at this time to incorporate the symbols and figures of local tradition into their own festivities.[207] But what everyone shared, each could also claim to be his or her own. The conflicts of the political realm came increasingly to obtrude on the deliberately nonpolitical activities of Heimat, and the politicization that before the war was only implicit in the movement began after the war to dominate it entirely.

207. Lidtke, *Alternative Culture*, p. 92.

FOUR

The Great War
on the Home Front

The Pfalz was one of the first regions of Europe to know what the outbreak of war between modern nations would entail. On 31 July 1914, all Bavarian troops in the border province went on full alert, and on 2 August the trains from the rest of Germany began to roll through—twenty-five hundred of them by 16 August, with one hundred forty thousand cars bearing equipment, supplies, horses, and, above all, men to a war of shifting place, uncertain cause, but undoubted justification.[1] Although the Pfalz never became the scene of actual fighting, as many of its inhabitants initially feared, its proximity to the front for four years brought it not only the sounds of this loudest of wars, but also a constant stream of prisoners and wounded and dying soldiers from one direction, and supplies and ever more troops from the other. It witnessed also the end of the war with all the unresolved and irresolvable hostilities that the years of death and deprivation had occasioned. For twelve years after the peace, the region was occupied by foreign troops and officials, who were themselves replaced within six years of their departure by more troops, albeit German ones, and soon, war again. Indeed, August 1914 began a second Thirty Years' War for the region, more destructive of the people and the land than its historical predecessor and more devastating to the society, its institutions and beliefs, than could ever have been anticipated by those who saw its beginnings.

War had scant place in the world and worldview of Heimat, and in 1914,

---

1. Bayerisches Kriegsarchiv, ed., *Die Bayern im Großen Kriege 1914–1918. Auf Grund der Kriegsakten dargestellt* (Munich, 1923), p. 8.

ironically, the Heimat movement was flourishing. In the Pfalz, it had reached what in retrospect would be its zenith, with more members in its organizations, more activities, publications, and festivities than ever before or after. The Pfälzerwald Verein's commemoration of the Hambach Festival in June 1914—which had been an enormous success, drawing thousands of Pfälzers from all parts of the region—elevated Heimat sentiment above any other human loyalty or emotion; the Verein's celebration of Germans' attachment to the land and people of their home reflected little of the bellicose nationalism that characterized many public pronouncements all over Europe in the months—and years—preceding the outbreak of war. Certainly war was featured in the collective memory that the Heimat movement had enshrined in its museums and ruins, but the movement itself represented essentially nonaggressive impulses, inward turning and quietly civic. Yet within six months it, too, had mobilized its resources to succor the soldiers at the front and, perhaps more important, to explain the war to those not directly involved in the fighting. In the end, the circumstances of the war transformed a general and passive Heimat feeling into an explicit Heimat ideology. Heimat organizations ceased to exist for themselves and for the purposes they had invented and began an apprenticeship to the state that continued throughout the 1920s, culminating in National Socialist Germany.

The initial response of the Heimat movement to the war was simply to shut down. Monthly meetings, outings, and convivial evenings were canceled until further notice, and funds from both the state and private individuals quickly dried up.[2] Heimat enthusiasts, like everyone else, had anticipated a short interruption of normal life, to be followed by a return to old routines and activities after the war was quickly won. But the winter of 1914–15 dispelled that illusion. In the course of 1915, the Heimat associations, in common with much of the nation, "followed the necessity" of long-term adaptation to the war of position, or *Stellungskrieg*.[3] In October 1914, the editors of the leading Heimat magazine urged their readers to "remain true" to the Heimat associations, "which also serve the greater German Fatherland."[4] In February 1915 the literary and historical societies began holding meetings again. Both groups, and with them the Pfälzerwald Verein, began to find new projects and purposes appropriate to a society at war and yet conceivable within the old framework of provincial associational life.

The Historical Association conceived of its wartime duties in terms of preparing a future depiction of these "great times" as they happened in the Heimat. "It will be the meritorious assignment of the Historical Association

2. Budget for 1914, *MHVP* 34/35 (1915): xv; the budget for the museum was also considerably reduced (Budgets of the HVP [1914–17], PLAS, T1, no 4).

3. Ludwig Eid, "Geschäftsbericht des Literarischen Vereins der Pfalz über die Jahre 1914, 1915, und 1916," *Mitteilungen Literarischen Vereins der Pfalz* (hereafter cited as *MLVP*) 4 (1916): 34.

4. "An unsere Mitglieder," *PM* 31 (1914): cover page of October issue.

of the Pfalz," wrote its secretary, Albert Pfeiffer, in the spring of 1915, "when the weapons are still and peace again holds sway, to convey to the world after us, unfalsified, the history of these days, events and experiences, impressions and moods, in the way they happened and intermingled in the Pfalz."[5] The Historical Association also took on itself the duty of combating the Allied depiction of Germany as a nation of barbarians.[6] Its monthly lectures, which were resumed in 1915, became exercises in self-conscious cultivation and dignified patriotism: while Allied propaganda shrieked about the advancing Huns, the Germans responded with scholarly analyses of French aggression over the last centuries, the restrained and objective style of which was to be the surest refutation of the anti-German imagery.[7]

The same desire to affirm the nobility of German *Kultur* informed the wartime activities of the Literary Association of the Pfalz, which had played only a minor role in the Heimat movement before the war. In the fall of 1915, declaring that the "muses need no longer be silent in the midst of fighting," it launched a series of projects under the rubric of "Pfälzer Literature for the Field and the Fatherland" to bring the "good book" to the soldiers at the front and to the wounded in local military hospitals.[8] In addition to collecting the classics of German literature, the association prepared its own offering of poetry, pictures, and prose about the beauties of the Pfalz, under the title *Heimatgrüße* (Heimat Greetings). "We know the enormous hunger of the German soldier for good literature," wrote the editor of *Heimatgrüße*, "so we need not ask... 'what is the use of these songs after such suffering?'"[9] "A piece of Heimat earth, of the father's house, of childhood's joy and youth's peace," the book proved enormously popular at least among those at home, who purchased it for relatives at the front. The Literary Association sold ten thousand copies of the book within six weeks of its publication.[10] In 1917, it prepared a new edition, in response to the probable prolongation of the war. Printed in a form "more suitable to the trench," the new *Heimatgrüße*, accord-

---

5. "Bericht über die Vereinstätigkeit, 1913–1915," *MHVP* 34/35 (1915): ii. On the plans for what would be included in this collection, see Friedrich Sprater, "Pfälzer Kriegssammlung in Speyer," *PM* 35 (1918): 16.

6. Remarks of Regierungspräsident von Neuffer, *PM* 32 (1915): 56.

7. "Vaterländisches Abend des Historischen Verein der Pfalz und des Verein Historischen Museum der Pfalz," *PM* 32 (1915): 56. Wartime lectures often played on the notorious German distinction between their own deeply inner *Kultur* and the French *civilisation*, a state of mere material and technological advancement. The most thorough exploration of that distinction is of course Thomas Mann's *Betrachtungen eines Unpolitischen* (Berlin, 1918); see the recent translation by Walter D. Morris, *Reflections of a Nonpolitical Man* (New York, 1983).

8. Eid, "Geschäftsbericht," 34–36. In June 1916, it also participated in the *Reichsbuchwoche*, a collection drive to send books to soldiers at the front.

9. Introduction, *Heimatgrüße* (1916), p. 1.

10. Eid, "Geschäftsbericht," 35.

ing to its editors, Ludwig Eid and Albert Becker, "should enchant the hearts of our countrymen in battle outside our sunny Heimat . . . and show that the Heimat . . . with its cultural treasures and natural beauties is worthy of the defense and of the defenders."[11]

But although the wartime activities of the Heimat associations were ostensibly directed to an audience outside the Heimat—either to soldiers for the alleviation of their homesickness or to the world as a whole, as proof of German culture—they implicitly aimed at combating civilian dissatisfaction and low morale. From the winter of 1914–15 on, the most important determinant of public mood at home was not the news of events at the front, which people learned to judge solely in terms of whether the war would be prolonged or shortened, but the state of the civilian food supply.[12] Food shortages, which had begun in Bavaria in 1915 and reached their height in the terrible "Turnip Winter" of 1916–17, were blamed on the government, the bureaucracy, the Prussians, the war planners in Berlin, or the speculators, but rarely on the enemy.[13] Already by December 1915, the Bavarian Ministry of War was concerned that soldiers' letters to their families were "poisoning the mood of whole localities."[14] Evidently few soldiers concealed from their families the hopeless terror of their situation; some even urged relatives to shrink food production and to refuse war bond subscriptions in order to shorten the war.

Bread shortages were felt in the Pfalz in the first year of the war, and by early 1916 potato shortages too were widespread, in spite of the Pfalz's own considerable contribution to German potato production.[15] Peasants held back their crops in protest against government price fixing and confiscation, and municipal authorities all over the region found it impossible to obtain enough food of any kind. Reports of low public morale and low support for the war, along with widespread refusal to subscribe to war bonds, came to the Bavarian Ministry of War from governmental and episcopal authorities in the region.[16] Contributing to the further souring of the public mood was a renewal of Pfälzer grievances against Bavarian rule. Pfälzers believed that their needs as inhabitants of a border region required particular attention, yet a special council formed by the Bavarian government in June

---

11. Introduction, *Heimatgrüße aus der Pfalz fürs Feld*, ed. Literarischer Verein der Pfalz (Speyer, 1917): 4.

12. Karl Ludwig Ay, *Die Entstehung einer Revolution. Die Volksstimmung in Bayern während des Ersten Weltkrieges* (Berlin, 1968), p. 23.

13. Ibid., pp. 26–29.

14. Cited by F. L. Carsten, *War Against War: British and German Radical Movements in the First World War* (Berkeley and Los Angeles, 1982), p. 78; Ay, *Entstehung einer Revolution*, pp. 25–26.

15. Carsten, *War Against War*, p. 76.

16. Ibid., p. 78.

1916 to consider questions of food supply included no Pfälzer representative.[17]

The Bavarian government first paid serious attention to the problem of civilian morale in February 1916.[18] Undersecretary of War Kress, author of a memorandum on the subject, wanted a "mobilization of the entire intellectual and moral powers of the home front [*Heimatkräfte*]," involving teachers, clergymen, government officials, and members of "patriotically minded" associations and leagues.[19] Such groups might perhaps restore the euphoria of August 1914; at the very least they could help to distract attention from the food shortages and even raise money for the war.[20] Moreover, the mobilization of private organizations would allow state officials themselves to remain discreetly in the background, appearing publicly neither on their own nor on any one else's behalf.[21] Perhaps the Bavarian government thought that the mendacity of its reports from the front would go unnoticed in the mouths of such guardians of moral rectitude as teachers and pastors. In any case, by the end of 1916 the chief coordinator of Bavarian propaganda had become the Bayerische Landesverein für Heimatschutz (Bavarian Regional Association for the Protection of the Heimat), an ostensibly private organization, founded at the height of prewar Heimat euphoria to coordinate local Heimat associations. The newly mobilized association put most of its energies into the countryside, for instance urging peasants not to hoard food. But it also tried—through slide shows, lectures, writings, and meetings—to instill an enthusiasm for the war into a populace that responded with indifference, if not outright hostility.[22]

In the Pfalz, the organizations that had made up the prewar Heimat movement came gradually to be drawn into a similar relationship to the state and district officials, whose chief concerns were low public morale and a growing hostility to Bavarian rule. The impending arrival of the one hundredth anniversary of the treaty that had made the Pfalz part of the Bavarian state posed a real dilemma for home-front propagandists. Would it be better to ignore the occasion, thus diplomatically avoiding a public demonstration of anti-Bavarianism, or would such deference to the sour popular mood be an admission of defeat, a foolish squandering of an opportunity tailor made to affirm Bavarian-Pfälzer ties? In the end, actual public celebrations of the centenary were muted, officially because public joy was declared inappropriate in the midst of war. The government itself did not openly sponsor any

17. Willy Albrecht, *Landtag und Regierung in Bayern am Vorabend der Revolution von 1918* (Berlin, 1968), p. 151.
18. Ay, *Entstehung einer Revolution*, pp. 63–64.
19. Cited in ibid., p. 63.
20. Ibid., pp. 63–66.
21. Ibid., p. 64.
22. Ay, *Entstehung einer Revolution*, p. 65; Albrecht, *Landtag und Regierung*, pp. 206, 245.

festivity, although a few schools did take minimal notice of the occasion.[23] And certainly plenty of ink was spilled in the production of *Festschriften* and histories of the last century, some more honest than others.[24] Needless to say, such writings did not dispel Pfälzer disgruntlement with Bavarian rule, but they managed to suggest that Bavarian, Pfälzer, and German interests were, from the patriotic point of view, at one.

That message was underlined in a variety of patriotic activities sponsored by the Heimat associations in the war years. All regularly urged their members to subscribe to war bonds, printing full-page advertisements at their own expense. Most touching, all maintained correspondence with the soldiers in the field who had belonged to the groups before the war. The soldiers' replies were then printed in the club newspapers; intended to refute rumors of bad morale, bad conditions, and food shortages at the front, they nevertheless conveyed something of the emotional precariousness of the relations between home and front. Less willing perhaps to confide their fears and their sufferings to the public at large than to their families, these letters to club leaders were, though not cheerful, at least silent about the grimmer aspects of the war. They spoke of love for the Pfalz, loyalty to the crown prince and Kaiser, and an unflagging will to victory. As Corporal Jakob Breinig wrote to the editors of *Wald-Heil!*, "things are going well here, and by God's grace, after a victorious peace we will return to our dear Heimat, in our glorious Pfälzerland. . . . Then I will devote every hour to that blessed ground for which we fight and for which we are also ready to die."[25]

In the face of such sentiment, civilian disgruntlement naturally appeared mean-spirited and petty. The editors of *Wald-Heil!* told their readers that they ought not to complain to sons, husbands, and brothers in the field of food shortages, for "real hunger" had been and would continue to be kept at bay.[26] Indeed, as the war dragged on the Heimat publications increasingly became vehicles for boosting civilian morale and invigorating a flagging patriotism. To some extent, the activities around which Heimat clubs gathered remained formally what they had been before the war, but their leaders and

23. *PM* 33 (1916), p. 80; A. Herzer, "Festanspruch," in Albert Becker, *Wiedererstehung der Pfalz*.

24. Schreibmüller, *Bayern und Pfalz*; on commemorative lectures, see Johann Keiper, "Der Historische Verein während des Krieges," *Zur 100-Jahr Feier des Historischen Vereins der Pfalz* (special edition), *Palatina*, no. 34 (1927); Albert Becker, *Wiedererstehung der Pfalz*, which interestingly warned against "exaggerated Germania [*Deutschtümelei*]" and "unchecked hatred for the French" (p. 27). Becker received a medal for his efforts; see *WH*, no. 6 (8 June 1917): 2.

25. "Aus Feldpostbriefen," *WH*, no. 3 (7 March 1917): 7.

26. *WH*, no. 1 (25 January 1917): 5. Real hunger was not, in fact, kept at bay. For an analysis of malnutrition and starvation in Germany—and interesting speculation on the possibility that actual brain damage figured into the political extremism of the 1920s and 1930s—see C. Paul Vincent, *The Politics of Hunger: The Allied Blockade of Germany, 1915–1919* (Athens, Ohio, 1985). See also Vernon Kellogg, *Germany in the War and After* (New York, 1919), pp. 35–47.

editors produced a continual barrage of pamphlets, articles, and speeches that forced on old activities a new wartime significance. Hikes were no longer just outings but opportunities for youth to train for mountain campaigns and the "outdoor living" of the trenches.[27] The familiar club hikes served other new functions as well: the Pfälzerwald Verein felt that one of its most important wartime contributions was to educate people on the nutritive qualities and availability of wild mushrooms. Members of the Verein were encouraged to collect them on their walks and bring them to mushroom-testing installations run by the Verein. Better yet, they could help farm the neglected fields of the region instead of taking purely recreational (hence not nearly as patriotic) strolls in the woods.[28] Local art exhibitions displayed drawings from the front by Pfälzer soldiers.[29] Even the institution of the *Heimatabend*, or Heimat evening, became an occasion for the further dissemination of inspiring sentiment and misleading report.

Thus, by 1918 the Heimat movement had thoroughly adapted itself to the seemingly permanent state of war. Its organizations had established regular functions for members to fulfill within a society at war and had retained to the extent possible the old styles and forms of association. Further, in the course of adjusting their institutional forms to a war of indefinite duration, the Heimat associations gradually adjusted their organizing ideas also. Though requiring far less drastic a mental and cultural reordering than did the experience of the trenches, the Great War in the Heimat nevertheless forced civil society to accept unprecedented degrees of regulation, militarization, and, ultimately, deprivation.[30] For soldier and civilian alike, cause and effect became increasingly dissociated in the experience of the war: things happened impersonally, without agent, whether sudden death from a shell emerging out of nowhere and launched by no man or, less lethal but hardly more comprehensible, a sudden shortage of cabbage or an abrupt cessation of postal or rail service, often to be followed by their equally sudden recommencement. Civilians—like the soldiers who were trapped in a war of impersonal violence—experienced the psychologically damaging frustration of having no outlet for the aggressive feelings that wartime propaganda incited. The central bureaucrats seemed to possess some of the same mysterious yet inept omnipotence over the civilian population as did the army staff over the

27. Report of the local chapter in Ludwigshafen for 1916 *WH*, no. 1 (25 January 1917): 2.
28. "Wer hilft der Landwirtschaft? Ein Aufruf an unsere Mitglieder," *WH*, no. 5 (8 May 1917): 1–2.
29. *PM* 32 (1915), Beilage.
30. For the cultural and psychological significance of the front, see esp. Eric J. Leed, *No Man's Land: Combat and Identity in World War I* (Cambridge, 1979). Although he discusses the reordering of the significance of "home" for soldiers, the complementary subject of how the home redefined itself is outside his subject.

soldier in the trenches. For the civilian population, however, the anonymity of the war and their uncertainty about their function in it were even more pronounced. They witnessed only the final results of the fighting, those hundreds of thousands of wounded, maimed, and absent dead—symbols of the war, to be sure, but ones whose meaning was ambiguous. Apart from purely practical arrangements, like hospitals and cemeteries, civil society was unprepared to absorb these people, just as the survivors were often unable to be absorbed.

To explain the war and to make sense out of what was coming to seem increasingly senseless became the task of the Heimat organizations, whose cultural role, after all, had always been to reconcile a local world with the larger, more impersonal national one. Under their sponsorship, the home front evolved from a transient set of social and political circumstances to an entire world that served as an alternative to the world of the soldier in the trenches. The term *Heimat* took on all the counterweight necessary to balance the new concept—and place: the front. "The field and the Heimat live in the closest of complementary relationships," wrote Hermann Schreibmüller in 1916.[31] As a regular feature, *Wald-Heil!* posed its "News from the Front" next to its "News from the Heimat." All over Germany, small journals and newsletters were founded, representing region or town, business or parish, and bearing such names as *Die Heimatglocke: Grüße an Heer und Flotte, Gruß aus der Heimat, Aus der Heimat und dem Felde, Stimmen der Heimat an die Mendener Krieger, Heer und Heimat,* or *Sachsen im Feld und Heimat.*[32] Their purposes and contents varied: some carried religious homilies, some told of marriages and deaths at home, some devoted themselves to the exploits of local boys at the front. But all were informed by that essential dichotomy between here and there, between the fighting and the home, a dichotomy over which the commonly shared state of war ruled and hence one whose only resolution would be victory or defeat.[33]

In shaping an understanding of the essential elements of that war, Heimat propagandists continued to draw heavily on experiences of war in the past, regardless of—or perhaps because of—the almost incomprehensible newness of this "war of peoples" (*Völkerkrieg*), as they called it. Illusions about the fighting itself, long since abandoned by the soldiers at the front, were cherished and nurtured in the home literature: clichés of heroism and bravery, of an evil and identifiable enemy confronted face to face, of decisive engagements and unambiguous victories. But Heimat writers mostly excluded fighting, bloodshed, and death from their portrait of wartime Ger-

31. *Heimatgrüße* (1916): 3.

32. Selection of wartime periodicals in the Hoover Institution Library, serials collection.

33. Paul Fussell has discussed the resonance of this same dichotomy in the English context; see his *The Great War and Modern Memory* (New York, 1975).

many. Their main subject was instead the pastoral beauty of the Heimat, in almost obscene contrast to the perverted pastoral of the scarred earth at Verdun. The rhetorical device that made such unviolated beauty bearable was its vulnerability, and the message it conveyed was the necessity of patriotic ardor to protect the home and keep away the enemy. In every province of Germany, these features became characteristic of a transmogrified Heimat genre. The actual content of the idyll—its inhabitants, their particular fears and hopes—varied according to the historical experience and Heimat traditions of the area. In the Pfalz, the nearness of the front and the devastations of its past gave its homefront propaganda an identifiably Pfälzer character: the sense of menace intrinsic to wartime was intensified; the identity of the enemy, France, well known.

In all such wartime writings and activities, the Heimat remained the center of attention and the point of reference, despite the tragic urgency of events at the front. This Pfalz was a land of beautiful vistas and peaceful agricultural and industrial scenes. In absolute contrast to the battlefield, wartime literature and art depicted wheatfields and vineyards, rivers and hills, cities and villages infused with the warm sunlight and peaceful mood of Heimat sentiment. The Literary Association's *Heimatgrüße*, for instance, devoted most of its offerings to pastoral poetry, introduced by prints of landscape watercolors by the local artist August Croissant. A sketch for the membership cards of the Pfälzerwald Verein in 1917 showed a quiet scene in the Pfälzer hills, where a young woman sat with a uniformed young man, his arm so inobtrusively swathed in bandage that no irony could have been intended in the juxtaposition of nature and war's wounds. In the political realm, the pastoral image had its counterpart in the state of *Burgfrieden*, the "single-minded lifting up of the whole nation without difference of party or confession," according to a Pfälzer politician.[34] Internal strife had no place in this scene; even to suggest conflict of interests in the Heimat was to violate the basis on which the image was built.

But like the wartime truce among domestic enemies, the Pfälzer idyll achieved its transcendent peace only through the fact of destruction elsewhere. The Pfalz, in particular its natural beauty, became the reason for which its sons fought, just as its beauty existed only thanks to their efforts. In a lecture to the Historical Association of the Pfalz on January 17, 1916, Daniel Häberle took as his subject "The Landscape of the Pfalz," whose beauty remained inviolate because of "the courage of our army on the western front."[35] The second edition of *Heimatgrüße* had a place inside the front cover to write the name of the soldier to whom one was sending the book

34. Remarks of the district president, Ritter von Conrad, to the regional council, *MHVP* 34/35 (1916): iii.
35. *MHVP* 36 (1916): iii.

"with thanks for your protection of the Heimat, with best greetings from the Pfalz and all good wishes for a victorious return home soon." Its editors greeted those "Pfälzer hearts...near and far from the Heimat," whose bravery in the field sustained the peace of the home to which they would ultimately return. In their appeals for subscriptions to war bonds, the editors of *Wald-Heil!* juxtaposed the tranquillity of the Heimat and the terror of the war, which would threaten the peace of home should citizens not do their duty.[36] The juxtaposition—one whose inner meaning was mutual dependence—of an undisturbed home and a distant, unseen battle characterized most starkly the "Letters from the Field" that were printed in each issue of *Wald-Heil!*; indeed, the letters were meant to create and sustain that contrast. Sergeant August Schwarz confided to the editors of the paper that after the war "many of my companions, whose bravery has spared the beautiful German forests from war's fury, will bring even more love and interest [to the Pfälzerwald Verein's undertakings]. . . . For," he concluded, in bitter though unintended irony, "most of us have first learned of the beauty of nature, and above all of the beauty of the forests, only here in the war."[37]

The vulnerability of the Pfälzer garden was, like the image of the garden itself, a convention rooted in prewar Heimat self-creation. Drawing on the experience of the left-Rhenish lands in centuries past, Pfälzer Heimat historians, both academic and popular, had produced a provincial historical canon, of which the most persistent refrain was French iniquity. During the war, this refrain was to be heard in all its old variations as well as some new ones. Articles in the journal of the Historical Association found evidence of France's destructive and acquisitive impulses toward the Rhenish Pfalz as far back as the Late Middle Ages. French misbehavior in the Rhineland became a general theme not just of Pfälzer wartime writings: in *Das eiserne Buch*, a propagandistic collection of articles from academics in Germany, Bodo Ebhardt wrote that the ruins on the Rhine banks "teach us what our fate would be if the hordes of our enemy descended upon us again. . . . Think on the picturesque image of the Heidelberg castle ruins . . . and let it, along with the silenced and deserted towns and castles of the Pfalz . . . be a call to hatred, to revenge, and to battle to the bitter end."[38]

Nevertheless, Heimat writers rarely indulged in the violent rhetoric characteristic of Ebhardt's appropriation of Pfälzer symbols. The victimization of the Pfalz by the French could at times simply dramatize the general problem of the region's vulnerability to war—as well as its enforced passivity in the

36. "Unsere Pflicht," *WH*, no. 22 (8 October 1918): 1; "Zeichnet Kriegs-Anleihe," *WH*, no. 10 (8 October 1917): 1.

37. *WH*, no 3 (1917): 7. The remark in its context seems to share the same wishful thinking—and denial—that led the Verein to see trench warfare as a form of "outdoor living."

38. Bodo Ebhardt, "Deutsche Burgen als Vorbilder," in *Das eiserne Buch. Die führenden Männer und Frauen zum Weltkrieg 1914/15*, ed. Georg Gellert (Hamburg, 1915), p. 204.

face of it. Here the Heimat writers showed perhaps a surer understanding of their audience than did more prominent propagandists on the national scene, whose calls to hatred and death fell on the increasingly jaded ears of soldier and civilian alike. Though mobilized for war, the Heimat and its promoters never glorified battle itself, and part of the effectiveness of the Heimat message in wartime was that it implicitly sided with the little man (or what is the same thing, the little region) swept along by events that brought as much loss and sorrow as patriotic satisfaction.[39]

Yet the cultivation of patriotism, both local and national, was by no means absent from the wartime mission of Heimat organizations. If Pfälzer history taught that the French were belligerent and greedy, it also taught that Pfälzers were loyal, idealistic, energetic, and ready to die for the home they loved.[40] In the natural beauties of the Pfalz, Heimat propagandists found not only the pathos of war but an exaltation of national and local feeling. A member of the Pfälzerwald Verein told of how he and his companions had been standing atop Kalmit Mountain overlooking the Rhine plain when they heard the news that the United States had broken off diplomatic relations with Germany. In this moral fable, reported in the pages of *Wald-Heil!*, such news in such a setting brought not discouragement but the spontaneous singing of the national anthem.[41] The highest good for both man and province, according to Hermann Schreibmüller, was to work fully and selflessly for the good of the whole, and this the Pfalz and Pfälzers, whether at home or at war, had done: "And so field and Heimat have worked together, to the glory and the honor of nation and of the Heimat."[42]

Yet field and Heimat could not forever remain so completely sealed off from each other as they were in wartime Heimat imaginings. For Germans at least, the final months of the war brought the two ever closer together, making the myth of an inviolate Heimat ever more difficult to maintain. Even as they parted with their precious gold coins from the museum or stood by as the old bells of historic churches were removed and melted down to make cannon fodder, the Historical Association had been acquiescent and patriotically dutiful.[43] The home front of cheerful sacrifice was easier to maintain than the real front, as long as the enemy was still in France and shells exploded only in the distance. But malnutrition, epidemics, food riots, walkouts, scattered rumors of mutinies, the abdication of monarchs, the gradual

39. The war poems in *Heimatgrüße* reveal this tendency, with such titles as "Soldatenabschied," "Der Feldsoldat," "Der Geworbende," that adopted the perspective of the simple soldier, off to war or in the war.
40. E.g., *Heimatgrüße* (1916): 4.
41. *WH*, no. 2 (28 February 1917): 8.
42. *Heimatgrüße* (1916): 7.
43. Memorandum from Keiper, Nortz, and Sprater (14 July 1917), PLAS, T1, no. 15; *PM* 34 (1917): 59.

return of troops, and finally the arrival of the enemy itself all made clear that
the Heimat was not and never had been an idyll of peace, protected from
hardship by the bravery of soldiers. In the end, tragically for Germany's
future, the Heimat itself assumed the blame for defeat: "And so the unde-
feated soldiers return to the defeated people," wrote the editors of *Wald-Heil!*,
in an article of December 1918 bitterly entitled "Welcome to the Heimat."[44]

"They return to a new Heimat," the article continued, "a Heimat much
changed from that they left in August of 1914." The organizations and individuals who had done so much to promote awareness of the Heimat were
themselves subtly changed in purpose, though not in form. The "new
Heimatbund" that they had hoped to forge in wartime between front and
home now in fact bound them ever more closely to the state, whose own
position in the Pfalz had become increasingly vulnerable, disputed, and in
need of advocates. The Pfälzerwald Verein spoke in December 1918 of the
urgent need to rebuild neglected forest paths, but the task on which it, along
with the Historical Association and many lesser Heimat groups, soon
embarked was the rebuilding of the German nation. In the Pfalz, the outcome of the war, indeed the war itself, had undermined to the point of col-
lapse the edifice of national feeling that the Heimat movement had helped to
construct. In the years of revolution, political insecurity, military occupation,
and separatism that followed, the Heimat movement tried again, with much
less unabashed optimism and much more anxiety, to redefine the bases of
their national and provincial communities.

---

44. "Willkommen in der Heimat!" *WH* no. 24 (8 December 1918): 1. Note that this is the
first intentional piece of irony in a Heimat periodical, and it comes at the expense of the genre
itself, not of those who conducted the war.

FIVE

Saving
the Heimat

The ten-year occupation of Germany's western regions after its defeat in the First World War tested the strength of national integration in ways that students of the Weimar Republic have been slow to appreciate—much slower, indeed, than those who lived through it. That the occupation was a volatile diplomatic issue has not been doubted, nor that it was a condition easily exploited by rabid nationalists on all sides, nor even that it burdened the German economy with an extra load it could ill afford to carry. What has been lost, however, is the sense in which the occupation forced Germans to reassess the nature of their national belonging. Where German identity came from and what it implied about the most desirable form of national government were both issues thrown open by the obtrusive presence of foreign troops on soil long considered part of the national patrimony. The issue of loyalties was the easiest to address, and the chapter that follows tells the story of the successful efforts to maintain the Germanness of the Pfalz in the face of various contrary pressures, mostly from the French. Less easily settled was the question of whether loyalty to Germany and hatred of the occupation required allegiance to the new German republic: the local answers to that dilemma—some positive, some cautiously neutral, and some emphatically negative—form the subject of the next chapter. In every case, the language of Heimat, whether expressing national patriotism, local republicanism, or cultural privatism, remained central to the self-understanding of the participants.

The Pfalz and its French occupiers were, of course, only one part of a much larger scene. The occupied area of Germany stretched from the Pfalz's southern border several hundred miles to the north, encompassing five times as much territory as the Pfalz and involving at least three other nations—the United States, Britain, and Belgium—whose representatives made scant appearance in the Pfalz. Some contemporaries nevertheless believed that the fate of the German republic hung on the occupation-induced identity crisis of a few hundred thousand Pfälzer grape growers and shopkeepers.[1] Throughout the 1920s, officials of both Bavaria and the Reich expended considerable time and money to secure the loyalty of the Pfälzers, and indeed Pfälzers themselves mobilized all the patriotic resources at hand, important among them the Heimat associations, to build a solid wall of pro-German sentiment. To understand their alarm and their response, one must begin with the cause: the arrival in the Pfalz, once again, of the French army.

On 1 December 1918, twenty days after the signing of the armistice, French troops of the Eighth Army under General E. M. Gérard entered the Pfalz from the south and occupied Landau, the old fortified town of the Sun King. For the French, it was a moment richly historic, a moment to be savored and celebrated by speeches filled with reference to past association and present promise. "To a people bowed down under a hundred years of tyranny," Gérard declared to his troops on the eve of the occupation, "you will show what a nation conscious of its power and its honor can and wants to do. . . . Republican France shines not only in the brilliance of its bravery; it is and has remained throughout history the eternal Fatherland of Justice."[2] Convinced, at least officially, that their mission was to liberate, not to occupy, French commanders immediately laid claim to the obedience and loyalty of the local population. In the heated rhetoric of the moment, *le Palatinat rhénan* was rejoining its spiritual homeland; Napoleon had returned. "You Pfälzers have the greatest happiness in store," Gérard repeated to the population itself; "after one hundred years of German tyranny, you return to the arms of generous mother France, who brings you Freedom and Justice."[3]

Whatever the merits of the French appeal to history, it at least recognized on a propagandistic level the potentially volatile state of national and regional loyalties in the Pfalz at the end of 1918. In the Rhenish cities hunger approaching starvation was destroying health and morale. Within days of the events of 7 November in Munich, councils of workers, soldiers, and peasants had been founded all over the Pfalz; for much of the Pfälzer middle

1. See, for instance, the assertion of Bavarian official Theodor von Winterstein in 1920 that the Pfalz was bearing the brunt of the French propagandistic attack and hence that the Pfalz was also the key to the defense of all Germany ("Niederschrift über die Besprechung im preus. Ministerium des Innern" [18 November 1920], Bayerische Hauptstaatsarchiv, München, Staatsministerium des Äussern [hereafter cited as BHStAM, MA] 108372).

2. Cited by, among others, Albert Pfeiffer, "Die Pfalz unter französischer Besatzung, 1918–1930," *Zeitschrift für bayerische Landesgeschichte* 5 (1932): 110.

3. *Franzosenzeit. 10 Aufsätze und 30 Bilder zur Räumung der Pfalz von den Franzosen*, special edition of the *Landauer Anzeiger* (Landau/Pfalz, 1930), p. 3.

class these represented the beginnings of the chaos that seemed to rule over the rest of Germany. Indeed, Germany as a national state seemed to those people on its edges barely to exist. Bavaria, too, was floundering economically and politically and seemed prepared to jettison the Pfalz altogether, into whose embrace no one knew. Only the scheduled arrival of French troops was certain. Large sectors of the population came to associate their arrival with the restoration of political stability and the promise of economic advantage, expectations that the French hastened to reinforce.[4]

The French hoped to use the time between the signing of the armistice and the convening of peace negotiations in Versailles to strengthen their position in Germany, and in particular to give substance to their claim that the natural state of the Rhineland was to be either French or neutral.[5] Militarily, the French presence in the region had been ratified by the terms of the armistice. Gérard and his successors attempted to strengthen that presence economically, culturally, and politically through a policy they came to call the "peaceful penetration" of the Rhineland. Already by December, the French had forbidden trade between the left bank of the Rhine and the rest of Germany, supposedly substituting French trade for what was lost.[6] Gérard also promised training programs to combat unemployment and emergency relief programs to bring food to the local people.[7]

But his actions proved mere gestures of which the positive value was overshadowed by the real economic burdens that the occupation—not liberation—placed on local society. In fact, the Allied blockade continued for months after the armistice, effectively cutting off the Rhineland from trade to the east and west. French businessmen rushed into the vacuum and with Allied-backed French money and Allied concessions established themselves in the wreckage of the German economy.[8] Occupation control of German railroads, water transport, post, telegraph, telephone, and presses further hindered recovery from wartime devastation. The quartering of troops and administrators in tens of thousands of apartments, rooms, and school buildings created resentment that promises of work programs could not over-

4. Theodor von Winterstein, "Der 18. Mai 1919, ein Gedanktag der pfälzischen Geschichte," in *Dokumente aus dem Befreiungskampf der Pfalz*, special edition of the *Pfälzische Rundschau* (Ludwigshafen, 1930), p. 6.

5. Klaus Reimer, *Rheinlandfrage und Rheinlandbewegung, 1918–1933. Ein Beitrag zur Geschichte der regionalistischen Bestrebungen in Deutschland* (Frankfurt, 1979), pp. 62–63; see also the comprehensive account of French aims in the Rhineland in Walter McDougall, *France's Rhineland Diplomacy, 1914–1924: The Last Bid for a Balance of Power in Europe* (Princeton, 1978).

6. Faber, "Die südlichen Rheinlande," p. 430.

7. Josef Wysocki, "Zwischen zwei Weltkriegen: Wirtschaftliche Probleme der Pfalz 1918–1939," in *125 Jahre Industrie- und Handelskammer für die Pfalz. Beitrag zur pfälzischen Wirtschaftsgeschichte*, ed. Martin Denger (Speyer, 1968), pp. 259–60.

8. Keith Nelson, *Victors Divided: America and the Allies in Germany, 1918–1923* (Berkeley and Los Angeles, 1975), p. 44.

come.[9] Finally, the formation in Paris of a central economic administration for the Rhineland undermined Gérard's efforts to treat the individual problems of the Pfalz.[10]

His policy of peaceful penetration had to rely, then, on the appeal of French civilization. Over the next three years, the French brought their own language courses, concerts, theater, reading rooms, cinema, newspapers, magazines, and horse racing to the region. They sponsored German-language periodicals and tried to establish a local university.[11] French cultural propaganda in the Pfalz itself, distinct in tone and in substance from the writings of such well-known nationalist publicists as Maurice Barrès, appealed to the peculiarities of Pfälzer character that had already been established by several generations of regional writers. It often relied on the folklorist and Heimat novelist August Becker, for instance, for descriptions of the allegedly Gallic character traits of the Pfälzers—their wit, argumentative liveliness, egalitarianism, devotion to Napoleon, and preference for wine over beer.[12] Dredging up all evidence of Prussian and Bavarian suspicion of the region in the nineteenth century, French propagandists easily established the artificiality of the Pfalz's bonds with Germany east of the Rhine. Pfälzer sympathy for the French, then, seemed axiomatic.

But cultural programs and economic measures, however convincing or successful, served the French cause only if they led to firm political commitments, and in that respect Gérard, like his superiors, proved inept. Although he made the most of conservative fears of the German revolution, abolishing the fledgling council movement and spreading exaggerated accounts of the chaos in Bavaria, all he ever obtained of mainstream political commitment was an anodyne testimony from a local assembly in February 1919 to the "irreproachable conduct and benevolent correctness" of the French occupiers.[13] Bishop Sebastian of Speyer may have greeted a French commander with the words "Avant tout catholique, mon Général," and another

9. Wysocki, "Zwischen zwei Weltkriegen," p. 257.

10. Ibid., p. 260.

11. "Kulturelle Durchdringung des besetzten Gebietes," misc. memoranda (1919–22), BHStAM, MA 108363; "Französische Kulturpropaganda in der Pfalz, Französische Wohltätig-keitsunternehmungen in besetzten Gebiet" (1922–28), BHStAM, Staatsministerium des Unterricht und Kultus (hereafter cited as MK) 15566; Paul Jacquot, *Général Gérard et le Palatinat,* trans. into German as *Enthüllungen aus dem französischen Generalstabs,* ed. Dr. Ritter [von Eberlein] (Berlin, 1920), p. 43.

12. Jacquot, *Enthüllungen,* pp. 25–27, 34–35.

13. Reimer, *Rheinlandfrage,* p. 136. The assembly also declared itself in favor of a separation from Bavaria, but the declaration was never put to a formal vote, even within this dubiously representative group of notables. See also Dietrich Schlegel, "Der Separatismus in der Pfalz nach dem Ersten Weltkrieg," *MHVP* 71 (1973): 223–25; Allan Mitchell, *Revolution in Bavaria, 1918–1919: The Eisner Regime and the Soviet Republic* (Princeton, 1965), pp. 145–46; Albert Pfeiffer, "Die Pfalz unter französischer Besatzung," p. 91.

cleric may have declared the French far less objectionable than the Prussians, but on the whole, Pfälzers remained politically aloof.[14] Indeed, working against any stable or powerful alliance with the French was the very volatility of political affairs from which the French had initially benefited. Anti-Bavarian, anti-Prussian, or anti-German, anti-Bolshevik or antibureaucratic, the rationale behind cooperation with the French was neither consistent nor clear. Conservative Catholics had little to gain by turning against the essentially Catholic state of Bavaria, despite its temporary control by the Socialists.[15] Nor did Social Democrats, who in 1919 were the major political force in the Pfalz, see any appeal in the neutralism offered by the French, particularly at a time when Germany itself seemed to be moving toward a Social Democrat future.[16] Moreover, the occupation rule came down with special severity on urban workers, leaving them with less food, less work, and less freedom of movement and expression than any other major social group.

The convening of the National Assembly in Weimar clinched the matter, undermining what little support had ever existed in the Pfalz for secession from the Reich itself.[17] On 6 February 1919, the Association of Pfälzer Industrialists recognized the "indissoluble unity of the Pfalz and the German Reich" and further called for the quick restoration of central authority under a new constitution.[18] By the end of March, the situation in Munich too had stabilized. The new prime minister was Johannes Hoffmann, a Pfälzer and a moderate Social Democrat, who might in Catholic eyes be guilty of militant secularism but could not be accused either of Bolshevism or of indifference to the Pfalz.[19]

Meanwhile Gérard, alienated from the mainstream of political opinion in

14. Faber, "Die südlichen Rheinlande," p. 431; miscellaneous reports on Catholic activities in the Pfalz, Papers of the Staatskommissariat für die Pfalz (1919–20), BHStAM, MA 107710.

15. Erwin Goebbel, *Die pfälzische Presse im Abwehrkampf der Pfalz gegen Franzosen und Separatisten, 1918–1924* (Ludwigshafen, 1931), p. 88.

16. For figures on the electoral strength of the SPD in the Pfalz, see Mitchell, *Revolution in Bavaria*, p. 215.

17. Faber, "Die südlichen Rheinlande," p. 430.

18. Minutes of meeting, Staatskommissariat für die Pfalz (6 February 1919), BHStAM, MA 107709. A Bavarian official entrusted with observing political developments in the Pfalz called this event "the first gathering in support of the unconditional unity of the Pfalz and Germany" and the "basis for the entrance of a united political front" into the struggle against French-sponsored separatism.

19. Hoffmann had earned the enmity of Catholic politicians before the war by his parliamentary harangues in the Bavarian Landtag against Catholic schooling. A radical in the prewar and war context, he began to seem moderate in the context of Eisner's cabinet, where he was minister of culture and education, and by March 1919 was welcomed even by the conservatives as a compromise candidate. See Peter Kritzer, *Die bayerische Sozialdemokratie und die bayerische Politik in den Jahren 1918 bis 1923* (Munich, 1969), pp. 53, 100; Mitchell, *Revolution in Bavaria*, p. 290; Ernst Müller-Meiningen, *Aus Bayerns schwersten Tagen. Erinnerungen und Betrachtungen aus der Revolutionszeit* (Berlin, 1923), p. 147.

the region, was thrown back on an otherwise insignificant group that grandly called itself the Free Pfalz movement. The inspiration of a chemist in Landau, Dr. Eberhard Haas, the Free Pfalz movement had only a handful of supporters—most of them small property owners from Landau and the surrounding villages—and virtually no ties to the northern Rhenish separatists of the Catholic and Francophilic Hans Adam Dorten. Gérard liked the Free Pfälzers chiefly for their utter dependence on French patronage. Dilettantish in its organization, the group would have sunk into obscurity among other immediate postwar wonders had not Gérard pressed it into publicly demanding Pfälzer neutrality.[20] District president Theodor von Winterstein, together with the Pfälzer deputies to the local and Bavarian parliaments, responded with an unambiguous denunciation of all autonomist initiatives. The SPD leader Friedrich Profit made the keynote address to the assembled deputies, declaring that "in the midst of Germany's and Bavaria's deepest distress Pfälzer Social Democracy stands now just as it has always stood in the past, true to its Fatherland."[21] "With great decisiveness," the assembly affirmed that "the Pfalz belong[ed] indissolubly to Germany" and that its relations with Bavaria were no concern of the French.[22]

The episode did not end there, however, but continued with a series of arrests and retaliations, culminating in Winterstein's expulsion from the Pfalz and the seizure of the government building in Speyer by Haas and his followers, who then declared the foundation of the Free Pfalz Republic. On 1 June 1919, union leaders in Ludwigshafen and Speyer mobilized hundreds of workers to mill threateningly around the Free Pfalz headquarters. The next day ten thousand people, again mostly workers, gathered in the main square of Speyer, shouting threats at the putschists (invisible in the building heavily guarded by French soldiers) and singing the national anthem. These shows of resolve, accompanied by union leader Fischer's threats of a general strike, dislodged the putschists from the government building, if not altogether from government. For the next three months, governmental affairs limped along, conducted by an awkward combination of Free Pfälzers, French, and uncooperative Bavarian officials—a situation bearable only given the fact of occupation rule. Protest demonstrations and strikes became regular occurrences: in August, a violent and prolonged general strike in

20. The day before the meeting of the local council, a Free Pfälzer pamphlet entitled "The Future of the Pfalz" was distributed throughout Speyer and other Pfälzer cities. It addressed itself to Winterstein, asserting that the Pfalz was doomed unless it sought neutrality under French protection. Its anonymous authors purported to be representatives of "agriculture, viniculture, the wine trade, industry, trade, commerce, and the workers." See "Die Zukunft der Pfalz" (17 May 1919), PLBS, collection of 1920s pamphlets (*Flugblätter*).

21. Goebbel, *Die pfälzische Presse*, p. 88.

22. Karl-Heinz Lintz, *Großkampftage aus der Separatistenzeit in der Pfalz* (Edenkoben/Pfalz, 1930), p. 25.

Ludwigshafen; in Neustadt, a patriotic rallying of three thousand for "the Pfalz, the pearl of the Reich"; and so on.[23] The French occupation authorities tried to discourage such actions through harsh reprisals.[24] By now thoroughly divided on the best course of action, they had ceased to hide their rule behind the façade of the Free Pfalz Republic, which had in any case received no recognition and precious little attention from the rest of Germany. On 12 October, Gérard was relieved of his duties. His successor and former deputy, General de Metz, abandoned the political front temporarily in pursuit of further cultural and economic influence.

These events, shaped as much by folly and pride as by unfolding necessity, set the terms within which local affairs were conducted throughout the years of the republic—and indeed, well into the era of Nazi rule. The dichotomy thus established between traitor and patriot dominated political rhetoric, making it impossible to sustain public debate on any other terms. Although one finds in Pfälzer political rhetoric surprisingly little of the stab-in-the-back legend of internal betrayal and defeat (one wonders if the Pfälzers' proximity to the warfront made them better acquainted with the real state of the army), its place was fully taken up by the figure of the separatist, the autonomist, the traitor to the Heimat, conspiring with the French after the armistice to turn national defeat into national disintegration. Against this figure was posed a variety of defenders, from Social Democrats to agrarian conservatives. In common opposition to French interference in local affairs, they managed to achieve a fragile consensus that lasted until the French left in 1930.

At the heart of this consensus was a commitment to the Germanness of the Pfalz, and the word, concept, and emotion that came to express this sense of loyalty and belonging was Heimat. Heimat and love for Heimat were not French but German—and only German—attributes. Referring to both regional loyalties and national patriotism, Heimat encapsulated the struggle against French efforts to invoke a regional heritage friendly to their own interests. Just as important, it symbolized the agreement of all conflicting parties on certain assumptions. As Friedrich Profit declared in his speech of 18 May 1919, "The party struggles must in this hour cease; today party passions must find no room in our midst. Beyond party programs, our hearts and minds sense other inspiring ideals in human life: *the love for our Heimat, for our Pfalz!* [Bravo, cheers from the audience.] We desire to proclaim loudly and joyfully that we are not just good Pfälzers, but good and true Germans, now and always."[25]

23. *Die Pfalz unter französischer Besatzung. Kalendarische Darstellung der Ereignisse vom Einmarsch 1918 bis November 1924*, ed. Lorenz Wappes, Bayerischer Staatskommissar für die Pfalz (Munich, 1925), pp. 28–30.

24. Faber, "Die südlichen Rheinlande," p. 431.

25. Speech of Friedrich Profit in the form of a pamphlet entitled "Die Zukunft der Pfalz" (18 May 1919), PLBS.

The full mobilization of Heimat sentiments against the foreign invader, however, fell not to the local politicians but to the Bavarian government in the early years of the occupation. In 1919, shortly after the French expelled District President von Winterstein from the Pfalz, Bavaria established a new Central Office for Pfälzer Affairs across the Rhine in Mannheim; in the words of one official, its job would be "enlightenment, education, and encouragement," to promote the "economic and moral strengthening of the Pfälzers."[26] The exiled Winterstein became its first head, with the title of *Staatskommissar für die Pfalz* (state commissioner for the Pfalz), and was given 10 million marks to administer as a "Pfälzer Aid Fund."[27] At the outset the purposes to which this money would be put were clear to no one, but the new state commissioner tended to favor cultural propaganda, spending little more than 2 million marks on economic aid and welfare programs, in contrast to over 5.5 million on schools, teachers' colleges, scholarly and popular-educational organizations, theaters, orchestras, and libraries.[28]

This initial preference for cultural programs owed much to the French themselves. For every language class, lecture, pamphlet, or piano recital that the French sponsored in the Pfalz, the Germans felt they ought to have one of their own. The evident slump into which such cultural activities had fallen since the war came to symbolize the decay of German loyalties and the eclipse of patriotic sensibilities. In the language of official reports and publications, concern for "culture" represented an implicit code for political, patriotic identity; cultural programs, however constituted, aimed to shore this identity up, to reaffirm the Germanness of those who happened to live on the wrong side of the Rhine. In this sense, the occupation represented for both French and Germans a continuation of the war, which had in any case only distracted people from the "real" struggle being waged between the propagandists of German and French culture, or, in the formulation made famous by Thomas Mann, between French *civilisation* and German *Kultur*.

But beyond this generally held attitude toward culture and its significance—the small change of patriotic discourse at the time—cultural programs were considerably cheaper than economic ones for an office like Winterstein's to administer. Without real political or constitutional legitimacy outside of Bavaria itself, Winterstein could not undertake extensive programs of economic aid to the region, even had he had the money, the inclination, or the staff to do so.[29] In the Pfalz itself, he had only a secret network of *Vertrauensmänner*, or confidential agents, drawn mostly from sym-

26. Secret memorandum of Wappes (8 August 1924), BHStAM, MA 107712.

27. Johannes Hoffmann (*Ministerpräsident*) to Winterstein (2 August 1919), BHStAM, MA 107709; "Bayerische finanzielle Leistungen aus Anlaß der Besetzung der Pfalz und der Abtrennung der Saarpfalz," BHStAM, MA 107785.

28. Winterstein to the Reichsinnenministerium (Berlin) (21 February 1920), BHStAM, MK 15557.

29. Memorandum of Wappes (8 August 1924), BHStAM, MA 107712.

pathetic trade unionists and Social Democrats, other bureaucrats, teachers, and not least of all, members of patriotic associations like the Pfälzerwald Verein or the Historical Association.[30] His chief of operations in the Pfalz, Lorenz Wappes, was a ranking forestry official, well known locally for his civic and patriotic activities as chairman of the ten-thousand-member Pfälzerwald Verein.[31] Voluntary associations provided networks of friendship ready-made for the discreet gathering and dissemination of information—both primary functions of Winterstein's office. Their membership included all those who might be expected to have a strong interest in the Pfalz remaining German; indeed, the leaders of the Pfalz in economic and political terms, with a few exceptions, might just as well have devised their plans at meetings of the Historical Association, where they all met regularly throughout the successive crises of the early 1920s, ostensibly to discuss such subjects as the seventeenth-century hunting accomplishments of Pfalzgraf Johann Casimir.[32] Then too, voluntary associations like the Pfälzerwald Verein had been able to pay their own way before the war. Winterstein's limited funds had only to supplement the regular structure of private dues and contributions, thereby shifting much of the expense of cultural defense away from the state and onto the shoulders of the besieged themselves.

Nor were Pfälzer Heimat associations at all unwilling to put themselves at the service of the Bavarian government's anti-French actions. During the war, they had shown their worth as guardians of civilian morale, and after the war, when funds were needed even for a limited resumption of everyday activities, the promise of small government subventions meant a great deal.[33] In short, a near-perfect mutuality of interests characterized the relations between Bavarian government and Pfälzer associations. The Heimat associations could go on doing what they had always done, with the added fillip of

30. Winterstein, "Bericht über die Sitzung zw. Mitglieder der Reichsregierung und Herren aus dem französisch-besetzten links-rhein. Gebiet" (28 August 1919), BHStAM, MA 107709.

31. See, e.g., *WH*, no. 5 (18 May 1917): 3–4. On Wappes's career, see *PH* 3 (1952): 90; and *Pfälzische Heimatblätter* 7 (1960): 5. In January 1920, in a letter recommending Wappes for promotion to the high rank of *Geheimer Rat* "for extraordinary service in the political defense of the Pfalz," Winterstein emphasized the importance of Wappes's local standing in gaining the trust of the middle class in the Pfalz; see Winterstein to Bayerischer Ministerpräsident (30 January 1920), BHStAM, MA 107709.

32. Ernst Bilfinger, "Schießregister des Pfalzgrafen Johann Casimir," *MHVP* 37/38 (1918): 129–46; lecture by Albert Becker, reported in *PM* 36 (1919): 17. Even after his removal from the Pfalz, Winterstein retained close ties to the Historical Association, of which he was the former chairman; see Miscellaneous records of membership and correspondence (1918–22), PLAS, T1, no. 4.

33. Monthly meetings of the HVP, for instance, were filled with references to the "hard times" and the difficulties of meeting even routine expenditures; see "Vereinsnachrichten," *PM* 36–38 (1919, 1920, 1921): passim; miscellaneous records of the museum and historical associations, PLAS, T1, no. 4.

defying the French. Government sponsorship, kept discreetly in the background, also made possible the undertaking of new projects—like the establishment of a central Pfälzer research library or an inventory of local castles—and the founding of new organizations—like a league for adult education.[34]

Bavaria was not, however, the only state concerned about the popular mood in the Rhineland. In 1920, with the immediate political crisis of Rhenish separatism passed, the Reich Ministry of the Interior had begun to take some interest in the "cultivation and preservation of German culture and German traditions [*Volkstum*]" in the occupied territories.[35] Operating through the innocuously named Reichszentrale für Heimatdienst (National Center for Heimat Services)—an organization founded in 1918 to invigorate civilian morale—the German government aimed to reestablish a strong German presence in the Rhineland and eventually to restore full German sovereignty.[36] In Frankfurt, Darmstadt, and Heidelberg, the Center established "information centers" and maintained a group of "Heimat Service" agents—mostly people whose work regularly took them into the occupied areas—to disseminate German news, propaganda tracts, and posters on the other side of the Rhine. These traveling salesmen, railroad workers, and union and party functionaries would attempt both to infiltrate separatist movements and to bring back with them as much documentary evidence of French "atrocities" as they could assemble. The National Center for Heimat Services would then publish this evidence with great fanfare or give it to the German commissioner for the occupied areas to lay before the Allied high commissioners.[37] The National Center also published a periodical called *Heimataufbau* (literally, Heimat Building-up), an "information bulletin" distributed on both sides of the Rhine that carried articles on the true German nature of various Rhenish peoples and regions.[38] Its "Rhenish cultural conferences,"

34. The castle project, in the words of Oberforstrat Keiper, would "strengthen our Pfälzer population in their patriotism for Bavaria and for the German Reich." See the confidential summary of his letter of 15 February 1920 to the Landesamt für Denkmalpflege, PLAS, T1, no. 11. On the importance of the Historical Association ascribed to the project, see also "Bericht über die Vereinstätigkeit von Spätherbst 1918 bis zum Frühjahr 1922," *MHVP* 39/42 (1922): 6.

35. Reichsinnenministerium to Landesregierung Bayern (6 February 1920), BHStAM, MK 15557.

36. Reimer, *Rheinlandfrage*, p. 174.

37. A selection of such pamphlets, bound into one volume by the Hoover War Library, is titled *Pamphlets on the Rhineland Question* and includes, for instance, a pamphlet ostensibly assembled by the Rhenish Women's League that enumerated cases of aggravated assault and rape upon Rhenish women, especially by black troops from the French colonies (Hoover Library, Stanford, Calif.); on the functions of the Reichskommissar für die besetzten Gebiete, see Ernst Fraenkel, *Military Occupation and the Rule of Law: Occupation Government in the Rhineland, 1918–1924* (London, 1944), p. 117.

38. The edition on the Pfalz, "Die Deutsche Pfalz," came out in early 1921: *Heimataufbau: Mitteilungsblatt der Reichszentrale für Heimatdienst* 1 (14 February 1921).

the first held in May 1920 in Fulda, conveyed further assertions of German devotion to the region, and its subsidiary organizations, like the Rheinische Heimatbund, founded in Düsseldorf in August 1920, engaged in covert activities on the left bank of the Rhine.[39] The National Center itself did not effectively promote German interests and German consciousness in the Rhineland, mainly because it did not fool the French. Heimat Service agents were regularly exposed, and by the autumn of 1920 the Reich had reached the point where it would have to end all Heimat Service operations in the occupied areas or face disciplining by the High Commission.[40] In addition, the strongly anti-Catholic—and in particular anti–Center party—attitudes of many of its organizers aroused opposition even within the German government.[41] In the Rhineland itself, such attitudes merely played into the hands of French propagandists, who already contrasted Prussian hatred for Rhenish Catholics to the purported sympathy of their French coreligionists.[42]

But by the time it had become clear that the National Center for Heimat Services was a failure, each of the state governments with an interest in the Rhineland (most importantly, Prussia and Bavaria) had already established operations of their own, to which the Reich government could simply add its support. At a series of meetings in 1920 and 1921, representatives from the states and the Reich (in particular from the Commission for the Occupied Areas) agreed with great difficulty on a common set of goals and guidelines for a "national cultural defense."[43] Bavaria sent representatives both from its regular ministries and from its special state commissioner for the Pfalz. The assembled officials gave the direction of cultural defense to the states, not the

39. Reimer, *Rheinlandfrage*, p. 177.
40. Ibid.
41. The Volksvereinigung für Katholische Deutschland mounted a particularly effective attack on the Heimatdienst (ibid., p. 177).
42. On French propaganda, see the contemporary account by Peter Hartmann, *Französische Kulturarbeit am Rhein* (Leipzig, 1921); see also, e.g., J. Aulneau, *Le Rhin et la France: Histoire politique et économique* (Paris, 1922), a book identified by the Germans as a piece of propaganda financed by the Quai d'Orsay (Rheinische Volkspflege representative to Bayerisches Staatsministerium des Unterricht und Kultus [hereafter cited as BavMinUK] [30 May 1922], BHStAM, MK 15557); and the Prussian government's own report on anti-Prussian sentiment in French propaganda, Ministerium für Wissenschaft, Kunst und Volksbildung (hereafter cited as PrusMinWKB), "Kulturpflege im besetzten Rheinlande" (18 November 1920), BHStAM, MK 15557 (hereafter cited as "Kulturpflege" [18 November 1920]), esp. pp. 2–4.
43. Notes from Knoch, Bavarian representative to the Reichskommissar für die besetzte Gebiete to BavMinUK (15 June 1920), BHStAM, MK 15557; "Kulturpflege" (18 November 1920); "Niederschrift über die Besprechung im preus. Ministerium des Innern" (18 November 1920), BHStAM, MA 108372; and Minutes from meeting in the Ministerium für Wissenschaft, Kunst und Volksbildung, Berlin (15 February 1921); Kaestner to BavMinUK (14 April 1921); Kaestner to BavMinUK (18 April 1921); BavMinUK to sämtliche Referate, "Betr. Kulturpflege in der besetzten Pfalz" (20 February 1921)—all in BHStAM, MK 15557.

Reich—an arrangement that satisfied Bavaria's insistence on the treasured prerogatives of the states.[44] The Reich would simply allocate a certain amount of money each year to "cultural purposes in the occupied areas"— 10 million marks in 1922—which would be divided among the states and matched, in turn, by equal funds from their governments.[45] This general plan was ratified by representatives from the Center party, the German People's party, the German Democratic party, the German National People's party, and the Socialist party.[46]

The common guidelines so achieved had two major tenets, the first called "local initiative," or *Eigeninitiative*, the second "mutual relations," or *Wechselbeziehungen*.[47] Cultural propaganda that ignored local cultural particularity, thought the Prussian officials who articulated these principles, would be a disaster; the National Center for Heimat Services had proven this. Moreover, the French (or so believed the Germans) were unfortunately the masters of cultural propaganda. They had already succeeded in the Orient, Latin America, Belgium, and, above all, Alsace-Lorraine in spreading their superficially attractive "civilization."[48] Indeed, Alsace-Lorraine stood as a constant reminder to these German officials of their failure as a nation to be persuasive. According to one representative, speaking of his experience as a German official in Colmar before the war, "we lost the struggle in Alsace: we never won over their souls." The teaching of everything, from mathematics to history, was "overwhelmingly Prussian," filled with "the usual Hohenzollern adoration and unreflective war enthusiasm." Not only was no account taken of local Alsatian culture, but no attempt was made to bridge the enormous cleft that developed between it and the rest of Germany.[49] In Holland, too, during the war, the German newspaper failed utterly because it was immediately recognized as propaganda and derided by the local population,

---

44. For the political dimensions of Bavaria's aggressive particularism, see Wolfgang Benz, *Süddeutschland in der Weimarer Republik. Ein Beitrag zur deutschen Innenpolitik 1923–1925* (Berlin, 1970), pp. 325–30; Reimer, *Rheinlandfrage*, p. 223. On the Bayerische Volkspartei in opposition to the Weimar Republic, see Klaus Schönhoven, *Die Bayerische Volkspartei, 1924–1932* (Düsseldorf, 1972); Werner Gabriel Zimmerman, *Bayern und das Reich 1918–1923. Der bayerische Föderalismus zwischen Revolution und Reaktion* (Munich, 1953), pp. 81–82; Falk Wiesemann, *Die Vorgeschichte der nationalsozialistischen Machtübernahme in Bayern, 1932–1933* (Berlin, 1975), pp. 34–39.

45. "Ergebnis der Besprechung in Reichsministerium des Innern" (12 May 1922), BHStAM, MK 15557. Bavaria received 22 percent of the money, or 2.2 million marks, to Prussia's 40 percent, half of which was committed to the Saarland. Thus, among the regions within the occupied area as a whole (Rheinhessen, the Prussian Rheinland, Saarland, and the Pfalz), the Pfalz actually received 2 percent, or 2 million marks more than the others.

46. Reimer, *Rheinlandfrage*, p. 179.

47. See the first extensive development of these terms in "Kulturpflege" (18 November 1920), passim.

48. Ibid., p. 3.

49. Minutes of the meeting in Darmstadt (22–23 April 1921), BHStAM, MK 15557, p. 3.

in contrast to the enormously successful papers sponsored by the French and British.[50]

The policies of "local initiative" and "mutual relations" promised a way out of the pattern of past failure and present inferiority; they also take us straight to the provincial heart of German national patriotism. According to the Prussian report, cultural propaganda of the entente variety should have been abandoned altogether as "pointless and destructive"—insulting to the Rhinelanders and productive only of further divisiveness.[51] The Rhinelander was "well aware of the national danger and the necessity of self-assertion," but he was also "conscious of standing in his own land on the soil of an ancient, constantly lively culture that must be maintained to be preserved." Similarly, the Pfälzers, according to one Bavarian official, were characterized by "a strongly developed attachment to the Heimat," which he attributed to the Pfalz's characteristic structure of settlement in small towns, its "companionable natural setting" manifested in extensive "Verein activity" (specifically, the Pfälzerwald Verein), and, most of all, its "strongly developed sense of self. . . that regards things familiar and local as the best."[52] The national and the state governments should engage in "cultural promotion" through the encouragement of local cultural associations ("local initiative") and in the "protection of the many ties between the Rhenish and the general German culture" ("mutual relations"). They should not inadvertently assist the French in turning the Rhineland into a "cultural borderland"; nor could they allow the "narrow Heimat" of Rhinelanders to become "encapsulated," isolated from "the broader Heimat" of Germany.[53] In short, "resistance had to come from the people themselves."[54]

Here the civil servants of the new republic found themselves in the same dilemma as the founding politicians of the old Second Empire: how to reconcile diversity with unity, how to bind the national and the particular in mutually satisfactory relations. Their efforts in the 1920s, under unusually tense political circumstances, drew on the cultural vocabulary of the 1860s and 1870s, in fact constituted part of a continuous process of national integration of a peculiarly German variety. Its defining characteristic was the cultivation of cultural diversity without the encouragement of political autonomy. "The thoughts, indeed the warm-hearted feelings, that we must care for and strengthen in the Rhineland, are consciousness of the distinctive character [*Eigenleben*] of this much pressured and threatened land and its

---

50. Ibid.
51. "Kulturpflege" (18 November 1920), p. 6.
52. BavMinUK, "Betreff: Kulturpflege in der besetzten Pfalz," no. 7495 (13 April 1921), BHStAM, MK 1557 (hereafter cited as "Kulturpflege in der Pfalz").
53. "Kulturpflege" (18 November 1920), pp. 6–7.
54. "Niederschrift über die Besprechung im preus. Ministerium des Innern" (18 November 1920), BHStAM, MA 108372.

interconnectedness with the entire organism of the German people," the
Prussian report emphasized. The initiatives of the local population, as well as
exchange between them and the population of unoccupied Germany, were
predicated first on the "principle of cultural distinctiveness" and second—
"at least as important"—on the principle of Heimatpflege. "This latter is of
the highest ethical value," continued the report. "For in Heimat thoughts the
people's character [*Volkstum*] is rooted, out of which develops the greater
interconnectedness."[55]

From the outset of their involvement in the "cultural defense" of the
Rhenish Pfalz, the Bavarians had given such Heimatpflege—with its attention both to the locality and to the rest of Germany—more attention and
funding than did even their Prussian and German counterparts. With the
addition in 1921 of Reich funding, they could simply do more than they had
done previously. Teachers in lower schools, now encouraged by special semi-
nars and attractive vacation plans, were to make their goal "the awakening
of understanding and love for the Heimat," as well as the "awakening of
lively ties to German culture on the foundation of Heimat-thinking."[56] The
new association for adult education, which was funded partly by the Bavarian government, devoted itself to German civic education through the
"Bodenständige und Heimatliche," the things rooted in the earth, the things
of the Heimat.[57] According to one Bavarian report, castles and architectural
monuments, "well known to be intimately tied to the Heimat feelings of the
local population," should be given particular attention, especially since the
French had "tried to exploit" such local feelings, even embarking on a highly
symbolic restoration of the great cathedral in Speyer.[58] And all the local
voluntary associations engaged in Heimat protection, whether of nature,
folklore, literature, festivals, or history, received further encouragement in
the form of more extensive grants and the adoption of their periodicals for use
in the Pfälzer schools.[59]

Bavaria also encouraged such traditional cultural undertakings as a regional orchestra and a new regional library, but even these paid homage to
Heimat sentiment. The library's collection was shaped almost entirely

55. "Kulturpflege" (18 November 1920), pp. 9–10.
56. "Kulturpflege in der Pfalz"; "Deutsche Kulturpflege im besetzten rheinischen Gebiet"
(14 April 1921), BHStAM, MK 1557, p. 6.
57. An extended discussion of adult education in the Pfalz may be found in Chapter 6
below. The quotation is from Hermann Fitz, "Was will der Pfälzische Verband für Freie Volksbildung?" *Der Pfälzische Heimatkalender 1922* (Neustadt/Pfalz, 1921), p. 72.
58. Korn (BavMinUK) to Regierungsrat Trendelenburg (PrusMinWKB) (13 April 1921),
BHStAM, MK 15557.
59. The intention was expressed in "Kulturpflege in der Pfalz"; the results can be judged in
the "Vereinsmitteilungen," reported in *Pfälzisches Museum*; in the records of the Historical Association, PLAS, T1; and in miscellaneous correspondence between the BavMinUK and the
Staatskommissar für die Pfalz, BHStAM, esp. MA 107709–12, MA 108078.

around the Pfalz itself, its history, its neighboring lands, its literature, landscape, and natural resources.[60] The books, in the militant imagination of the library's new director, Hermann Reismüller, were soldiers, standing in orderly line along the bookshelves, ready to resist the French. As he saw it, the library was "a further important link in the chain of cultural measures" that would "extend the cultural potential of the Pfälzer borderland, give scholarly efforts there a stronger foundation, and, most important, strengthen the national defense against energetic and determined attacks from our western neighbor."[61]

Although French annexationism remained the most important reason behind the state sponsorship of Heimatpflege in the Rhineland throughout the 1920s, Bavarian and Prussian officials would not have worried about the French influence on the Rhenish population were it not for the troubled state of their own relations with their Rhenish districts. To put the case otherwise, the cultural policies of the 1920s reveal more about the difficulties of German integration after the First World War than merely the consequences of French interference. The Weimar constitution had by no means solved the perennial German problem of balancing state and national power, and the tensions of intra-German affairs tended to make themselves felt in even the most unlikely contexts. Mention has already been made of Bavaria's resistance to a centralized policy of Heimatpflege, a resistance rooted in a desire for state autonomy within the German nation. The general concept at issue in that debate was how German nationalism should be understood and encouraged. The answer the national and state representatives came up with was largely decentralist, emphatic in its insistence on the importance of local particularity in the construction of a general German identity.

But even while they may have approved of such a vision of German nationalism in its cultural aspect, Pfälzers found themselves more and more dismayed at its political aspect, which is to say, the refusal of the conservative Bavarian state to grant the Weimar government the full recognition that most Pfälzers felt it deserved. Here was the revival of a century-old suspicion between the two regions, rooted in the Pfalz's far greater enthusiasm for a strong national state. As in the 1860s, Pfälzer political opinion in the 1920s, with some exceptions, supported the unified, indivisible state that Bavaria

60. "Die Schaffung einer Pfälzischen Kreisbibliothek, Denkschrift des Bibliothek-Ausschußes," *PM* 36 (1919): 42; "Niederschrift über die Sitzung des Ausschuß zur Schaffung einer pfälzischen Kreisbibliothek" (16 February 1920), BHStAM, MA 107924; Reismüller, "Bericht über die Bibliotheksverhältnisse der Pfalz und Denkschrift über die Schaffung einer pfälzischen Kreisbibliothek" (June 1920), BHStAM, MA 107924. One owner of a large private collection, Jakob Baumann, publicist, historian, and cathedral cleric, refused to sell his collection to the French, who wanted their own Pfalz collection. Baumann, according to Reismüller, the teller of this story, was "kerndeutsch." See Georg Reismüller, "Die Pfälzische Landesbibliothek in der Separatistenzeit: Ein Erinnerungsblatt" (1930), PLBS, unpublished MSS. ("Rara"), pp. 2–3.
61. Reismüller, "Die Pfälzische Landesbibliothek," p. 1.

rejected. This time the Socialists, not the National Liberals, were the strongest representatives of unitarian opinion in both regions, and as their influence waned in Bavaria in the course of 1919, the hostility between the Pfalz and Bavaria grew. Chronic Pfälzer complaints against the government—that Bavaria neglected their economy, discriminated against their Protestants, harbored generally hostile attitudes toward their culture—again came to the surface, but this time accompained by the threat of Pfälzer defection to other states or to an autonomous position in the German nation itself: in October 1919, for instance, an editorial in the *Speyerer Zeitung* declared that "the economic abandonment of the Pfalz by Bavaria as well as the pressure of Center party domination that has hung heavy on this land for so many years has turned a large portion of the population against Bavaria and awakened the wish for secession."[62]

In Bavaria, meanwhile, the growing influence of the Bavarian People's party (BVP), which had become openly hostile to the republic, even to the point of breaking with the German Center party, confirmed Pfälzer alarm.[63] Such programs as the Pfälzer Aid Fund, established at just this juncture, could do little to combat the deepening suspicions. In May 1920, at the first meeting of the Pfälzer local council, Social Democrat Profit condemned Bavarian efforts to undermine the unity of the Reich and affirmed the Pfalz's devotion to the Reich and to Bavaria if the latter chose the right course.[64] In language that echoed the liberals of 1848, Pfälzer Social Democrats declared themselves to be "with Bavaria for the Reich, yes; with Bavaria against the Reich, never!"[65] The worst crisis in this tense situation came in late 1920, when rumors of BVP leader Georg Heim's negotiations with the French to establish a "Rhine-Danube block" against Prussia reached the Pfalz.[66] An advisor to the district presidium reported that the Heim episode had seriously damaged "pro-Bavarian thinking": "One hears everywhere in the educated and hence in the loyal German circles of the citizenry the fear that the Pfalz will be 'negotiated' away by Bavaria; the circles of Heimat-loving, Pfalz-born civil servants, especially of the higher ranks, are particularly fearful; they have the bitter feeling that their heads are in a noose and after all their loyalty and conscientiousness they will in the end be betrayed."[67]

Thus Bavaria's plans for the "cultural defense" of the Pfalz, like Prussia's

62. Cited by Georg Steigner, *Presse zwischen Rhein und Saar. Angriff und Abwehr der Sonderbündler im Spiegel der Publizistik* (Zweibrücken, 1962), p. 7.

63. Kritzer, *Bayerische Sozialdemokratie*, p. 148ff.; Zimmermann, *Bayern und das Reich*, p. 81.

64. "Niederschrift über die Verhandlungen des Kreistages der Pfalz am 10. Mai 1920, in Speyer" (10 May 1920), BHStAM, MA 107710.

65. Cited by Steigner, *Presse zwischen Rhein und Saar*, p. 6.

66. Wiesemann, *Vorgeschichte*, p. 28; Reimer, *Rheinlandfrage*, p. 223.

67. Memorandum from "Dr. K" (i.e., Knoch, the Bavarian representative to the Reichskommissar für die besetzten Gebiete) (20 December 1920), BHStAM, MA 107737. At the same time, the reactionary Gustav von Kahr was rumored to be trying to trade away the Pfalz for the Tyrol (Memorandum from Knoch [11 November 1920], BHStAM, MA 108363).

for the defense of its Rhineland, proceeded within a context of disintegrating loyalty and even outright hostility to the rule of a right-Rhenish state. The confessional issues may have differed widely, the political alignments taken divergent patterns, and the attitudes in the two Rhenish districts over the desirability of a unified state not been in accord, but both situations highlighted the dilemmas of Germany's inconsistently federal structure. Under the pressures of French occupation, the weak points in the interlocking levels of local, regional, state, and national government became weaker, and the many oddities of an uneven political development even odder. With the French pushing them one way and the Bavarians another, the Pfälzers had hardly space or strength enough simply to affirm that their loyalties were all for Germany. As one Pfälzer civil servant warned the Bavarian state commissioner, "The Reich matters to us Pfälzers more than anything, in the unity of the Reich our Germanness is incorporated, our love for the Heimat seeks in it a foundation, our economic life is built upon it; the Reich matters to us more than party, religion, and, in the final analysis, the borders of this state."[68]

Bavarian officials, for their part, tended to lose sight of the question of German survival in pursuit of the nearer goal of holding on to the Pfalz for Bavaria. Many, for instance, were reluctant to admit to Pfälzer organizations that money for cultural promotion came from the Reich as well as from themselves. In March 1921, a Bavarian cultural official wrote to his Prussian counterpart that the point of cultural propaganda was "to create a close dependence" of the occupied districts on the governments of the individual states, not on Germany as a whole.[69] This indeed was the true inner logic of the principle of Wechselbeziehungen, or mutual relations: to strengthen the Prussian-Rhenish and the Bavarian-Pfälzer bonds. And from the start, the struggle for Bavarian officials had two fronts: against anti-Pfälzerism in Bavaria and anti-Bavarianism in the Pfalz. Ridden as it was with economic and political crises, not to mention Social Democrats, the Pfalz seemed no great prize to many conservative Bavarians. Already in 1919, Winterstein's office, with the Bavarian Regional Association for Heimat Protection, was producing propaganda for consumption in both regions—for instance, the *Pfalz-Bayerische Heimgarten*, an almanac for the home the basic message of which was that "the peoples of the Pfalz and Bavaria are essentially the same and share a two-thousand-year history."[70]

68. Oberregierungsrat Dr. Künkele (Pfälz. Reg. Kammer des Forsten) to Wappes (18 July 1922), BHStAM, MA 107806.

69. Korn (BavMinUK) to Regierungsrat Trendelenberg (PrusMinWKB) (31 March 1921), BHStAM, MK 15557.

70. Georg Berthold, "Bayern und Pfalz," in *Pfalz-Bayerischer Heimgarten*, p. 3. The Staatskommissar arranged for its distribution in schools and elsewhere (Jolas [Staatskommissar für die Saarpfalz] to BavMinUK [20 August 1920], and Matt [BavMinUK] to Staatskommissar für

But ultimately the goal of "mutual relations" depended on the Landsmannschaften, organizations of "compatriots" or "fellow countrymen" that formed an essential part of the associational landscape of German cities. A Landsmannschaft usually had its beginnings in gatherings of displaced provincials at a favorite restaurant or pub—at the so-called *Stammtisch*. The Stammtisch could of course also be a venue for the cultivating of advantageous business relationships and the forwarding of political ambitions. In many ways the prototypical expression of the German preoccupation with Heimat and a communalism that was both nostalgic and strategic, the Landsmannschaft rested on the conceit that its members were all strangers in a foreign city, whether it be Stuttgart, Berlin, or San Francisco (where the notion at least made some sense), and distinct from the rest of the population in their locally formed traits of personality as well as their shared memories of home.

The Pfälzer Landsmannschaften had been founded in the first decade of the century as chapters of the Pfälzerwald Verein, and thus had unusually well developed ties to the Heimat itself. The war and the subsequent occupation of the Pfalz gave them a renewed sense of mission, while the steady movement of Pfälzers out of the economically beleaguered region into the cities of unoccupied Germany increased their membership far beyond its prewar level. Already in 1919, the Association of Pfälzers in Berlin held a demonstration in front of the Reichstag to protest the conditions of occupation in the Pfalz, with the Pfälzer Maximilian Pfeiffer, then general secretary of the Center party and member of the Reichstag, presiding.[71]

To turn such expressions of mutual loyalty into support for Bavaria was only a matter of emphasis. The majority of the Pfälzer Landsmannschaften were in Bavaria anyway, their chairmen and activists often Pfälzers who had left the region to pursue careers in the Bavarian civil service.[72] The same was also true of the so-called Pfälzer Hilfsvereine (Pfälzer Aid Associations), new organizations founded specifically to relieve distress in the occupied regions. From 1920 on, Winterstein and Wappes (who succeeded Winterstein as the Pfälzer state commissioner in November 1921) had extensive contact with all these organizations, providing them with the occasional contribution or speaker for their meetings.[73] At one point, Winterstein even had ambitions to

---

die Pfalz [16 September 1920], BHStAM, MA 107710). Another example of such propaganda was the book *Der Wert der Pfalz für Bayern und das Reich*, by BVP politician Michael Horlacher (Diessen vor München, 1920).

71. "Such gatherings," wrote a Pfälzerwald member in *Wald-Heil!* "can fill us left-Rhenish Pfälzers with thanks and joy" ("Die Pfälzer im Reiche," *WH*, no. 9 [1920]: 4).

72. Of the ten groups in Bavaria, six were led by men in the higher ranks of the civil service (*PM–PH* 38/17 (1921): 126).

73. See, e.g., the extensive contact between the Bavarian government and the Verein der Pfälzer in Berlin, BHStAM, MA 108048.

bring them all together into a Westmarkenbund (roughly, a League of the Western Marches), but their main tie remained the associative rituals of the Pfälzerwald Verein.[74] The limitations of relying on essentially nonpolitical associations to shore up Bavaria's reputation in the Pfalz were made clear in the summer of 1922, when the logic of "mutual relations" across the Rhine threatened to encourage the Pfalz right into the arms of Baden. The episode, which was set off by Bavaria's failure to show any enthusiasm for the Law for the Protection of the Republic, a tremendously popular law in the Pfalz, demonstrates the malleability of regional traditions in Germany as well as the arbitrary nature of many inner-German relations.[75] In May 1922, the city of Mannheim had hosted a "Badenese-Pfälzer May Day," in which artistic exhibitions and folkloric festivities were combined, according to the mayor of Ludwigshafen, with political efforts "in the direction of the reestablishment of the old Kurpfalz."[76] In July, civic and Heimat organizations in cities of the southern Pfalz began making similar plans for a "Pfälzer Sunday" in Karlsruhe that would be the culmination of an autumn festival. Plans were also in the air for a new "Rhineland committee" at the University of Heidelberg, which would give academic expression to the long historical ties between Heidelberg and the left-Rhenish Pfalz. Even the Pfälzerwald Verein had stated not long before at a "Pfälzer evening" in Mannheim that "we left-Rhenish Pfälzers are delighted that 'Pfälzer thoughts' live on with such vigor in Mannheim, proving after all that blood is always thicker than water."[77]

Perfectly ready to exploit the invented traditions of a common Pfälzer-Bavarian past for their own political ends, Bavarian officials now found themselves in the uncomfortable position of standing by while the Badenese and their supporters in the Pfalz played the same game. The planners of the Karlsruhe "Alemannic-Pfälzer Sunday" spoke, ostensibly in reference to the French, of producing "an eloquent expression of the will to inde-

74. Winterstein to Reichsinnenministerium (21 February 1920), BHStAM, MK 15557. Not until the Nazi era did such centralization occur, and then not voluntarily.

75. On anti-Bavarian feeling attendant upon Rathenau's murder, see Knoch to Lerchenfeld (18 July 1922), BHStAM, MA 107806; see also Bruno Körner in the *Pfälzische Post* (13 July 1922); on similar anti-Bavarian feeling flaring up at the time of Erzberger's murder in 1921, see Faber, "Die südlichen Rheinlande," p. 433; and Albert Pfeiffer, "Die Pfalz unter französischer Besatzung," p. 94. Pfälzer civil servants, for instance, were adamantly in favor of the law; see Minutes of meeting of Pfälzer chapter of the Bayerische Beamten Bund (23 July 1922), BHStAM, MA 107806.

76. Mathéus to the Bayerische Staatsministerium für Handel, Industrie und Gewerbe (Commerce, Industry, and Occupations) (30 June 1922), BHStAM, MK 15557; on the Staatskommissar's suspicions of Badenese businessmen, see Knoch to Wappes (29 April 1922), and Mathéus (Präsidium der Pfalz) to BavMin für Handel etc. (30 June 1922), both in BHStAM, MK 15557.

77. *WH*, no. 28 (1919): 3; "Ein Rheinlandausschuß an der Universität Heidelberg," *PM–PH* 37/18 (1921): 143; *Pfälzer in Berlin* (November 1922): 2.

pendence . . . in which the main emphases will be the qualities of rootedness and fellow-feeling [*Landsmannschaftlichkeit*] in Pfälzer-Badenese cooperation."[78] The Pfälzerwald Verein, too, involved itself in the preparations
for the celebration of "the Alemannic component of the Pfälzer people [*Volks-
stamm*]." Displays of traditional costume, parades of dressed-up historical
figures, singing of folksongs and patriotic songs—all part of the standard
repertoire of the Verein's Heimat activities—suggested in the Badenese context the marginality of Bavaria to the Pfalz and indeed to Germany.[79] State
Commissioner Wappes, after an initial panic, decided that the best course of
action would be to participate in the celebrations, making them as blandly
patriotic as possible. But he never approved of them, for although a "Greater
Baden" never emerged in Germany, the celebratory argument for its historical truth did in fact undermine Bavaria's attempt to claim the Pfalz for its
own. "Their costume parade has no artistic or historical value whatsoever,"
wrote an outraged Bavarian official in response to the Karlsruhe celebration.[80] Momentarily preempted, the Bavarians still maintained their claim to
the rituals and traditions of the Pfälzer Heimat.

But the campaign to save the Pfälzer Heimat specifically for Bavaria was
bound for failure, even if that failure did not become clear until 1933. It
depended on a delicate balance—difficult to maintain in the best of times, let
alone the worst—between Pfälzer self-consciousness and Pfälzer submission
to Bavaria, between pro-German loyalties and pro-Bavarian ones, between
cultural exchange and political stability, between national unity and regional
autonomy. The relations between Bavaria and the Pfalz never again
achieved the relative peace enjoyed before the war, even if by the end of 1922
the efforts of the state commissioner for the Pfalz to overcome at least the
French challenge had obviously succeeded. When the Reich secretary for the
occupied areas discreetly toured the Pfalz to see the programs he was financ-
ing, he encountered everywhere "a splendid feeling for the Fatherland . . .
the true reflection of the German soul of the Pfalz." In expecting to arouse
affinities between themselves and the Pfälzers, the French, he thought, had
mistaken "appearance for essence and form for content." The Rhinelander
was, "to paraphrase the Nuremberger poet on the working class, 'Germany's
poorest but also truest son.'"[81]

After January 1923, he could not have been so sanguine. The near col-
lapse of the economy and the political structure of the occupied regions under
the strain of passive resistance greatly complicated the maintenance of a

78. Knoch to Ministerpräsident von Lerchenfeld (3 August 1922), BHStAM, MK 15557.

79. Adding insult to injury, the Reich was all set to support Badenese-Pfälzer friendship
days, evidently in ignorance of Bavaria's extreme pique (ibid.); see also Wappes to BavMinUK
(19 September 1922), BHStAM, MK 15557.

80. Korn (BavMinUK) to Staatssekretär Brugger (3 September 1922), BHStAM, MK
15557.

81. Report of Knoch (14 November 1922), BHStAM, MA 107812.

united German front in the face of French aggression. Indeed, German unity survived only at a high cost, not just to Rhinelanders but to all Germans. The events of 1923 and 1924 sharpened the distinction between traitor and patriot, threatening to dissociate patriotism and love for Heimat from the tenuously established institutions of the German republic. Starting with a mass lynching in the Pfälzer town of Pirmasens that put a terrifying end to the second wave of separatism in the region, right-wing violence became ever more a feature of the Pfälzer scene, eventually proving the final, most compelling argument against a purely "cultural defense."

The national crisis of 1923 thus represented both climax and defeat for the essentially domestic and pacifistic nationalism of Heimat. Its events are familiar, and only the particular form they took in the occupied Pfalz need be considered here. In January 1923, the French, not content with the Ruhr, also impounded the customs duties, export and import revenues, and returns on public forests in the Pfalz.[82] By the end of January, most of the leading Bavarian administrators had been expelled, and civil servants in railroad, finance, and forest administration were subordinated to the direct orders of the Interallied Rhineland Commission. In response, Pfälzer workers adopted the strategy of passive resistance along with the rest of the occupied areas, refusing to carry on their duties under French supervision. In March 1923, the French simply took complete control of the railways, revenues, and forests, firing, then expelling from the Pfalz, some 8,400 civil employees. The expulsion of most town mayors and of many Bavarian administrators and civil servants immediately followed. By November, over 21,000 people (or approximately 2.5 percent of the population) had been forcibly removed to the other side of the Rhine.[83] The great inflation, which had begun in the Pfalz by the end of 1922 (and proceeded with especial severity, with currency devaluations sometimes 25 percent greater than in unoccupied Germany), accelerated an already powerful trend toward the complete displacement of German currency by French.[84] In the six months after the onset of passive resistance, unemployment, though hardly uniform, was generally severe. In the shoe-manufacturing town of Pirmasens, where the sole industry was brought to a standstill by the combination of trade barriers, passive resistance, and shortages of crucial raw and ready-made materials, unemployment was almost 100 percent between April and December 1923.[85]

The practice of passive resistance and the expulsion of so many civil servants came close to destroying the administrative structure of Bavarian-Pfälzer relations. The Rhineland Commission had forced the office of the

82. Wysocki, "Zwischen zwei Weltkriegen," p. 261.
83. Ibid.; Albert Pfeiffer, "Die Pfalz unter französischer Besatzung," pp. 94–95; Faber, "Die südlichen Rheinlande," p. 434.
84. Rudolf Fendler, "Die Pfalz in der Weimarer Zeit," in *Pfälzische Landeskunde*, vol. 3 (Landau/Pfalz, 1983), p. 328.
85. A. Seibel, "Die Cunozeit," *Pfälzische Heimatblätter* 7 (1959): 28.

state commissioner for the Pfalz to disband in the fall of 1922 because of alleged activities in violation of the treaty. The office secretly relocated to Heidelberg, where it continued to operate behind the cover of ostensibly private organizations like the Oberrheinische Nachrichtenbüro (Upper-Rhenish Information Service).[86] With the flood of Bavarian civil servants to the right bank of the Rhine, the Heidelberg operation took on the character of a shadow government, staffed by the old administrators and in clandestine contact with influential circles in the Pfalz. Without any increase in funds, State Commissioner Wappes ministered to Pfälzer morale and loyalty as well as to the welfare of the expelled Bavarian employees and their families; he also coordinated political parties, unions, and professional organizations within the Pfalz, and maintained regular contact with the other German states that had authority in the occupied areas.

The Heidelberg "Watch," as it patriotically called itself, received support from private voluntary associations in its struggles to maintain "Heimat loyalty."[87] Outside the Pfalz, the Landsmannschaften took over many welfare functions for expelled Pfälzers, raised money for people in the Pfalz, and kept up a steady stream of propaganda on the region's sufferings.[88] In June 1923, a number of civil servants and businessmen living in Munich formed a new organization they called the Pfälzer Treubund (Pfälzer Loyalty League), the aims of which were to maintain ties to the Pfalz and to coordinate the many Pfälzer voluntary associations already in Bavaria. Their appropriation of the Pfälzer cause constituted a significant departure from previous efforts, which had been shaped by a primarily convivial tradition. They modeled the Loyalty League on organizations more aggressively nationalistic and outward-turning than most local Heimat clubs—chiefly the Deutsche Schutzbund für das Grenz- und Auslandsdeutschtum (German Protective League for Germans in Borderlands and Foreign Countries), whose Munich chief, Major Gilardone, helped to found the new Pfälzer group. Gilardone introduced the word *völkisch* into the discussion, a term with racial and exclusionary implications absent in the preferred words of Heimat organizations, *volkstümlich* or *heimatlich*.[89] Calling for a "*völkisch* resistance in the west," Gilardone wanted to create a "single mass" out of the sixty thousand or so Pfälzers in unoccupied Bavaria.[90] His choice for leader of the new organization was Munich police president Eduard Nortz, a Pfälzer who had risen through the ranks of the Bavarian civil service. Nortz was

86. Wappes to Ministerpräsident Knilling (5 September 1923), BHStAM, MA 107711.

87. Jakob Mathéus, "Auf Wache in Heidelberg," in *Dokumente aus dem Befreiungskampf der Pfalz*, p. 89.

88. *PB* (1923): passim.

89. Ernst Ritter, *Das Deutsche Auslands-Institut in Stuttgart 1917–1945. Ein Beispiel deutscher Volkstumsarbeit zwischen den Weltkriegen* (Wiesbaden, 1976), p. 3.

90. "Niederschrift über eine Besprechung zur Bildung eines pfälzischen Treubundes" (18 June 1923), BHStAM, MA 108046.

by reputation a conscientious civil servant, a traditional conservative rather than a right-wing radical, but in the aftermath of his handling of the May Day demonstrations in Munich he had been criticized for leniency toward Hitler's National Socialists.[91] Outside the Loyalty League, certain people within the Heidelberg Watch began to have contacts with even more explicitly right-wing, antitreaty, antirepublican groups in Bavaria. This trend, epitomized by the Pfälzer Loyalty League, betrayed the growing influence of prescriptive rather than descriptive notions of Pfälzer identity: no longer seeking the commonalities of an admittedly diverse population, the Loyalty League set rigid and ultimately exclusionary conditions for membership. In 1923, the shift in emphasis was subtle, and it was aimed, moreover, against the French. Its implications, however, turned ultimately against other Germans.

Meanwhile, in the Pfalz itself, the organized assertion of Pfälzer character was subordinated to the struggle of daily life under the conditions of passive resistance. The boycott of French-operated rail, mail, and bus services made most associational activities impossible—or at least impolitic, given the ironic necessity to ride a French train to attend a patriotic meeting. In addition, the rapid devaluation of the currency put a nearly unmanageable burden on local Heimat publications.[92] Most people actively engaged in associational activities—particularly those concerned with the character and traditions of the Pfalz—had to accustom themselves to the constant scrutiny of the French. As the prominent Pfälzer Maximilian Pfeiffer expressed it in his letter to the German foreign minister, these men and women lived "standing on a powder keg, . . . daily placing their entire legal existence on the line."[93]

But the full impact of 1923 on the local population, particularly that part of it engaged in Heimat associational activities, cannot be understood without some consideration of the psychological effects of the runaway inflation. As Gordon Craig has written, the wildly declining currency created "a lunatic world in which all the familiar landmarks assumed crazy new forms and all the old signposts became meaningless."[94] To be sure, the presence of foreign troops in old familiar places had already altered the world of the local population, a fact that required its own psychological adjustments, but the state of occupation and siege was a historically precedented one that evoked easily understandable emotions and well-rehearsed responses. Inflation, in

91. Harold J. Gordon, Jr., *Hitler and the Beer Hall Putsch* (Princeton, 1972), pp. 125, 195–97, 204–6.

92. In 1923, for instance, the paper *Pfälzisches Museum* nearly went bankrupt and was saved only through special Reich funds (Miscellaneous correspondence [1923], PLBS, Papers of Albert Pfeiffer and Maximilian Pfeiffer).

93. Max Pfeiffer to Reichsminister des Auswärtigen Amt (8 March 1923), PLBS, Maximilian Pfeiffer Papers.

94. Gordon Craig, *Germany: 1866–1945* (New York, 1978), pp. 450–51.

contrast, undermined the world of local self-understanding, suggesting an arbitrary and rootless quality to social position, communal organization, and personality itself. As one Pfälzer writer exclaimed, "In the value of the American dollar and the English pound, see your own worth, O people of Germany, O German nation!"[95] The victims of the rapidly devaluing currency filled the ranks of the Heimat associations: middle-class people of limited horizons and unadventurous fiscal behavior, living on fixed incomes or small salaries or self-employment; people who had already lost considerable savings through their conscientious investment in war bonds, people who now lived trapped between French economic exploitation and their own ruined national economy. Certainly a frenetic disregard for social prescriptions could have been one reaction to the situation, but a far more accessible response for hometown people was a kind of grim resignation—and in public, a clinging to old certainties about the Heimat. The deliberately folksy almanac published yearly by the adult educational league always began with a letter, sprinkled with folk wisdom, from the "Kalendermann." In 1923, he indulged in a fantasy about the return of the Huntsman of the Kurpfalz from the misty past, not to save the maiden from the dragon or even the Pfälzer from the Frenchman, but to intervene in a food purchase between a villager and a shopkeeper charging millions of marks. "In this hour of need, falling hard on our ears like the sound of funeral bells, comes the word *Heimat*," the Kalendermann wrote. Like the elm tree (a recurrent metaphor in Heimat writings of this year), the Heimat endured storm, war, and hunger by pressing its roots ever deeper and growing ever upward. "With the Heimat, one doesn't gamble, winning then losing, losing then winning. The Heimat was bequeathed to us by our fathers, and we pass it on to our children. . . . The Heimat survives, as long as you have breath left in you, it survives."[96]

In September, the new German chancellor, Gustav Stresemann, called an end to the economically crippling practice of passive resistance, a decision that made financial reform possible in the rest of Germany but deliberately abandoned the Rhenish economy to follow its own declining course. In the Pfalz, unemployment, already a more severe economic problem than in the Reich, rose from 15,000 in March 1923 to nearly 70,000 by October, then by December to more than 119,000, a figure never again reached even in the severe crisis of the early 1930s.[97] Meanwhile, the continuing crisis had revived the interest of the French—Tirard in Coblenz and de Metz in the Pfalz—in establishing a neutral Rhenish state. In the late summer, the

95. Franz Hartmann, "Das Prüfungsjahr 1923," in *Der Jäger aus Kurpfalz: Pfälzischer Heimatkalender 1924*, (Neustadt/Pfalz, 1923), pp. 78–79.

96. "Lieber Heiner," *Der Jäger aus Kurpfalz 1924*, p. 1.

97. Faber, "Die südlichen Rheinlande," p. 435. The total population of the Pfalz was somewhat less than 950,000; the December figure thus represented unemployment of about 12 percent.

northern Rhenish separatists Josef Smeets, Josef Matthes, and Hans Adam Dorten regrouped, also approaching representatives of disaffected economic groups in the Pfalz, especially the unemployed and the struggling farmers.[98]

Ironically and unfortunately, the first bid for a political reordering of the Pfalz in 1923 came not from separatists but from the Social Democratic deputy and former Bavarian prime minister Johannes Hoffmann and two of his party colleagues. Hoffmann had long felt that "the Pfalz question" had been raised by "the open constitutional crimes of the Bavarian government" and hence that Pfälzers should not "fear the French" but rather "the Bavarian government with its Reich-damning, Reich-destroying politics."[99] When in the fall of 1923 Hoffmann's old nemesis Gustav von Kahr took on the semi-dictatorial powers of general state commissioner in Bavaria, Hoffmann began to fear that Bavaria would secede from the Reich, leaving the Pfalz stranded.[100] He decided to forestall such a disaster by leading the Pfalz out of the Bavarian polity, and the logic of the situation led him to seek French support. In October 1923, Hoffmann and his allies proposed the formation of an independent Pfälzer state within the German republic, but the Pfälzer council, unwilling to take such a radical measure, unanimously rejected the motion, an action that made Hoffmann into a political pariah.[101]

The defeat of Hoffmann's initiative again forced the French to shift their attention to elements on the fringes of Pfälzer political life. The second separatist episode in the Pfalz, which began less than two weeks after Hoffmann's failure, was much more unsettling and violent than had been the Free Pfalz movement of 1919, in part because of the increasing polarization of local politics, in part because of the disastrous economic situation. The Social Democrats, once the crucial force in the united German front in the Pfalz, were demoralized by recent events, and trade unions could no longer be depended on to mobilize in the face of a French-supported coup. The Bavarian People's party and the Center party were in the midst of a bitter fraternal feud. The party that had succeeded to National Liberal support in the region, the German People's party, was turning further to the right, gathering support from elements normally associated with the reactionary National German People's party (unrepresented in the Pfalz).[102] Other former

98. Ibid., p. 434; see also the general study McDougall, *France's Rhineland Diplomacy*, esp. chap. 8.

99. Speech of Reichstag Deputy Hoffmann, reprinted in the *Pfälzische Post*, no. 184 (9 August 1922).

100. Kritzer, *Bayerische Sozialdemokratie*, pp. 153–54, 183.

101. Hoffmann even lost the support of his own party. Later he lost his job as a schoolteacher in Ludwigshafen, and after his death in 1930 his widow received no state pension. See Hans Fenske, "Der Konflikt zwischen Bayern und dem Reich im Herbst 1923 und die pfälzische Sozialdemokratie," *MHVP* 71 (1973): 203–16; and Kritzer, *Bayerische Sozialdemokratie*, p. 154.

102. Faber, "Die südlichen Rheinlande," p. 434.

National Liberal voters split off into farmers' organizations, especially
the Freie Bauernschaft (Free Peasantry), a group tending simultaneously to
the right and to the French.[103] In short, if a consensus could be said to have
existed in 1919 in support of the new German government, it was attenuated
to the point of vanishing by late 1923, leaving only a variety of groups fixated
as much on their internal enemies as on the national threat.

The national threat came in the form of a vagabond, disorderly army
under a landless farmer named Franz-Josef Heinz from the village of Orbis.
In early November, shortly after the Dorten-Matthes coup in the Rhineland,
it entered the Pfalz from the already "liberated" north, taking over town
halls with French rifles, extracting oaths of loyalty from cowed or indifferent
town mayors, and finally arriving at the government building in Speyer on 10
November. Seizing the building and expelling its inhabitants, the separatists
proclaimed the foundation of the "Pfälzer Republic in Federation with
the Rhenish Republic," under the "autonomous government" of President
Heinz-Orbis. The new government adopted a currency based on the French
franc and promised to make good what the inflation had destroyed. At the
same time it consolidated its essentially military control over the towns and
countryside.[104] By early December, under the sponsorship of the French, it
had requested recognition from the Rhineland Commission as the legitimate
government of the Pfalz.

In early January, a few days before the commission's decision on formal
recognition of the Pfälzer Republic was due to be made public, Heinz-Orbis
and his chief advisors were shot down while enjoying after-dinner drinks at a
hotel dining room in Speyer. The assassination was carried out by a handful
of radical nationalists probably recruited from various extremist organizations—among them the Nazis, who after 1933 took full credit for the affair.[105]
It had been carefully planned by officials in the Heidelberg Watch, even to
the point of assuring the presence in the hotel that night of a *London Times*
correspondent sympathetic to the Germans.[106] It effectively meant the end of
the separatist regime. The Agreement of Speyer, ratified on 14 February

103. Jonathan Osmond, "Geman Peasant Farmers in War and Inflation, 1914–1924: Stability or Stagnation?" in *Die deutsche Inflation—Ein Zwischenbilanz/The German Inflation Reconsidered—
A Preliminary Balance*, ed. G. Feldman et al. (Berlin, 1982).
104. Pamphlet (30 November 1923), PLBS, collection of 1920s *Flugblätter*. The appeal was
largely to the petty bourgeoisie and the worker, as well as to war widows and veterans. It
denounced Bavarian neglect and indifference, quoting an unnamed Bavarian official's response
to appeals from the depressed region, "The Pfälzers are used to going hungry."
105. For a profile of one of the people involved in the vigilante action, see Friedrich Graß,
"Edgar J. Jung," in *Pfälzer Lebensbilder*, ed. Kurt Baumann, vol. 1 (Speyer, 1964), pp. 302–49.
See also Reimer, *Rheinlandfrage*, p. 372; McDougall, *France's Rhineland Diplomacy*, p. 322.
106. The reporter, G. E. R. Gedye, published his account of the bloodbath, carried out by
courteous young men who asked the other restaurant guests to get under their tables, in *The
Revolver Republic: France's Bid for the Rhine* (London, 1930).

1924 by the Allied High Commission, brought an official end to the autonomous government and gave the Pfälzer local council the authority to restore order, which it did by restoring Bavarian government in the region and bringing back the officials and civil servants expelled since January 1923.[107]

Regardless of whether the Heidelberg officials maintained regular ties to extreme nationalist organizations—an alliance that Wappes, a reliable and moderate participant, vigorously denied—the vigilante tactics to which these government officials in Heidelberg resorted eloquently bespoke the general level of anarchy and demoralization that obtained throughout the occupied area.[108] In 1919, coordinated resistance from all the major groups of the population had immobilized a similarly hodgepodge group of autonomists, who had also been armed by the French. In 1923, resistance was sporadic, isolated, and ineffectual. The separatists of 1923 did not hold on to power through the French, though they could not have held on without them, and certainly not through popular support. A week after the assassinations, the British consul in Munich toured the Pfalz and reported that no significant part of the population—neither the unions nor the newspapers—had ever supported the separatists, more than three-quarters of whom had come from outside the region.[109] The French aside, then, the separatists seem to have prevailed at least partly because no popular consensus existed on which to build a concerted resistance. Indeed, almost immediately after the separatists had seized power, the Pfälzer population was treated to the spectacle of its own government in Bavaria seeming to condone the similarly lawless activities of Adolf Hitler and his National Socialist movement. Nor was the comparison overlooked either by the left or the bourgeois middle in the Pfalz, who saw little difference between that group of fanatics and their own.[110]

Two months later, in the violent, anarchic dénouement to the whole crisis-ridden year, a mob in the town of Pirmasens, possibly incited to action by Nazi agitators, trapped the remaining separatists in the town hall and set it on fire, lynching those men who tried to escape the burning building. It was a

---

107. Albert Pfeiffer, "Die Pfalz unter französischer Besatzung," p. 97.

108. The groups in question were the Bund Oberland, the Jungdeutsche Orden, and the Werwolf, Wicking, or Treuhand organizations. Both the French and subsequent historians have too quickly assumed a close affinity between these groups and the Heidelberg Watch.Wappes's distancing from radical nationalism deserves consideration, not least because it was made not publicly but to a closed meeting at the Bavarian Foreign Ministry. See "Niederschrift über die Sitzung im Staatsministerium des Äussern" (1 May 1924), BHStAM, MA 107712.

109. "Die Separatistenbewegung in der Pfalz," esp. Clive Protokolle (14 January 1924), BHStAM, MK 15575; Dietrich Schlegel, "Der Separatismus in der Pfalz nach dem Ersten Weltkrieg," *MHVP* 71 (1973): 228–46. See also Steigner, *Presse zwischen Rhein und Saar*; and Goebbel, *Pfälzische Presse*, passim.

110. For an expression of Pfälzer dissatisfaction with Bavaria's tolerance of the Nazis, see, e.g., the editorial in the *Pfälzische Rundschau*, "Hitler und seine Leute," on 11 November 1923.

frenzy of violence that appalled contemporary observers, even as they tried to believe the separatists had it coming to them. The murderous conflagration in Pirmasens betrayed a growing rift that had opened in the course of 1923 between the purveyors of a conventional Heimat patriotism, of mountain wanderings and local artistic exhibitions, and a small but growing number of Germans too radically disaffected from the political and economic order to find answers to their grievances in the consolations of a local world.

But by March 1924 all this was either officially forgotten or transformed into a tale of "sober, decent patriotism."[111] In the years between 1923 and 1933, as internal strife increasingly immobilized the Weimar governments, a new literature developed in the Pfalz that recounted the events of 1918 to 1923, memorialized their participants, and shaped these events with the logic of Pfälzer historical understanding. As in 1689, when the French general Mélac had laid waste to the Pfalz, so in 1791, in 1919, and in 1923. By these accounts, what had taken place had been the "heroic struggle of the Pfälzer people for their Germanness and their freedom," the victory of "a defenseless, weaponless," but "true German" population.[112] This moral battle "of spirit and sensibility against brute strength" was won through "their love for their Heimat": "loyalty to the Heimat triumphed over storms of lightning and thunder that broke over us time and again."[113] One former district president reminisced in 1927 how his government's "Heimat work" (referring to the encouragement of local festivities, traditions, historical consciousness) had been the key to victory over the French.[114] Another recounted his experience of administering the Pfalz from the Heidelberg Watch fully within the conventions of Heimat writings about local nature: like the Heimat poet, he stands at a distance, admiring the full spectacle of the Pfalz's natural beauty from his vantage point across the Rhine, feeling the "blue mountains of the Haardt" evoke in him "a deep Heimat feeling" for "the suffering spirit in a battle of Right with Power."[115] The symbols of the Pfalz—the cathedral in Speyer, the Rhine, the vine-covered hillsides—became symbols for Germany also in this literature of nostalgia and veiled justification. And presiding over the years of struggle, "rising ever over the most delicate lines of our mountains, over the bows of our dark, melancholy forests, over the music of the winds, reviving the most downtrodden victim, delighting future generations,

111. Gedye, *Revolver Republic*, p. 63.
112. Lintz, *Großkampftage aus der Separatistenzeit*, p. 7; Georg Germann (pseud.), *Im Gefängnis der Separatisten. Wahre Begebenheit aus den Leidensjahren der Pfalz* (Nuremberg, 1927), pp. 10–11.
113. Lintz, *Großkampftage aus der Separatistenzeit*, p. 7; Franz Hartmann, "Großkampftage," in *Dokumente aus dem Befreiungskampf der Pfalz*, p. 69.
114. Friedrich von Chlingensperg auf Berg, "Heimatarbeit in der Pfalz," in Manz, Mitterweiser, and Zeiss, *Heimatarbeit und Heimatforschung*, pp. 35–42.
115. Hartmann, "Großkampftage," p. 91.

spoken from loving lips comes one word, conveying at once wish and fulfillment, the word: *Heimat!*"[116]

For the Bavarian administrators who returned to the Pfalz, eager to
reassert their own government's legitimacy, that word with all its unifying,
summarizing, mystifying potential continued to hold a powerful attraction.
They immediately set about trying to salvage the mission of the early years of
the occupation—the struggle of patriotic Germans against a repressive, insi-
dious foreign occupier, the saving of the Heimat. In the months and years
that followed, the Bavarian government continued to stage demonstrations,
festivals, and cultural events that emphasized both the Germanness of the
Pfalz and Bavaria's devotion to the region. In April 1924, after two months of
intensive planning, Pfälzer clubs in all the cities of Bavaria celebrated a
"Pfalz week," during which distinguished politicians and scholars gave public speeches on the distinctive cultural and historical heritage of the beleaguered region and popular festivities raised money for Pfälzer families.[117]
At the end of 1924 the government launched its most ambitious program of
Pfälzer support yet, with the establishment of a large fund for loans to small
businesses in the Pfalz, the interest from which would go to Pfälzer cultural
and Heimat programs.[118] In 1925 Pfälzer groups, albeit cautiously, joined in
the Prussian Rhineland's celebration of a thousand years of participation in
German culture and history.[119] The next year saw the founding, with great
fanfare, of the Pfälzische Gesellschaft zur Förderung der Wissenschaften
(Pfälzer Society for the Promotion of Learning), dedicated to the study of
the Pfalz, its history, its natural resources, its people and traditions.[120] In
1927 the Historical Association celebrated a hundred years of Bavarian commitment to the preservation of the Pfälzer past.[121] And so on it went, in every
town in the Pfalz, for every conceivable anniversary or historically resonant
occasion—this celebration of the Pfälzer heritage, defying the foreign enemy
while making increasingly unconvincing assertions of domestic accord. By
1930, the actual French departure from the Rhineland came almost as an
anticlimax, so perfunctory had been their presence in the last years of the
occupation, so well anticipated and well rehearsed the celebrations attendant
on this "liberation" of the Pfalz. The Heimat had been saved, as jubilant
publicists proclaimed all over the Pfalz in 1930; but in the process, it had also
been lost.

116. Lintz, *Großkampftage aus der Separatistenzeit*, p. 75.
117. "Pfalzwoche" (1923–24), BHStAM, MK 15541.
118. "Pfalzhilfe" (1924–26), BHStAM, MK 15530–31.
119. "Tausendjahrfeier der Rheinlande," BHStAM, MK 15584.
120. "Gründung einer pfälzischen Gesellschaft zur Förderung der Wissenschaften" (1924–
June 1926), BHStAM, MK 15549.
121. "Hundertjahrfeier des Historischen Vereins der Pfalz" (1927), BHStAM, MA 107935.

SIX

A Republic
of Hometownsmen

The cultural defenders of the Rhineland elevated local identity to the level of national destiny, recruiting the homespun virtues of Heimat to the patriotic cause of German survival. Nevertheless, within the political culture of the Weimar Republic the encouragement of localism—local loyalties, identities, and cultures—was more than a clever tactic of anti-French propagandists. For a variety of Germans, some of them outspoken republicans, some self-conscious guardians of high culture, and others simply anxious defenders of the community, the common good had to be pursued locally, in the more intimate circles of one's collective life. *Heimat* was the term that called forth a vision of this common good; it was the moral dimension of mere geographical closeness, the common obligations, duties, and values implied by a "feeling of belonging together." In the words of Lorenz Wappes, a public official in the Pfalz, Heimat was the "common good, . . . the foundation on which man strives upward, and the goal for which man struggles," the basis for a "coming together of hearts and minds."[1] The unification of German hearts, in this idiom, depended not on politics, or on "science, art, the economy, the public bureaucracy," but on the Heimat "as the living part of the great whole, of the people and fatherland": in order to "bring our people to a state of unity, that is to say, to the agreement of popular feelings and the integrity of state affairs," he concluded, "we must turn our minds to the idea of Heimat."

---

1. Lorenz Wappes, "Zum Geleit," in *Die Pfalz: Ihre Entwicklung und Ihre Zukunft. Ein Sammelwerk unter Mitwirkung führender Persönlichkeiten der Pfalz und mit besonderer Beförderung der Staatsbehörden*, ed. Erich Köhrer and Franz Hartmann (Berlin, 1926), p. 5.

Despite the quasi-mystical tone of this kind of language, neither Heimat nor the hopeful localism to which it belonged necessarily reflected a tendency to apolitical retreat in the troubled years of German democracy. The term *apolitical*, as it has been used in recent efforts to define the public disposition of localist Germans, refers to the "desire to make party political concerns, practices, and structures inapplicable to public life."[2] The apolitical German was, then, not so much the immature German of Weberian analysis as the determinedly consensualist German, who tried to exclude party conflict from public affairs by refusing to speak in public about the economic and political issues that would inevitably provoke disagreement. That consensualism, in turn, helped to maintain a bourgeois hegemony in the hometown: those who would challenge the cultural and political preeminence of the bourgeoisie simply could not make themselves heard. Wappes's call to "turn our minds to the idea of Heimat" would seem on the face of it an eloquent testimony to such apoliticism; indeed, the whole edifice of Heimat cultivation before and after the war included no room for the expression of grievances against the political and economic order.

Nevertheless, one must pause for a moment to ask why, in fact, it should have. Wappes's "Heimat thoughts" could and did exist, in the same person, alongside partisan political opinion; the advocates of Heimat patriotism included people who joined national parties and people who did not, as well as people who felt no solidarity with the bourgeoisie as such. More important, if we would label "Heimat thoughts" as apolitical, we would learn only what something is not—a perilously incomplete understanding to be sure. Precisely because the term *apolitical* is essentially negative, describing an "is not" rather than an "is," it leaves an interpretive vacuum into which rush all variety of inappropriate and unintended assumptions: the observation that Heimat was not political in the partisan or power-wielding sense can carry the strong implication that it *ought* to have been. As a conceptual category, then, apoliticism runs the danger of implying failure where there is just absence, deviation where there is just difference.

One can reduce this danger by employing a vocabulary capable of expressing and interpreting the actual content of what passes as apoliticism. The public realm need not be understood, implicitly or explicitly, as properly constituted by competing economic interests and identities; political theory allows for a publicness defined by the effort to achieve commonality, mutual dependence, and responsibility. The localists of Weimar certainly saw the public realm in such a way and consequently devoted themselves to community rather than (and as well as) to party. "Heimat ideas" in their positive form were the expression of communal integrity, the conscious imagining of a

2. Rudy Koshar, *Social Life, Local Politics, and Nazism: Marburg, 1880–1935* (Chapel Hill, N.C., 1986), p. 6.

whole. During the years of the Weimar Republic, Heimat was at the center of deliberate efforts to nourish a public morality appropriate to the new form of government and yet mindful of German traditions. Heimat rhetoric and Heimat activities encouraged a public-mindedness, a desire for moral elevation, and, not least of all, a search for security in a society ridden by crisis. Heimat defined a certain kind of identity, neither private nor partisan but "political" in its dependence on a common public space: to be conscious of one's Heimat and solicitous of its welfare was continually to seek the implications for action that followed from the sharing of a land and a historical tradition.

The encouragement of Heimat thus reveals a public activism very different from the bitter party struggles that dominate our image of Weimar public life. The failure of Weimar governments to win widespread agreement on such symbols of the common life as a national flag or a national anthem is of course notorious, the most telling case being the painful absence of unquestioning support for the "Law for the Protection of the Republic."[3] But efforts to achieve a republican consensus also took a localist turn, where they met with modest successes before being undermined by sustained economic crisis and resultant political extremism. Heimat ideas and organizations played a crucial role in sustaining public loyalty to the Republic, both as the legitimate form of government in Germany and, less cautiously, as the government most consistent with German traditions.

Heimat also served the ideological purposes of local men and women who were hardly enthusiastic about Germany's republican experiment but were nevertheless hostile to the radical alternative of Nazism. To take the full measure of Heimat's significance in Weimar culture, then, one must also consider its role in expressing established values, in representing a vision of political and social stasis. The turmoil of the Weimar years brought cultural conservatives and troubled republicans into a strange alliance that did not survive the onslaught of the National Socialist movement. How the ideas and institutions of Heimat cultivation served the consensual needs of the Weimar Republic and in turn fell victim to the Republic's inherent instability is the subject of what follows.

Writing in the fall of 1918, a representative of the Pfälzerwald Verein declared that "a new Heimat" awaited the soldiers returning defeated from the field, a Heimat "totally changed" from that which they had left in 1914.[4] The revolutionary aftermath of the German defeat had loosened the bonds be-

3. The best book-length treatment of the problem of legitimacy is Gotthard Jasper, *Der Schutz der Republik: Studien zur staatlichen Sicherung der Demokratie in der Weimarer Republik* (Tübingen, 1963).

4. "Wilkommen," *WH*, no. 24 (8 December 1918): 1.

tween local loyalty and the national state that fifty years of Heimat activities had tried to secure. For the Heimat associations, the uncertainty of late 1918 over whether a German state existed—and if so, where—posed a severe challenge to their capacity to articulate feelings of patriotic loyalty. What did it mean in November 1918 to be a patriotic German, loyal to Heimat and Fatherland, concerned about the common good of both? The author of the Pfälzerwald Verein's welcome to homecoming soldiers hoped for an "order of rights . . . better than we have heretofore had, which will guarantee freedom to everyone, without distinction of rank, an order of rights that the hard-pressed citizen of this severely tested land may claim as his own."[5] To take part in this rebuilding, reestablishing the communal harmony on which citizenship was based, was at least part of the mission of the Verein in the subsequent months. In March 1919, the Verein paper proudly announced that four club members had been elected to the National Assembly in Weimar.[6] Regardless of how it eventually came to regard the Republic in its last years, in 1918 the Pfälzerwald Verein, then the premier Heimat organization in the region with some fifteen thousand members in the Pfalz and outside of it, was prepared to accept the Republic as the legitimate expression of German sovereignty and the heir to Heimat loyalties.

This tentative convergence of Heimat sensibilities with republicanism owed something, to be sure, to the threat of French annexation of the Pfalz, but patriotic expedience alone accounts for neither the extent nor the nature of the phenomenon. Certain groups in the Pfalz, especially though not exclusively those on the left, believed that the notion of Heimat, properly understood and propagated, could strengthen the civic consciousness and the democratic capabilities of Germans, producing good Germans and good citizens too. Responsible public behavior would follow from the study of the Heimat, and an enhanced public consciousness from its celebration. The Pfälzische Verband für freie Volksbildung (Pfälzer League for Popular Education), a new adult educational association founded initially to nourish anti-French patriotism, argued that the "most significant holes in the spiritual armor of the German people" were to be found in the area of popular knowledge of civic and state affairs; its leaders proposed the remedy of popular education first in matters of the Heimat, then of the nation altogether.[7] Encouraging a local newspaper's Heimat celebration, Maximilian Pfeiffer, the German ambassador to Vienna and a native Pfälzer, wrote that "Heimat love and Heimat pride alone enable the state citizen to become a citizen of

5. Ibid.
6. *WH*, no. 26 (8 March 1919): 4.
7. Hermann Fitz, "Die Volksbildungsbestrebungen in der Pfalz," *Pfälzische Post*, no. 225 (26 September 1919).

the world, for the path to the understanding of peoples is open only to those who in their deepest soul understand and exalt their own identity."[8] Consciousness of one's local identity, one's *Pfalztum*, thus seemed to hold implications for political and social behavior beyond the mere sentimentality of hometown patriotism.

The Pfälzers who tried to articulate the civic implications of "the idea of Heimat" shared this set of assumptions about local life and politics with the founders of the Weimar Republic itself. Hugo Preuss, first author of the Republic's constitution, brought to his practical effort at state building a preoccupation with the contemporary implications of German traditions of local self-government. A student of Otto von Gierke, Preuss had pursued the democratic implications of Gierke's work in his prewar scholarship on German cities and in his early political career as a municipal politician in Berlin.[9] His initial constitutional draft (which did not survive even the first round of constitutional consultations with the German states) had contained his solution to the twin German problems of territoriality and citizenship. He proposed to devolve many administrative and self-governing powers from the central state, past the intermediary states, to the municipalities, communes, and districts, from whose local embrace the new citizen would step forth. And although this balance of local autonomy within a unified state fell afoul of small-state particularism, Preuss's vision of the citizen as an updated hometownsman, responsible to the ever-widening spheres of communal life from the town to the Republic, survived implicitly in the Weimar constitution's statement of the rights and duties of citizens. For Preuss, as for the Pfälzer Heimatlers, the ethical and political locality could be the location of "a universal national-pedagogical system of education, bringing the participating citizens out of the narrow circle of their communal experience step by step into the great matter of national politics."[10]

Indeed the "idea of Heimat," with various emphases and flavors, permeated the educational reforms and experiments of the Weimar period. Article 146 of the Weimar constitution had set the agenda for a major recasting of the German public school system, calling for a reformed curriculum, expanded educational opportunities, and careers open to talent. Although many specific reforms, particularly those intended for high schools and universities, were quickly lost amid confessional, ideological, and sectional conflicts, early Weimar governments agreed on the need for the inclusion of

8. Dr. Maximilian Pfeiffer to the *Pfälzische Rundschau*, printed in *25 Jahre "Pfälzische Rundschau."*

9. See, e.g., Heinrich Heffter, *Die deutsche Selbstverwaltung im 19. Jahrhundert. Geschichte der Ideen und Institutionen* (Stuttgart, 1950), pp. 731–67; and Gerhard Schulz, *Zwischen Demokratie und Diktatur. Verfassungspolitik und Reichsreform in der Weimarer Republik* (Berlin, 1963), pp. 9–17.

10. Preuss, cited in Schulz, *Zwischen Demokratie und Diktatur*, p. 128.

Staatsbürgerkunde, or civics, in schools at all levels, and they managed to create a national elementary school system.[11] In addition, a startling variety of programs in adult education, open education, and vocational education began to take hold alongside the old structure of confessional and elite education.[12] The general tendency of both reform and experiment was to dismantle the system that had created a nation of "subjects" (*Untertanen*) and replace it with one that would cultivate the German citizen, capable of independent thought but conscious of his or her role in society, educated in practical matters but committed to ideals, particularly republican ones. Social Democratic reformer Konrad Haenisch called this paragon "the new German character [*Menschentyp*]": not with Hamlet's "unworldliness" (*Weltfremdheit*), nor yet materialistic, but rather a union of the "most solemn fulfillment of duty, the most sober sense of facts, and the most elevated idealism," a synthesis of "Old-Potsdam, Old-Weimar, and New-Berlin," a person of "political-economic and civic thought and of social and democratic feelings."[13]

For reformers and experimenters alike, the field of Heimatkunde seemed to offer the means and the subject materials with which to begin this education in public-mindedness. Heimat studies as such had been invented by the Heimat movement of the late nineteenth and early twentieth centuries, and involved the teaching of geography, science, and history through the firsthand experience of one's surroundings—methods already advocated by the likes of Rousseau and Pestalozzi but little adopted in the pedagogically unimaginative Wilhelmine schools.[14] Apart from a few Heimat textbooks that appeared at the turn of the century, Heimatkunde made scant appearance in school curricula until the Weimar period.[15] Its first adoption came in the experimental *Gemeinschaftschulen* (community schools), the Dewey-influenced *Arbeitsschulen* (work or activity schools), and new *Deutsche Oberschulen* (German upper schools), like the Lichtwarkschule in Hamburg that one observer called "perhaps the most radical state secondary school in all of Germany."[16] Reflecting an emphasis on not only geography and natural sci-

11. Thomas Alexander and Beryl Parker, *The New Education in the German Republic* (New York, 1929), pp. vii–x; Manfred Abelein, *Die Kulturpolitik des Deutschen Reiches und der Bundesrepublik Deutschland* (Cologne, 1968), pp. 69–74; R. H. Samuel and R. Hinton Thomas, *Education and Society in Modern Germany* (London, 1949): Kurt Düwell, "Staat und Wissenschaft in der Weimarer Republik: Zur Kulturpolitik des Ministers C. H. Becker," *Historische Zeitschrift*, Beiheft 1 (1971): 32, 46–47; Cecilia Hatrick Bason, *Study of the Homeland and Civilization in the Elementary Schools of Germany* (New York, 1937), p. 26.

12. Alexander and Parker, *New Education*, pp. 3–11, 67–83, 119–242.

13. Konrad Haenisch, *Sozialdemokratische Kulturpolitik* (Berlin, 1918), pp. 23–24.

14. See Chapter 3 above; and Bason, *Study of the Homeland*, pp. 8–10.

15. Bason, *Study of the Homeland*, p. 8.

16. Anderson and Parker, *New Education*, pp. 5–7, 121–128, 156–160; Bason, *Study of the Homeland*, p. 15.

ence but social relations as well, Heimatkunde suited the nonregimented plans of study in the new schools, which directed the student's attention "in ever-widening circles" from schoolroom to city to province to nation, with frequent stops to observe the out-of-doors.[17] In the course of the 1920s, Heimatkunde achieved even wider dissemination, particularly in the education of young children. The Reich *Grundschulgesetz* (Basic School Law) of 1921, which abolished state and private preparatory schools and established national standards for the first four years of a child's education, suggested that the early school should encourage "moral advancement, the spirit of citizenship, and individual and vocational qualification in the spirit of German culture and international conciliation"; the principles of nationality, Heimat, and childhood should integrate the curriculum.[18] The principle of Heimat required that all human activities be introduced and understood in relation to the local and the familiar. As an educator in the national *Zeitschrift für die Bildung* wrote in 1925, "Our goal today in education is to form not only a civilized person [*Gemeinschaftsmensch*] but a conscious citizen of the German state. Along the path of educating a German citizen lies an education in the German national consciousness, which in turn is accomplished by an education in the German Heimat-consciousness."[19] The details of such an education were left to the individual regions to legislate; by 1928, Baden, Prussia, Württemberg, Thuringia, Saxony, and Bavaria had developed guidelines that included Heimatkunde as a special subject for older children and a method of learning for the younger ones.[20]

Bavaria issued its guidelines on the teaching of Heimatkunde in secondary schools in 1921.[21] The ministerial announcement called for the replacement of *Bürger- und Lebenskunde* (civic and life studies) with *Heimat- und Lebenskunde* (Heimat and life studies), a shift that one textbook writer called the "official recognition of the Heimat principle."[22] Heimatkunde was to form the "core of the entire secular instruction," instilling "knowledge and understanding" of the world through the local perspective and evoking "respect and love . . . for the culture and the history of our people . . . which will be the surest foundation for a new building of our fatherland."[23] The initiative was wel-

17. Bason, *Study of the Homeland*, p. 15.

18. Quoted in ibid., p. 27.

19. Cited in Wolfgang Emmerich, *Germanische Volkstumsideologie* (Tübingen, 1968), pp. 135–36.

20. Bason, *Study of the Homeland*, pp. 27–28.

21. In 1922, it issued similar guidelines for the elementary schools. Ibid., p. 27; Jakob Böshenz, *Heimat-Lebenskunde und Stoffverteilung für die Volksfortbildungsschulen Bayerns*, 3 vols. (Grünstadt/Pfalz, 1921–22), introduction; Friedrich Pfister, "Volkskunde und Volksschule," in Manz, Mitterweiser, and Zeiss, *Heimatarbeit und Heimatforschung*, p. 137.

22. Böshenz, *Heimat-Lebenskunde*, introduction.

23. Pfister, "Volkskunde und Volksschule," pp. 137–38.

156										A NATION OF PROVINCIALS

comed in the Bavarian Pfalz. Since 1920 teachers' organizations had been encouraging Bavarian authorities to "throw out history, geology, and biology and bring in simple Heimatkunde, so that our schoolchildren will develop love for their Heimat" yet still learn about the rest of the world.[24] Rejecting previous Bavarian textbooks as "boring," a teacher in the Pfalz argued for the importance of leaving the classroom occasionally and taking to the roads of the region, in order to instruct "each individual Pfälzer in the German quality of his own nature and his own land."[25] The idea of community and commonality would thus take on an actual physical dimension. Journeys, we know from anthropologists, create meaning; this particular journey through the Pfalz was to establish the interconnectedness of many personal histories to that of the imagined whole, the Pfalz—with roads and long vistas as an appropriate embodiment of the unity across space and time.[26]

The Heimat associations of the Pfalz—the Historical Association and the smaller literary and antiquarian societies—also maintained in the pages of their magazines a lively discussion about educational reform and Heimat-kunde. One writer suggested that an experimental residential school, a *Landes-erziehungsheim*, be founded in one of the old Pfälzer castles. The method of teaching would be "living observation, not book learning"; "the study of nature, of the Heimat, its social relationships and its history" would "give to humanistic education a new meaning" and would establish "the golden mid-dle way," "the proper balance between freedom and law."[27] Albert Becker of Zweibrücken, the most prolific of local Heimat scholars, emphasized the im-portance of teaching a "psychological understanding" of the German char-acter (*Volkstum*); the "highest purpose" of such instruction would be to make students understand that "out of the many-sidedness of the individual folk groups a unified community of people reveals itself, existing behind all changes in family and life forms and all differences in estate and education."[28] Support for Heimatkunde in the regular schools stretched from the Catholic head of the teachers' association to the Social Democratic party (SPD) of the Pfalz.[29] In 1924, for instance, the Educational Committee of the regional SPD had added a "children's Heimat edition" to their local news-

24. "Wir brauchen ein Pfälzisches Heimatbuch," *Pfälzische Lehrerzeitung*, no. 45 (1920): 264.
25. Ibid. The notion of such education immediately brings to mind W. H. Riehl and his method of "knowing" the Pfalz, i.e., walking its roads. See Chapter 2 above.
26. See Benedict Anderson's thoughts on the establishment of new group identities in *Imagined Communities*, esp. p. 55 on journeying.
27. E. Schramm, "Burg Berwartstein als Erziehungsheim," *PM–PH* 38/17 (1921): 123–24.
28. Becker also discouraged too great a fixation on peasant life in the teaching of Heimat-kunde; see his "Volkskunde und Unterricht," *PM–PH* 44/23 (1927): 65.
29. See Ludwig Eid, *Heimatliches Volkstum und der Lehrer in der Pfalz* (Ludwigshafen, 1925); and Ludwig Eid, *Pfälzer Volk. Vortrag im Ferienkurs der bayerischen Lehrerbildner zu Speyer* (Bayreuth, 1926).

paper; the same Albert Becker, writing in the leading Heimat magazine of the Pfalz, approved of its "warm heart for the youth, its open spirit, and its true Heimat love."[30]

One of the first and most complete of the Heimat textbooks written in the 1920s was the work of Jakob Böshenz, a poet, author of one of several "Pfälzer songs" ("Es liegt ein Land am grünen Rhein"), and an active participant in the "discovery of the Heimat" at the turn of the century.[31] By profession Böshenz was a teacher, and his textbook *Bürger- und Lebenskunde* had been widely used in Pfälzer continuation schools (for those not bound for university) before the war. In 1921, in line with Bavarian policy, Böshenz retitled the work *Heimat- und Lebenskunde*, adding sections on democracy, citizenship, and social organization.[32] The purpose of the book and the three-year course of study it prescribed was to teach students about the practical and ethical aspects of "occupational" and "communal" life.

Böshenz's essential message was one of communal responsibility and moral obligation, which was at the same time a message of social reconciliation and reformism. The principal lesson that Böshenz drew from occupational life was the need for cooperative effort: "Bound together so also will the weak be powerful." What he called *Vereinsgedanken*, or associational attitudes, ought, he thought, to pervade the economic sphere, leading men to join together in trade, agricultural, recreational, and philanthropic organizations to advance their own cause as well as that of the whole.[33] Association was for Böshenz both the secret to progress and the principle that explained the whole complex interweaving of state, industry, agriculture, trade, and commerce in modern society. Men did not pursue their own interests in disregard or ignorance of countless other discrete economic individuals; rather, they formed various kinds of groups, which together made up the whole.

The principle of association—a prescription disguised as a description—received its fullest treatment in Böshenz's three sections on "communal life" in family, Heimat, and Fatherland. All good feelings and all cooperative impulses emanated, by his account, from the family house outward into hometown and nation. Both family and community membership exacted duties as well as bestowed privileges: respect, gratitude, care for elders, punctuality, cleanliness, and consideration were featured on the list of "foundations of a lasting Heimat peace," along with "community feeling, peaceableness, help-fulness, dependability, and integrity." The hometown ought to satisfy one's private and public needs; its streetlights and sewage system, its town hall, marketplace, and churches, "Catholic, Protestant, and Israelite," together

30. *Die Welt der Kleinen* (ed. Bildungsausschuß der SPD Bezirk Pfalz) 1 (1924), intro.; review of same by Albert Becker, *PM–PH* 41/20 (1924): 187.
31. Biographical sketches in *PP* 2 (1951): 16; and *PH* 7 (1956): 71.
32. Böshenz, *Heimat-Lebenskunde*.
33. Ibid., 1:40–44.

defined the "Heimat place" and in the process saved man from "that most horrifying of all human feelings," homesickness (*Heimweh*).[34]
Democracy first entered onto this conventionally harmonious scene protectively clothed in "old German ways."[35] According to Böshenz, the new German state had reestablished the hometown on the basis of a communal and egalitarian self-government with ancient though unspecified roots. Democracy itself he nevertheless saw as something new, the "great turning point" for Bavaria and Germany.[36] Germany had become "the freest democracy in the world": "The old state has fallen, the authoritarian state has disappeared; there are no more rulers and no more subjects."[37] Democracy had brought civic and legal rights to the people, but Böshenz insisted that these rights also entailed duties, the fulfillment of which would secure the common good—notions that, again, harked back to much older German conceptions of communal peace and brotherhood.[38] Working for the good of the whole, whether "community, state, nation, or humanity," required "a readiness to serve and to sacrifice, which are the true civic virtues": "The protection of the rights of the individual require first and foremost respect for the fundamental rights of the whole."[39] The civic freedom of Böshenz's account, then, lay not in the absence of restraints on the citizen, but in the possibility of self-determination and ultimately in the citizen's ability to rule himself for the sake of his community.

Applied to actual social relations, Böshenz's insistence on duty as the essence of citizenship required that conflict among classes be resolved in the interest of the whole. The modern state, according to Böshenz, "more and more seeks to ward off such shocks [as class conflicts]" and to achieve "social justice" through "better living conditions" and other measures.[40] "Social thinking" in the life of the nation, like "associational thinking" in the life of the economy, was the key to public health. Not coincidentally, the articles of the Weimar constitution for which Böshenz reserved special praise were those assuring the freedom of assembly and association (Article 59) and the right of codetermination and worker's councils in the workplace (Article

34. Ibid., 1:48, 75–76; 2:158–60, 163, 182–84.
35. Ibid., 2:160–62. Böshenz's whole discussion of hometown autonomy bore more than coincidental resemblance to Otto von Gierke's fundamental distinction between community (*Genossenschaft*) and domination (*Herrschaft*) in the first volume of *Das deutsche Genossenschaftsrecht* (Berlin, 1868).
36. Böshenz, *Heimat-Lebenskunde* 3:110.
37. Ibid., p. 119.
38. See Antony Black, *Guilds and Civil Society in European Political Thought from the Twelfth Century to the Present* (Ithaca, N.Y., 1984).
39. Böshenz, *Heimat-Lebenskunde* 3:113–14.
40. Ibid., p. 124.

165). "With these," he optimistically instructed young Pfälzers, "the freest constitution in the world overcomes the hostile conflict between capital and work, between industrialist and employee."[41]

Heimatkunde, then, involved not just instruction through the example of local conditions but, more important, the projection onto the nation at large of a traditional, guild-inspired notion of communal harmony. Understanding the Heimat—"the foundation of the national state"—involved understanding one's own self and responsibilities in relation to the locality, the nation, and the world. "All the communal life of man," taught Böshenz, "is carried out in either the circle of the family or the community or the state— and each of these communities brings men face to face with their human fate, which is to be bound together for better and for worse by the bonds of love and loyalty, ready to protect and to help one another in the defense against unfriendly forces and in the fulfillment of common goals."[42] "State" or "civic" thinking, he concluded, was "eminently ethical."

The union of Heimatkunde with civics, and of ethical communalism with political education, was not confined to the education of young people in the Weimar Republic but extended into the new territory of adult education, or *freie Volksbildung*. The Volksbildung movement had begun before the war in efforts—first of the socialist adult education movement and later of a middle-class, reformist imitation of that movement—to bring advanced education and high culture to the working classes.[43] In the Weimar Republic, the adult education movement spread rapidly into all regions of Germany, reaching out to the peasantry and petty bourgeoisie as well as to its traditional constituency of urban workers.[44] One of the more important consequences of the new democratic constitution, the Volksbildung movement expressed for one observer the "right of all to a liberal education" and "assure[d] to all the citizens the opportunity of sharing in our cultural resources."[45] The "young Republic and the new trend in adult education were mutually necessary," wrote an activist in the movement, because "the urgent need for free and responsible citizens had to be met immediately" and could not wait for "a new generation . . . educated for the right combination of liberty and discipline."[46] "According to their right of self-determination, the people have taken their fate into their own hands and in the future want no more to abandon their political power to a highly privileged few," wrote a Pfälzer teacher and head of the new adult college in Kaiserslautern. The mission of

41. Ibid., pp. 125–26.
42. Ibid., p. 128.
43. Samuel and Thomas, *Education and Society*, pp. 135–37.
44. Ibid., pp. 140–47.
45. Alexander and Parker, *New Education*, pp. 215–19.
46. Fritz Borinski, cited in Samuel and Thomas, *Education and Society*, p. 140.

Volksbildung was to teach people about the "common cultural heritage," which would give a solid foundation to their new political rights and renewed "communal feeling."[47] The Weimar constitution itself specified in Article 148 that all levels of government should support adult education. Indeed, for a Pfälzer lawyer in Berlin, the Volksbildung movement had "finally made real the idea of the 'Great Coalition.'"[48]

The state did not, however, directly govern adult education; instead it provided financial and moral support to a variety of organizations, some affiliated with parties or religious groups, but many unaffiliated, or "frei," and gathered in regional coalitions like the Landesverband für freie Volksbildung (Regional League for Popular Education) in Bavaria and the Zentralstelle zur Förderung der Volksbildung und Jugendpflege (Central Office for the Promotion of Popular Education and Youth Activities) in Hesse. In the Pfalz, the Pfälzer League for Popular Education was founded in 1919 with Bavarian funds and democratic aspirations.[49] In the early 1920s it participated in local efforts to defend German culture against the invasion of French civilization, but the league also adopted a position critical of the German heritage of elite culture.[50] Its leaders saw the league as the organization of the future, suited to the "new democratic times" and ready to meet the challenge of the French occupation by appealing directly to the desire for Bildung in the people, the *Volksgenossen.*[51]

Adult education in the Pfalz, associated primarily with trade unionism, had had its beginnings in the industrial towns of Ludwigshafen and Kaiserslautern before the war, but the leaders of the new adult education movement, although mostly Social Democrats and Democrats, were determined to remain absolutely neutral in religious and political terms, as befitted the dignity of their task in a people's state.[52] Freie Volksbildung contrasted with state education, forced education, and any education that tried to impose particular opinions on other people. The league's members believed instead in rationality, open discourse, and above all *Sachlichkeit*, objectivity.[53] They believed also in the importance of shifting the ground of cultural education—

47. Ludwig Wagner, "Der Pfälzische Landesverband für Volksbildung," *Pfälzer Lehrerzeitung*, no. 26 (23 December 1919): 134.

48. Emil Dosenheimer, "Die Volksbildungsbestrebungen in der Pfalz," *PB* 8 (25 May 1928): 68.

49. See pp. 129 and 133 above.

50. Fitz, "Was will der Pfälzische Verband für Freie Volksbildung?" p. 71.

51. Ibid.; and Fitz, "Volksbildungsbestrebungen."

52. *Volksbildung in der Pfalz. 30 Jahre Kulturarbeit im Dienste unserer Heimat*, ed. Pfälzischer Verband für Freie Volksbildung (hereafter cited as PVFV) (Neustadt/Pfalz, 1952), pp. 12, 42; Fitz, "Pfälzischer Verband für freie Volksbildung," *PM–PH* 38/17 (1921): 89.

53. Fitz, "Was will der Pfälzische Verband für Freie Volksbildung?" p. 71.

and cultural defense—away from the artifacts of the privileged few to the artistry of the people, in both city and countryside. Consequently they advocated a decentralized organization—indeed, less an organization (even that sounded too regimented) than a spontaneous coming together of many efforts to promote "Pfälzer-German folk culture."[54]

Neither the league's decentralized structure nor its independence was achieved without a struggle. The Bavarian state commissioner for the Pfalz, Theodor von Winterstein, wanted adult education to be based in Speyer, from which cultural stronghold would go forth roving bands of professors delivering scholarly lectures across the region. In the Social Democratic newspaper of Ludwigshafen, league cofounder Dr. Hermann Fitz published a widely reprinted criticism of the plan, in which he argued for cultural promotion from "unten nach oben" (bottom to top) instead of "oben nach unten" (top to bottom). The Speyer plan, thought Fitz, would produce an organization "with the character of an Honoratioren club," consisting of "civil servants, professors, and moneybags [Geldgeber]." What Germany and the Pfalz needed was the active participation of "simple people" in their own further education, particularly in civics and history: "because in the realm of popular education in citizenship lies the most alarming hole in the spiritual armor of the German people."[55] The issue was finally decided at a public gathering, where the democratic model of adult education triumphed, albeit with some concessions to the advocates of scholarly lectures, and in July the league received 500,000 marks from Bavarian funds to "promote the lasting unity of the Pfalz, Bavaria, and the German Reich."[56]

Membership in the league consisted only of groups, one per locality, which supervised adult education courses and supported other activities deemed compatible with the league's goals.[57] Already in February 1920, the league and the city council of Kaiserslautern had founded a community college as a focal point for adult education in the Pfalz.[58] The league made pioneering efforts to establish public libraries all over the region, as well as

54. Ibid.; Fitz "Pfälzischer Verband," p. 89.

55. Fitz, "Volksbildungsbestrebungen"; the same article was reprinted in many newspapers in the Pfalz (see the newspaper clippings in the papers of the Staatskommissar für die Pfalz, BHStAM, MA 106019).

56. Winterstein to Bayerisches Staatsministerium des Innern (hereafter cited as BavMinInn) (14 January 1920), BHStAM, MA 107709; Fitz, "Zur Frage der Volksbildung in der Pfalz" (ca. December 1919), BHStAM, MA 106019; "Gründung einer freien Volksbildung Verein betreffend" (28 November 1919), BHStAM, MA 106019; "Bericht über die Besprechung der sachgemäßen Verwendung der 500.000 Mark: Volksbildungszwecke" (Mannheim, 13 June 1920), BHStAM, MA 106019; "Satzungen des Pfälz. Verbandes für Freie Volksbildung, e.V." (Neustadt, 1920).

57. "Satzungen," p. 3.

58. PVFV, Volksbildung in der Pfalz, pp. 14–15.

sending out a *Wandertheater* to bring German drama to the people.[59] It also published popular almanacs, sponsored concerts and poetry readings, organized folk costume and custom celebrations, led people to museums and historical sites—in short, engaged in all the activities falling under the rubric of Heimatpflege. "Under the unifying banner of love for Heimat," read the league statutes, the manifestations of a democratically shaped culture would gather.[60]

In its efforts to make local culture explicitly democratic and even republican, the Pfälzer League for Popular Education faced the opposition of those who read in the word *frei* an intemperate liberalism, godlessness, ethical neutrality, and anticommunitarianism. The Katholische Presseverein für Bayern (Catholic Press Association for Bavaria), a leading Volksbildung organization in Bavaria that claimed eight hundred chapters and over one hundred thousand members, objected in 1921 to the exclusive support that the *frei* Volksbildung movement of the Pfalz was receiving from the Bavarian government.[61] But against such criticism, the league always insisted that the word *frei* indicated neither liberalism nor anticlericalism but the pluralism of opinions and ideas in a democratic culture. "We represent a totally different kind of neutrality from that of the old liberal tendency," wrote its leader, Dr. Fitz, to the Catholics in 1921.[62] According to Fitz, "free" education involved an attempt to do more than either propagate one view of the world (as the Catholics did) or simply present opposing points of view (as, supposedly, liberals did); "freie Volksbildung" aimed rather at reaching some collective notion of "a true national-popular culture" through the consideration of all "worldviews and religions."[63]

Fitz called himself "a convinced follower" of the adult educational reformer and bureaucrat Robert von Erdberg, then administrator of Volksbildung in Prussia.[64] Erdberg's distinction between a "dispersed" Volksbildung and a "shaped" Volksbildung (formulated in the late nineteenth cen-

59. Eduard Feth, "Büchereiarbeit in der Pfalz" (lecture at the Volksbüchereikonferenz in Kaiserslautern, 20 October 1921), *PM–PH* 38/17 (1921): 155–58. The Wandertheater was eventually enormously successful, the first of its kind in Germany and the model for a number of later efforts like the Bavarian *Landesbühne*; see Spindler, *Handbuch der bayerischen Geschichte*, vol. 4, part 2, p. 1239.

60. "Satzungen," p. 3; Fitz, "Was will der Pfälzische Verband für Freie Volksbildung?" p. 72; Verein news, *PM–PH* 38/17 (1921): 89.

61. Müller of the Katholische Presseverein für Bayern e.V. to Kreisregierung der Pfalz (26 March 1921), BHStAM, MA 107924; same to BavMinUK (21 July 1921), BHStAM, MA 107924; same to Fitz of PVFV (22 July 1921, BHStAM, MA 107924. For its part the government was mostly concerned that educational efforts be centralized: Korn of BavMinUK to Kreisregierung der Pfalz, Kammer des Innern (8 September 1921) BHStAM, MA 107924.

62. Fitz to Müller (26 July 1921), BHStAM, MA 107924.

63. Ibid.

64. Ibid.; Samuel and Thomas, *Education and Society*, p. 140.

tury to clarify his own program of ethical, intuitive, and national values) was similar to that struck by Fitz between an empty neutrality and a productive toleration. And Fitz did at first succeed in gathering together Democrats, Social Democrats, and Communists, as well as Christian trade unionists and non-Bavarian Catholics, under the banner of a "shaped" Volksbildung.[65] Another founder of the Pfälzer league, the jurist Emil Dosenheimer, described the scene at the community college in Kaiserslautern, where "representatives of the most divergent religious confessions and worldviews— Jesuits and freethinkers—discussed religious problems from their own personal standpoint, without concealing their differences. . . . It is indeed a sign that true education is taking place," he continued, "when one sees this capacity and desire to understand and to respect the convictions of another." Volksbildung, he concluded, had brought together "people of different religious and political outlooks—making no distinction between bourgeois and worker—into one unanimous voice."[66]

Given the familiarly communal ring to these words, reminiscent of Böshenz's call for a harmonious citizenry, one is not surprised to find that the "leading and integrating" concept that would accomplish this transformation, indeed this transcendence, of conflict was Heimat: "We are all citizens, Pfälzers—and the Pfälzer loves his Heimat," intoned Dosenheimer. More, "we are all Germans, no matter to which estate we belong, to which party, religion, or worldview we confess."[67] And even though Dosenheimer's sketch of the community college may read more like a fantasy than a factual report, the aspiration to a unified diversity was there: in Heimat, Pfälzers found a commonality sufficiently open-ended to accommodate as many different opinions as would admit to loving their homeland. Like the national unifiers of the 1860s and 1870s, these adult educators sought to create a single entity out of fragmentation. But in the intervening half-century, the diagnosis for what caused fragmentation had changed from regional diversity as such to religious and political differences. To overcome them without "repressing" them was the challenge facing the new democracy, and that challenge could be met not only through the open discourse and Sachlichkeit of adult educational methods, but through a concentration on the "Bodenständige und Heimatliche" as well.[68]

The league's insistence on the achievement of freedom only within a community of people belongs, then, in the context of this German preoccupation with unity and fragmentation. Fitz believed that without "communal life"

65. Fitz to Kreisregierung der Pfalz, Kammer des Innern (22 July 1920), BHStAM, MA 106019; Fitz to Müller (16, 22 July 1921), BHStAM, MA 107924.
66. Dosenheimer, "Volksbildungsbestrebungen," p. 68.
67. Ibid.
68. Fitz to Müller (22 July 1921), BHStAM, MA 107924: Fitz, "Was will der Pfälzische Verband für Freie Volksbildung?" p. 71.

individual education and self-fulfillment were impossible: the chief goal of
freie Volksbildung should be "to develop individuals into full personalities
and into worthy members of the community of people." The whole man was
one who not only had the inner resources to understand his own potential
and survive disappointment but had also "found in his inner self a relation to
the commonality of his fellow creatures."[69] A common love for one's Heimat
was one such relation; in the Weimar Republic, one's citizenship or role in
the state—though poorly understood and less cultivated than Heimat
loyalties—joined with love for the Heimat as another "relation to the commonality of fellow creatures."

The league, as a consequence, set about the task of educating the German
people in public responsibility.[70] In 1923 the folksy almanac *Jäger aus Kurpfalz*, one of the chief means by which the league cultivated "Heimat thinking," included alongside its Heimat poetry and weather reports a "civic
chat" from Fitz.[71] In it he discussed the newly acquired rights and—just as
important for Fitz as for Böshenz—the newly expanded duties of the
citizen.[72] The failure to recognize these duties was in Fitz's opinion the
greatest threat to the Republic's survival, for it lent credence to the authoritarian assertion that the masses were not fit for self-rule. Obedience to the
laws of the nation was the essential duty of the citizen, even more crucial in a
democracy than in an "authoritarian state" because "one controls oneself."
Such self-control flowed not from enlightened self-interest but from a carefully cultivated altruism; a citizen, then, was to be contrasted to an indi-
vidualist and a particularist.[73] Fitz's civic education was, like Böshenz's,
essentially ethical, an instruction in democratic morality. "Morals," he
argued, "are a cultural good, a commonly held and pursued good, that
makes possible the flourishing of human life." They derived from the restraint of a natural, but destructive, egoism. Without that restraint—
voluntary in a *Volksstaat*—there would be no community, no culture, no human existence. In any community, from the family to the workplace, the
town, and the state, the will of the people must be directed "to the preserva-

69. Fitz, "Was will der Pfälzische Verband für Freie Volksbildung?" pp. 71–72.
70. Fitz, "Volksbildungsbestrebungen."
71. *Bezirksamtmann* Dr. Hermann Fitz, "Eine staatsbürgerliche Plauderei," *Der Jäger aus
Kurpfalz* (1923), pp. 80–84.
72. He divided these rights, conventionally, into "positive" and "negative" ones: the latter
were freedoms of religion, assembly, speech, thought, person, economic conduct, and press; the
former, representing the state as "union of free citizens," were equality before the law, equal
participation in the suffrage, and equal claim to protection from attack. He perceived the most
change from before 1918 in the realm of positive rights (ibid., pp. 80–81).
73. In the words of Prussian minister of education C. H. Becker, who in 1922, shortly after
the murder of Walter Rathenau, had pushed through a program of civic education in the schools
and universities, "this kind of learning will be our way from individualism and particularism to
a true citizenly character" (cited by Düwell, "Staat und Wissenschaft," p. 47).

tion and the promotion of the whole in which each lives." In conclusion, Fitz directed the attention of his readers to Article 163 of the Weimar constitution: "Each German has the moral duty so to direct his intellectual and physical powers that without damage to his personal freedom the good of the whole will be promoted." "Can you, reader, call yourself a citizen in this sense? Have you deserved the rights of our *Volksstaat?*" he asked Pfälzers.[74] The answer was not self-evident in 1922; eleven more years of democracy would make it hardly more so.

Thus, a Heimat education brought the singularity of one's immediate experience of the world together with the diversity and generality of greater horizons and grander purposes. The point of such self-understanding was to emphasize the concepts of belonging and commonality, through them teaching responsibility. For the Weimar educators, one's Heimat was the most basic component of identity: "Ours is the education of Germans to be Germans, the rooting of the German individual characters in the German folk character," declared an author in the *Zeitschrift für die Bildung* in 1925; "from the narrow Heimat to the German people and from the German people to the German state, that is the way our youth should go."[75]

Although incompatible with classic liberalism, such attitudes did not necessarily preclude either equality, toleration, or self-government, as Böshenz's textbook and Fitz's chat sought to demonstrate. The civic teachings of Heimat-minded educators in the Weimar Republic made up for any philosophical inconsistencies by their sincerity in searching for some source of common identity; they should not be faulted for their consequent failure to encourage individual dissent—an intellectual commodity that in any case seemed plentiful enough to contemporaries. The Weimar Republic had its vigorous opponents as well as its reasoned advocates, the *Vernunftsrepublikaner*; what it lacked, what Fitz was trying to produce, was passionate supporters, people committed intellectually and emotionally to a "people's state." Fitz's and Böshenz's constant talk of the whole man, of community and communal feeling, coupled as it was with their enthusiasm for the Weimar constitution, makes sense only in light of such a mission.

The compatibility of Heimat and democracy also revealed itself in the activities of Pfälzer Heimat associations. For the duration of the Weimar period they, too, bestowed a degree of legitimacy on the government, if only by proving that Heimat loyalties and Heimat patriotism could flourish in the Republic. The field of Heimat history was a case in point. Recounting the misdeeds of the French took up much Heimat-historical energy during the 1920s, but local historians also discovered the Pfalz's own democratic tradition. The black-gold-and-red flag of the new Republic had, after all, once

74. Fitz, "Staatsbürgerliche Plauderei," p. 84.
75. Cited in Emmerich, *Germanische Volkstumsideologie*, pp. 135–6.

been raised over a Pfälzer castle (Hambach in 1832), and Pfälzers were inclined to interpret contemporary German republicanism as the outgrowth of some locally cultivated variety.[76] At a well-attended lecture in Speyer in 1923, for instance, Professor Hermann Schreibmüller argued that nationalism and republicanism had long been allied in the Pfalz in such figures as the Hambachers Johann Wirth and Philipp Siebenpfeiffer (this lecture, incidentally, contributed to the French decision to expel him from the Pfalz later that year).[77] The Heimat novelist August Becker, locally celebrated since the late nineteenth century for his romantic stories of Pfälzer customs and people, was suddenly discovered to have been a "forty-eighter" who remembered as a young boy hearing the townspeople cry, "Up with freedom! Freedom in our land!"[78] There was also an upsurge in public ceremonies commemorating municipal charters granted some six or seven hundred years earlier; the precedent may not have been as apt as planners wished, but as in Böshenz's textbook, democracy and self-government were celebrated as old German traditions, to be welcomed and respected as such.[79]

Consolidating this alliance between Heimat and democracy, the Social Democratic party of the Pfalz founded its own Heimat newspaper in 1925, comfortably named *Bei uns daheim* (At Home with Us), which published histories of Pfälzer socialists and popular uprisings.[80] What was notable about the party's effort in the field of Heimat history was its participation in a recognizable mainstream. The same authors—Daniel Häberle, Ernst Christmann, Kurt Baumann, Albert Zink, Lina Staab, and the redoubtable Albert Becker, to name but a few—that appeared in *Bei uns daheim* appeared in *Pfälzisches Museum–Pfälzische Heimatkunde* as well. The same unmistakable Heimat mixture of sentimental poetry, folklore, and popular science accompanied the local histories. In 1929, the grandfather of Heimat history in the Pfalz, Theodor Zink, formally bestowed his approval on the "Heimat newspaper" *Bei uns daheim* for having brought "the ideals that we all try to serve into circles that heretofore were torn out of the Heimat earth, uprooted, but nevertheless possessed of an unfulfilled longing for the unattainable values of the things of the Heimat." The benefits of the undertaking were not confined

76. Albert Becker, "Das tolle Jahr der weinseligen Anarchie," *PB*, no. 5 (1929): 64ff.

77. *PM–PH* 40/19 (1923): 52.

78. The anti-French resonance of this phrase should not drown out its democratic overtones. See his story "Der Freiheitsbaum," and accompanying biographical sketch, in *Der Jäger aus Kurpfalz 1928*, pp. 28ff.; *PB*, nos. 20 (25 December 1927): 244–45 and 5 (25 May 1928): 71.

79. See, e.g., the accounts of the *Stadtsjubiläum* of Kaiserslautern in *PM–PH* 43/22 (1926): 245, and of Neustadt in *PM–PH* 42/21 (1925): 323.

80. These were contained in a regular section, "Kulturgeschichtliches aus alter und neuer Zeit," *Bei uns daheim*, Heimat beilage of the *Pfälzische Post* 1–8 (1925–32). In 1929, for instance, the articles addressed the subjects "Ferdinand Lassalle and the Pfalz" (Kurt Baumann, *Bei uns daheim* 5 [21 August 1929]: 22) and "Proletarian Currents in the Pfälzer Movement of 1848/49" (*Bei uns daheim* 5 [6 February 1929]: 3).

to workers but were mutual, indeed, Pfalz-wide. Reading the paper, Zink asserted, "I have been able for the first time to look into a world that most of us know only by hearsay. In their sections of stories, sketches, and tales they have brought together, so far as I can see, the best of our Heimat talents; in no other paper have so many been combined so fruitfully."[81]

Heimat history had always tended toward social history, certainly more so than its academic counterpart in the German universities; in the Weimar period this tendency mirrored the aspirations of the new political order to egalitarian representation. A historical subject need claim neither power, wealth, nor genius (with which the Pfalz was ill-supplied) to attract the attention of Heimat historians, but only Pfalztum, the quality of "typical Pfälzerness." In 1925, for instance, teacher and Heimatler Ludwig Eid celebrated the lives and personalities of two "men of the people," Aloys Weisenburger and Johannes Schiller, for embodying "the high excellence of the folk character."[82]

Indeed, the more Heimat history turned away from a celebration of Bavarian dukes and their dynastic concerns, the more indistinguishable it became from its close cousin Volkskunde, which reached a peak of popularity and intellectual legitimacy in the Weimar Republic.[83] Closely tied to the teaching of Heimatkunde in the schools, Volkskunde took as its subject the manners and mores of the "people." And like Heimatkunde, it represented for many of its practitioners "a breath of fresh air" in the desiccated academic halls of "intellectualism" and "rational culture."[84] It promised to unite the modern call for "a youthfully fresh culture" with the equally strong impulse to seek out the past for its revelations of the "German spirit": "Like a tree that sends its roots deep beneath it to acquire strength and life," wrote one Weimar practitioner of Volkskunde, "so do we seek life forces out of the past, while our gaze is nevertheless on the future. . . . [Our] goal is a culture that is rooted in our people and has as its centerpoint the Heimat."[85] For Albert Becker, Volkskunde was the academic fulfillment of Heimatkunde: "it leads from the geographically bound to the general-human."[86] Inextricable from other contemporary intellectual strivings for categorization and synthesis,

81. *Pfälzische Lehrerzeitung*, no. 45 (7 November 1929).

82. "Männer des Volkes," *PM–PH* 42/21 (1925): 155. The enduring popularity of Liselotte von der Pfalz can be attributed to this same tendency in Heimat historical consciousness to celebrate people for their Pfalztum (see also Chapter 3 above).

83. Albert Becker, "Um die Seele des Volkes und der Heimat: Neues vom Arbeitsfeld der Volkskunde in Deutschland," *PM–PH* 47/26 (1930): 263.

84. E. Fehrle, "Zur Stellung der Volkskunde in der Gegenwart," in Manz, Mitterweiser, and Zeiss, *Heimatarbeit und Heimatforschung*, p. 74.

85. Ibid., pp. 75–76.

86. "Um die Seele des Volkes und der Heimat: Gedanken zur Geschichte der Pfälzer volkskundlichen Bestrebungen," *PM–PH* 42/21 (1925): 285.

from Karl Jaspers to Werner Sombart, Volkskunde was for Becker the climax of the collective intellectual history of the last two centuries. Through its examination of the intersections between high and low culture, one would arrive at a definition of the Volk that could encompass individual creativity, high cultural development, and the ineffable, associative spirit of the collectivity—a goal shared, for instance, by Ludwig Eid in his admiring account of talented "men of the people."

For the average member of a Heimat association, however, Volkskunde provided an excuse to dwell on everyday phenomena and was thus eminently suited to the cheerful self-absorption of the Heimat turn-of-mind. The subject of the Pfälzer personality became a virtual obsession of popular Heimat writings. Albert Pfeiffer, a severe critic of the excesses of popularized folklore, considered it a "fad" riddled with spurious claims to authenticity.[87] Pfeiffer was surely right in seeing that the subject gave even the lowliest representative of Pfälzer culture license to expressive indulgence. In a rare congruence of subject and object, these Pfälzer self-analysts irreverently described their irreverence—or directness, playfulness, feistiness, open-mindedness, whatever seemed appropriate.[88] More than that, the methods of Heimatkunde that were pushed in popular courses and textbooks of the 1920s represented a do-it-yourself attitude toward local history.[89] In 1923, the Pfälzer League for Popular Education came out with a book entitled *How I Research the History of My Heimat*. A Badenese Heimatler, Michael Walter, promised in his *Brief Guide for the Heimat Researcher* to help the beginner avoid "detours and dead ends" and to "incorporate him into the whole Heimat movement."[90] Heimat activists encouraged women and peasants to become conscious of their irreplaceable knowledge of Heimat traditions and folklore.[91] The family itself became an object of research, as well as a method for understanding one's own personal ties to the Heimat, that is, to the commonality of all families.[92]

87. Albert Pfeiffer, "Der Pfälzer Character," *PM–PH* 39/18 (1922): 64–65.

88. For a good selection, see *25 Jahre "Pfälzische Rundschau."*

89. See, e.g., the "heimatkundliche Kurs" given by the Verein Historisches Museum der Pfalz in 1924 ("Vereinsnachrichten," *PM–PH* 41/20 [1924]: 88), or the "Volksbildungskurs-Ferienkurs für Heimatkunde" given by the Pfälzische Verband für Freie Volksbildung every year starting in 1921 ("Auszug aus dem Reisetagebuch des Regierungspräsidenten" [1921], BHStAM, MA 108372).

90. *PM–PH* 40/19 (1923): 103–4; M. Walter, *Kleiner Führer für Heimatforscher. Winke, Stoffe und Hilfsmittel* (Karlsruhe, 1924), p. 2.

91. See, e.g., Hedwig Buller-Hoefler, "Frau und Heimat," in Manz, Mitterweiser, and Zeiss, *Heimatarbeit und Heimatforschung*, pp. 30–34; and F. J. Ehleuter, "Wie ein Bauer Heimatarbeit treiben kann und soll, und wie ich dazu kam," in ibid., pp. 66–73.

92. In 1921, the Heimat magazine *Pfälzisches Museum–Pfälzische Heimatkunde* established a regular section on *Familienforschung* (*PM–PH* 38/17 [1921]: 148); see also the March/April issue of 1925 devoted to family research, esp. Dr. August Sperl, "Die Sinn der Familienforschung," *PM–PH* 42/21 (1925): 43–44; and E. L. Antz, "Familienkunde," ibid., p. 45.

The lively interest in Mundart or dialect, the speech of the people, epitomized the folkloric egalitarianism of this period. Dialect literature and poetry, long a haven for sentimentality as well as a measure of vulgarity, flourished as a truly popular art form, appropriate to the "now-current democratic sensibilities."[93] "No part of our German Fatherland has so much dialect poetry as the Pfalz," boasted an editor of *Pfälzisches Museum–Pfälzische Heimatkunde*. To preserve it, to encourage new production of it, and to make it available to the rest of Germany became a major task of the Heimat associations.[94]

Of course, the affinities between the Heimat turn-of-mind and democracy did not necessarily translate into enthusiasm for the particular government of the Weimar Republic. The folkloric activities of the 1920s had no such explicitly partisan content. Pursued largely irrespective of political implications, their political reputation has subsequently derived from an antiliberalism and antiparliamentarianism attributed to them by the genealogy-building propagandists of Nazism.[95] But the Nazi interpretation says little about the actual role of Heimatkunde and folkloric enthusiasms in provincial societies. Moreover, if anti-Weimarism was all there was to this folkoric activity, what then is one to make of a group of costume and dance enthusiasts of the 1920s who dubbed themselves "the Hambachers" and traveled around the Pfalz performing "revived" versions of folk celebration?[96] Their deliberate identification with a local landmark most prominently known for a nineteenth-century democratic demonstration betrayed an almost naive readiness to fuse onto the serious questions of government in the Weimar Republic an all-embracing sentimentality, sinister only in retrospect—and perhaps not even then. Similarly, the Social Democrats' enthusiastic adoption of folklore into their festive occasions reflected both their effort to participate in a mainstream of German popular culture and, it follows, the preoccupation of that mainstream with Volkskunde, the cultivation of popular traditions.[97] Folkloric activities would strengthen "feelings of togetherness" and "consciousness of a common German fate," according to the Reich Committee for Socialist Cultural Work, thereby creating a true *Volksgemeinschaft*—a true national community.[98]

The Pfälzer preoccupation with the United States of America in the 1920s

93. Otto Mausser, "Die Mundarten der Pfalz," *Pfalz-Bayerischer Heimgarten*, p. 67.
94. *PM–PH* 38/17 (1921): 126.
95. See Chapter 7 below.
96. "Die Hambacher," *PM–PH* 41/20 (1924): 69.
97. See, e.g., the Pfälzer preparations for a *Kulturwoche* in Leipzig in 1924, sponsored by the Reichsausschuß für sozialistische Bildungsarbeit and devoted in part to the "echt volkskündlich" (BavMinUK [July 1924], BHStAM, MK 15558).
98. Ibid. It is worth noting that the vocabulary of a Volksgemeinschaft was not the exclusive property of the radical right.

reflected better than anything the tentative steps of the Heimat community toward democratic consciousness and republican sensibilities. Early in the decade, local interest in America had tended to take the form of an appeal (encouraged by the Bavarian and German governments) for help against the French.[99] Heimat clubs in Germany sent publications and information to German societies in America, like the American and German Federation for Culture and Commerce, which in turn raised money and lobbied for political support for the occupied region.[100] In 1920, for instance, a German-American society in New York sponsored a money-raising "Volksfest in the manner of the Dürkheimer Wurstmarkt [a celebrated Pfälzer fall festival]" in Astoria Park. Back in Germany, the Pfälzers claimed to be heartened: "In our times," wrote a *Wald-Heil!* editorialist, "when the hard-pressed German people stand alone in the world, we find consolation and good cheer only in our inner connection to the Fatherland and the Heimat. . . . We must never forget that we are Germans and in the Pfalz also Pfälzers, and this we cannot forget as long as there are still Pfälzers in the rest of the world, standing strong and true to their identity [*Volkstum*]."[101]

But from the outset, the act of cultivating ties to America—a kind of journey of the collective Pfälzer imagination—created new meaning, new significance for the quality of Pfälzerness itself.[102] The simple fact that there were "Pfälzer-Americans" reinforced the primary conceit of Heimat cultivation, that Pfalztum preceded and indeed transcended the mere political boundaries of the region: many Pfälzer-Americans were, after all, descendants of people who had left the Rhineland long before the Pfalz as such existed.[103] But the most important extension of meaning that the American connection realized was toward an essentially democratic definition of Pfalztum. America became, in the frequent accounts of emigration to America,

99. The Oberrheinische Nachrichtenbüro—an arm of the Staatskommissariat für die Pfalz—provided "objective" (i.e., not French-sponsored) information on the events in Germany to German-American newspapers; the Bavarian government also collected and sometimes published letters from Americans incensed about French occupational practices, especially the use of black troops (Bayerisches Staatsministerium des Äussern [hereafter cited as BavMinAus], misc. papers, BHStAM, MA 108326).

100. "Vereinsnachrichten," *PM–PH* 38/17 (1921): 145; Robert Paul Sachs, Präsident des Amerikanischen und Deutschen Bundes für Kultur und Wirtschaft, misc. papers, BHStAM, MA 108326.

101. "Pfälzer in Amerika," *WH*, no. 9 (8 September 1920): 4.

102. On the role of "journeys" in creating meaning, see Victor Turner, *Dramas, Fields, and Metaphors: Symbolic Action in Human Society* (Ithaca, N.Y., 1974), esp. chaps. 5 and 6.

103. As Albert Becker put it, "Political borders cannot define the limits of culture"—though in the case of the "Pfälzer character" that is precisely what they did do ("Von Pfälzerlands Natur und Geschichte," *PM–PH* 44/23 [1927]: 59). The extension of the term *Pfälzer* indefinitely and imprecisely into the Rhenish past led to such meaningless statistics as that two to three times as many Pfälzers lived in Pennsylvania as in the Pfalz (cited by Ludwig Eid in *Pfälzer Volk*)—meaningless, that is, only *out* of the context of the cultivation of local identity.

the nation most expressive of the German soul.[104] And America was a democracy. Early Pfälzers in America, of whom much was made in the 1920s, had also been democrats: from Nikolaus Herchheimer, a Revolutionary War general, to the dukes Christian and Philipp Wilhelm von Forbach, who also participated in the "North American war for Freedom," even to Oskar Straus, a Jewish-American businessman and public servant whose Pfälzer forefathers had been active in the 1848–49 revolution and who left considerable money to a Pfälzer charity when he died in 1926.[105] The identification of the Pfalz with the United States through its favorite sons reached a kind of apotheosis in 1930, when the Heimat researcher Daniel Häberle laboriously uncovered the Pfälzer ancestry of then-President Herbert Hoover, revealing him to be the first American president of German descent.[106]

America was also prosperous and hard-working, qualities that Pfälzers liked to claim and, in the 1920s, wished desperately to recover. When in 1929 the industrial city of Ludwigshafen celebrated its seventy-fifth birthday, a Heimat newspaper compared its rapid growth to that of the United States: both had a "healthy moral center"—which accounted for their success—a soberness of purpose, and a productive cooperation between industry and learning, technology and art.[107] Indeed, the incorporation of the United States into the world of the Pfälzer Heimat can serve as an analogue for the whole ambiguous role of democracy and the Weimar Republic in the Heimat imagination. A middle ground, where the United States could appear as something other than a behemoth of unrestrained modernism and the Weimar Republic something more than an unsatisfactory and un-German compromise, sometimes, for a few moments, came into view behind the fogs of social resentment and political extremism.

Had democracy, equality, citizenship, and civic responsibility been the only or even the most prominent of "Heimat thoughts" (*Heimatgedanken*) during the Weimar period, Fitz's vision of a regionally rooted republican consensus in Germany might have been realized. But posed sometimes in conjunction

104. An incomplete list of emigration articles in the Heimat press would have to begin with the November/December issue of *PM–PH* 39/18 (1922), devoted to Pfälzer emigration to America; see also *PM–PH* 41/20 (1924): 137; *PB*, nos. 3 (1 February 1925): 36; 5 (March 1929): 64; 5 (March 1931): 52; 1 (January 1932): 3; *PM–PH* 45/24 (1929): 162–64.

105. Daniel Häberle, "Die Heimat der Familie Herchheimer und des Bauerngenerals Niklaus Herchheimer festgestellt," *PM–PH* 43/22 (1926): 90; *PM–PH* 39/18 (1922): 169; "Oskar S. Straus," *PM–PH* 43/22 (1926): 244.

106. Hoover apparently did acknowledge the kinship; "Dank des Präsidenten Hoover an Professor Dr. Häberle," *PM–PH* 47/26 (1930): 43. He also received an invitation to participate in a Berlin celebration of the "liberation" of the Rhineland; needless to say, he declined it. See *PB*, nos. 2 (January 1930): 22 and 4 (February 1930): 45.

107. "75-Jahre Ludwigshafen-am-Rhein," *Die Pfalz am Rhein: Touristen-Zeitung* 12 (May 1929): 202.

with and sometimes at odds with a Heimat egalitarianism was the problem of cultural excellence and spiritual renewal. *Heimatpolitik*, like *Kulturpolitik* on the national level, had addressed itself after the war to the dual problem of consolidating republicanism and preventing the decline of the "cultural nation," the commonality of aspiration to that most German of qualities, Bildung.[108] Unlike Kulturpolitik, however, no explicit Heimatpolitik really existed, only an ill-defined effort by Bavarian cultural bureaucrats and their allies to encourage Heimat activism. "We must reawaken pride in our cultural community," said a Prussian official at a meeting of the representatives of the occupied territories in 1921: "pride not just in our technical superiority, but deeply within, where the holiest and most valuable goods of humanity dwell. . . . Let us infuse the German republic with the German spirit and the German soul, and only then can they continue to exist!"[109]

The French were not the only enemies of German culture in the 1920s. French civilization did often play the role of whipping boy, standing in for all the absent or abstract modernisms that threatened to undermine the foundations of the cultural nation. Materialism was the chief problem, though to a much greater extent than they themselves acknowledged Heimat activists participated in material culture, carrying advertisements in their newspapers, praising industry and commerce, savoring the Pfälzer wines and *Saumagen* (a local delicacy, similar to the Scottish haggis) along with the rest of the masses—in short, selling Heimat on the market of modern material society. Nevertheless, in the "fiery struggle of materialism with humanism," most Heimat clubs and their members would have placed themselves firmly on the side of humanism, idealism, and the cultivation of the inner man.[110] And along with materialism came a host of lesser vices to be resisted, from emotional depression and spiritual demoralization to trashy and porno-

---

108. Bildung, of course, means more than mere education; it means cultivation of the intellect, the sensibilities and emotions, and the soul or spirit; it refers to a consensus on how that could be achieved, through extensive formal education, through the absorption of a body of literature and history. Unlike cultivation in the English sense, which involves some notion of good breeding, "gentle birth," and an internalized set of manners and mores, Bildung was available to anyone who could obtain the education and so, under a democratically minded regime, to all the people—potentially. On the German concept of Bildung, see Fritz K. Ringer, *The Decline of the German Mandarins: The German Academic Community 1890–1933* (Cambridge, Mass., 1969), esp. pp. 6–13, 86–89. On national Kulturpolitik, see Düwell, "Staat und Wissenschaft," pp. 31–32.

109. Minutes from meeting in the (Prussian) Ministerium für Wissenschaft, Kunst, und Volksbildung, Berlin (15 February 1921), BHStAM, MK 15557.

110. Albert Becker, "Das Ende einer altpfälzischen Lateinschule," *PM–PH* 43/22 (1926): 141. According to Becker, the struggle had begun already in the mid–nineteenth century, when an attempt had been made to turn the *Lateinschule* into a *Gewerbeschule*, or trade school. In 1926, finally, the school "that had survived even during the terrible times of the Thirty Years' War" succumbed to the spirit of the age.

graphic literature. In April 1922, the Literary Association of the Pfalz warned that despite the relative success of its most recent Heimat evening, "many who should participate still keep their distance: the souls of even the best in our midst are depressed, and rightly so. . . . But let us not allow total pessimism to rule," the editorialist continued; "no one who wishes to take part in the spiritual rebuilding of Germany ought to neglect the task of combating the greedy drive of the masses toward cheap entertainment."[111]

Religion provided the most obvious avenue to German souls, and Heimat enthusiasts did not ignore its importance in maintaining German culture—indeed, a priest or minister was the mainstay of many a Heimat association. In his celebrated *Rembrandt als Erzieher* (1891), Julius Langbehn had stated that "the wine of religion is best savored in the chalice of the Heimat"; attempting to extend this metaphor further some twenty-five years later, a Bavarian cleric added: "the taps through which knowledge of the Heimat flows are the church, the cemetery, the chapel, and the sacred year of festivals and customs."[112] A local priest should consider Heimatpflege part of his sacred duty, this writer continued, lest drinking halls replace houses of God in shaping the people's spiritual lives.[113] From the start, the Bavarian officials concerned with supporting German culture in the Pfalz included in their package of subsidy a generous grant to religious institutions—Catholic, Protestant, or Jewish, according to population distribution.[114] In 1928, a memorandum on "economic and cultural emergency in the threatened western border regions and in the occupied region" declared that "spiritual distress" had turned people ever more toward the churches, which as "monuments" to Heimat culture and spirit were eligible for state aid.[115]

But the advocates of spiritual renewal through Heimat cultivation found in the nurturing of local identity reason enough for their activities. Though its boundaries may have been fully physical, Pfälzerness, like the Heimat feelings that went with it, was a state of mind or, as the Germans more often put it, of heart and of soul. "Heimat work is educating work," wrote a Bavarian Heimatler, "and the Heimatler is a missionary, whose Bible are his Heimat notebooks, out of which he creates the spirit and draws his

111. "Vereinsnachrichten des Literarischen Vereins der Pfalz," *WH* 7 (April 1922): 8.

112. Dr. Peter Dörfler, "Der Pfarrer und der Heimatgedanke," in Manz, Mitterweiser, and Zeiss, *Heimatarbeit und Heimatforschung*, pp. 50–52.

113. Ibid.

114. BavMinUK, "Übersichten: Reichs und Landesmittel für kulturelle Fürsorge im besetzten Gebiet," BHStAM, MK 15533.

115. BavMinAus, "Denkschriften der Länder Preussen, Bayern, Hessen, Baden und Oldenburg über die wirtschaftliche und kulturelle Notlage in den bedrängten westlichen Grenzgebiete und im besetzten Gebiet" (1928), BHStAM, MA 107971; in addition, Domkapitular [and Landtag member] Hildenbrand to Ministerpräsident Held (17 December 1924), BHStAM, MA 106032.

strength."[116] The Pfälzer Heimat was not just a place but an *Erbe*, an inheritance, on the preservation of which the Heimat activists staked the moral health of their nation. Reflecting on the widespread feeling of cultural, as well as political and economic, crisis, one contemporary observer wrote of a "general longing for inwardness and profundity" in the people, who naturally turn to the "creative treasures of the Heimat" to recover their "cultural pride."[117] For the Pfälzer bureaucrat and naturalist Theodor Künkele, the contemplation of localness, especially local nature, would assure the Germans of spiritual victory over hostile forces: "Joy in nature and in its immutable truth and noble purity, investigation of its being in its most general and most particular . . . manifestations can elevate us above all the wretchedness of our humiliation in Germany and our misfortunes in the Pfalz and make us strong in love for the Heimat, in belief in our people, and in the hope of a peace not of the sword and of force but rather of the spirit and of all humanity."[118]

For others, the inheritance of the Heimat was chiefly historical and traditional. To rediscover the many-sidedness of German history and folklore was to keep alive a consciousness of German worth. In 1927, a Pfälzer historian wrote that "within the unity of the nation" the "cultural progress" of a people depended on the quality of its understanding of its past; historical study had to address itself to the "individual character [*Eigenart*] of lands and peoples, the particularities of the Heimat."[119] Similarly for a school official in Passau, "the forces for awakening the spirit of healthy progress" lay in "Heimat history": "it is the task of the Heimatler to reach into economic life with an educational purpose, directing men's minds toward the spiritual necessities of life." Against the increasingly uprooted character of men's lives, the Heimatler "must create a tradition"; he must ensure "that the Heimat is *felt* as the center of the cares, the sorrows, and the struggles of past generations. . . . For then, out of the history of the Heimat will grow pride in the Heimat and loyalty to the land."[120]

The first group to try to establish a new context for the preservation of Pfälzer culture was, not surprisingly, the local adult education league. At its founding in 1919, the league's leaders declared its main objective to be the

116. Wilhelm Leidel, "Von der bayerischen Ostmark," in Manz, Mitterweiser, and Zeiss, *Heimatarbeit und Heimatforschung*, p. 99.

117. Dr. Anton Weiher, Vorsitzender der Pfälzischen Verband für Freie Volksbildung, "Besatzung und Volksbildung," *Dokumente aus dem Befreiungskampf der Pfalz*, p. 152; the same sentiments are echoed by Josef Oswald, "Bayerische Heimatbewegung und -forschung zwischen den zwei Weltkriegen," *Historisches Jahrbuch* 72 (1953): 604.

118. Theodor Künkele, "Der innere Wert naturkundlicher Arbeit in der Pfalz," *PM-PH* 38/17 (1921): 1.

119. Fr. Jung, "Die historische Wissenschaft und die Heimatpflege," *Hundertjahr Feier der Gründung des Historischen Vereins der Pfalz* (Speyer, 1927), pp. 6–7.

120. Leidel, "Von der bayerischen Ostmark," pp. 96–99.

"improvement and deepening of the intellectual, artistic, and moral cultivation of the Pfälzer people"; to this end it would become "an intellectual and
creative center" for the Pfalz, helping to save "the rich treasures of the Pfälzer spirit from their disastrous fragmentation."[121] It pledged to "bring the
good book to as broad a cross-section of people as possible." The league's
own "Advisory Board for the Discouragement of Trashy Writing" would
seek to elevate the moral and artistic taste of the population, providing classic and Heimat literature as sounder alternatives.[122]

But the league received little support from the traditional guardians of
Pfälzer culture in Speyer. Hermann Fitz had from the start defended his
project against the charge of purveying "inflated half-cultivation" for mass
consumption. He asserted that Bildung ought not to be the exclusive domain
of an "Honoratioren-Club" of "civil servants, professors, and moneybags."
Government officials, eager for a truly popular offensive against the French,
seem to have agreed with him; in any case, they gave the organization broad
support.[123] But governmental fiat could not so easily overcome the tension
between equality and excellence that remained central to local discussions of
culture, nor did it intend to undermine the prestige of Speyer as the capital of
the Pfalz.[124] Consequently, government policy never tried to shift the balance
of cultural power that had obtained since the 1870s. A select group of the
educated middle class continued to dominate local cultural institutions. The
sociological character of the region's scholarly associations, for instance, did
not change significantly after the war. In 1918, the membership of the
Historical Association consisted of a reasonably broad range of middle-class
professionals, businessmen, and white-collar workers, but moving up the
hierarchy of the association the atmosphere became increasingly rarefied,
until at the very top, in the ruling committee, one encountered only the highest Bavarian officials, the wealthiest businessmen, the most distinguished
academics of the region.[125] The pattern repeated itself in the association supporting the Historical Museum.

But then, neither by design nor by purpose were these meant to be popu-

121. Dosenheimer, "Volksbildungsbestrebungen," p. 66; Fitz, "Pfälzischer Verband," p. 89.
122. Dosenheimer, "Volksbildungsbestrebungen," p. 67; "Vereinsnachrichten," *PM–PH*
39/18 (1922): 303.
123. Ludwig Wagner, "Pfälzischer Landesverband"; Fitz, "Volksbildungsbestrebungen."
124. Out of practical necessity, the Verband itself soon sought out the support of the "civil
servants, professors, and moneybags," gradually winning over to the cause of popular education
the head of the new Pfälzische Landesbibliothek and the editor of the leading Heimat publication, *Pfälzisches Museum–Pfälzische Heimatkunde*; see Reismüller, "Die Pfälzische Landesbibliothek," p. 11; BavMinUK to Staatskommissar der Pfalz, BHStAM, MA 107924.
125. "Verzeichnis der Mitglieder des Historischen Vereins der Pfalz nach dem Stande vom
1 October 1918" (Speyer, 1918). The organization membership stood at 1,130. Of the 38 *Sach-
waltern* in the localities, most were higher-level civil servants, mayors, and school directors
("Vereinsnachrichten," *PM–PH* 38/17 [1921]: 125).

lar organizations. More the patrons of culture than its creators or consumers, the historical and artistic associations of the Pfalz combined small numbers with large influence. All Pfälzer museums and most Pfälzer writing and research went on under their auspices and those of the churches and schools from which they drew their support.[126] In 1924, moreover, the Bavarian government renewed its support of high culture in the region, in effect tightening the grip of Speyer and its educated elite over cultural life in the Pfalz.

The Bavarian government reentered Pfälzer cultural affairs after the crisis year of 1923 both to continue the rhetorical battle against the French and to combat a pervasive sense of cultural depression in the Pfalz, which threatened—or so the Bavarians thought—the political stability of the region.[127] The state of the local economy was alarming enough. District President Mathéus reported that it "was totally beaten down": large industries he thought could eventually recover on their own, but the middle ranks of agriculture and trade would need considerable help.[128] At his and the government's urging, the Landtag in February 1925 approved the appropriation of 10 million marks to combat both cultural and economic decline.[129] These *Pfalzhilfe* funds were to be divided among individuals, communities, cooperatives, and firms in the form of readily available, variable-term loans, the interest on which would be given outright to cultural organizations in the region. The district president of the Pfalz, together with representatives of the local assembly, trade unions, and farmers' and independent businessmen's organizations, would extend the loans; the Bavarian Ministry of Culture, together with the State Commission for the Pfalz, would distribute the interest.[130]

Within only four years, the conflicts inherent in the scheme had manifested themselves, but in the meantime this balance between indebtedness and outright subsidy seemed a brilliant solution for the Bavarian govern-

126. The cultural preeminence of Speyer and its elite comes through clearly, for instance, in the account of Prof. Ludwig Fränkel, "Pfälzische Kleinstadt-Kultur," *Das Bayerland: Illustrierte Zeitschrift für Bayerns Volk und Land* (1921): 145–46.

127. On the reorganization of the Pfalzkommissariat and Wappes's warnings for the future, see the exchanges of 1924 in the BavMinAus, BHStAM, MA 107712, esp. Wappes to BavMinAus, (8 August 1924), "Betr. Die Neugestaltung der nationalen Abwehr in der Pfalz und für die Pfalz," BHStAM, MA 107712; also "Ministerialratssitzung" (23 January 1925), BHStAM, MK 15530, in which the prime minister held forth on the "special importance to be laid upon the cultivation of cultural and intellectual ties between Bavaria and the Pfalz for its great political significance in the strengthening of the feeling of belonging together."

128. "Niederschrift über die Sitzung im Staatsministerium des Äussern" (16 January 1925), BHStAM, MA 106032.

129. Bayerischer Landtag, 46. Sitzung (20 February 1925), BHStAM, MK 15530.

130. Statutes of the "Pfalzhilfe" (20 January 1925), BHStAM, MK 15530; see also "Niederschrift über die Sitzung im Staatsministerium des Äussern" (16 January 1925), BHStAM, MA 106032.

ment, generating more goodwill than was paid for by, in effect, making Pfälzers support their own culture while Bavaria took the credit. The Pfalzhilfe subsidized only those cultural undertakings that were both locally prominent and "patriotic." The Pfälzer orchestra and opera, the recently established regional library, the scholarly associations, the Historical Museum, the most prominent Heimat journal, and the league for adult education had all proven their usefulness to Bavaria and their antipathy to anything French. Their funding was never in question.[131]

But the centerpiece of Bavaria's renewed Kulturpolitik—the establishment of a "Pfälzer Academy," eventually named the Pfälzische Gesellschaft zur Förderung der Wissenschaften (Pfälzer Society for the Promotion of Learning)—generated considerably more controversy. The proposed academy's promoters claimed that it would provide a "necessary union of scholarly and artistic work in the Pfalz" and "answer the long-felt need to consolidate the fragmented scholarly works in the field of Pfalzkunde."[132] But skeptics heard in this echo of the Volksbildung movement's statement of mission an implicit rejection of the egalitarian premises of open adult education. There seems, at the very least, to have been a clear intent on the part of Bavarian officials to appeal to the elitist cultural sensibilities of the "educated and art-loving middle class," whose loyalty the Bavarian state was eager to secure.[133] And by 1924 the political support for a democratic Kulturpolitik had dissipated, leaving the way open for such conservative cultural projects as the proposed academy.[134]

A renewed call for cultural excellence and scholarly distinction, then, was the public expression of a resurgent Honoratioren Kulturpolitik in the 1920s. The new society's founders liked, somewhat speciously, to trace its ancestry back to the Kurpfälzische Akademie der Wissenschaften of the eighteenth

---

131. Bavaria also supported churches, sporting activities, singing groups, and a variety of special events and projects; see Misc. financial reports of BavMinUK (1925–26), BHStAM, MK 15530; financial report of the Pfalzhilfe (1925–26), BHStAM, MK 15534; financial report of the Pfalzhilfe (1926–35), BHStAM, MK 15535. Bavarian officials were quick to point out that these monies represented not even half of what their actual support for culture in the Pfalz came to, if one counted regular appropriations to cultural and educational institutions; see "Aufzeichnungen über die Berücksichtigung der Pfalz im Bereiche des Staatsministeriums für Unterricht und Kultus 1924–26," BHStAM, MK 15530.

132. BavMinUK to BavMinAus (23 December 1924 and 1 August 1925), BHStAM, MK 15530.

133. BavMinUK to Jolas (Staatskommissar für die Pfalz) (22 December 1924), BHStAM, MK 15530.

134. The adult education movement had so successfully proven its "patriotic importance" that no outright attack on its democratic principles materialized. Likewise, the popular Pfälzerwald Verein continued to be funded, despite its irrelevance to high culture. See Reg. Pfalz to BavMinUK (3 April 1925), BHStAM, MK 15530; BavMinUK to BavMinAus (9 June 1925), BHStAM, MK 15530.

century; they invoked also a late-nineteenth-century call for the establishment of a prestigious and scholarly "Historical Commission" for the Pfalz.[135] A "national Heimat problem" (as one contemporary account put it), the lack of a "scholarly center" in the region contrasted miserably to the "love for the Heimat" that informed the region's distinguished literary and historical work.[136] Cultural leaders claimed to be "dismayed" by the diminishing number of Pfälzers active in Heimat scholarship and the generally low level of much that appeared in the daily newspapers and journals.[137] However well intentioned, the overwhelming majority of what passed as Heimatkunde and Heimatpflege, the head of the regional library declared, "has no significance and no value in the field of true learning."[138]

Jealousy of Baden's cultural and academic brilliance presented Bavaria with further reason to move quickly before the educated Pfälzer elite discovered there was more than a fine university to admire in Heidelberg.[139] Whether or not such anxieties were grounded in political reality, Bavaria maintained its suspicions even to the point of excluding the rector of the University of Heidelberg from the opening ceremonies of the new Pfälzer Society for the Promotion of Learning in October 1925—whose presence, so they reasoned, would give the impression that Bavaria could not pursue a Pfälzer Kulturpolitik without Baden's aid.[140] The impression they sought instead was that of Pfälzers and Bavarians united in cultural aspiration and

---

135. Emil Heuser, "Eine historische Kommission für die Pfalz," *PM* 16 (1899): 1–3, and misc. letters in response, pp. 25–27, 43; HVP committee minutes (22 February 1905), PLAS, T1, no. 14. See the account of the new society's historical origins in Meeting of the Gesellschaft on its 50th anniversary, published in the series *Veröffentlichungen der Pfälzischen Gesellschaft zur Förderung der Wissenschaften*, vol. 69 (Speyer, 1975), p. 7.

136. "Ein nationales Heimatproblem," *Neue Pfälzische Landeszeitung* (29 September 1924); Matt (BavMinUK) to Mathéus (Reg. Pfalz) (20 April 1925), BHStAM, MA 107932.

137. Wappes Memorandum, "Betr. Pfälzisches Institut zu Speyer" (30 December 1924), BHStAM, MA 107932; Reismüller (Direktor des Landesbibliothek) to Decker (BavMinUK) (3 January 1925), BHStAM, MK 15549; also Ludwig Eid, "Über eine geistige Aufgabe in der Pfalz" (17 December 1924), BHStAM, MK 15549.

138. Reismüller, "Der Pfälzische Gesellschaft zur Förderung der Wissenschaften zum Geleit! Der Stand der wissenschaftlichen Pfalzkunde," *Pfälzer Zeitung* 76 (24 October 1925): 3.

139. In 1924 Bavarian suspicions of Baden seemed to be confirmed. A wealthy patron of scholarship and Democratic party politics in Heidelberg, Dr. Goldschmidt, opened negotiations with Daniel Häberle, Pfälzer geologist and Heimatkundler, to found a Pfälzer institute in Heidelberg. Häberle was thought to be harboring feelings of resentment toward Bavaria for failure to honor him sufficiently for his Heimat scholarship. The plan eventually came to nothing. See the tempest it nevertheless occasioned in the cultural bureaucracy in BHStAM, MA 107932 and MK 15549.

140. Decker (BavMinUK) to Jakob (Präs. Pfalz) (2 October 1925), BHStAM, MK 15549. On the founding itself, see Reismüller to Wappes, "Organisationsplan für die Wissenschaftliche Kommission für Pfalzkunde" (3 January 1925), BHStAM, MA 107932; Mathéus (Pres. Pfalz) to BavMinUK, "Zusammenfassung der wiss. Arbeit in der Pfalz" (15 May 1925), BHStAM,

achievement. Most of the twenty-two founding members, who were not self-selected but appointed, were the beneficiaries of Bavarian education and the promoters of Bavarian-Pfälzer cultural ties. The new chairman was Friedrich von Bassermann-Jordan, wine magnate, gentleman scholar, and heir to the only real political dynasty in the region; the secretary was Albert Pfeiffer, head of the state archives in Speyer, brother to a leader of the Bavarian People's party (Anton Pfeiffer) and to a leader of the Center party (Maximilian Pfeiffer), and editor of the Pfalz's best journal of Heimat studies. Leading industrialists and cultural patrons, heads of cultural and educational institutions, and eminent local scholars made up the balance of the membership in this exclusive group.[141]

The opening ceremonies, and the week of scholarly lectures in Pfälzer cities that followed, presented a vision of the Pfalz as a community of culture and imagination, of tradition and creation, but also as a community with recognized leaders and elite standards.[142] The opening-day audience included the entire spectrum of Pfälzer notables, political and economic, sacred and secular, academic and practical—a quite literal gathering of those on whose political loyalty the Bavarian government depended. What these men heard was an affirmation of the unity and antiquity of the geographical region, defined as a heritage of Bildung and Kultur common to all Pfälzers; what they participated in themselves was an affirmation of the power of a select few to protect and preserve the Pfalz so defined. "The love of Heimat, Volk, and Fatherland has brought us all together here," said District President Mathéus. New chairman Friedrich von Bassermann-Jordan thought that "no one [could] outdo us in attachment to our earth and Fatherland" and, more, that "for us the society [would] itself be a Pfalz—a *Palatium* not only of united scholarly activity but a *Palatium* of German thought." "It is a joy for my German and especially my old Pfälzer heart," said Franz Matt, the Bavarian minister of culture, to witness this revival of interest in the history of our "forebears and *Volkstum*," which springs from "a longing for the spiritual" and "a love for the Heimat." For Matt, the task of

---

MK 15549; Schmitt (BavMinJust) to BavMinUK (22 July 1925), BHStAM, MA 107932; Matt (BavMinUK) to BavMinAus (21 August 1925), BHStAM, MA 107932; Matt to Mathéus (20 October 1925), BHStAM, MA 107932.

141. "Die Gründung der Pfälzischen Gesellschaft zur Förderung der Wissenschaften [PGFW]," *PM–PH* 42/21 (1925): 279–81 (this full account of opening festivities, statutes, and members was also reprinted in pamphlet form in 1926). Regular members were to be nominated by the Ministry of Culture and ratified by two-thirds of the PGFW membership; the Ministry of Culture would also name the chairman and secretary of the society (Draft of the PGFW organizational structure, BHStAM, MK 15549).

142. The latter part, the *Hochschulwoche* as it was known, was a revival of the ministry's original conception for adult education in the region, a notion that Fitz had managed several years earlier to quash.

saving the past and with it the future was not for every man but for "a small and united group of men, . . . not seeking honor but fulfilling duty and service to their compatriots."[143] The Pfälzer people should acknowledge the superior claims of such excellent and dedicated men to guard its cultural identity. "In their hands," reported the *Pfälzische Rundschau*, a paper chronically affirmative of the government's position, "lies the spiritual reawakening of our life in the Pfalz."[144]

Similarly, a laudatory editorial in the *Pfälzer Zeitung* assured its readers that this had not been a scholarly event for the benefit of "a narrow circle of academically trained and academically active men": "What happened yesterday in this historical setting must be considered a general Pfälzer event, can indeed with full justification be seen as a Bavarian event, and, like all cultural occurrences on the Rhine, it is also a German event."[145] The shapers of the new society saw themselves transcending the particularities of class and region not through democracy but through the universality of their high cultural aspirations. Invoking the cultural authority of Goethe, Schiller, Melanchthon, and, surprisingly, the Koran, Friedrich von Bassermann-Jordan argued that "'learning and art belong to the world and before them disperse the boundaries of nations.'"[146] Yet such a transcendence of particularity for the most part ended at the borders of Germany, the cultural significance of which the society continually reaffirmed. The nationally circumscribed knowledge it promoted held the key to national regeneration. The new society, proclaimed Mathéus, will not just serve "our narrow Heimat, but will participate in the revival and prospering of our Bavarian and greater German Fatherland. . . . The weapons of the spirit are left to us," he continued; "German learning and German culture will lead us out of the expanses of rubble that the world war left behind."[147]

Between 1925 and 1933, the society sponsored publications, a handful of historic festivals and commemorations, and a few major projects like the compilation of a dictionary of Pfälzer dialect. It also probably contributed to a general reinvigoration of the scholarly associations of the region. "It is a high service and a cultural necessity," wrote the cultural minister of Bavaria to the Pfälzer Society for the Promotion of Learning,

> that in these times, in which all traditions find fundamental opposition and are put aside in preference for the present, there are still nationally minded men willing to devote themselves to the cultivation of Heimat history, never tiring in

---

143. "Die Gründung der PGFW," *PM–PH* 42/21 (1925): 272–73.
144. Ibid., p. 283.
145. Ibid.
146. That particular line—"Wissenschaft und Kunst gehören der Welt an und vor ihnen verschwinden die Schranken der Nationen"—he attributed to Goethe (ibid., p. 280).
147. Ibid.

their maintenance of the ties between our generation and the past. From these ties come not only the courage, the self-consciousness, and the Heimat joy of our people, but also the proper public sense, in short, every fundamental power that is identical with culture and with prosperity.[148]

But the efforts of the adult education league and the academy to realize a Heimat community in the Pfalz inevitably came up short when confronted by the incapacity of the whole society, deeply divided on the pragmatics of politics and economics, to sustain any common understanding of its collective life. Political disagreements in and of themselves do not necessarily preclude a society's achieving some consensus on its civic responsibilities and its cultural values. But the citizens of the Weimar Republic notably failed to agree on a common language with which to discuss the larger aspirations and responsibilities of their society, despite much talk about the importance of traditions and "belonging-togetherness" (*Zusammengehörigkeitsgefühl*). Those who shared a language of Heimat shared it only in a limited sense: they had inherited a mixed legacy of Heimat cultivation from the Wilhelmine period, the ambiguity of which continued to manifest itself in considerable disagreement over whether Heimat implied democracy, cultural pluralism, spiritual regeneration, or simply escape. A pervasive, multifaceted discontent undermined even tentative efforts toward consensus. The enemy of any and all Heimat exhortations to collective contentment, such discontent ultimately proved the greatest strength of the otherwise incoherent and self-contradictory National Socialist movement.

The intractability of specifically political divisiveness in the Pfalz had become obvious to Bavarian officials by November 1924, less than a year after the separatist incidents. The state commissioner for the Pfalz, entrusted with overseeing Bavarian interests in the region, wrote to his superiors that his office would have to disband the special political action committees, with whose cooperation many of the cultural and economic programs for the Pfalz had been implemented: "The party splinterings in the Pfalz are so strong, the conflicts between individual parties so deep, that it is becoming too difficult to direct them toward a profitable cooperative effort."[149] Even though flawed, the collective effort to combat the French from 1919 to 1923 proved to be the last occasion on which political factions in the Pfalz came together in the Weimar Republic. After 1924, the political life of the region was marked by continual party feuding and periodic political crises: from 1924 on, an acrimonious fraternal battle between the Center party and the Bavarian People's party; in 1925, Social Democratic uproar over rumors of a monarchist putsch; in 1925, 1926, and 1927, the proliferation of new right-wing splinter

148. BavMinUK to PGFW (28 October 1931), BHStAM, MK 15551.
149. Jolas to Staatsrat Schmelzle (24 November 1924), BHStAM, MA 107712.

parties; periodic witch-hunts of alleged separatists, incidents between right-wing groups and the French authorities, clashes between the Nazi *Sturmab-teilung* (SA), the Reichsbanner (the Socialists' answer to the SA), and the *Pfalzwacht*, a Catholic semimilitary group; and finally, persistent rumors of an imminent Nazi coup.[150] Both the Catholic parties and the socialist parties held on to their constituencies until the final years of the Republic, losing voters to one another (Center to the Bavarian People's party, the Social Democrats to the Communists) but not significantly to splinter groups. The Protestant bourgeois parties of the Pfalz, the dominant political force of the nineteenth century, enjoyed no such stability. Sooner and more rapidly than in Germany as a whole, liberalism lost its strength, the few democratic liber-als tending toward social democracy and the once powerful National Liberal constituency drawn ever more to the right and into a variety of racialist-nationalist (*völkisch*) groups, including the German National People's party, the Economic party, the Bavarian League of Peasants and Proprietors, and, of course, the National Socialists.[151]

The development of National Socialism in the Pfalz largely confirms the current scholarly opinion that the movement represented, as Thomas Childers recently expressed it, "less. . . a distinctly lower-middle-class phe-nomenon than. . . a remarkably successful catchall party of protest."[152] Cer-tainly strong support from the largely Protestant Mittelstand in the Pfalz brought an important block of otherwise fluctuating voters to the National Socialists, but well-to-do, well-educated Pfälzers as well as dirt-poor farmers and unemployed shoemakers also voted for the Nazis.[153] The founding mem-bers of the party in Kaiserslautern, the Pfalz's second industrial city, in-

150. Schönhoven, *Die Bayerische Volkspartei*, p. 182; BHStAM, MA 108076, MA 107816; Faber, "Die südlicher Rheinlande," pp. 437–42; NSDAP Hauptarchiv, Hoover Institution Microfilm Collection, reel 32A, folder no. 1786 (1926–32); reel 48, folder no. 1105 (1931); and reel 86, folder no. 1776 (1932).

151. Faber, "Die südlichen Rheinlande," pp. 439–40.

152. Foreword to 1986 reissue of Theodore Abel's *Why Hitler Came into Power*, reprint ed. Thomas Childers (1938; Cambridge, Mass., 1986), p. xvii; Abel's own observations in 1939 on the diversity of National Socialism's social composition have, starting in the mid-1970s, been reaffirmed. Also relevant are Thomas Childers, *The Nazi Voter: The Social Foundations of Fascism in Germany, 1919–1933* (Chapel Hill, N.C., 1983); Thomas Childers, ed., *The Formation of the Nazi Constituency 1919–1933* (Totowa, N.J., 1986); Richard Hamilton, *Who Voted for Hitler?* (Princeton, 1982); and Peter Merkl, *Political Violence Under the Swastika: 581 Early Nazis* (Princeton, 1975). See also the review article of books on the social composition of Nazism, by James J. Sheehan in *Theory and Society* 13 (1985): 851–67.

153. Hamilton has suggested that the strong National Socialist showings in the wine region reflect the presence of well-to-do travelers in resort towns like Neustadt, Landau, and Bad Bergzabern, thus down-playing the significance of the lower-middle-class vote in those regions (*Who Voted for Hitler?* pp. 227–28). The Nazis' greatest successes nevertheless came in the eco-nomically most depressed parts of the Pfalz—the north and the town of Pirmasens in the south, neither of which was by any stretch of the imagination a resort area.

cluded along with the small businessmen and midlevel bureaucrats several academically trained professionals.[154] Electoral success for the National Socialists came early and fast in the Pfalz. The party won its first victory in 1924, taking a mayoralty in the northern community of Dannenfels (and thereby giving the Pfalz the dubious distinction of having elected the first Nazi town mayor in all of Germany).[155] Largely independent of its Bavarian counterpart, the Pfälzer party avoided the period of stagnation that set in after 1925 among Bavarian Nazis; Pfälzer Nazis regrouped in 1925 under schoolteacher Josef Bürckel and his cronies Ernst Leyser and Richard Imbt, a trio that dominated Nazi affairs in the region until 1944.[156] Between 1928 and 1930 the party had made enough inroads into the multiple parties of the Protestant electorate to run a close second behind the Catholic parties in the 1930 elections, overtaking the Social Democrats by a narrow margin. By 1932 they were far and away the strongest single party in the region and had begun to win away some of the Catholic-Bavarian vote itself.[157] In March 1933, the Nazis almost achieved an absolute majority against the combined votes of Catholic, socialist, and bourgeois parties:[158] this was an electoral victory unparalleled in any region of such mixed confessional and occupational structure and exceeded only in the entirely Protestant regions of Schleswig-Holstein, East Hannover, Chemnitz-Zwickau, and Pomerania.[159]

The success of the Nazi party in the Pfalz had particular causes as well as general implications, but certainly the character of the local leader, Josef Bürckel, who maintained extraordinary personal control over the shape of the local movement, was of fundamental importance.[160] A populist, social revolutionary, and virulent anti-Catholic, Bürckel was closely allied to the Strasser brothers' wing of the Nazi movement, with its emphasis on the "Arbeiter" component of NSDAP and its radical critique of capitalism. In

154. Heinz Friedel, *Die Machtergreifung 1933 in Kaiserslautern Ein Beitrag zum Werden des Nationalsozialismus in der Westpfalz* (Otterbach/Kaiserslautern, 1983), p. 11.

155. Faber, "Die südlichen Rheinlande," p. 442.

156. Wiesemann, *Vorgeschichte*, pp. 88–90.

157. On the potential susceptibility of Catholic voters to the Nazi appeal, see Günther Plum, *Gesellschaftsstruktur und politisches Bewußtsein in einer katholischen Region, 1928–1933* (Stuttgart, 1972). His study concerns the Prussian-Rhenish district of Aachen, but certain social characteristics of his Catholic sample obtained also in the southeast corner of the Pfalz. Plum argues that the church, perhaps inadvertently, made it easier for voters to switch to the Nazi party by excluding loyalty to parliamentary democracy from the program and outlook of the Center party. On the antiparliamentarianism of the Bayerische Volkspartei, see also Wiesemann, *Vorgeschichte*, pp. 284–85.

158. Wiesemann, *Vorgeschichte*, pp. 270–71.

159. Faber, "Die südlichen Rheinlande," p. 440.

160. Peter Hüttenberger has identified two styles among the Nazi Gauleiter, the first toward bureaucratization and the second—the pattern Bürckel embodied—of clique formation, where a few people held power in their hands and distributed it among their friends. See his *Die Gauleiter. Studie zum Wandel des Machtgefüges in der NSDAP* (Stuttgart, 1969), p. 39.

1926, Gregor Strasser spoke at a rally in the industrial town of Kaiserslautern and to the catcalls of Social Democrats and Communists accused them of being the pillars of capital in Germany.[161] Indeed, Pfälzer Nazism under Bürckel in some ways represented a striking revival of an old local political tendency toward volatility, radical populism, and grass-roots mobilization—qualities that had surfaced at various points in the nineteenth century in protest against Bavarian monarchism.[162] A travestied Jacobinism, stripped of concern for liberty or civic virtue, Nazism in the Pfalz fed on the chronic economic depression in the region and on the continuing presence of the French occupation, against which local Nazis managed by sheer repetition and audacious prevarication to establish themselves as the most German of national patriots.

The economic difficulties of the Pfalz in fact derived in large part from the conditions of occupation. Occupational restrictions on trade had exacerbated postwar problems of readjustment, cutting off the industries of the Pfalz from raw materials, coal supplies, and markets and contributing to high rates of unemployment in 1922 and 1923.[163] After the disastrous inflation of 1923, the occupied regions were slow to benefit from the advantages of the new currency because both the French and German governments resisted its introduction into the Rhineland. In the Pfalz, the Chamber of Commerce was driven in January 1924 to invent its own currency, the short-lived "Pfälzische Handelskammerdollar"; without a settled currency, overall recovery was delayed and a decline in levels of unemployment agonizingly slow.[164] Only in 1927 did the region begin to see the possibility of a return to prosperity—the building trades revived, and French actions somewhat relieved the commercial isolation of local industries. Thanks to unrelenting propaganda, the tourist trade had begun to pick up, and Pfälzer wine was enjoying a patriotic vogue in unoccupied Germany. But even before the American stock market crash in October 1929, the tenuous prosperity of the Pfalz began to falter. In late 1928, unemployment rose again. The reports from Bavarian prime minister Held's official tour of the region in September 1929 attested to the pessimism of trade unionists, white-collar workers, and industry and trade leaders alike: Friedrich von Bassermann-Jordan himself led the prime minister around the stricken vineyards in the southeastern Pfalz.[165] The crash, like

161. Account in *Pfälzer Tageblatt*, no. 226 (8 September 1926).

162. Many of the Pfälzer respondents to Theodore Abel's 1936 survey of early Nazis revealed a decided concern for social justice, as well as a general belief in the virtues of the German worker; see, e.g., nos. 178, 183, 331, and 410, Hoover Institution Archives, Stanford, Abel Collection.

163. Wysocki, "Zwischen zwei Weltkriegen," pp. 267–80.

164. Ibid., p. 289.

165. "Pfalzbereisung durch den Herrn Ministerpräsidenten Dr. Held" (September 1929), BHStAM, MA 107820; also, "Denkschriften der Länder Preußen, Bayern, Hessen, Baden und Oldenburg," (1928), BHStAM, MA 107971.

the postwar depression, hit the Pfalz particularly hard: chronic capital shortages in small and medium industries became more acute; industries closed or
went on short time; the building industry practically shut down; wages sank,
and the percentage of day laborers rose; the number of unemployed workers
reached 84,280 at the end of 1930 (the figure in December 1923 had been
slightly higher at 84,900).[166] In 1930, a journalist in Munich reported that
the Pfalz stood far above the national average in receipt of unemployment
compensation; in Kaiserslautern, as much as a third of the population received it, in Ludwigshafen, a seventh.[167]

In Pirmasens, the "shoe capital" of Germany, that figure would reach
almost 100 percent by 1932. A case study in the growth of right-wing radicalism, Pirmasens had a Protestant, lower-middle-class population that stood
out in the largely Catholic southern Pfalz. Its economy depended exclusively
on the shoe industry, organized in small-scale, labor-intensive production
with many family members participating. Hard economic times came after
the war. The Nazi movement had gained adherents in the town already in
1924.[168] Future *Gauleiter* Bürckel came from a neighboring village; he regarded the town as his political birthplace.[169] The town's shoes were bought
and distributed in the national market by middlemen, most of them Jews. By
1930, anti-Semitic incidents—including not only harassment and insults but
beatings of Jewish businessmen—had become so frequent and blatant that
the Jewish middlemen began to avoid Pirmasens altogether, farming out
their contracts to Catholic producers in surrounding areas. This "boycott,"
as Nazi agitators termed it, exacerbated the town's economic decline and
hatred for both Jews and Catholics.[170]

The Nazis of Pirmasens tended to be young, hard hit by the chronic economic problems in the town, and involved in violent paramilitary groups,
some of the left and some of the right.[171] But the growth of Nazism in Pirmasens reveals more than the impact of economic crisis on political behavior.
By far the most significant formative experience for Nazis of Pirmasens and

166. Wysocki, "Zwischen zwei Weltkriegen," pp. 287, 293.

167. "Die Pfalz, Bayerns Sorgenkind," *Münchener Zeitung* (1930), newspaper clipping in
BHStAM, MA 107785. See also Friedel, *Machtergreifung*, pp. 21–25.

168. Theodore Abel's remarkable series of Nazi vitae, solicited in 1934, included what Peter
Merkl has called a "grossly disproportionate" number of responses from the Pfalz and neighboring Saarland (about 60 out of 581 life stories) attesting undoubtedly to the efforts of Bürckel
himself to encourage participation in the project. Several of these respondents were from Pirmasens; one (no. 410) was the founder of that town's SA group in 1925. See Merkl, *Political
Violence*, pp. 16, 198. The responses themselves, in their original form, can be read at the Hoover
Institution Archives in Stanford, Calif.

169. Hüttenberger, *Die Gauleiter*, p. 185.

170. For a full account, see the *Deutschland Berichte der Sozialdemokratischen Partei Deutschland*
(Frankfurt, 1980), vol. 4 (1937), pp. 984–85. (hereafter cited as *Sopade*).

171. Merkl, *Political Violence*, pp. 198–203.

the Pfalz as a whole had been the French occupation. This obvious, but often unattended, fact of 1920s German life also proved crucial to the involvement of almost every one of Theodore Abel's Pfälzer respondents in a 1934 survey of ordinary Nazis: drawing on these life histories, Peter Merkl asserts that the antioccupation struggle was a "school for political violence" as well as a "major recruiting vehicle" that brought the young Nazi movement early adherents and quick legitimacy.[172] Whatever the civilities of relations between French and German officials in the Rhineland, the mere presence of occupation troops suggested that in the last analysis political rule was based on force. Occupational rule also subtly undermined the legitimacy of the courts, elections, and other civic apparatus of the Weimar Republic. Abel's Pfälzer respondents displayed extreme hostility not only to foreigners, political parties, the Catholic church, and to a lesser degree Jews, but also—and unlike respondents from other regions of Germany—to the German police and government proper.[173] In light of its cooperation with the occupiers, however reluctant and pragmatically motivated it may have been, the German government's authority as the "conventional wielders of violence" seemed illegitimate; reliance on "one's own physical force" came to seem not merely a justified but a welcome alternative.[174]

Abel's respondents for the most part confirm the general pattern of Nazi activism in the Pfalz in the 1920s. The early years of the occupation, from 1919 to 1924, had been marked by an extraordinary amount of violence, between French troops and Germans as well as between Germans of various labels and identities—Socialists, Communists, separatists, right-wing paramilitarists, and so on. National Socialists as such caught only the tail end of this half-decade of uproar, but many who eventually drifted into the Nazi party had begun in other antiestablishment groups or simply as individual agitators, passive resisters, or rowdies. The sociological character of the early Nazi party in the Pfalz thus bore curious and more-than-coincidental resemblance to the separatist gang, for both were groups of radically disaffected, often unemployed or underemployed young men. Without too much psychological second-guessing, one can regard this close resemblance as crucial to the Nazi obsession with the separatists, an obsession that did not abate but grew in the course of the 1920s and persisted well after 1933.[175]

---

172. Ibid., p. 203. Abel's survey (see note 168 above) took the form of a contest for pre-1933 party members to write an account of their life and involvement in the National Socialist movement. An American sociologist at Columbia University, Abel published his analysis of the life histories in *Why Hitler Came into Power* in 1938.

173. Ibid., p. 206.

174. Ibid., pp. 203–6.

175. When the French left the Pfalz in 1930, the Nazis declared a kind of unofficial free-for-all against former separatists, many of whom had been granted amnesty in 1924 in a short-lived spirit of reconciliation. On 24 March 1933, the new Nazi government of the Pfalz ordered the

Nor did the possibility, real or imagined, of some kinship between the fledgling National Socialist movement and the defunct separatists escape the attention of contemporaries. Various Pfälzer Nazis periodically refuted accusations that they were former members of separatist groups.[176] Bürckel himself was dogged by this suspicion, which he took the trouble to refute in court in 1931. By his own account, his antiseparatist credentials were proven by his participation in the mob's lynching and burning of separatists in Pirmasens in early 1924.[177]

The contribution of the occupation to the Nazi movement, Merkl argues, was "an extreme degree of leader worship, a sense of personal insecurity and self-pitying masochism, and a touch of irrational paranoia."[178] Add to that the unsavory and brutal character of many early Nazis in the Pfalz and the picture is not one to attract the Heimat and fresh air–loving *Kulturmenschen* who flocked to less violent forms of associational life. Yet the Nazis' championing of the antioccupation cause, in however unheroic and unpleasant a fashion, contributed enormously to winning over the self-consciously respectable Pfälzers.[179] At the very least, the Nazis' self-representation as *the* patriotic defense organization ultimately frustrated the capacity of the legitimate government and the mainstream political parties of the region to combat Nazi fanaticism. The Pfalz did, after all, have well-established Catholic and Social Democratic parties that could, with much greater justification than the Nazis, claim to have "saved" the Pfalz from the French. Compared to their systematic efforts, through legitimate political, cultural, economic, and diplomatic channels, to frustrate French ambitions and gather Pfälzer loyalty, the Nazis' occasional ambushing of a French soldier or harassment of a suspected former separatist looked paltry indeed.

But the political mainstream never got the credit it deserved—the story, of course, of the Weimar government all over Germany. The Bavarian government, moreover, increasingly sought to avoid confrontation with the Nazis rather than risk a showdown that might conceivably benefit the far left.[180] In April 1927, for instance, Pfälzer district president Mathéus and the

---

arrest of all known or suspected separatists; many were subsequently sent to concentration camps where they died or were executed (Reimer, *Rheinlandfrage*, pp. 407–9).

176. *Sopade* (1936), 3:225, e.g.

177. *Pfälzische Rundschau* (20 April 1931), account of fines imposed on Editor Neubauer of the *Rheinpfälzer* for having printed an article in 1930 suggesting Bürckel was a separatist; see also accounts of Bürckel's successful refutation of such rumors in the courts in NSDAP Hauptarchiv, Hoover Institution Microfilm Collection, reel 81, folder no. 1610 (1930–32).

178. Merkl, *Political Violence*, p. 206.

179. Faber also argues that the anti-separatist stance of the Nazis won them instant credibility among the respectable classes (p. 442).

180. Geoffrey Pridham, *Hitler's Rise to Power: The Nazi Movement in Bavaria, 1923–1933* (London, 1973), pp. 146–84.

Bavarian minister of the interior agreed on the necessity of banning a Nazi rally in Landau for fear it would provoke the working class and the occupation authorities; but, Mathéus emphasized, *"we must not use the objections of the occupation authorities as a reason,* or we will invite the criticism especially of the National Socialists."[181] In the face of the ostentatious "patriotism" of Nazi agitators and bullyboys, the very legitimacy of the Pfälzer and Bavarian governmental authorities as the guarantors of public order and justice seemed uncertain. Prosecution of Nazis for crimes against French occupation personnel became a politically hazardous undertaking, and eventually the government and the police were reluctant to pursue cases against the Nazis even for attacks on other Germans.[182] Only at the insistence of the Interallied Rhineland Commission did the Bavarian government impose a ban on the wearing of brown shirts in 1929.[183] In 1930, the Bavarian Catholic defense organization, Bayernwacht, expanded into the Pfalz, changing its name to Pfalzwacht in deference to the Center party and gathering extensive membership from Catholic organizations to combat the "godlessness and immorality of the revolutionary new-barbarism."[184] Yet neither the Pfalzwacht nor the Pfälzer SPD Reichsbanner units were as strong as the Nazi SA, nor were they willing to join forces against the SA, as their fathers and elders had in the early part of the decade against the separatists and French. Few, if any, perceived the National Socialists as a force so destructive as to warrant the temporary transcendence of an older antipathy between the traditional right and the equally traditional left.

Against this foreground of growing hostility to the established authority of government and rising legitimacy of antiestablishment agitators like the Nazis, the Heimat movement stands in bizarre contrast, providing a background of steady exhortations to peaceableness, contentment, conservationism, self-knowledge, acceptance, and resignation. Certainly the gap between this symbolic depiction of Pfälzer society and its splintered, unhappy reality was enormous, but so too was the gap between most of the Heimat movement's leaders and the proponents of political extremism. Although it remains difficult to gauge the extent to which the membership of comparatively large organizations like the Pfälzerwald Verein was infiltrated by Nazi

181. Mathéus to BavMinInn (8 April [and 4 May 1927]), BHStAM, MA 108076. The occupation authorities had closely monitored the Nazi party from its start, and had frequently put pressure on the local government to ban Nazi rallies and the like. See, e.g., a series of incidents in 1926 recounted in BHStAM, MA 108076.

182. NSDAP Hauptarchiv, Hoover Institution Microfilm Collection, reel 32A, folder no. 1786 (1926–32).

183. Memorandum of the Interallierte Rhein. Kommission (May 1929) and accounts of incidents in the Pfalz and the protest in the Bavarian Landtag (July–Sept. 1929), BHStAM, MA 108076.

184. Wiesemann, *Vorgeschichte*, pp. 199–200.

party members, several factors speak against any significant National Socialist presence in any of the Heimat organizations in the Pfalz. In the first place,
the actual number of Nazi party members before 1933 was relatively small:
people may have voted for the National Socialists without joining the party,
an act of distancing that allowed them, tragically, to continue to benefit from
the institutions and values of the Weimar Republic while undermining them
with their vote. And certainly the Heimat organizations were part and parcel
of Weimar, whatever transmutations they underwent after 1933. The historical and scholarly associations were too Catholic or too pro-Bavarian, the
adult education league too democratic, the hiking, singing, and folklore
groups too apolitical, and all were too conservative in the literal sense of the
word to attract much support from committed Nazi party members, dis-
gusted with the status quo and increasingly busy with party rallies, street
fighting, and political organizing.[185]

Indeed, in the course of the 1920s, Heimat activities themselves came
under attack, from the Nazis as well as from a variety of individuals and
groups sympathetic to the Nazis and unable to find either merit or consolation in the invented traditions of an earlier generation. The most obvious
source of conflict was the money for cultural undertakings that Bavaria and
the Reich distributed in the Pfalz.[186] The Cultural Ministry's policy of
restricting funds to a few umbrella organizations, which had been designed
at least in part to consolidate Bavaria's political supporters, necessarily left
individuals and smaller, less well established organizations without state
support.[187] A number of the government's critics, including for the time
being the Social Democrats, saw in the policy a deliberate neglect of avant-
garde cultural efforts in favor of convention, tradition, and hopelessly narrow
provincialism. The failure in 1926 of a literary magazine called *Heimaterde*
(Heimat Earth), which had tried to encourage young and experimental writers, led the Social Democratic *Pfälzische Post* to denounce angrily "those
upper classes, those educated people, and especially those circles who [took]
every opportunity to lay claim to literary sophistication, Heimat love, and
popular education" yet stood by and let *Heimaterde* down in their silence. The
Pfälzische Merkur similarly deplored the demise of *Heimaterde* and the cultural
exile of its editor to Baden: "A few people, always pushing themselves to the
front, think themselves to be the only true representatives of Pfälzer cultural
life, and they take great pains to insure that no one disturbs their exclusive

---

185. Hoover Institution Archives, Stanford, Abel Collection.
186. Hüttenberger points out that fully half of the Bavarian Gauleiter were, like the Pfalz's
Bürckel, schoolteachers—a statistic he thinks may reveal a great deal of alienation from Bavarian cultural policy, for schoolteachers were, after all, state servants (*Die Gauleiter*, p. 88).
187. The files are full of such requests and rejections. For a typical exchange, see BavMinUK
to A. Roediger of E. Kaussler'schen Verlag, Landau (19 January 1926), BHStAM, MK 15530.

circles, snuffing out any work that does not bear the holy mark of their clique."[188]

Nothing revealed the existence and the power of this "clique" more than the new Pfälzer Society for the Promotion of Learning. From the start, it drew the anger of Bavaria's cultural critics, predictably those of the Social Democratic left, and more profoundly in the end from a nascent group of cultural radicals who were drifting closer to the National Socialist camp in their call for a revolutionary reawakening of German culture. The leading representative of this attitude was a young scholar, poet, and writer named Gert Buchheit, who had studied under the literary critic Friedrich Gundolf and had become possessed of the spiritual ambitions of the George Circle, those advocates of a poetic regeneration of civilization.[189] Buchheit had returned to the Pfalz after his education to try to ignite his stodgy Heimat with the fire of art. He settled in Pirmasens and there tried to establish his own association, the Rheinpfälzer Society for Literature and Art, for whose financial support he applied to the Bavarian Cultural Ministry.[190]

Unsuccessful in his plans, Buchheit began publicly to denounce the Bavarian cultural establishment and the new Pfälzer academy.[191] Published in the anti-Bavarian press, Buchheit's attacks revealed a self-consciousness of youth, change, and the greater Germany, all of which were inimical to the insiders' cultural Heimat. Buchheit denounced the new Society for the Promotion of Learning as a "purely provincial, local undertaking," whose leaders dishonestly evaded his criticism by deploying their "ingratiating Pfälzer ways."[192] He repeated a Social Democratic accusation that the society merely represented the backstage maneuverings of the Bavarian People's party to gain popularity in the region, but his critique otherwise bore little resemblance to calls for a more democratic cultural policy.[193] "Germany can only be thought united through common work, given that this work takes the whole nation into account," wrote Buchheit (following Paul de Lagarde); the "Pfälzer Society for Heimatkunde," as he contemptuously referred to it,

188. "Zum Ende der *Heimaterde," Bei uns daheim* 6 (19 May 1926); "Aus heimatlichen Gauen," *Pfälzischer Merkur,* no. 13 (1926).

189. Biographical notice in *Rhein-pfälzische Monatshefte* 6 (January 1955): 25.

190. Buchheit to Geheimrat Gruber, Bayerische Akademie der Wissenschaft (11 October 1925), BHStAM, MK 15549; clipping from the *Landauer Anzeiger* [Buchheit probable author] (20 October 1925), BHStAM, MK 15549.

191. Buchheit seems nevertheless to have continued to try to wield cultural influence in the Pfalz. See, for instance, a Buchheit petition in 1926 to obtain recognition for a young painter named Bürckel from Pirmasens (*not* the future Gauleiter, though likely a relation). The petition was refused. See PGFW, Niederschrift, Zweite Sitzung, BHStAM, MK 15549.

192. Dr. Gert Buchheit, "Grundsätzliches über meine Kritik an der Pfälzische Gesellschaft zur Förderung der Wissenschaften," *Landauer Anzeiger,* no. 28 (2 February 1926).

193. See also Studienrat Rudolf Thiel, "Pfälzische Wissenschaft! Pfälzische Wissenschaft?" reprinted in *Landauer Anzeiger,* no. 289 (10 December 1927).

failed to recognize the perilous times facing Germany. The younger generation, survivors of war and the "horrific national suffering" of revolution, had
no patience for the "pointless historical nit-picking of the Pfälzer character"
and the "hobby mentality" of the Heimat researcher. "It seems more important to us to secure all forces for the conscious rearmament and renewal of
German culture and the German state," he wrote, urging Germans not to
"elevate truth over its consequences, value over usefulness, or the Heimat
over the whole Volk." He argued, invoking Lagarde, the "warrior [*Vorkämpfer*] of German learning," that the youth did not lack idealism, but their
statesmen lacked the capacity or the will to inspire idealism.[194]

In 1933, having cast the old Pfälzer Society for the Promotion of Learning
by the wayside, the Nazis would expand on Buchheit's critique, but for the
time being he spoke, if not just for himself, then for a cultural radicalism
as yet unclaimed by National Socialism. For its part, the society decided
privately not to respond to the attacks from the Landau press; the general
consensus among its members was that envy alone had inspired this
aggression.[195] In 1928, in a gesture meant to be conciliatory but appearing
only patronizing, the society held its annual meeting in Landau, replete with
speeches on Heimat, culture, and Fatherland. But the ceremonial did not
evoke the worshipful admiration that such ritualistic celebrations of culture
always had before—and that its organizers had anticipated. Instead it provoked Buchheit and his supporters to further invective. The whole episode
exemplified the inability of the society's members to come to grips with the
extent of the disaffection they were facing. Buchheit and his supporters did
not want promises of eventual inclusion in the most exclusive of Heimat
clubs; what they wanted was to have done with the whole complacent, self-
perpetuating fiction of local identity and national harmony.

The affinities between the radical discontent of an intellectual like Buchheit and an unemployed shoemaker like the Pirmasenser respondent to
Abel's survey of early Nazis emerged clearly after 1929. Without the severe
depression that devastated the already-tenuous German economic recovery,
the Buchheits and Bürckels of the Pfalz might have gone on indefinitely rail-
ing against the black plague of Bavarianism and the curse of the Weimar
system. But economic distress, helped along by the peculiarities of the Pfälzer situation, promoted an alliance of the discontented. The practical basis
for such an alliance was conveniently provided by the Bavarians themselves,
whose Pfalzhilfe programs seemed designed to force small proprietors into
economic enslavement to the cultural doyens of Speyer. The interest from the

194. Ibid.
195. Pfeiffer to the Amtliche Pressestelle Pfalz, "vertraulich" (1 February 1926), BHStAM,
MK 15549. The old specter of Badenese scheming was also invoked; see Dr. Albert Pfeiffer,
"Ziel und Arbeit der PGFW" and others, Festsitzung der PGFW (28 January 1928), BHStAM,
MK 15550; "Festsitzung der PGFW in Landau," *Der Rheinpfälzer*, no. 25 (30 January 1928): 5.

loans to small producers and tradesmen, after all, was what actually supported organizations like the local orchestra and the learned society. As the
economic situation worsened, Pfälzer debtors began to clamor for relief from
interest payments, or at the very least a reduction in interest rates.[196] The
Bavarian government refused, ostensibly on the ground that the ensuing deprivation of cultural life would provoke an uproar in the Pfalz. In fact, an
uproar was far more likely to come from those who would have happily seen
the Pfälzer Society for the Promotion of Learning sink into the Isar (from
whence it seemed to them to have come) if that would have brought some
small measure of economic relief. Even in the face of an appeal from the
minister of finance in late 1931 to reduce the budget of the Pfalzhilfe altogether, the prime minister insisted on retaining the cultural support in
order to avoid "unpleasant political consequences."[197]

The Bavarian government's stubborn support of the cultural and Heimat-
promoting organizations of the Pfalz, despite increasing signs that an alienated lower middle class was drifting out of the Bavarian People's party and
into the National Socialist camp, represented a fateful miscalculation. Never
skillful in its handling of Pfälzer popular opinion, the government in Munich
mistook its own clients and official retainers in the Pfalz for the Pfalz itself
and, while trying to placate them, inevitably ignored large parts of the
population. Moreover, its preoccupation with organized life in what had always been the cultural and political mainstream led it to misinterpret the
nature of anti-Bavarian sentiment in the region, attributing it to Social
Democratic and Badenese mischief or to traditional Pfälzer unitarism. Nor
did the prime minister or his advisors on the Pfalz doubt that Catholic opinion, regardless of social class, was behind him. But by 1933 the party of the
Bavarian government in the Pfalz, the Bavarian People's party, had lost significant electoral force even in its stronghold of Speyer.[198] Culture alone,
even when delivered in the familiar garb of Heimat promotion, could not
hold the electorate of the late Weimar Republic.

Indeed, the Heimat that since the turn of the century had expressed the
peculiarly provincial character of German national identity seemed by the
late Weimar period to have lost its constituency and, with it, its cultural
resonance. The problem was not that Heimat activities had abated in any
significant way, but that Heimat sentimentality in the population at large
had become increasingly separated from associational life. Abel's early Nazis
in the Pfalz, for instance, commonly expressed love for Heimat and Father-

196. Auszug aus der Niederschrift über die 136. Sitzung des Ausschuß für den Staats-
haushalt (30 January 1931), BHStAM, MK 15533.

197. BavMinFinanz to Held (23 August 1931), BavMinUK to Held (3 September 1931),
and Ministerratsitzung (3 September 1931, BHStAM, MK 15533.

198. Wiesemann, *Vorgeschichte*, pp. 270–71.

land but spoke simultaneously of an inability to "fit in," to find companions in everyday life, indeed even to recognize the Pfalz itself, overrun as it was by "villains," as their true Heimat.[199] The whole edifice of Heimat promotion presupposed something that did not exist in the Weimar period: that elusive quality of consensus and, perhaps more important, a measure of goodwill toward the existing system, a capacity to seek out and celebrate commonality within it. Plenty of people longed for some kind of unity in Germany—the vocabulary of Volksgemeinschaft was by no means the exclusive rhetoric of the Nazi movement. But fewer and fewer sought that unity in the Weimar Republic.

The Heimat movement in the Pfalz for the most part did still look for solidarity in the Republic; but even when the Heimat believers gave their support to the Weimar system, it was by 1929 passive, limited, or indifferent. Heimat rhetoric, as well as Heimat activities, characteristically conveyed the innocuous injunction to set aside differences, to love one's surroundings, and to cherish one's country. Yet active support for the Weimar Republic as such may not in the end be a particularly useful criterion by which to assess the meaning of Heimat activity, much of which could just as well have been carried on under a monarchy as a democracy—or for that matter, a dictatorship. Heimat symbols attempted to embody not the state but the nation and could not, by their very nature, be the source of any critique of the state that happened at the moment to rule the nation. The essence of the Heimat movement was to legitimate what existed and what had existed, not to undermine it. Insofar as the Weimar Republic was the legal and established representative of the German nation, the Heimat movement's celebration of German nationhood was perfectly consistent with the institutions of the 1920s: a Heimat event like the gigantic *Trachtenfest* of 1931 in Berlin brought together thousands of Germans dressed in "traditional" regional costume, not to criticize the modernity of Weimar society, but rather to symbolize the egalitarian togetherness that was the essence of the imagined national community. Unfortunately, national symbols alone are not enough to insure the survival of the nation-state, and the Heimat movement of the 1920s could do nothing but mirror in its increasing ineffectualness the terminal crises of the political state.

In the Pfalz, the saddest demonstration of the hollowness of the public symbols of Weimar came in 1932 at the attempted celebration of the centenary of the Hambach Festival. An event and a place at once locally beloved and nationally acknowledged, Hambach had given the Weimar Republic its flag as well as demonstrated the possibility of a democratic and liberal patriotism. Although, as with everything associated with the Weimar Republic,

199. See, e.g., nos. 181, 183, 184, 413, 416, and 417, Hoover Institution Archives, Stanford, Abel Collection.

not everyone had accepted the legitimacy of the riotous demonstrations of 1832 as a national symbol, the impending arrival of their hundredth anniversary was not an event to be taken lightly by any concerned German, whether that citizen were anxious for the Republic's survival or eager for its demise.

Local preparations for some kind of centennial were under way already in 1929: the Pfälzer historical associations planned to organize a Hambach exhibition in the Neustadt Heimat Museum; the Pfälzerwald Verein hoped to repeat their festivities of 1914; various Heimat newspapers, especially the Social Democratic *Bei uns daheim,* began to carry articles on the events and participants of 1832; Albert Becker, ever prolific, added two new books on Hambach—*Hambach und Pirmasens* and *Deutschlands Wiedergeburt* (Germany's Rebirth)—to his series of "Contributions to the Heimat Studies of the Pfalz" and delivered a much-reprinted lecture entitled "The Spirit of Hambach." But in early 1931 the anticipated shape of the centennial changed drastically when the Reichs minister of the interior, Joseph Wirth, decided to try to stage a national celebration at Hambach and recruited the local press club to manage the affair. Heading this effort was Franz Hartmann, also leader of the adult education league and a convinced democrat. Hartmann envisioned a celebration not simply patriotic or narrowly historical, but imbued with the ideas of "German unity and German freedom" and concentrated on the theme of freedom of the press.[200] Deeply conscious of the dire political situation, he hoped to attract as broad a base of participation as possible "to secure [the celebration's] transcendence of political conflict and to protect it against political exploitation by any one party."[201]

Long before the actual celebration, planned for May 1932, any illusion that the political battles of the day could be sidestepped or overcome had dissipated. The national government's sponsorship of the event went the way of Wirth himself, who lost his office in October 1931. The Communists announced their refusal to participate in an event that would falsify the ideas of Hambach;[202] conservative and Catholic circles held back, finding nothing to support either in the liberal and enlightened rhetoric of the original Hambach Festival or in the democratic, antimonarchical, egalitarian emphasis of the contemporary one. The National Socialists, originally inclined to appropriate Hambach for its nationalistic potential, were by 1932 denouncing the original event for the weakness of its leaders, the "foreign, liberal, and Marxist" nature of its ideology, and above all the influence on it of "the Jews Heinrich Heine (alias Chaim Bückeburg) and Ludwig Börne (Löw

200. Minutes of meeting in BavMinAus (30 June 1931), BHStAM, MA 108074; see also Baumann, "Hambacher Erinnerungsfeiern," p. 54.

201. Meeting of 30 June 1931, BHStAM, MA 108074.

202. Baumann, "Hambacher Erinnerungsfeiern," p. 55.

Baruch)."[203] Finally, the Bavarian government decided to maintain its distance from the celebration, despite the participation of groups it had long supported through the Pfalzhilfe. Accurate enough in their interpretation of the historical record, though, as always, inept in their gauging of contemporary significance, Bavarian officials expressed to Hartmann their fear that the event would become "a demonstration for the unified state" and an occasion for centralists to denounce federalism, the rights of the smaller states, and, of course, Bavaria itself.[204]

All that was left to Hartmann, still intent on his vision of a festivity in which all could participate, was nationalism and that most durable of political opinions in the Pfalz, Francophobia. In an effort to placate a radical and a conservative right, who themselves were willing to make no concessions, the Hambach centenary of 1932 became a watered-down celebration of Bismarck's nation of 1870 (arguably without relevance to either 1832 or 1932) and Germany's freedom (defined as freedom from French occupation). The essential incoherence of the final result was aptly captured in the title-page drawing by Max Slevogt for a commemorative history of 1832: it pictured the arm of a man holding three flags, the black-white-and-red of the old Reich, the black-red-and-gold of Hambach and Weimar, and the blue-and-white lozenges of Bavaria.[205] As the Pfälzer historian Kurt Baumann wryly observed in 1957, Slevogt might just as well have drawn in a swastika as well.[206] On the day itself, May 6, 1932, the last gathering of democratically minded people in the republican Pfalz was disrupted by gangs of SA men who lined the narrow path to the castle, harassing the people attending the rally and shouting, "Deutschland erwache," throughout the festival speeches.[207] The Nazi press triumphantly foresaw the day when "a fresh wind will blow away the whole revolting episode . . . and bring fluttering in the air over the castle the swastika flag." The day after the festival, the news came that Brüning's government had fallen in Berlin; within a few months, the Republic itself would follow.

Only the Heimat organizations and those democrats still willing to show themselves in public embraced the Hambach centenary wholeheartedly; only the Heimat organizations still believed—or claimed to believe—that the rec-

203. Cited in Emil Strauss, "150 Jahre Erinnerungsfeiern zum Hambacher Fest," Die Pfalz am Rhein: Pfälzische Verkehrs- und Heimatzeitschrift 55 (May 1982): 278.

204. Meeting of 30 June 1931, BHStAM, MA 108074.

205. Johannes Bühler, Das Hambacher Fest. Deutsche Sehnsucht vor hundert Jahren (Ludwigshafen, 1932). Veit Valentin also wrote a commemorative history for the event, but was forbidden access to all Bavarian and Pfälzer archives by the Bavarian government; see his Das Hambacher Nationalfest.

206. Baumann, "Hambacher Erinnerungsfeiern," p. 55.

207. Ibid., Strauss, "150 Jahre Erinnerungsfeiern," p. 278; miscellaneous remembrances from participants, or descendants thereof. The future president of the Bundesrepublik, Theodor Heuss, was one of the speakers.

onciliation of all Germans was possible. In October of the previous year, Franz Hartmann and the members of the adult education league had questioned whether their organization's work could be continued in the poisonous political climate of the day, but they had resolved to carry on: "Precisely in the face of conflicts, we must emphasize the common goods of our culture; precisely because of the social and political fragmentation, our work has its particular importance."[208] At the meeting's close, the Heimat poet Leopold Reitz spoke of the ideals of adult education and Heimat promotion in the Weimar Republic, in words hopeful, futile, and soon forgotten:

> We do not want the battle, we want the peace. We are not a party, we are over parties and between parties. We do not have a worldview, we have a view of humanity. The party wants division, we want reconciliation. Over there, party comrades; here, only the man next to you. There, party organization; here, free will. The party wants to rule, we want to serve. The party says: who is not for me is against me. We say: who is not for me can still be for the whole. Parties say: Marx, Lenin, Hitler. We say: Pestalozzi, Goethe, Mozart. The party makes enemies of father and son. We want each to be the other's brother. The party is dissatisfied with everything and everyone; we are dissatisfied only with ourselves, that we have not yet encouraged enough forgiveness and love and still run the danger of believing ourselves to be always in the right.
>
> We must not dispute but discuss. Not to be right but to be kind, that is everything.

208. Record of the Hauptversammlung (18 October 1931), *PM–PH* 49/28 (1932): 83–84.

SEVEN

From Homeland
to Borderland

The National Socialists, in common with the shopkeeper who invented the Billigheim Purzelmarkt in 1907 or the artist who designed a Pfälzer flag in 1909, showed a propensity for public rituals and invented traditions that embodied some notion of Volksgemeinschaft. Like all Pfälzer Heimatlers, they claimed to value the soil of Germany, the customs and ways of its people, and the integrity of the whole. A festival of folk costume looked much the same under Nazi rule as it had in earlier times; the castles of the Pfalz got equal care and attention. To be sure, the National Socialists asserted the legitimacy of their rituals, revivals, and historical interpretations with rather more determination and single-mindedness than had the shopkeeper, artist, or amateur archeologist: no Georg Berthold of the Historical Association dared inform the Nazis that their swastika flag, their claims to the contrary notwithstanding, had no basis in German heraldry; no Albert Pfeiffer of the state archives could chide the choreographers of Nazi folk costume parades for the rank amateurism and historical inaccuracy of their efforts. But such distinctions may simply have been ones of power. If those thousands of Pfälzer Wäldlers, those hundreds of Heimat-historical enthusiasts, had possessed the power of the Nazis, would they not have behaved similarly? Perhaps in fact the Heimat movement prepared the ground for National Socialism, by denying the importance of individual identity and attempting to subordinate all Germans to an essentially patriarchal, authoritarian system of obedience and collective anonymity.[1]

1. This in essence is Ina-Maria Greverus's argument about the Heimatschutz and Heimatkunde phenomena (*Auf der Suche nach Heimat*, pp. 9–10).

In the agonized retrospection that the Nazi regime has occasioned, such a conclusion is not out of place. Indeed, the Nazis, with their grandiose claims to have brought to a culmination the culture of Central Europe, themselves insured that posterity would treat the German past as their prologue, judging it in light of their deeds and understanding its significance by their own standards. But clearly, the earlier entrepreneurs of tradition in the Pfalz aimed neither at complete domination of the German state nor at the destruction of all its enemies, domestic and foreign. Are their evident affinities in ideology and social understanding with the Nazis not then invalid, irrelevant, or coincidental? Somewhere in between the two extremes—Heimat as, on the one hand, necessary to Nazism and, on the other, irrelevant to it—lies the real history of the appropriation and exploitation of Heimat symbols, ideas, and people by the confused and self-contradictory political culture of Nazism. It is a history that brings together the revolutionary intent of the Nazi recasting of German local life with the ultimate failure of the regime to be anything but destructive.[2] The integrity of local culture and identity that lay at the heart of the Heimat movement was an early and in some sense willing victim of the National Socialist revolution; its forms persisted, but now infused with the rhetoric of racial superiority and the rituals of German power.

On 30 January 1933, Adolf Hitler became chancellor of Germany; on 23 March, after two months of high-pitched propaganda and calculated terror in the streets, the Reichstag passed the Enabling Act that made him in effect Germany's dictator, "created by democracy and appointed by parliament."[3] Even before the passage of the Enabling Act, the dual process of *Ausschaltung* and *Gleichschaltung*—of excluding some groups from public life and bringing others into conformity with Nazi standards—had begun. The undesirables—Jews, Socialists, Communists, Catholics, and Freemasons, among others—were forced out of the civil service and judiciary; the Weimar party system was destroyed; the state governments and local councils were disbanded or robbed of any independence; all the associations, leagues, societies, unions, and circles that crowded the landscape of local and national German public life were either replaced by Nazi organizations or persuaded to pose no autonomous principle of their own against the National Socialist world view.

2. A major trend in recent scholarship on Nazi rule has been to examine the patterns and pathologies of everyday life in an effort to determine the extent of Nazi transformation of society. The material in this chapter on the confusion and the incompleteness of Nazi intervention in social organizations bears affinities to Detlev Peukert's *Inside Nazi Germany: Conformity, Opposition, and Racism in Everyday Life*, trans. Richard Deveson (New Haven, 1987). In his treatment of the Edelweiss Pirates, for instance, Peukert suggests that the retreat to groups based on the locality or the "territorial principle" was a form of rejection of Nazi centralization (p. 155).

3. Konrad Heiden, *Der Fuehrer: Hitler's Rise to Power*, trans. Ralph Manheim (Boston, 1944), p. 579.

In Bavaria, Heinrich Held's government resisted the Nazi takeover relatively strenuously, unsuccessfully appealing at the last minute to Hinden-
burg to block the appointment of a new Nazi Reichs commissioner.[4] But the
Bavarian government had already lost much of its authority in the Pfalz, and
by early March Gauleiter Bürckel was flying the swastika flag from all public
buildings in the district, in defiance of the explicit orders of the minister of
the interior.[5] After the elections of 5 March, Bürckel began in earnest to
replace Bavarian authority in the region with his own, relying on the efficacy
of his combination of anti-Bavarianism, arms, and intimidation. A rash of
early retirements, job changes, and leaves of absence (in the case of socialist
mayors, alarmingly literal ones) thinned the ranks of Pfälzer town mayors
and regional officials.[6] Bürckel himself appropriated no new titles, retaining
his independence as the local party boss.[7] His electioneering practices
brought stunningly affirmative results in the plebiscites of the following
years, and his programs of social relief and employment were popular if not
as effective as was claimed.[8] Deeply provincial in outlook, he did not aspire to
much beyond the securing of his own personal fiefdom in the Pfalz and the
promotion of its economic well-being.

Securing the fiefdom meant above all suppressing the opposition. The
March elections had shown that despite Nazi efforts to intimidate the presses
and break up public meetings, Social Democracy, Communism, and political
Catholicism were all still alive in the Pfalz. By July, they were dead. In
Kaiserslautern, the only Pfälzer town for which a study of any depth of the
Nazi seizure of power has been undertaken, the SA and the *Schutzstaffel* (SS)
seized the public buildings in early March 1933 and launched a series of
raids against the socialist newspaper that ended in its closing on 13 March.
Dissolution of the Reichsbanner and the Catholic Pfalzwacht followed, then
of Social Democratic associations, trade unions, and finally, on 22 June, the
Social Democratic party itself. In early July 1933, the Bavarian People's
party and the Center party dissolved themselves.[9] The Social Democratic

---

4. Karl Schwend, *Bayern zwischen Monarchie und Diktatur. Beiträge zur bayerischen Frage in der
Zeit von 1918 bis 1933* (Munich, 1954), pp. 506ff

5. Rothenberger, "Aus der Nationalsozialistischen Zeit," p. 352.

6. Hüttenberger, *Die Gauleiter*, pp. 92, 98.

7. On Bürckel's position, see Faber, "Die südlichen Rheinlande," pp. 452–53; Hüttenberger, *Die Gauleiter*, pp. 39, 77–79, 119, 213; *Sopade* (1935), 2:1477.

8. Rothenberger, "Aus der Nazionalsozialistischen Zeit," pp. 357–61; see also notices in
Pfälzer in Berlin of the high Pfälzer turnouts and "yes" votes ([1933]:143; [1934]:98). The secret
reports of the Social Democratic party contain numerous accounts of electioneering fraud and
intimidation in the Pfalz—Bürckel's trademarks (*Sopade* [1934], 1:199, 279, 283, 349, 392). He
took effective if not official control of the Bavarian Pfalzhilfe funds, insisting on a reduction in the
interest rates on loans, hence a reduction in cultural expenditures (misc. docs., BHStAM, MK
15534–35).

9. Friedel, *Machtergreifung*, pp. 50–69.

party's secret reports from the Pfalz attested throughout 1934 to wide-spread hatred of the regime and the imminence of revolt, but by the end of the year even an optimistic reporter had to acknowledge the disarray among his Social Democratic comrades, many of whom were in jail or in concentration camps, and the likelihood that the regime would survive for a while longer.[10]

Accompanying the suppression of political opposition was the persecution of cultural diversity. The Protestant church organization in the Pfalz succumbed internally, gradually giving way to the influence of Nazi party members in the church officiate.[11] The Catholic church and its organizations were more of a problem for the furiously anti-Catholic leaders of Nazism in the Pfalz. Catholicism was "the greatest and most dangerous opponent of our world view," declared a Nazi text on "the enemies of the movement."[12] Acts of terror against Catholic clergy, a smear campaign against the Catholic church, and the forcible integration of Catholic youth groups into the Hitler Youth, all played a role in the marginalization of what had once been a politically potent minority in the Pfalz.[13] The top church officials fluctuated between courageous opposition and what they thought was limited cooperation, always in the hope that conditions would improve for Catholics in the near future—once the SA was brought under control, once the Saar vote was over, once the defensive works of the Westwall had been built, and so on.[14]

But Bürckel's particular obsession with Catholicism (he was himself the son of Catholics) did not lessen his anti-Semitism; the Jewish community of the Pfalz suffered the full measure of Nazi hatred. The first anti-Semitic campaigns in the Pfalz centered on the economic role of the Jews. As middlemen, they were blamed for the economic problems of small-scale producers: their businesses were boycotted and destroyed; their lawyers and doctors were barred from practice; some were arrested, some beaten, many harassed.[15] In 1935, the Social Democrats reported that as many as four-fifths of the Pfälzer

10. *Sopade* (1934), 1:396; for expressions of optimism, see pp. 111, 114, 187, 253 (here the reporter admits that "a quick end" to the regime cannot be expected).

11. Karl-Georg Faber, "Überlegungen zu einer Geschichte der Pfälzischen Landeskirche unter dem Nationalsozialismus," *Blätter für pfälzische Kirchengeschichte und religiöse Volkskunde* 41 (1974): 29–58.

12. 1935, PLAS, T65, no. 9; reprinted in *Nationalsozialismus im Alltag. Quellen zur Geschichte der NS-Herrschaft im Gebiet des Landes Rheinland-Pfalz*, ed. Anton Doll (Speyer, 1983).

13. See esp. Helmut Prantl, "Zur Geschichte der katholischen Kirche in der Pfalz unter Nationalsozialistischer Herrschaft," *Blätter für pfälzische Kirchengeschichte und religiöse Volkskunde* 42 (1975): 79–117. The *Sopade* reports refer to incidents in the suppression of Catholic youth groups in the Pfalz ([1935], 2:680, 695).

14. *Sopade* (1935), 2:235. In fact, Nazi attacks on the Catholic church and its hierarchy increased in number and intensity after the Saar vote.

15. Faber, "Die südlichen Rheinlande," p. 455; *Sopade* (1935), 2:921, 924–25, 1030; (1936), 3:1657. See also Hermann Arnold, *Von den Juden in der Pfalz* (Speyer, 1967).

vintners refused to participate in the anti-Jewish agitation and resented the boycott of Jewish merchants because it forced them to sell their grapes at deflated prices to the Nazi-controlled collective.[16] But such opposition went mostly unexpressed. Even before the implementation of the Final Solution, Bürckel had devised his own answer to the Jewish question, the *Aktion Bürckel*, which by a series of massive deportations beginning in October 1940 had removed all Jews from the Pfalz within a year.[17]

Bürckel's energy and inventiveness in the establishment of his own petty Pfälzer principality were mirrored in the gradual promotion of the region from a minor district of distant Bavaria to a major bulwark of the German western front.[18] The promotion began in 1934, when Hitler chose Bürckel over several other Nazi loyalists to manage the Saar plebiscite of 1935 and bring the disputed territory back under German control.[19] The Allies made scant effort to monitor the plebiscitary process, leaving Bürckel free to employ the electioneering practices he had used to such good effect in the Pfalz: massive propaganda, mobilization of non voters, intimidation and slandering of opponents, thuggery and fraud at the polls. The final vote was overwhelmingly in favor of a return to Germany, and Bürckel, more than ever a favorite of Hitler, became the new Reichs commissioner of the Saar and party leader of the new *Reichsgau* Pfalz-Saar. In 1937 the region metamorphosed again, this time into Gau Saarpfalz der NSDAP, a term that reflected the dominance of Bürckel's Nazi party over any other state authority in the region. This it remained until Bürckel returned from a temporary appointment in Vienna, where he had helped to engineer the annexation of Austria and to organize the first deportations of Austrian Jews.[20] Finally, in 1940, the Pfalz disappeared altogether, replaced in official usage, if not in popular consciousness, by the appropriately grandiose and implicitly militaristic notion of the Westmark.

The evolution from Pfalz to Westmark in the space of about six years required the participation of the old Heimat associations in the destruction of a century's worth of Pfälzer invention. The Heimat museums, Heimat clubs,

---

16. *Sopade* (1935), 2:1029.

17. Faber, "Die südlichen Rheinlande," p. 455; Karl-Heinz Debus, "Christen und Juden in der Pfalz zur Zeit des Nationalsozialismus," *Pfälzische Landeskunde*, vol. 3 (Landau/Pfalz), pp. 377–82.

18. One can follow this evolution in the maps of the period, from a depiction of the greater Pfalz, entitled "Rheinfront," in 1934 (Neustadt), which expressed the aspiration, to another entitled "Gau Westmark" in 1941 (Kaiserslautern), which reflected its realization.

19. Hüttenberger, *Die Gauleiter*, pp. 139ff.

20. Ibid. The SPD-in-exile reported overhearing in the Pfalz just prior to the Austrian plebiscite the remark that "der Bürckel wird schon 110 Prozent Stimmen herausholen, der ist geeignet für einen solchen Wahlschwindel" ("Bürckel will undoubtedly bring in 110 percent of the votes; he's the man for election fraud like this"; *Sopade* [1938], 5:262–63.)

and Heimat publications represented a distinctively Pfälzer version of the Volksgemeinschaft that was not entirely consonant with that of National Socialism. Having achieved power, the Nazis moved quickly to insure that all imaginings of the whole were in line with their own, and this meant bringing Heimat organizations under their control, along with singing clubs, youth groups, hiking fellowships, and all other expressions of German sociability. The Gleichschaltung, or coordination, of the German Heimat consciousness proceeded in the Pfalz in three stages, each a further intensification of Nazi influence on local institutions. From the consolidation and centralization of some groups to the transformation of others and finally the invention of new ones, the Nazis attempted to appropriate and organize the sentiments of hometown patriots.

The Pfälzer Heimat organizations subjected to the least amount of change after 1933 were the primarily convivial organizations, the most prominent of which was the Pfälzerwald Verein. Its hikes and its Heimat evenings seemed to take place as before, with only the occasional reference to the "national revolution" in progress. Yet more than the quiet hegemony of everyday life over political drama seems to have been responsible for this continuity, for members of such organizations often considered themselves to be active participants in Germany's fate as a nation—before and after 1933—and many enthusiastically endorsed what they called the regeneration of Germany under Nazi rule. Part of the answer lay in the common fund of German nationalist rhetoric from which both Nazis and groups like the Pfälzerwald Verein had long drawn. But part lay as well in the tendency of the Nazis, after 1933, to fashion their rhetorical Volksgemeinschaft out of the available materials, of which one of the most important was the highly developed infrastructure of German associational life. Hence, organizations like the Pfälzerwald Verein could go on as before because the Nazis approved of some of their activities and were indifferent to others. In minor matters the Verein even continued to assert a conviviality outside the grasp of the Nazi revolution: witness their continued preference in greeting one another for the simple "Deutsche Grüße" (German greetings), or even "Fröhliche Pfalz, Gott erhalt's" (Happy Pfalz, may God preserve it), to "Heil Hitler."

The problem of interpreting the lack of change in certain Heimat associations is further complicated when one considers that their stability was in some sense only apparent, an assertion of normalcy in the face of a darker reality. In 1933, for instance, *Pfälzer in Berlin*, an organ of the Heimat association, printed a small notice between hometown news and subscription pleas entitled "Against the Atrocity Slanders Abroad": "We ask all our members and countrymen to help us in the battle against the atrocity stories; especially in letters to relatives and friends outside of Germany, everyone should emphasize that the national revolution has completed itself in a fully orderly fashion and that all the reports of horrors are mere inventions, intended to damage our German Fatherland."[21] Similarly, in 1935 a retrospective look at the twenty-five-year history of the Berlin club of Pfälzers emphasized the *abnormality* of the Weimar period, with its continual strikes and street battles (no mention that the Nazis had themselves been responsible for most of these): "Much of it today sounds to us like a fairy tale [*Märchen*]; one can hardly believe that such times really existed."[22] In both these examples, the truth of the matter is at least partly acknowledged by the protest itself; the effort to disguise that truth results in the ludicrous notion of a "revolution" (*Umwälzung*) conducted in "an orderly fashion" and in the revealing comparison of the past to a fairy tale—a notion that resonates with suppressed longings.

In the specific context of club activities, the apparent lack of change could and did legitimate that Nazi regime by giving it an appearance of rootedness in the structure of everyday life. At the same time, to assert the continuity of their experience, as Heimat associations often did, allowed them self-servingly to claim to have prefigured the Nazi revolution. The effort to appear unchanged yet revolutionized inevitably involved people in more vague and self-contradictory assertions about the situation in Germany. In the same paragraph, the editor of *Pfälzer in Berlin* could refer to the profound "internal rebuilding and new organization" brought about by the "national transformation" and assert that "in outer form we are little changed" and in inner form "our Landsmannschaft has always been völkisch in outlook and dedicated to the service of Volkstum"[23]—in other words, we have been through a profound change, but everything is the same as before. These eager conformists found themselves hopelessly caught in the contradictions of Nazi ideology itself, fruitlessly circling between the equally empty promises of revolution and of order.

For all was not, in fact, unchanged in the world of Heimat conviviality. The very fact that the new regime aspired to total control, regardless of whether they achieved it, altered the relation of association to state and with it the complexion of public life in Germany. The Nazis renamed and reorganized convivial associations as part of the drive to centralized administration that affected many other parts of institutionalized life in Germany. In 1934, for instance, a new Reichsbund Volkstum and Heimat absorbed the Berlin group of Pfälzers into its national structure.[24] Justifying his notionally voluntary decision to join the Reichsbund, association leader Flickinger wrote that "the national-socialist revolution has inserted itself into all areas of public

21. "Gegen die Greuelhetze im Ausland!" *PB* (25 April 1933): 48.
22. "1910–1935: 25 Jahre Arbeit der Landsmannschaft der Rheinpfälzer in Berlin," *PB* (25 February 1935): 30.
23. Ibid. On the distinction between *völkisch* and *volkstümlich*, see below, pp. 141–42.
24. On the Reichsbund, see NSDAP Hauptarchiv, Hoover Institution Microfilm Collection, reel 14, folder no. 276.

life, and it must do so if it is to achieve a full redesigning of our collective life; everything that can be useful in this new building of the national character must put itself at the service of the revolution. Indeed, it would certainly have been a grave error had the Führer not turned to the Landsmannschaften, with all their experience in the work of Volkstum, to serve in the revolution."[25] Flickinger went on to announce that since the new umbrella organization was part of the National Socialist party, so too had the Landsmannschaft become National Socialist, and "its leadership will henceforth follow National Socialist principles." Adherence to the *Führerprinzip* justified reshuffling the internal organization of the club to give it a more hierarchical character than before—a change that went a long way toward destroying the spirit of egalitarian comradeship that Landsmannschaften had supposedly represented.[26] Membership, too, would no longer be simply a question of one's Pfalztum; lip service to these so-called principles of National Socialism, if not actual membership in the party, became a requirement for admission to the now-exclusive group.[27] Here, certainly, the Nazi regime had effected a profound, albeit invisible, transmutation in the purpose and spirit of the Landsmannschaft. Simply by altering the definition of a member from a Pfälzer to a Nazi (albeit a Pfälzer one), the Nazis reordered the priorities of the organization, and with them the balance between provincial identity and national consciousness.

The incipient chaos of Nazi administration, with its proliferating authorities and umbrella organizations, also undermined the localist autonomy of the Heimat associations. The Pfälzer Landsmannschaft in Berlin was swallowed up twice, first by the Reichsbund Volkstum und Heimat and then by the new Bund Deutscher Westen.[28] In the Pfalz, the various historical and botanical associations amalgamated to become the Arbeitsgemeinschaft der völkischen Wissenschaft im Kampfbund für deutsche Kultur in der Westmark (Working Community of Völkisch Learning in the League of Struggle for German Culture in the Western March), itself part of several national organizations; the Literary Association became the Arbeitsgemeinschaft des deutschen Schrifttums in der Pfalz, part of a national literary organization; the many local singing groups became a single Sängerbund Westmark. All, in turn, became subsidiaries of the recast adult education association, which was itself subordinate to, among others, the Reichskulturkammer, the Landespropagandastelle Rheinpfalz, the Gaukulturamt der NSDAP, the Deutsche Arbeitsfront, the Deutsche Bühne, the "Kraft durch Freude" campaign, and

25. J. Flickinger, "Im Reichsbund Volkstum und Heimat," *PB* (25 April 1934): 37–38.
26. "Jahresbericht für 1934," *PB* (25 January 1935): 3.
27. "Im Reichsbund Volkstum und Heimat," *PB* (25 April 1934): 38.
28. President Speiwok of the "Bund Deutscher Westen," speech printed in *PB* (25 July 1933): 77–79.

the Reichsbund Volkstum und Heimat.[29] A preference for the gigantic and national in place of the small and local corresponded to this elaborate centralization and rationalization of institutions. In 1934, for instance, the central propaganda agency of the Reich staged a large exhibition in Berlin called "The Pfalz in the New Reich" to coincide with the intensification of the campaign to win the Saar plebiscite. The old Heimat associations of the Pfalz had little to do with the exhibition, apart from attending, publicizing, and praising it; indeed, the only local organization that had any hand at all in shaping the exhibition was the Nazified professional tourist association, headed by Bürckel's deputy, Richard Imbt.

The Nazi reorganization effectively robbed Heimat activities of their particularity and their local independence, both qualities at the heart of the idea of Heimat itself. At its most ridiculous, the subsumption of German Heimat sociability under myriad groups and subgroups could be simply unwieldy: take for example an announcement of a brief performance of Pfälzer folk customs put on not just by the local Landsmannschaft, but by "the Landsmannschaft of Rheinpfälzers in Berlin, in the Reichsbund Volk and Heimat," in conjunction with "the Office for Heimatkunde and Volkstum in the Cultural Division of the Berlin Area of the Hitler Youth" and "the Cultural Office of the NSDAP Rheinpfalz."[30] Most manifestations of Nazi encroachment, however, ranged from the unpleasant to the vicious. In the literary organization, such old leaders as Ludwig Eid were forced to give way to men like Roland Betsch (the new chairman), Paul Ginthum, and Gerd Buchheit, all leading voices of disaffection in the Weimar period.[31] The "Folk music movement" in Pirmasens, according to one report, was languishing under a proliferation and politicization of music clubs that had led to "the falling apart of associations, a drying up of interest, and a dying out of the joy in singing."[32] In 1935, a Pfälzer group called the "Friends of Nature" had set out on a bus trip to the graves at Verdun, only to be stopped and arrested en masse by the Gestapo. The arrests were evidently a mistake, for everyone was soon released; as a parting gesture, the Gestapo revoked their passports and told them to keep their mouths shut.[33] The message, in any case, was clear enough. Associational activities continued only on the forbearance of the regime; they could end at any time. In 1936, Bürckel's crony Imbt, the

29. R. Jung, "Jahresbericht," *Die Westmark: Monatsschrift des Volksbildungsverbandes Pfalz-Saar/Kampfbund für Deutsche Kultur in der Westmark*, Sonderdruck (1934): 4.
30. "Jahresbericht für 1934," *PB* (25 January 1935): 3.
31. *Pfalz am Rhein* 16 (June 1933): 272. See also Chapter 6 above.
32. Attributed to the *Pirmasenser Zeitung* in *Sopade* (1935), 2:717–18. The SPD reporter was, of course, particularly concerned about the dissolution of workers' singing groups and folk music choirs, which he said had once been strong in the Pfalz and Baden.
33. *Sopade* (1935), 2:831.

new director of the Dürkheimer Wurstmarkt, the most famous of the Pfalz's folk festivals, fired the publican in charge of provision because he had bought meats from a Jewish butcher. When the publican appealed the firing, some local SA men took matters into their own hands, forcing him to close his business and pillaging the house of the Jewish butcher.[34] The festival went on.

The public world over which the Nazi regime presided may not have reflected the Nazi world view in all its parts and processes; but the principle of conformity had been propagated, and its consequences were significant. In January 1933, five days before Hitler was suddenly appointed Reichs chancellor, the editor of *Pfälzer in Berlin* had pleaded with members to respect the non-political character of the group by not wearing uniforms to club meetings and not turning meetings and outings into political gatherings: "Have consideration for the opinions of your neighbors. Everyone who belongs to the Verein loves his Heimat and serves its interest. With that, let us be content."[35] That understanding of the notion of *Überparteilichkeit*, in which "suprapolitical" meant the toleration of political differences, did not long survive in National Socialist Germany. Within the year, *überparteilich* better described the position of the Nazi party itself—the party above parties— whose transcendence had been achieved at the cost of political and cultural dissent. The Pfälzer Landsmannschaft, in contrast, had become *unterparteilich*, just one more mouthpiece for the National Socialist "principles" now presumed to be at one with those of all Heimat-loving people. Perhaps the "apoliticism" of the association in the days of the Weimar Republic—its insistence then on remaining above the fray—had helped to make for Nazi success.[36] Certainly it allowed groups like the Heimat associations to adjust to Nazi society with seeming effortlessness. But such continuities do not preclude change, and what began by destroying the old context in which Heimat associations had flourished quickly altered their internal tissue also.

The cultural organizations of the Pfalz felt the effects of Nazi power more immediately and directly. For those who in the Weimar period had devoted themselves to cultivating and preserving more than just the conviviality of countrymen, the advent of Nazism did not offer the possibility of life-as-usual, with a blind eye to one side and a blinkered one to the other. Nazi Kulturpolitik in the Pfalz was from the start aggressive and wide-ranging. Kurt Kölsch, the new *Gaukulturwart*, or warden of culture, declared that the entire culture of the region had been polluted by foreign propaganda over the past centuries, and by democracy and "racial chaos" in the past decade.

34. Ibid. (1936), 3:1030.
35. The stricture was almost certainly directed against Nazi party members, for whom the kind of behavior inveighed against here was usual. See "Jahresbericht für 1932," *PB* (25 January 1933): 4.
36. See esp. Koshar, *Social Life, Local Politics, and Nazism*.

Since its inception, he asserted, National Socialism had tried to defend the true German culture of the region; in the "new Germany," it "went without saying" that "the propaganda apparatus of the party must be mobilized for cultural purposes, since not only is culture a task of propaganda, but propaganda is itself a cultural act and must be an essential piece of our völkisch reeducation."[37]

The process of transforming Pfälzer culture, rather than merely centralizing it, began with the liberal adult educational league. Almost everything about the league, from its egalitarian structure to the repertoire of its theater company, was repugnant to the Nazis; there was never any question that it would have to change radically, if not close down entirely. In May 1933, Franz Hartmann, doubly implicated as head of the league and leader of the Pfälzer press club, went into quasi exile in Saarbrücken, where he carried on as a freelance journalist and anti-Nazi publicist until the Saar plebiscite made that region no longer a refuge.[38] He was succeeded by two newcomers to Pfälzer cultural organization, Hermann Emrich and Kurt Kölsch—one a self-styled scholar, the other a local poet desiring larger audiences, and both willing agents of party bosses Bürckel and Imbt. Emrich at once discarded the offensive word *frei* from the organization's name, dubbing it instead the Kampfbund für deutsche Kultur in der Westmark (League of Struggle for German Culture in the Western March). He purged the association's libraries of all undesirable literature; abolished the education courses; substituted dramas like *Schlageter*, the story of an occupation-period saboteur, for the classical offerings of the old theater company; and inserted Hitler's birthday, among other new events, into the popular almanac *Jäger aus Kurpfalz*.[39] The Nazi wardens of culture in the Pfalz also tightened what had been the loosely associative structure of the old league into a hierarchy of titles and functions that underscored the militarism in the new organization's name.

The effect of the reforming zeal of Emrich and Kölsch was to gut the old adult educational league of its adult educational functions, turning it instead into a heavy-handed propaganda organization. "There is no longer an adult education movement in the old sense with so and so many contradictory and artificially integrated liberal organizations," wrote Kölsch in 1934; "there is only national-socialist and racially conscious cultural work, which has brought into conformity and subordination to it all organizations and associations."[40] Another Kampfbund official described the organization as a

37. Kurt Kölsch, "Kultur aus Volkstum und Heimat," *Westmark*, no. 12 (1933–34): 642.

38. BavMinAus, "Betr. Pf. Volksbildungsverband" (1 June 1933) BHStAM, MA 106019. After the plebiscite of 1935, he moved on to Munich and then to a small village outside of Passau, where he died in 1944.

39. Emrich to BavMinUK (summer 1933, 27 October 1933, 12 January 1934) BHStAM, MK 15534; "Jahresbericht," *Westmark* Sonderdruck (1934): 4–9.

40. "Kultur aus Volkstum und Heimat," *Westmark* (September 1934): 642.

"cultural wall" against outside incursions. Behind this wall, Pfälzer culture would develop in ever greater conformity with the "German soul"; the cultural "new order" in the Pfalz would reflect "a single point of view."[41] As both the new name and the new rhetoric accompanying it suggested, the distinctively Pfälzer—the "things of the Heimat and the things of the earth," as Hermann Fitz had written in 1919—now played a decidedly subordinate role to the national and the German. The balance had always been delicate, sustained by the belief that the national soul had many aspects, many forms. The Nazis spoke of their *Volksnähe*, or closeness to the people, but the Volk of the Nazis bore only one aspect. Indeed, the notion of diversity, the "many-sidedness" of W. H. Riehl, disappeared entirely from the public vocabulary of German culture. The distinctiveness of the Pfalz, at least in the new Kampfbund, survived only as the peculiar problems of a border region.

The Kampfbund gave an overall ideological shape to cultural promotion in the Pfalz; a transformed Pfälzer Society for the Promotion of Learning gave it intellectual underpinnings. The "new ordering" of the scholarly society involved a thoroughgoing replacement of old members with ideologically fit new ones, as well as a redefinition of its purpose. The exclusivity and elitism of the society persisted, a curious anomaly in the context of the "national revolution," which, strictly speaking, had rendered the distinction between high and low culture meaningless.[42] Other scholarly institutions, like the old Historical Association, had gone the way of assimilation and centralization, disappearing into the anonymity of the ponderously titled Working Community for Völkisch Learning in the League of Struggle for German Culture in the Western March.[43] But the Society for the Promotion of Learning remained, keeping its original name and structure throughout the 1930s. "The *Neugestaltung* [rearrangement] of the society was no *Gleichschaltung* [putting-in-the-same-gear]," wrote a new member, but rather a "*Neuformung* [reshaping]" that permitted its "*Eingliederung* [incorporation] into the new cultural tasks of our Heimat" and the "*Anknüpfung* [tying on]" to past traditions.[44] The distinctions may have been more imagined than real, but that they were made at all was testimony to the new regime's desire for the imprimatur of the past.

Hermann Emrich, who took charge of this internal "rearrangement" of the society, drew inspiration from the radical critique of it in the 1920s.[45] Its

---

41. Emrich to BavMinUK (Summer 1933), BHStAM, MK 15534.

42. For the invocation of the "revolution," see Hermann Emrich, "Denkschrift: Neuordnung der PGFW" (1 June 1933), BHStAM, MK 15551.

43. Ibid.

44. E. F. Rasche, "Die Neuordnung der Pfälzischen Gesellschaft zur Förderung Wissenschaften," *Völkische Wissenschaft: Periodische Beilage zur Monatsschrift "Die Westmark"* 1 (1934): 22.

45. Gert Buchheit, the original critic, had himself become a subregional head of a department of the new literary association that was part of the new Kampfbund, no very exalted post;

Bavarianism, its conservatism, its narrowness of vision and timidity of purpose, and most of all its provincialism aroused Emrich's scorn: the "purpose of the society," he asserted, had been "to control scholarly life to the benefit of the Bavarian People's party," and under such circumstances "no real progress in scholarship could take place, no real creative drive could exist."[46] The many studies that the society had sponsored all suffered from the flaws of "literal-mindedness," "objectivity," and "specialization."[47] Without sufficient regard to "philosophy" (which in this context meant National Socialism), "the consciousness of the whole," and "the requirements of the present," scholarship had degenerated into mere "Pfalzkunde," which was "a dead, museum-bound science."[48] Most damning, the old leaders of Pfälzer scholarship, prejudiced by the "ruling liberal attitude toward learning," had neglected to study the importance of race in folk life; hence they had failed "to deepen the racial self-consciousness of the population."[49] Emrich intended that future scholarship would deal only with the "living ties to the life problems of our people" and represent only "the ideological and racialist points of view."[50] The "completely meaningless concept of a Pfalzkunde," he noted with unconcealed contempt for the Heimat tradition, would be abandoned; "purely Pfälzer themes" would henceforth attract the Society's attention only "as expressions of the Westmark, itself an organically adapted member of the Reichs-whole."[51]

By the end of the summer of 1933, Emrich had accomplished at least part of his plan for the "spiritual renewal" of the Westmark: the replacement of "unacceptable" members of the society with "völkisch scholars."[52] He apparently drew inspiration from the purging, then in process, of the Literature Section of the Prussian Academy of Arts. There a combination of internal pressure toward conformity and external threats had driven out half the membership, among them Germany's most distinguished writers.[53] In the Pfalz, the blow to German culture may not have been as severe, but cultural integrity was equally compromised. Ten of the twenty-five members of the society resigned under various forms of pressure; several more were allowed

---

in fact, Emrich referred to Buchheit's criticism of the PGFW in the 1920s as coming from "non-National Socialist sources." See Emrich to BavMinUk, "Denkschrift" (31 July 1933), BHStAM, MK 15551.

46. Ibid.

47. What Emrich seemed to mean by "ideel-sachlich" was simply that Pfälzer scholars had been too interested in the facts.

48. Ibid.; Emrich and Kölsch (1 June 1933), "Denkschrift," BHStAM, MK 15551.

49. Emrich, "Denkschrift" (31 July 1933), BHStAM, MK 15551.

50. Emrich and Kölsch, "Denkschrift" (1 June 1933), BHStAM, MK 15551.

51. Emrich (31 July 1933), BHStAM, MK 15551.

52. Emrich and Kölsch (1 June 1933), BHStAM, MK 15551.

53. On the Prussian Academy, see Craig, *Germany*, pp. 646–8.

to stay on only because they were expected to die soon, and those who did stay were relegated to minor subdivisions, where they discovered the benefits of obscurity and absenteeism.[54] The president, Friedrich von Bassermann-Jordan, was given to understand that the society could not develop under his leadership; he resigned politely and promptly.[55] As a reward, he was permitted to continue to attend meetings as "honorary president." The title gave far more credence to the Nazis than balm to his wounded self-esteem, for such apparent approval of the new order by the old did the Nazis no harm and their supine opponents no good.[56] The secretary, archivist Albert Pfeiffer, of a prominent Catholic family, tendered his resignation at the same time as Bassermann-Jordan, but he received no false civilities in return, just a notice of reassignment to an obscure archive in rural eastern Bavaria. By the end of 1934, the turnover in membership since 1932 exceeded 50 percent, and if one counted the rate of chronic absenteeism at the frequent meetings called by Emrich, the figure would be even higher.[57] The new members included a few prominent Nazi scholars: Eugen von Herrigel, philosopher and author of *Zen and the Art of Archery*; Kurt von Raumer and K. A. von Müller, both historians, the latter the new editor of the *Historische Zeitschrift*.[58] Others, like Karl Roth of Kaiserslautern, who had spent much of the 1920s measuring Pfälzer heads, had expertise in the arcana of intellectual racialism, or were simply disgruntled scholars whose accomplishments had received no recognition under the old regime.

In 1938, when Emrich finally got around to cleaning out the society's basement, he found piles of old publications from the Weimar period, most of them flawed by what he called "liberal attitudes" and "outdated approaches to Heimat research," and one even tainted by "the participation of Jews" in its preparation.[59] Since the enthusiasm for public book burning had never been great and even such ineffectual preservers of culture as the Bavarian Ministry of Culture were raising objections to wholesale cultural destruction, Emrich decided to stamp the lot as "old paper" and sell it to

54. BavMinUK to Präsidium Pfalz (23 June 1933), Präs. Pfalz to BavMinUK (4 July 1933), and Emrich to BavMinUK (1 September 1933), BHStAM, MK 15551.

55. BavMinUK to Präsidium Pfalz (23 June 1933), Präs. Pfalz to BavMinUK (4 July 1933), BavMinUK to Bassermann-Jordan (23 July 1933), and Bassermann-Jordan to BavMinUK (4 August 1933), BHStAM, MK 15551.

56. The new corresponding secretary of the society in fact boasted of this coup in his article, "Die Neuordnung der Pfälzischen Gesellschaft," p. 23.

57. PGFW, Minutes of meeting of regular members (5 January 1935), BHStAM, MK 15552.

58. Emrich to BavMinUK (1 September 1933), BHStAM, MK 15551.

59. The volume so described was Fritz Heeger and Wilhelm Wüst's *Pfälzische Volkslieder*; Emrich, "Begründung für den Antrag, betr. Revision der von der PGFW verlegten Veröffentlichung" (16 December 1938), BHStAM, MK 15553.

junk dealers.[60] As he well knew, the designation aptly expressed the transformation in local scholarship that he had brought about. *Völkische Wissenschaft*, *Die Westmark*, and *Unsere Heimat*, the three periodicals that replaced the Heimat-historical journals of the Weimar period, were filled with shrilly racist and nationalist articles, programmatic statements and ideological harangues, and "reinterpretations" of Pfälzer figures of the past that recruited them to the ranks of Nazi heralds. The lecture offerings of the society were similarly transformed: in 1934 the subjects included "A View into Western Racial Chaos," "The Reich as Longing and Fulfillment of Pfälzer Volkstum," and "The Thousand-Year Struggle for the Rhine as a Struggle for the Reich."[61] Amid all this *weltanschaulich* clamor, the notion of the Pfalz, too, was gradually becoming as obsolete as the old-paper publications that had sought to preserve it. Research may have taken as its conscious point of departure "the details of the landscape," but the "thematic, totalizing goal," as Emrich put it, effectively obscured one's view of anything else.

Nevertheless, even though centralized, consolidated, regulated, and revolutionized, the old institutions of Pfälzer Heimat cultivation evidently did not prove equal to the task of realizing the Nazi vision of the Pfalz, or Westmark, in a dynamic greater Germany. In 1936, Emrich created an entirely new scholarly organization, the Saarpfälzische Institut für Landes- und Volksforschung (Saar-Pfälzer Institute for Regional and Ethnographic Research), which was dedicated to the study of the racial characteristics and "fate" of the "Saar-Pfälzer" German type at home and abroad.[62] The new institute's scholars were known as "experts" and "specialists" rather than simply "Heimatpfleger"—a terminological innovation that speaks generally to the Nazis' technocratic and ideological distance from local life.[63] From the start, the Nazis systematically undercut the autonomy of associations by submerging them in national organizations and by substituting a language at once bureaucratic and grandiose for the locally rooted, deliberately nostalgic language of Heimat.[64] The Nazi "revolution," as arbitrary and incomplete

60. Ibid.; cf. Bavarian objections, BavMinUK to Präs. Pfalz (13 January 1939), BHStAM, MK 15553.

61. PGFW, Minutes of meeting (24 March 1934), BHStAM, MK 15552.

62. Correspondence between Emrich of PGFW and the BavMinUK (December 1935–37), in BHStAM, MK 15536, 15552, and MA 106035. One could possibly argue that ample precedent existed for such an institute in the various right-wing organizations devoted to the study of Alsace-Lorraine as well as the German "borderland" study groups, but none of these had specifically Pfälzer roots or Pfälzer interests. On the Westdeutsche Forschungsgemeinschaft and the Bund der Elsaß-Lothringens im Reich, see esp. Lothar Kettenacker, *Nationalsozialistische Volkstumspolitik im Elsaß* (Stuttgart, 1973), pp. 39–49, 76.

63. On the debates over nomenclature in the institute's hierarchy, see BavMinUK to Präs. Pfalz (6 February 1940), BHStAM, MK 15553.

64. The question of language is a vexed one; for every example of a technocratic euphemism there is a counterexample of a deliberate archaism, like *Gau* or *Wart*.

as it was, did render the institutions of Heimat cultivation in Germany mar-
ginal to local society and unresponsive to the needs or desires of participants
themselves. Moreover, the marginalization of Heimat cultivation was itself
part of the larger process of the "fracturing or atomization of opinion" that in
the long run reduced opposition to grumblings about bits and pieces of Nazism, rather than systematic resistance.[65] Against the claims of locality,
whether political, economic, or merely cultural, the Nazis insisted on the
absolute priority of the nation, which they defined from a fictive center—the
Führer—on outward and downward. In the face of such a world view there
remained little point to the cultivation of Heimat at all.

Thus, although Heimat cultivation did persist in the Third Reich, its
meaning—politicized, paganized, and nationalized—became ultimately abstract. All that had once been vital to Heimat cultivation, from civic pride to
a respect for the particularity of local life and tradition, had little resonance
in a regime attentive to national grandeur and racial, not simply local, pride.
Heimat, because it implied little about race, tribe, or any other of the categories favored by Nazi ideology, became a term of distinctly subsidiary importance: the locus of race, perhaps, but not its essence, and not a concept
with any intrinsically prior claim to the loyalties of the German Volk. *Boden*
(earth), in the final analysis, meant nothing without *Blut* (blood).[66] Moreover, one need not give undue credence to the incoherent ramblings of its
ideology to see in the Nazi state the systematic undermining of local society
and locally referential worldviews. In all aspects of their lives, as breadwin-
ners, as churchgoers, as family members, as citizens, as human beings, Germans were told to see themselves in terms of the nation and the nation's
destiny. And as practiced by the Nazi leadership, that national destiny had
in fact an enormous capacity to disrupt the lives of even the most provincial
of Germans.

The ways by which the "Heimat" was cultivated during the Nazi years
subtly (and sometimes not so subtly) discouraged the enjoyment of local
particularism, even in its politically neutral aspects. The Nazi year of festivals, for instance, imposed itself on such traditional (at least since 1900)
expressions of Heimat consciousness as the almanac and the town festival.[67]

65. Ian Kershaw, *Popular Opinion and Political Dissent in the Third Reich: Bavaria 1933–1945*
(Oxford, 1983), pp. 384–85. This is also an essential part of Peukert's perspective on everyday
life in *Inside Nazi Germany*.

66. See also Max Braubach, *Landesgeschichtliche Bestrebungen und historische Vereine im Rheinland*
(Düsseldorf, 1954), p. 91.

67. See *Der Jäger aus Kurpfalz*, the almanac put out by the Kampfbund für Deutsche Kultur,
after 1933. Randall L. Bytwerk argues that the Nazi "Feier inflation," by which he means the
proliferation of Nazi celebrations—on Hitler's birthday, on the day of "national Regeneration,"
on May Day, and so on—loosened local ties and transformed civic rituals into religious ones; see
his "Rhetorical Aspects of Nazi Holidays," *Journal of Popular Culture* 13 (1979): 243.

In the Nazi period, the local almanacs featured swastikas and Nazi youth in the middle of the sketches of local nature, wisdom from the mouth of Hitler in place of the folk sayings, pseudopagan designations for the months, and announcements of dates significant in the history of the Nazi party alongside the Pfälzer anniversaries. Hermann Emrich justified the various paganisms the Nazis had introduced into the *Jäger aus Kurpfalz* as an expression of "the powerful movement toward renewal in the German people," which had awakened a longing "to connect with the eternal symbols of Being... the *urdeutsch*-mythical lore of the yearly cycle."[68] Although the Nazis were simply replacing one set of invented traditions for another, theirs served a different principle. The pseudopaganisms tied Pfälzers into a cultural identity purportedly more ancient, more essential than the epiphenomena of regional distinctions. At the same time, the insistence on the non-Christian *urdeutsch* lore undermined the symbiosis between Christianity and Heimat that had been so crucial to its rootedness in local life.

A similar disruption of local patterns characterized the public festivals in provincial Nazi Germany. The celebration of Hitler's birthday with a mandatory flying of flags and banners is a case in point: it symbolized the power of the center distributed across the whole. The old local events, whose historical and cultural references did not extend beyond a limited geographical area, had, as I have argued, provided occasion to reflect on the larger communities to which one also belonged, but they had not celebrated a homogeneous set of values and political norms. Such genuinely local events as the Billigheim Purzelmarkt were infrequent in the frenetically festive 1930s, pushed to the margins on the one hand and decked out with swastika flags on the other. In 1938, the author of a dissertation on turn-of-the-century Heimat literature summed up the prevailing attitude when she concluded that "present-day literature is völkisch literature and belongs to a single-minded people, while the old Heimat poets [of the prewar period] were only weak and incomplete voices in the battle." And yet, she continued, "the Heimat art movement [was] certainly one of the most promising currents that indicated even before the war a spiritual preparation for what was coming, and hence should be honored for its service to a national future."[69] Heimat was assimilable, but with reservations, alterations, and provisos.

The Nazi worldview and Nazi state dynamism made themselves felt throughout the threefold categories of local self-understanding that I have considered in the context of the Heimat movement: tourism and the promotion of local nature; folkloric activities and the interpretation of local culture; historical endeavors and the creation of a usable past. Of the three, tourism underwent by far the most banal and thus perhaps most enduring trans-

---

68. Introduction, *Der Jäger aus Kurpfalz* (1934), p. 1.
69. Dieck, "Die Literargeschichtliche Stellung der Heimatkunst," p. 85.

formation. Gone were the happily solipsistic days when the castle ruin was a local monument, site of picnics and goal of Sunday afternoon strolls, when the town fathers were the tourist agents, content with the occasional visitor from Mannheim or Karlsruhe. The Nazification of nature involved the subordination of the civic and communal to the economic exploitation of the outdoors—a tendency already evident, to be sure, in the first decade of the century, but not dominant.[70] The effect of forcing local nature clubs, like the Pfälzerwald Verein, into national organizations and centralized patterns of administration was not, as Nazi rhetoric suggested, to deepen the German appreciation of nature's mysteries, but to bring greater sophistication—by way of greater awareness of the national market—into the promotion of the Pfalz's charms. The most mystical declarations of "the experience of landscape" would now appear in tourist magazines alongside crass calculations of its salability.[71] The Nazis were naturally talented tourist agents and succeeded throughout the Pfalz in transforming civic boosterism into professional tourism.[72] In tourism, as in many other aspects of social life, the Nazis achieved a degree of modernization that had eluded previous promoters of consumerism, and they laid the basis for the atomized but materially sated culture that flourished long after they had gone down in the flames of their own making.[73]

Without question, the greatest triumph of Nazi touristic naturalism in the Pfalz was the construction of the *Deutsche Weinstraße* (German Wine Road), an assertion of national coherence on an unruly natural setting that persists to this day. Completed in 1935, the Weinstraße formed part of Bürckel's overall efforts toward the economic recovery of the region, the much-vaunted "socialism of the deed."[74] Its building was a public works project of considerable proportions, and its completion promised to make accessible the tiny villages and vineyards of the Pfälzer wine-producing region, which were set far back from the Rhine in-the-hills of the Haardt and had thus never attracted many visitors. Its opening in October 1935 gave Bürckel a chance to boast of his recent successes and hint at his future ambitions. The midpoint of the Weinstraße just happened to coincide with his party headquar-

70. See also analyses of everyday life that emphasize the acceleration of modernization under the Nazis (e.g., David Schoenbaum, *Hitler's Social Revolution* [Garden City, N.Y., 1966]) and the structural contradictions that that entailed (e.g., Peukert, *Inside Nazi Germany*; and, on female labor, Tim Mason, "Women in Germany, 1925–1940: Family, Welfare, and Work," *History Workshop Journal*, nos. 1 and 2 [1976]).

71. *Pfalz am Rhein* was the professional tourist publication, but *Unsere Heimat* and *Der Pfälzer in Berlin* also served the functions of advertising hotels, wines, tourist spots, and the like.

72. See, e.g., the speeches from Imbt of the Pfälzische Verkehrsverband, a new information guide to touristic promotion, and a variety of other schemes in *PB* (1934–38).

73. See also Peukert, *Inside Nazi Germany*, pp. 241–42.

74. See report on economic conditions in the Sudpfalz by local party official Karl Kleeman, BHStAM, MA 106035.

ters in Neustadt, no longer in the Haardt but now "an-der-Weinstraße." The road's starting point, where the opening ceremonies took place, lay as close to the French-Alsatian border as one could come without crossing over it, and it was marked by a gigantic gate, or *Tor*, in a modified monumental style with such oblique references to vernacular architecture as a gabled roof in stone atop massive pillars. Whether the *Weintor* faced inward, opening onto the Weinstraße as it headed north, or outward, a gateway to Alsace and to France, was left ambiguous; the town where it sat was appropriately named Schweigen (to keep silent), and Bürckel was not talking either, except to reiterate that thanks to him new times had arrived for the Pfalz. "In wine is truth," he declared, prefatory to a brief exposition of the historical development of the Westmark: "The political rises and falls, the Good and the Evil are mirrored in the wine itself." His point was not so much that men make wine and hence can spoil it; rather, wine was seen as manifestation of nature's own bounty, and its quality an expression of nature's approbation of the state of men's affairs. "Where a pure will clearly and deliberately serves the people, then purity again characterizes the life principle, and the corrupted and false are all the more hateful to us," he concluded.[75] The wine of 1935 was by many accounts excellent—but then, after such a speech, one could hardly have suggested otherwise.

"Wine is the symbol of blood," added the chairman of the club of Pfälzers in Berlin at the time of the Deutsche Weinstraße's completion, and blood was the reality behind the deceptively diverse manifestations of German culture.[76] The need to awaken Pfälzers to the significance of "blood" in their social identity, to, as Emrich put it, "deepen the racial self-consciousness of the population," informed the practice of Volkskunde in the Nazi period and its interpretation of local identity.[77]

A recent scholar, Ernst Ritter, has struck a distinction between "volkstümlich" and "völkisch." The former, he argues, implied "historical and cultural shaping processes"; the latter reflected an "ahistorical and racist ideology" that in practice was "militantly anti-Semitic."[78] The distinction is a telling one and crucial to understanding the path along which the interpreters of regional identity traveled in the years of Nazi rule. Unlike other parts of Germany, where anti-Semitism had long characterized the Heimatkunde genre, the Pfalz had until 1933 been mostly free of racialist, that is to say völkisch, interpretations of local culture. Karl Roth, who became the

---

75. "Die deutsche Weinstraße: Rede des Gauleiters Bürckel beim Eröffnungsakt in Bad Dürkheim," *PB* (25 October 1935): 134–35.

76. "Ansprache unseres Vorsitzenden J. Flickinger im Berliner Lustgarten am 21 Oct. 1935," *PB* (25 October 1935): 131.

77. Emrich, "Denkschrift" (31 July 1933), BHStAM, MK 15551.

78. Ernst Ritter, *Das Deutsche Auslands-Institut in Stuttgart 1917–1945: Ein Beispiel deutscher Volkstumsarbeit zwischen den Weltkriegen* (Wiesbaden, 1976), p. 3.

leading Pfälzer practitioner of *Rassenkunde* (racial ethnology) in the Nazi period, had campaigned unsuccessfully in the 1920s for recognition by the leading cultural organizations: the most he achieved was the acceptance of one article in the minor Heimat journal of Kaiserslautern, *Unsere Pfalz*, and one book review in *Pfälzisches Museum–Pfälzische Heimatkunde* in 1928. In the article, Roth laid out the results of his survey of Pfälzer heads, 62 percent of which, he revealed, were covered with brown hair.[79] In the review, Roth argued that the discipline of Rassenkunde deserved more attention than it got in the Pfalz, where, significantly, none of the books under review had been published.[80] To Roth's disappointment, the Volkskunde of men like Albert Becker and Emil Heuser amounted to mere cultural interpretation with eclectic theoretical tendencies. Pfälzer culture emerged in their works as the sum of many influences and cross-currents over the centuries that were engaged neither in a Darwinian process of cultural selection nor in a Spenglerian struggle with chaos and decline. Moreover, Pfälzer Heimat associations generally acknowledged the contributions of Jewish culture to that of the Pfalz and preserved its remains along with those of court and peasant culture.[81] The ancient *Judenbad* in Speyer had been restored in the 1920s; the sufferings of the twelfth-century Jews of Speyer were the subject of a sympathetic novel in the Heimat-historical genre, published in 1925 by Maximilian Pfeiffer, a prominent Center party leader and well-known Pfälzer.[82]

In short, when in 1933 Emrich and Kölsch announced the advent of a new science, a *völkische Wissenschaft*, their sense of a radical break with the past was for once accurate; indeed, in some ways the break with traditions of interpreting the Pfälzer character and culture was even more complete than they portrayed it. Here as elsewhere, the newly empowered Nazis were caught in a rhetorical battle between the wish to appear revolutionary and hence responsible for the complete regeneration of German society and the wish to

79. One suspects that all dark-haired people were measured as brown-haired, in order to come up with the figure of 0.3 percent black-haired, proof for Roth of the essentially Nordic character of the local people; nevertheless, only 35.6 percent were blond-haired, and only 36.5 percent were blue-eyed. See "Über Rassenzugehörigkeit und Körperbauformen des Pfälzer Volkes," *Unsere Pfalz* (21 May 1926).

80. "Neue rassenkundliche Literatur in ihren Beziehungen zur rassenkundlichen Allgemeinsituation," *PM* 45/24 (1928): 270–71.

81. In 1921, for instance, Albert Becker wrote that "it would be a gratefully received project for someone to undertake a thorough investigation of the far-ranging influences of the morals and customs of the Jews on *heimatlich* customs of the Rhineland—that our Mundart is filled with Jewish words and expressions is so well known that I need hardly even mention it" (*PM–PH* 38/17 [1921]: 119). In a similar spirit, the philanthropic activities in the Pfalz of the American-German-Jewish family of Strauss were often acknowledged in the Heimat press; see *PM–PH* 43/22 (1926): 244 and 47/26 (1931): 44; *PB* (25 June 1931): 55.

82. Albert Becker, review of F. J. Hildenbrand's *Das romanische Judenbad im alten Synagogenhofe zu Speyer am Rhein*, in *PM* 37 (1920): 40; the title of the novel was *Kyrie Eleison*.

appear traditional and hence responsible for fulfilling German destiny. To further the latter self-image, an early article in *Die Westmark* credited Wilhelm Heinrich Riehl with directing German scholarship away from "false paths" and toward an understanding of "the unchangeable spirit of the people, rooted in blood and race," though even the extracts from Riehl's writings cited in the article hardly supported such an interpretation.[83] Albert Becker, consciously or not, helped to legitimate the Nazi interpretation of Riehl, and of the whole discipline of Volkskunde, by continuing to publish short pieces in Nazi magazines and, more significantly, by allowing himself to be claimed as an early practitioner of völkische Wissenschaft in spite of the fact that before and even during the Nazi period his writings were entirely cultural in emphasis and said nothing about race and blood, except in the most perfunctory fashion.[84]

Although neither revolutionary nor regenerative, the Nazi folklorists in the Pfalz did manage to transform the categories within which local culture was understood and its significance judged. In their school textbooks, popular publications, and lectures, they encouraged the reading of folktales, the singing of folksongs, and the preservation of folk customs.[85] So of course had the Heimat movement, but in the Nazi state folklore existed only to illuminate a mystified past of racially pure societies.[86] Family research also was reestablished on the basis of investigation into one's racial background, a task with frighteningly practical consequences.[87] German emigration, another area in which the Nazi scholars and teachers seemed merely to take over a long-established interest of Heimat research, now illustrated the principle of "blood ties," over and above the social and cultural affinities that had struck the Heimatkundlers of the Weimar period.[88] Indeed, the example of

83. Kurt von Raumer, "Wilhelm Heinrich Riehl und die Volkskunde der Pfalz," *Westmark* 1 (1933–34): 350.

84. Brief biographical notice on his sixtieth birthday, *Westmark* 6 (1938–39): 754.

85. Bason argues that while the writers of Nazi textbooks tried to wipe out any trace of the Weimar Republic, they were immeasurably helped in their task of securing national loyalty by the emphasis the Weimar schools had placed on homeland and nation, and in the end only shifted emphases and wordings, not substance (*Study of the Homeland*, pp. 38–45, 120–121). See also Gilmer W. Blackburn, *Education in the Third Reich: A Study of Race and History in Nazi Textbooks* (Albany, N.Y., 1985).

86. For the Pfalz, see Hermann Kohl, *Pfälzer Land und Volk in der Schule erlebt. Die neue Heimatkunde für die Westmark, auf nationalsozialistischer Grundlage* (Pirmasens, 1935); "Blut und Boden als Grundlagen völkischer Erziehung des deutschen Volkes" (Speyer, ca. 1935), in Doll, *Nationalsozialismus im Alltag*; statement on importance of Volkstumspflege in *PB* (25 June 1934): 53.

87. E.g., "Vom Sinn und Wesen der Familienforschung"; and Antz, "Der Zweck der Geschlechterkunde"—both in *PB* (25 September 1933): 94, 104.

88. See, e.g., *Der Jäger aus Kurpfalz* (1938), the theme of which was "Saarpfälzer da und dort und überall in der Welt"; or the *Heimatbriefe* (1938), a publication produced in the Pfalz to be sent to "Saarpfälzer Volk" outside of Germany, with greetings from Bürckel, Imbt, Kölsch, and Fritz Braun, head of the Mittelstelle.

emigrants, distant from their culture only in geographical terms, made clear that blood and race, not land, were the ultimate determinants of cultural identity: it was not the Pfalz that mattered, but the racial heritage of its inhabitants.[89]

Ironically, the Nazi redefinition of the bases of cultural life did not in the end encourage the local celebration of folkways. In part Germans simply became *feiermüdig*, tired of the endless number of occasions on which they were to take to the streets in joyful celebration. Less obvious perhaps to those at the time was the growing irrelevance of local culture in the national state, despite the attention given it. Viewed from the perspective of blood and race, Pfälzer culture as such made little sense. Its particularities, so carefully catalogued over the decades, began to fade away under the light of the racial unity of the German people in their "blood-bound total community."[90] A deepening of the racial consciousness of local people, as Emrich desired, necessarily involved a weakening of their Pfälzer consciousness.

Riehl, who had spent an entire book arguing for the cultural reality of the term *Pfälzer*, would hardly have appreciated its subsumption into the "racial-historical movements" of Nazi imagination, but he could not without hypocrisy have caviled at the political calculation that lay beyond this ideological performance.[91] Just as the Bavarian government had used Riehl's interpretation to support its stake in the contemporary borders of the Pfalz, so too did the Nazis manipulate the categories of blood and race to support the political idea of the Westmark and the national policy of resettling Germans (among them Pfälzers) in unknown territories to the east. Race could be the basis for such expansion of political borders; attachment to a unit as enclosed and static as the Pfalz could not. The new völkische Wissenschaft thus sought finally to undermine that traditional inward-turning of the German, not just to his own soul but to his hometown, his province, his locality. In a state that had made expansion and aggression the basis of its economic recovery and political survival, such inwardness could not be allowed to persist.[92]

The past also contributed to the National Socialist depiction of locality

---

89. Emil Maenner, "Die Auswanderung aus dem pfälzischen Raum nach Galizien 1782–1785," in *Abhandlungen zur saarpfälzischen Landes- und Volksforschung*, ed. Günther Franz, Ernst Christmann, and Hermann Emrich (Kaiserslautern, 1937), pp. 129–53; *Völkische Wissenschaft* (1934–35), no. 12, an issue devoted to "Auslandsdeutschtum."

90. Karl Herzog, "Schule und Volkskunde," *Unsere Heimat* (August 1935): 3.

91. See, e.g., Fritz Hellwig, "Bevölkerungsgeschichte—Volksgeschichte," *Völkische Wissenschaft* (1936–37): 189–90.

92. Ritter also points out that the expansionary policies of the Nazis contradicted the ideal of state boundaries corresponding exactly to racial boundaries, the "Volksboden." To this he adds, the Nazis' "drive to expand . . . also contradicted the sentimentally loaded Heimat-term in Germany" (*Das Deutsche Auslands-Institut*, p. 16).

and nationality, or rather, the past served the Nazis, as it had every generation of tradition inventors since the Pfalz began, as the ultimate affirmation of
their creation. The Nazis set themselves apart from their predecessors not
only in the content of their interpretations but also in the frankness with
which they acknowledged the hold of the present upon them. Hermann
Emrich, the Pfalz's Dr. Goebbels, whose opening remarks and closing interpretations framed every cultural production, said that "the essence of our
time is history shaping to a degree hitherto unknown."[93] He referred to the
world-historical events and figures in whose midst he felt himself to be;
things were happening, so it seemed, and Emrich sought to argue, in that
inflated language characteristic of Nazi pronouncements, that people must
be changing also, becoming "open" to history-in-the-making, submitting
themselves to the "eternal racial-spiritual essence." But his words, taken
together with the lecture they introduced, conveyed another meaning as well.
The Nazis "shaped" history by rewriting it. History, Kurt von Raumer
argued in his address to the new Saarpfälzische Institut für Landes- und
Volksforschung, ought to reflect the political spirit of the period in which it
was perceived. Raumer was not, however, encouraging a decidedly un-Nazi
relativism. As he explained, politics had reached its final stage in the Nazi
regime, in the ultimate union of the people and the state. Therefore, history
writing also had achieved a state of perfection, not in its objective or truth-
telling character, but in its capacity at last to depict the destiny of the German nation, in its perception of the final outcome that the events of the past
had foreshadowed, and in its embodiment of the national will.[94]

   Landesgeschichte, or regional history, formed the subject of von Raumer's
exhortation, because it posed a potentially troubling opposition to this
national spirit and its historiography. To warn the members of the institute
of the dangers of regional history and to instruct them in its proper application was his explicit purpose.[95] The history of the Pfalz (or Saarpfalz) needed
to be "seen anew" from the perspective of the "destiny of the German people." To this end von Raumer suggested that contemporary historians look
at the Pfalz first as "keeper and protector of the idea of the Reich," second as
"guardian of the border, bearer of the conflict with the west," and third as
the embodiment of the Volksgemeinschaft, as the "history of the people."[96]
Certainly these first two would have been unlikely to give pause to a local
historian, and the third was so vague as to be universally acceptable. But as
recurrent themes of the local historical consciousness in the Pfalz, the impe-

---

   93. "Das Wesen unserer Zeit ist geschichtsbildend in einem bisher niegekannten Ausmaß"
(introduction to Kurt von Raumer, *Der politische Sinn der Landesgeschichte* [Kaiserslautern, 1938],
p. 5).
   94. Ibid., esp. pp. 17–21.
   95. Ibid., p. 7.
   96. Ibid., p. 22.

rial and, perhaps perversely, the war-ridden, many-times-invaded past had been sources of pride and claims to local distinction. This tendency toward solipsism, or *Selbstbespiegelung*, was precisely what von Raumer detested: "Local patriotism," he pronounced, "is the most dangerous restraint on regional history."[97] The Nazi rewriting of Pfälzer history thus set out to free it from its entrapment in local self-regard so that it might become the more appropriate reflection of the Nazis' supralocal grandeur. In 1938, the editors of a volume devoted to the lives of famous Pfälzers described their "duty" similarly: "We seek to depict the *heimatlich* past in the mirror of its great and its typical personalities in order that a supra-individual quality will find expression in all the many-sidedness and diversity of the individuals, that is to say, [we seek to depict] the share of our region in the historic destiny of the German nation."[98]

Accordingly, the Pfälzers' new historical identity would encourage them not in the "Heimat idea" but in the "Reich idea" and the "borderland idea." The promotion of the "Reich idea" took the form of extensive writings about the so-called First Reich, in particular the medieval empire of the Hohenstaufens that had its geographical fulcrum in the lands of the Pfalz. Even earlier manifestations of Germanic peoples in the area of the Rhine acquired new significance and a wholly undeserved imperial mystique.[99] These diffuse and often doggedly factual accounts of excavations and emperors received some much-needed glamor from the castle of Trifels in the south Pfalz. A medieval stronghold that for a few years in the twelfth century had housed the imperial crown jewels, Trifels came to serve the Nazis in an equally transitory and symbolic fashion. In 1934, the Bavarian historian Johannes Bühler published a long article entitled "Trifels as a Symbol of German Power" in the yearly *Wanderbuch* of the Pfälzerwald Verein.[100] Adopting the then-current clichés, Bühler argued that strength (*Kraft*) was the essential attribute of German peoples, but that in the last few centuries it had become tragically divorced from power (*Macht*), a state of affairs contrary to what nature had intended and hence responsible for the extreme tension in Europe. The recent developments in Germany had finally brought about the proper relations between German Kraft and political Macht. In the wake of this reordering, Germany needed a symbol, and Trifels, as the

    97. Ibid.

    98. Raumer and Baumann, *Deutscher Westen—Deutsches Reich* 1: iv.

    99. For some accounts of the early history of the Pfalz, see the articles by Ernst Wahle, Hermann Graf, and Friedrich Sprater in Franz, Christmann, and Emrich, *Abhandlungen; Wanderbuch* (1939): 25ff.; and articles by Dr. Keith, Wilhelm Tendt, and Sprater in *Völkische Wissenschaft* (1934).

    100. "Der Trifels als Symbol deutscher Macht," *Wanderbuch* (1934): 55–80. Bühler was also the author of the official Bavarian history of the Hambach Festival, published at the time of its centenary in 1932 (see Chapter 6 above).

most important survival from the time when German Kraft and Macht had first come together, ought to be it.

Bühler's article came to the attention of Kurt Kölsch, Gaukulturwart of the Pfalz, who began in 1935 to lobby for the ruined castle's extensive renovation to make it accessible to tourists.[101] Simultaneously, the archeologist and head of the Historical Museum, Friedrich Sprater, began excavations in the castle that yielded important, if politicized, results. By 1937, the Bavarian and Pfälzer authorities had spent 2 million marks on renovation, excavation, and construction of a new tower atop the castle. Whether or not Trifels really became, as one writer suggested, "a national place of consecration to the German people," the Nazis did succeed in linking its glorified imperial past to their imperial present.[102] And with Trifels came all the castles of the Pfalz, no longer as monuments to local distinctiveness but, as Bavarian prime minister Siebert put it, as "witnesses to the attachment between the long-gone imperial glory of the First Reich and the bold new Reich of Adolf Hitler."[103]

For categorical thinkers like the Nazis, every absolute good required the existence of its opposite, and the opposite of the *Reichsidee* was *Kleinstaaterei*, petty-statism. The Nazi image of the Pfälzer past consequently divided neatly at the Thirty Years' War, after which—until the Nazi seizure of power—Germany suffered to a greater or lesser degree under the "arbitrary rule" of petty princely particularism.[104] This "Germany of three hundred Fatherlands" was a perversion incapable of expressing the will of the German people—what Kurt von Raumer meant when he referred to the eighteenth century as "states without a people."[105] Princely mismanagement led, moreover, to the financial domination of the German people by Jews.[106] A few, like Franz von Sickingen, stood out by virtue of having struggled for the idea of a unified Reich, but for the most part the Nazi historians condemned the last centuries of localized rule and with it the whole idea of federalism.[107]

Kleinstaaterei also indirectly illuminated the second of von Raumer's

101. Correspondence between Kölsch, Sprater of the Historisches Museum, and the BavMinUK and BavMinAus (fall of 1935), BHStAM, MA 106018.

102. Albert Zink, *Die Pfalz am Rhein: Heimatkunde des Gaues Westmark* (Saarbrücken, 1943), p. 82. See also the issue of *Völkische Wissenschaft* (1937) devoted to Trifels, with Hermann Schreibmüller, "Der Trifels als Reichsburg"; Carl Pöhlmann, "Der Trifels als Territorialburg"; Johannes Postius, "Die Burg als politische Erscheinung"; and others.

103. Ludwig Siebert, quoted in *Völkische Wissenschaft* no. 10 (1937).

104. See, e.g., the depiction of Pfälzer sufferings in the eighteenth century in Maenner, "Auswanderung aus dem pfälzischen Raum," pp. 129, 153.

105. Raumer, *Politischer Sinn der Landesgeschichte*, p. 22.

106. The argument of Kurt Baumann, "Aaron Elias Seeligmanns Aufstieg: Ein Beitrag zur Geschichte der Judenemanzipation in der Kurpfalz," *Unsere Heimat* 1 (1935–36): 360–64.

107. On von Sickingen, see Albert Becker, *Hutten-Sickingen im Zeitenwandel: Ein Beitrag zur Pfälzer Geistesgeschichte*, Beiträge zur Heimatkunde der Pfalz, 16 (Heidelberg, 1936).

themes: the Pfalz as Germany's borderland in struggle with the west. The fact of German disunity linked together two essences that seemed at least discordant, if not actually contradictory—the depiction of the Pfalz as the heart of the German Reich on the one hand, and its long suffering as a border region on the other. The squabbles of princes and the ambitions of the French had destroyed the Reichsidee and condemned the lands on the Rhine to centuries of "bitter suffering and dreadful need."[108] The Reich, in other words, was a past that had been lost, then recovered; the borderland was a past that lived on, in Emrich's terms, as both "experience and assignment."[109] For Kurt von Raumer, the history of the Pfalz helped to illuminate the "struggle between peoples" on the Rhine, which since the "breakthrough of National Socialism" had become a "struggle of world-views."[110] On a more mundane level, towns commemorated the many times they had been attacked, burned, or looted by the French; hiking clubs lamented the destruction of the Pfälzer forest; entire organizations and institutes—like the Westdeutsche Grenzlandsmannschaft (West German Borderland Association)—devoted themselves exclusively to the representation of a besieged existence.[111]

The most recent chapter in this sorry tale of suffering had of course been the French occupation, along with the doings of those latter-day petty princes and mercenaries, the separatists. In the organic and predestined whole that was history, the separatists played the crucial role of ushering the Nazis onto the stage as the saviors, once and for all, of the western Reich. The Nazis' unusual insistence on the teaching of contemporary history in the schools stemmed from their recognition that here was an opportunity too good to be passed up—an immediate yet historically resonant demonstration of their absolute right to power. The obsessive commemorations of the killings at Speyer and Pirmasens also partook of that propaganda technique attributed to Goebbels as the Big Lie; recited often enough and with sufficient fervor, the heroic role of the Nazis in saving the Pfalz from Frenchness and particularism came to seem credible, even if not in fact true.[112]

Finally, the past revealed for the Nazis what the Bavarians had been

108. A. Zink, *Die Pfalz: Heimatkunde des Gaues Westmark*, p. 35.

109. Emrich, "Grenze als Erlebnis und Aufgabe," *Westmark*, no. 1 (1933); see also article by Raumer in the same issue. The border fate also provided the themes for the *Jäger aus Kurpfalz* in 1935 and 1937, and for *Unsere Heimat* in August 1936.

110. Kurt von Raumer, *Der Rhein im deutschen Schicksal. Reden und Aufsätze zur Westfrage* (Berlin, 1936).

111. For accounts of town festivals, see *PB* (1934): 86–87 and (1939): 16; on the various Grenzlandsmannschaften, see, e.g., *PB* (1933): 62–63, 71, 77–81, 86; *Unsere Heimat* (12 July 36); and *Völkische Wissenschaft* (1936–37): 147–50.

112. A. Zink, *Die Pfalz: Heimatkunde des Gaues Westmark*, pp. 36, 113–15; accounts of commemorations in *PB* (1933): 143, (1934): 2, (1935): 6–7, (1938): 6–8, (1939): 88–89, 98–99, (1940–41): 29–30, 89. The most ambitious intellectual account of the separatists as the culmina-

trying to obscure for more than a hundred years—that the Pfalz was just an invention, and one that had long outlived its usefulness. "In these times, when the internal border-stakes of Germany have all fallen and a decisive new territorial order has been prepared," wrote Kurt von Raumer about his book of biographies, *Deutscher Westen—Deutsches Reich,* "it was impossible to take as the basis of a significant study the accidental borders of 1816 from which the Rheinpfalz derived, more as an administrative unit than as an organic unity."[113] The Westmark, not the Pfalz, von Raumer argued, was just such an organic unity; "the chief task" of his book would be "to demonstrate to the people of the Südwestmark how clearly their past pointed to their common fate to act as guardians of the border, to do service for Volk and Reich."[114] Such assertions became ever more insistent with each new political event. By 1943 Albert Zink claimed that the seizure of Lorraine had "at last made possible the union of the two sides of the eternal east-west axis"—whatever that was.[115]

But what all the talk of history and destiny failed in the end to obscure was that the Nazi regime was bound by none of it. The Nazis demonstrated from the start an essential disregard for history, except as a reflection of their own ambitions and desires. The "community of fate" that supposedly bound together the land and the people of Bürckel's fiefdom in the west existed only as an expression of their common vulnerability to what the future would bring. And what the future brought was war.

Few Pfälzers failed to read the message behind the historical posing and the racial boasting of the Nazi regime. The renovation of Trifels in 1937 was seen by many simply as part of the ongoing war preparations; already going up less than ten kilometers from Trifels, after all, was a line of border fortifications known as the Westwall.[116] This perception of the actual purpose of Trifels accounted for the destruction one night of the neatly landscaped grounds around the castle—one of the minor acts of resistance so character-

---

tion of a "thousand-year struggle" was a dissertation by Robert Oberhauser (1932), republished in 1934 with a foreword by Bürckel as *Kampf der Westmark. Frankreich, Separatismus und Abwehrbewegung 1918–1922* (Neustadt, 1934). Compare the accounts in the *Sopade Berichten* of the Saar campaign in 1935, when old SPDers reported their disgust that the role of the Social Democrats and free unions in fighting separatism had been completely suppressed, allowing the Nazis to take all the credit (*Sopade* [1935], 2:11, 13, 16).

113. Raumer and Baumann, *Deutscher Westen—Deutsches Reich* 1: iv–v.

114. Ibid., p. v.

115. A. Zink, *Die Pfalz: Heimatkunde des Gaues Westmark,* p. 11; see also Franz Steinbach, "Das Land zwischen Saar und Rhein als Kernstellung der deutschen Westgrenze" and "Die Einheit der Oberrheinlande," *Völkische Wissenschaft,* no. 11 (1934–35).

116. The new tower the Nazis built onto the medieval ruins looked to the astute observer like an observation post; *Sopade* (1937), 4:1374.

istic of the Nazi period.[117] The Pfälzers' "borderland-consciousness," well developed, so it seemed, long before the Nazis coined the term, did not extend to a willingness to sacrifice themselves that the German race might survive. Instead it made them sensitive to signs of preparation for war and susceptible to war panics. Already in 1934 rumors of impending war were widespread in the region, as quasi-military exercises and increasingly stringent economic controls began to remind the local population of a not-so-bygone past.[118] The rumors reached a climax right before the Saar vote, in the form of fears of an imminent French invasion. Throughout the 1930s Nazi propaganda itself contributed to the growing *Kriegspsychose* by deliberately exaggerating the hostility and strength of other powers in order to justify German rearmament. Those who took Nazi propaganda literally, especially those in vulnerable border areas, beame first fearful, then fatalistic; those who took it all with a grain of salt still dreaded the seemingly inevitable conflict.[119]

When Hitler managed to pull off first the Saar *Anschluß*, then in 1936 the remilitarization of the Rhineland, without provoking a French response, such fears abated, though they were not replaced by uncritical acclamation.[120] From the perspective of the Rhenish population such "victories" had been accomplished at the cost of an unfree labor market, ever-broader controls over movement around the Pfalz, and shortages in food and raw materials for industry.[121] The usual grumblings about the privileges of Nazi *Bonzen* (bigwigs) and the high prices of goods were now met with arrests and even executions; constant troop movements and maneuvers put local people into an uproar; and by 1936 the public works projects of which Bürckel was so boastful consisted entirely of war-related construction: three new bridges over the Rhine, barracks, airstrips, new railroad lines, the celebrated *Autobahn*, and, most dramatically, the Westwall.[122] True, unemployment had practically

---

117. Ibid., p. 609.

118. Farmers were reportedly talking of seven-year cycles, first drought, as in 1911, then "soldier games," as in 1912, and then, "well, who knows what will happen next?" (ibid. [1934], 1:59, 114, 327).

119. Ibid., (1937), 4:1090. In March 1936, shortly after the remilitarization of the Rhineland, there were even some reports of rushes on banks and savings and loan associations; see ibid. (1936), 3:304.

120. Indeed, one report claimed there were "no signs of celebration" at the remilitarization, only "an intensification of the already existing fear of war and of the sacrifices it would require" (*Sopade* [1936], 3:300, 304). On acclamation for Hitler's foreign policy accomplishments, see Marlis G. Steinert, *Hilter's War and the Germans: Public Mood and Attitude During the Second World War*, trans. Thomas E. J. DeWitt (Athens, Ohio, 1977), p. 38.

121. Rothenberger, "Aus der Nationalsozialistischen Zeit," pp. 365–68.

122. Kershaw includes the grumbling phenomenon in his useful term *popular dissent*; the Nazis called it "popular mood," and it worried them (Steinert, *Hitler's War*, pp. 5–14). On the rising terror against the population, see *Sopade* (1937), 4:1086–87, 1374; (1938), 5:682.

disappeared, but in its place had come the institution of forced labor, often in mobile units completely cut off from family and home by the need for military security. The Westwall involved, moreover, a tremendous disruption of the patterns of everyday movement in the border area. In the twenty kilometers between Pirmasens and Zweibrücken, for instance, the labor and army units built nine hundred bunkers, sometimes between houses in villages; by the completion of the project, more than six thousand bunkers dotted the Pfalz.[123] Around them were barbed wire and zones of restricted access to civilians, including farmers. The mobile construction units had also to be housed and fed, the burden of which was all borne by the local population.

The coming of war, so long anticipated and so little celebrated, might have relieved the tension of waiting, but certainly it brought no other advantage. The fate of a borderland, as the Nazis had so often pointed out, was to experience war from its beginning to its end. On 1 September 1939, Hitler announced the invasion of Poland in response to the alleged Polish attack on a German radio station in Gleiwitz; two days and hundreds of miles from Poland, the entire population of a designated "Red Zone," an area about twenty kilometers deep in the southern Pfalz along the French border, was forcibly evacuated to rural areas east of the Rhine.[124] When these Pfälzers finally returned in July 1940, after a year of sporadic, sometimes intense fighting in the region, they found wrecked houses, fields of rotting crops, and empty yards where factories had been dismantled and moved farther into Germany. In the midst of his Aktion Bürckel—by which all the Pfälzer Jews were transported first to France, then to the death camps in Poland— Bürckel offered the returning Pfälzers yet another of his projects, this one called the "Village Renewal Action." He also forced many to relocate into newly conquered Lorraine, where he meant for them to replace the indigenous population of racially inferior "Celts." Certainly, the spectacular German victories had not brought back to the region that fleeting prosperity of 1935, nor had they secured it from war's destruction. The first enemy bombing raids hit the Pfalz, in particular its industrial areas along the Rhine, in the fall of 1940, intensifying gradually until their high point in the fall of 1944, when not just Ludwigshafen and Frankenthal but every other sizable town of the region went up in flames. In March and April 1945, heralded by several days of carpet bombings, American troops crossed over the French border into the Pfalz and established a second rule of occupation, fifteen years almost to the day since the last one had ended.

The Red Zone, the forced resettlement of Pfälzers, and the war itself each in its own way symbolized the ultimate perversion of the idea of Heimat,

123. Rothenberger, "Aus der Nationalsozialistischen Zeit," pp. 366–68.

124. Johannes Nosbüsch and Karl-Heinz Rothenberger, "Die Pfalz im Zweiten Weltkrieg," in *Pfälzische Landeskunde*, vol. 3 (Landau/Pfalz), pp. 386–87.

even while each was a logical extension of the policies and ideology of the Nazi years. Each required of Germans a nationalism that was literally uprooted from the local and familiar world, a nationalism to which all bonds of locality had necessarily to be sacrificed. Together they exposed the extent to which Nazism had broken with the German past and the German people, in the matter not only of hometown sentimentality but also of national traditions of far graver import. To be sure, past, people, nation, and homeland were socially constructed and socially maintained abstractions, by which the Nazis, no different from any other regime or collectivity, had understood themselves and justified their actions. Nazism, moreover, was of Germany, undeniably and tragically. And not just any past, but the German past, not any homeland, but the German Heimat, not any people, but the German Volk, had been its starting point and, one must presume, inspiration. Nevertheless, somewhere along the way to total war those symbolic representations of society had ceased to have any point of reference in the actions of the regime; in the end, the only "idea" with any force left to it was that of anti-Semitism, with its corresponding imperative to destroy the Jewish people. Heimat, Volk, and Nation had long since become just empty words.

Yet Heimat may finally have had the last word, for in the midst of the massive destruction that the war brought, the lines of obedience and submission to a central will inevitably broke down, leaving people in the rubble not of their nation, but of their locality. The full significance of that Nazi neologism *Heimatfront* revealed itself in the localization of experience—and survival—in the last year of the war.[125] Loyalties, too, underwent a kind of redirection under those circumstances, shrinking down to the visible world of one's immediate surroundings and companions. Oddly, the clearest representative of that process was Gauleiter Bürckel himself. With a long history of conflict with such figures of centralized authority as Bormann, Speer, and various SS commanders already behind him, Bürckel became almost rebellious during the last years of the war. He refused to send Pfälzer farmers to colonize Russia, concocting instead the Lorraine scheme; he discouraged Pfälzers from joining the SS because it "only did dishonorable things"; he tried to prevent the building of the Westwall, a "pointless work of fortification" that would almost certainly turn his region into a theater of war. Finally, in September 1944 two SS officers, under orders from Bormann, came to his office and purportedly offered him a pistol; by the next day, according to official reports, he was dead of pneumonia.[126] A fanatical racist and anti-

125. On the Nazi etymology of *Heimatfront*, see *Das Große Lexikon des Dritten Reiches*, ed. Christian Zentner and Fridemann Bedürftig (Munich, 1985), p. 244.
126. On Bürckel, see Hüttenberger, *Die Gauleiter*, pp. 179–80, 184–86, 195, 202, 210–11; Rothenberger, "Aus der Nationalsozialistischen Zeit, p. 363; Albert Speer, *Inside the Third Reich: Memoirs*, trans. Richard Winston and Clara Winston (New York, 1970), pp. 313, 402n.

Catholic, a brutal opponent of dissent in any form, a swindler, a liar, a brag-
gart, and a blindly obedient follower of Hitler himself, Bürckel was by no
reasonable standard of morality a good man. Yet he is remembered as a
"Pfälzer patriot," and for all his talk of the Westmark, he would not have
denied the title. As an epitaph for the Nazi regime it could hardly be less
adequate, but as a tribute to the resilience of the hometownsman it says all.

EIGHT

Heimat and the
Recovery of Identity

War, the last and most desperate assertion of national existence, had twice brought the Germans to the point of losing theirs, the second time more decisively than the first. The immediate postwar arrangements among the Allied leaders made official what bombing raids, Nazi excesses, and sheer weariness had already accomplished: the narrowing of political and social life to small regions unconnected to any whole, not even that of a single victorious power. The Pfalz came first under American occupation, then under French, was linked first to the Saar, then to Hesse and parts of the Rhineland. In 1947 it finally ended up a district of the state Rhineland-Pfalz.[1] For the first several years after the war, the French insisted that political parties and economic activities be restricted to the borders of their zone of occupation. The immediate postwar years also brought a modest revival of separatist activities in the region, as well as other movements of opinion for and against a variety of regional alliances—with Baden, with Bavaria, with Hesse, and so on.[2] A national state to which the Pfalz could belong was

1. On the occupation and the reestablishment of government in the Rhenish area, see Rainer Hudemann, "Zur Politik der französischen Besatzungsmacht," in *Rheinland-Pfalz entsteht. Beiträge zu den Anfängen des Landes Rheinland-Pfalz in Koblenz 1945–1951,* ed. Franz-Josef Heyen (Boppard am Rhein, 1984); Faber, "Die südliche Rheinlande," pp. 457–64; Gustav Wolff, "Die Pfalz in den Schicksalsjahren 1945/6," *Pfälzische Heimatblätter* 2 (1954): 49–53, 57–61, 81–84; Hans-Jürgen Wünschel, ed., *Schicksalsjahre der Pfalz. Dokumente zur Geschichte von Rheinland-Pfalz* (Neustadt/Pfalz, 1979); F. Roy Willis, *The French in Germany 1945–1949* (Stanford, 1962).

2. Peter Jakob Kock, *Bayerns Weg in die Bundesrepublik* (Stuttgart, 1983), pp. 98–99, 121, 126–28; Kurt Thomas Schmitz, *Opposition in Landtag. Merkmale oppositionellen Verhaltens in Länder-*

achieved only in 1949 after four years of political limbo. It claimed only some of those people accustomed to calling themselves Germans and boasted a constitution explicitly federalist, based on those regional governments that, at least in the case of Rhineland-Pfalz, had preceded it by several years.

Germany, in short, was rebuilt from the regions outward and upward. Within the western zones of occupation, the particular shape of the rebuilding derived as much from the Germans' own diagnosis of the national "sickness" as from the various schemes for German "pastoralization" or deindustrialization that were current in French and American governmental circles at the time.[3] Many of those Germans who were gradually reviving public life had come to understand Nazism (what Ludwig Reichert, the mayor of Ludwigshafen and the president of the constituent assembly for the Rhineland-Pfalz, called "our insanity beyond all conceiving and our consciencelessness beyond all measuring") as the disease of uprooted "mass man."[4] Thus democracy and "healthy" attitudes would have to begin in the family, the home, the locality, and grow from those "roots" into a new nation and a new national identity.[5]

Not surprisingly, one of the essential terms of this discussion was *Heimat.* Pulled out of the rubble of the Nazi Reich as a victim, not a perpetrator, Heimat once again expressed the particular claims of a traditional provincialism on the identity of Germans. "Out of our spiritual and material distress," observed a Bavarian historian in 1949, "has been born a new animation of Heimat thoughts."[6] These "Heimat thoughts" in turn informed the efforts of Germans in scholarly, cultural, and civic organizations to "unburden" themselves of the Nazi heritage, while at the same time strengthening the ties of German people to their locality. Heimat was not, however, as simple a cure as many claimed it to be, and in the interplay of reform and

---

parlamenten am Beispiel der SPD in Rheinland-Pfalz (Hannover, 1971), pp. 18–20; Horst-W. Jung, *Rheinland-Pfalz zwischen Antifaschismus und Antikommunismus. Zur Geschichte des Landesparlaments 1946–1948* (Meisenheim am Glan, 1976), p. 11; Hans-Jürgen Wünschel, "Der Separatismus in der Pfalz nach dem Zweiten Weltkrieg" (diss., Universität Heidelberg, 1975).

3. In 1949, for instance, in his *Goethejahr* address at the Paulskirche in Frankfurt, Thomas Mann spoke of standing "four years after the culmination of our sickness." On the language of sickness and convalescence, see the suggestive remarks in Kock, *Bayerns Weg,* p. 22; on the Allies, see Willis, *The French in Germany;* and Henry Morgenthau, Jr., *Germany Is Our Problem: A Plan for Germany* (New York, 1945).

4. Quoted in his obituary, *PH* 9 (1958): 34–35.

5. Kock, *Bayerns Weg,* pp. 22–23. He points in particular to J. J. Kindt-Kiefer, *Europas Wiedergeburt durch genossenschaftlichen Aufbau;* Wilhelm Hoegner and C. Silens, *Irrweg und Umkehr;* Otto Feger, *Schwäbisch-alemannische Demokratie. Aufruf und Programm;* and Wilhelm Röpke, *Die Deutsche Frage.*

6. Max Spindler, "Zur Lage der bayerischen Geschichtsvereine," *Zeitschrift für bayerische Landesgeschichte* 15 (1949): 263.

forgetfulness it mirrored both the accomplishments and the shortcomings of the German effort to move beyond their Nazi past.

That the locality should be the appropriate context for understanding the recasting of German national identity is not self-evident. National discussions in national publications among nationally prominent intellectuals and politicians have largely shaped our understanding of the process of *Vergangenheitsbewältigung*, or overcoming the past. Yet the structure of opinion at the national level was so attenuated in the immediate postwar years—and what there was, so preoccupied with the unfolding drama of cold war—that to understand the internal implications of recovery we must look to local papers, local organizations, and local public occasions. Regional public life had already begun to revive several years before anything approaching national public life reemerged in western Germany, and in the early postwar years localness itself became a subject of discussion, particulary discussion about the assimilable past. Germany, wherever and whatever it might be, still mattered; but the Pfalz was Heimat and the ruins of the Westmark were yet to be cleared away.

The issues of local identity and the Nazi past took shape in a number of different contexts, but most explicitly in the revival of scholarship on the Pfalz and in the revival of a specifically Pfälzer literature, art, and folk culture. In default of a regional university, the traditional representatives of scholarship in the Pfalz had been the historical and scientific associations and, since 1925, the Pfälzer Society for the Promotion of Learning. All had been subsumed within the Nazi vision of a centrally controlled "völkisch learning," and all had more or less shut down after 1940, barely managing to preserve anything in the final years of the war. By 1950, however, all had been restored to the form they had taken in the Weimar period. In 1949, six of the ten surviving members of the original, pre-Nazi Pfälzer Society met to revive the organization; the state government of Rhineland-Pfalz quietly took over the functions of a now-absent Bavarian government, and Friedrich von Bassermann-Jordan again became president.[7] The Historical Association reformed in 1950, officially voting out the statutes of 1937 and electing a new central committee.[8] In 1948, the Pfälzer Association for Natural History and Preservation also regrouped. In 1950, a new "Working Group for Pfälzer Heimat History" was founded for "all friends of Pfälzer history," a new "Working Group for Pfälzer Family Research" started up, and a local branch of the regional office of monuments opened in Speyer.[9]

A range of new publications was the most visible sign of this flurry of

7. *PH* 1 (1950): 64; *Veröffentlichungen der PGFW* 69:7; Ernst Christmann, "Wissenschaftlicher Mittelpunkt der Pfalz," *Pfälzische Heimatblätter* 1 (1952): 35.
8. *PH* 1 (1950): 31.
9. *PH* 1 (1950): 48; Rudolf Schreiber, "Bilanz der Pfälzer Wissenschaft," *Pfälzische Heimatblätter* 2 (1953): 4–5; Kurt Oberdorffer, "Bilanz der Pfälzer Wissenschaft," *Pfälzische Heimatblätter* 3 (1955): 11–12.

reorganization. In 1949, Friedrich Sprater, longtime director of the Historical Museum, founded a quarterly journal called *Pfälzer Heimat* that he conceived of as the heir to the magazine *Pfälzisches Museum–Pfälzische Heimatkunde*. In 1952, the *Pfälzische Heimatblätter* began to appear, a joint venture of the scholarly associations and the local press, aimed at a popular audience. In 1953, the Historical Association restarted its own yearly journal.[10]

Although no single purpose informed this writing and the subjects addressed were as varied as the inherent limitations of the Pfalz would permit, the new periodicals did reflect their editors' determination to restore to scholarship, particularly regional scholarship, the attachment to factual detail of which the Nazis had been so contemptuous. But publishing reassuringly antiquarian articles was not all they did. Such leading local scholars as Kurt Baumann and Rudolf Schreiber brought a critical realism, for the most part unprecedented, to their understanding of the entity "Pfalz" itself. No longer were the nineteenth-century origins of the region ignored or its troubled relations with Bavaria made to seem better than they had been.[11] These men's attitude reflected a profound distaste for the blatantly political function that regional scholarship had served in the Third Reich. Baumann consistently criticized local histories that in any way smacked of apologies for the new, old, or wished-for borders of the region.[12] In 1953, he lashed out at a book by Eugen Ewig on "the historical foundations of the state Rhineland-Pfalz" that argued—rather mildly—for the existence of historical precedents for the current political arrangements: "That the historical profession, after all the bleak experiences of the last decades, would still allow itself to serve as the underpinnings for whatever political opinion should happen to be current must strike all of us as alarming. Does our existence as a state really depend upon the construction of artificial and problematic prehistories to justify it?"[13] Similarly, the scholarly associations gave no comfort to the various postwar movements to reunite the Pfalz with Bavaria (the mission of a new Bund Bayern-Pfalz) or to establish a "new Kurpfalz" through the union of the Pfalz with Baden.[14] In many ways, Pfälzer scholarship after the war looked much like Pfälzer scholarship of the twenties. It did not, to the disgust

10. *PH* 1 (1950): 1; Rudolf Schreiber, "Zum Geleit," *MHVP* 51 (1953): 5–6.

11. See, e.g., Schreiber's "Grundlagen," pp. 35–40; and Kurt Baumann, "Die bayerische Oberrheinpolitik," *Pfälzische Heimatblätter* 2 (1954): 89–91.

12. See his criticism of the treatment of Pfälzer themes in Karl Bosl and Hermann Schreibmüller's *Geschichte Bayerns* (review in *PH* 5 [1954]: 140–41) and his harsh criticism of Rolk Gustav Haebler's *Badische Geschichte: Die alemannischen und pfälzisch-fränkischen Landschaften am Oberrhein* (review in *PH* 4 [1953]: 32).

13. Review of Ewig, *Die geschichtlichen Grundlagen des Landes Rheinland-Pfalz*, in *PH* 4 (1953): 125. On Baumann, see Hans Keller in a Festgabe für Kurt Baumann zum 70. Geburtstag, ed. Anton Doll, *MHVP* 77 (1979); and his collected essays, *Von Geschichte und Menschen der Pfalz. Ausgewählte Aufsätze*, ed. Kurt Andermann (Speyer, 1984).

14. See the journals *Bayern und Pfalz* and *Stimme der Pfalz* on the one hand and *Kurpfalz*, organ of the *Verein "Kurpfalz,"* on the other.

of some, address broad or burning historical issues, but retreated instead to the security of the small in scale and the local in range.[15] In that—divided Berlin and cold war notwithstanding—it differed little from the rest of German life.[16]

The dispassionate scholar of postwar local history nevertheless lived in tension with the locally patriotic preserver of the regional past. Often united in the same person, these two attitudes jostled each other in the publications themselves, where the objectivity of the articles was belied by the sentimentality of titles like *Pfälzer Heimat*. Individuals continued to describe their scholarly activities in terms of concern for the fate of the region. Walther Plümacher wrote in 1951, for instance, that "now, more than ever before, localities must cultivate their past in order that the historical consciousness of people, from which rises the capacity continually to renew our lives, may intensify and grow"; similarly, Otto Sartorius described work in Pfälzer natural history in terms of "the great need of the people of our time to cultivate and promote everything that expresses our German, Western culture."[17] The groups themselves continued to seek out connections to local public authority, as expressions of their representation of the region as a whole. The Historical Association again asked the district president to serve as honorary chairman: "[His participation] is the richly symbolic expression," wrote a chronicler in *Pfälzer Heimat*, "of the close attachment, over the past 125 years, of the Pfälzer government to the representatives of Pfälzer historical efforts."[18] It was an attachment, moreover, that, despite the obvious abuses of the Nazi period, the group saw no fundamental reason to distrust.

Of course, preservationism had a practical side to it, and the urgency of the need to restore wrecked and plundered Heimat museums, disintegrating archives, and bombed-out historical buildings obscured the equally urgent need to question what one preserved and why one preserved it.[19] In Siegfried Lenz's novel *Heimatmuseum*, the hero, a displaced person (*Heimatvertriebener*) from the eastern provinces, tells how he came ultimately to destroy the museum of Masurian culture that he had constructed in Schleswig-Holstein

15. Buchheit, "Nur engere Heimatforschung wie bisher? Zur Diskussion um die Arbeit im Historischen Verein der Pfalz," Ludwigshafener *General Anzeiger*, 10 March 1955, p. 6.

16. On the retreat from politics, "abstract ideas, programs, and organizations" in the postwar years, see Helmut Schelsky, *Wandlungen der deutschen Familie in der Gegenwart* (Stuttgart, 1953).

17. Walther Plümacher, "Die Ebernburg, Geschichte und Bedeutung," *PH* 2 (1951): 114; Otto Sartorius, "Unsere Heimatmuseen und Vereine," *PH* 1 (1950): 11. Sartorius's identification of German culture with a broader western tradition is itself new and remarkable.

18. *PH* 1 (1950): 32.

19. On the destruction of archives, museums, and buildings, both during and immediately after the war, see Friedrich Sprater, "Kriegsverluste," *MHVP* 51 (1953): 41–47; and miscellaneous accounts, e.g. *PP* 2 (November 1951): 8; and *PH* 1 (1950): 30–31 and 2 (1951): 28.

after the war.[20] In the Pfalz, such despair and disgust were never publicly acknowledged; with vigor, hope, and persistent self-regard, Pfälzers set about recovering what had been lost and restoring what had been damaged. In 1950, the Historical Museum in Speyer, whose collections had survived the war only to disappear in the chaos of 1945, reopened with an exhibition entitled "Pfälzer Land—Pfälzer Work."[21] The Cultural Ministry of Rhineland-Pfalz at the same time began a systematic effort to preserve historic buildings.[22] By 1951, the first town festival had been held, in celebration of an occasion deep in the past and in restorative disregard for the more recent and painful anniversaries that each passing year brought.[23]

Not just buildings, archives, and museums had to be preserved, but people also, a scarcely articulated truth of post-Nazi existence that the notion of denazification could not accommodate. Some of the more egregious sinners of the Nazi period disappeared—no trace of Hermann Emrich, for instance, can be found after 1945, for whatever reason. Others sought or were granted obscurity. Still others, the bulk of the population, considered themselves as much victims as participants in the Nazi era of German and Pfälzer history. Few disqualified themselves from participation in the postwar society just because they had failed to put up active resistance to the prewar one. The scholarly societies were filled with and even led by men who had published, researched, excavated, and lectured under the Nazi regime. Evidence of devotion to the Pfalz went a long way toward securing forgiveness even for those whose sins had been more than ones of omission. Hermann Moos, who had headed the folklore museum in Kaiserslautern in the Nazi period and had organized it around distinctly racialist principles, died in early 1950 in obscurity. The author of a long obituary in *Pfälzer Heimat* questioned whether "this true son of our Pfälzer Heimat, one of its experts and artists of a truly notable rank, whose life and work were deeply rooted in it and completely dedicated to it," ought really to be ignored and forgotten.[24] Such words should be read not as an apology for Nazism but rather as a plea for Pfalztum that stemmed from a sense—tinged with self-pity—of its vulnerability, its corruptibility, and, for all that, its essential worthiness. In a similar spirit, a regular section of the magazine *Pfälzer Heimat* celebrated the accomplishments of Pfälzers, living and dead, with scant regard to the Nazi

20. Lenz's work fits into a postwar literary genre of what one might call the anti-Heimat; Günter Grass's *Tin Drum* is another example. In them a sense of place and locality no longer provides consolation or identity but undermines one's ability to be at peace in the world.

21. Account in *PP* 1 (June 1950): 18.

22. See esp. Wolfgang Medding in *PH* 1 (1950): 113; 2 (1951): 90; 3 (1952): 119; 5(1954): 35; 6 (1955): 158; and on into the present.

23. *PH* 2 (1951): 64; and frequent accounts of such festivities in the following years, especially in 1958, when Kaiserslautern celebrated its eight hundredth anniversary.

24. Rudolf Ludwig, "Unsere Landsleute und Mitarbeiter," *PH* 1 (1950): 63.

234 A NATION OF PROVINCIALS

period. In those first years after the war, it seemed to Germans that their suffering had been punishment enough for their misjudgments, conceits, and ambitions. Healing, not hair rending, was the order of the day as far as the local societies were concerned, and part of that process, for all its disturbing overtones, was recapturing and preserving the past.

Those who were responsible for the revival of local art, literature, and music showed as much or more reluctance to stir up memories of the recent past, seeking instead in culture both consolation for their sorrows and vindication for their forgetfulness. "The German person takes the word of the poet with him on his way through life," wrote the Pfälzer Oskar Bischoff in 1950, "in order that he find new strength in his life and work when he is worn out."[25] Like Friedrich Meinecke with his vision of small circles of Goethe lovers in every German town and city, some Pfälzers believed that culture, specifically heimatlich culture, could turn people back to the best and truest of Germanness.[26] "A people is more than a mere political expression," declared the founder of the new Pfälzische Kulturgemeinde (Pfälzer Cultural Community), and life amounted to more than the struggle for existence.[27] Indeed, these promoters of culture thought that a preoccupation with mere existence in the postwar years had thrown Germans into a profound cultural crisis, the manifestations of which were the fragmentation of cultural endeavors, an indifference to cultural excellence, and a proliferation of bad literature, bad music, bad art. Few agreed on where the roots of this crisis were to be found—in Nazism generally, in Nazi materialism, in war and defeat, in postwar want and plenty, in the atom bomb—but few disputed that a crisis was upon them, and few doubted that salvation from it lay close to home.[28]

In the Pfalz, cultural renewal centered on the periodical *Pfalz und Pfälzer*, founded in 1950 and edited by Oskar Bischoff.[29] Its focus, as the title indicates, was explicitly Pfälzer; it was oriented toward the Heimat, in order, as Bischoff later explained it, to prove that "the landscape was still both artistically and spiritually valid."[30] Other projects and associations aimed at the renewal of local culture soon followed: the Pfälzer Cultural Community in late 1950, a refounded Pfälzer Literary Association in 1951. The promoters of Pfälzer culture worried that insufficient attention had been paid to the

25. *PP* 1 (June 1950): 15.
26. Friedrich Meinecke, *The German Catastrophe: Reflections and Recollections*, trans. Sidney B. Fay (Cambridge, Mass., 1950).
27. Joachim Körner, "Wie überwinden wir unsere 'Kulturkrise'?" *PP* 1 (November 1950): 10.
28. Ibid., pp. 10–13.
29. Later it was called the *Rheinisch-pfälzische Monatshefte*.
30. Bischoff, "Die Aufgaben und Ziele unsere Zeitschrift," *Rheinische-pfälzische Monatshefte* (coninuation of *Pfalz und Pfälzer* under a new title; hereafter cited as *RPM*) 4 (1953): 1.

importance of ineffable goods in the rebuilding of Germany after the war. For instance, Bischoff called the closure of a radio station specializing in cultural broadcasting "spiritual *démontage*," in reference to the widely resented French relocation of whole factories from the Pfalz to Lorraine.[31] In contrast to his countrymen in the 1920s, Bischoff did not blame the French for the threat to "Pfälzer culture and its traditions," but rather the Germans themselves, who had neglected to take the same care in recouping their spiritual losses as they had their material ones.

Pfalz und Pfälzer pursued spiritual regeneration for the most part through literature, publishing the writings of former and contemporary Heimat authors. Literary and art criticism and music history also appeared in its pages, along with frequent discussions of the essential value of looking to folk culture for inspiration and Pfalztum. "One thing is certain," began one such discussion in 1951: "if we would heal our wounded soul, if we, the straying ones, would again find ourselves, if we would again feel within ourselves the Volksgemeinschaft . . . then we cannot take seriously enough the problem of folk culture."[32] The notion of heimatlich culture encompassed all these diverse fields, from the folk song to the sculpture, positing a continuum of cultural experience in the landscape itself. More than anything else, the editors and writers of *Pfalz und Pfälzer* relied on the notion of Heimat to give coherence and unity to their work. Hence, when they spoke of cultural fragmentation in the Pfalz, as they frequently did, they referred only to institutions, and their prescriptions for improvement were likewise limited to practical matters like train schedules.[33] No one seemed ever to doubt that, given the opportunity, the essential Pfälzerness embedded in the land could not fail to find expression in a distinctive and worthy renaissance of local culture.[34]

Pfälzer culture may have been regenerative; it certainly was rehabilitative. In the new and renewed cultural organizations, many artists and poets who had put their work at the disposal of the Nazi regime reconstructed themselves through the forgiving genre of Heimat lyricism. "My dear friends," began an early essay in *Pfalz und Pfälzer*, "one cannot speak enough of the Heimat": "it is something like heaven, a nonrational, deep soulfulness," not a place, "neither mountain nor valley, neither tree nor hill," rather "rootedness in the earth"; "it is the strengthening of life and the original comfort from which all else flows that in this earthly corner affirms your existence; so let the world do as it will—the Heimat loves and confirms you

31. Oskar Bischoff, Hans Reetz, et al., "Wir protestieren gegen die Auflösung des Studio Kaiserslautern," *PP* 2 (March 1951), p. 16.

32. Prof. Arthur Berg, "Volksliedforschung—Volksliedpflege," *PP* 2 (April 1951): 16.

33. Hanz Reetz, "Pfälzische Kulturpropaganda auf Seitenwegen?" *PP* 1 (June 1950): 19; "Die Kulturaufgabe der Pfälzischen Presse," *PP* 2 (May 1951): p. 18.

34. Other regions, after all, claimed such a culture; indeed, most German literary histories were once organized by region.

without question, as its child."[35] The most prominent erring child to return to this Heimat, professing, probably in all sincerity, his love and his never-extinguished attachment to the Pfalz, was Kurt Kölsch, the former Gaukulturwart on the long road back from Nazi prominence. His arrival was marked by the publication in 1952, on the front page of *Pfalz und Pfälzer*, of a poem he had written in 1945. It was called *"Abendländische Elegie"* (An Elegy to the West), and it depicted a crisis of soul in all western culture, affirming in the end the essential goodness of the earth and the Fatherland: "Hier ist der Acker und hier ist die heilende Erde. / Langsam füllt sich Wort und reift in den Ähren das Korn. / Über dem Heimweg wölbt sich der Reichtum der Sterne. / Kühle der sanftesten Nacht umfängt uns abendlich schön. / Singe, du Künstler, das Lied von dem Heimweg der Seele!"[36]

In June 1952, again in *Pfalz und Pfälzer*, Kölsch made explicit the message of the poem. In a short piece, part autobiography, part apologia, he described times in prison camp right after the war when he had helped his companions assuage their homesickness by telling stories in Pfälzer dialect; later, after his return to the Pfalz in 1948, he had been able to find employment only in odd jobs, as a forester, gardener, stonecutter, delivery boy, and agricultural day laborer; nevertheless, although cut off from his real profession, he "rediscovered" in the vineyards of his beloved Pfalz and in the daily contact with Pfälzers "truly a deep and inner union with my Heimat, a mystical communion, a rediscovery of the powers and essences" of the land to which his poetry had always spoken.[37] Throughout the narrative—indeed, throughout his poems after 1945—the Heimat was a constant point of reference; his love for it, ever on display, legitimated him as an artist in postwar society. "I ask no more," he concluded, disingenuously, "than what I myself have always and under all circumstances been ready to grant to others: that one's work be justly received and recognized for the creativeness that is expressed not politically but artistically and—a little love, so that one feels that one is not entirely alone."[38]

35. Wilhelm Michel, "Lob der Heimat," *PP* 1 (August 1950): 13–14.
36. "Abendländische Elegie," *PP* 3 (January 1952): 1:

> Here are the fertile fields and here is the healing earth.
> Slowly the word fills up and the corn ripens in the ears.
> Above the way home arches the richness of the stars.
> Coolly the gentlest night wraps us around of an evening.
> Sing, you artist, the song of the soul's way home!

37. Kurt Kölsch, "Von mir—über mich," *PP* 3 (June 1952): 2–3. "He has always remained closely bound to his Pfälzer Heimat," affirmed Oskar Bischoff a few years later (*PP* 3 [June 1952]: 10).

38. Kölsch, "Von mir—über mich," p. 3. Kölsch could hardly have forgotten that such toleration was precisely what he rejected in his "inspirational" writings in *Die Westmark*, where he associated it with a destructively "liberal" outlook. See Chapter 7 above.

Nevertheless, the restorers of Pfälzer culture in the postwar Pfalz, affirming and forgiving though they certainly were, did not lack a critical distance from the task at hand, or a sense of ambivalence about the Heimat genre to which they were dedicated. An essential feature of Heimat endeavors had always been their solipsistic regionalism: written, painted, or composed by local artists on the subject of the locality, Heimat works of art had not found, nor were they intended for, an outside audience (except, possibly, the outside audience of tourists who came to visit and admire). True, these works consistently turned on the paradox of the representatively German within the particularly Pfälzer—a paradox that was the key to their dual patriotism—but recognition from Germans had not been essential to the maintenance of Pfälzer art. The French occupation and then, of course, Nazism had strained the Heimat genre to the point of breaking by demanding that it turn outward and promote the Pfalz, propagandistically, for an audience of non-Pfälzers. Bischoff, though he shared little else with his immediate predecessors, nevertheless believed that Pfälzer culture would thrive only if it gained the recognition of German society as a whole. "The acknowledgment of our narrow Heimat is not enough," he wrote in 1953; "we seek to gather together on one platform . . . all those engaged in the culture and Heimatpflege of the Pfälzer and Rhenish areas, in order to gain recognition of their worth beyond the local borders."[39]

Lying behind Bischoff's concern, one that he shared with many others in the Pfalz, was not mere Pfälzer boosterism but a recognition of the problem of cultural excellence and authenticity in postwar Germany. Too much literary and artistic production since 1945 had opted for triviality and frivolity in the face of destruction and atrocity. Against all that, Bischoff insisted that the Heimat and the landscape could be the basis of profound artistic expression, not just of popular movies about Alpine maidens and doggerel (*Reimerei*) about mischievous boys. Similarly, the truly Pfälzer existed not in the vulgar sense in which one found it depicted in much popular literature, but deeply embedded in a particular feel to the land and in a particular cast to the people. Landscape artists had also to learn to seek profundity, not prettiness.[40] The renewed interest in folklore took shape, at least in part, in an effort to locate authentic and profound cultural experiences that were also local and particular. When the radio studio in Kaiserslautern threatened to shut down in 1951, Bischoff and others claimed that their opposition to its closure sprang "not from provincial prejudice, but from an understanding of

39. Bischoff, "Die Aufgaben und Ziele unserer Zeitschrift," *RPM* 4 (January 1953): 1.

40. There was notably more interest in artistic modernism after the war: see esp. Hans Reetz, "Auch Hans Purrman hat die Bitternis erfahren müssen," *PP* 1 (August 1950): 12; and K. F. Ertel, "Die Pfälzische Sezession," *PP* 1 (June 1950): 9.

authentic Kulturpflege, which must be nourished directly from the Volkstum in order that its intellectual heights not be suspended, unsupported, in empty space."[41]

The existence of an outside audience would supposedly provide a check on too much local silliness, forcing Pfälzer artists simultaneously to think deeply about their local selves and strive toward universal standards of cultural excellence (whatever they might be). In a piece playfully entitled "Pfälzer, Over-Pfälzer, All-Too-Pfälzer," Hans Reetz addressed such an audience by making fun of stories in which the word Pfälzer became meaningless through its repetition: "the Pfälzer village, the Pfälzer heaven, the Pfälzer air, the Pfälzer bread (perhaps made out of American grain, ground in Mannheimer, thus Badenese, mills), the Pfälzer summer, the Pfälzer evenings, Pfälzer table gossip, a velvet-blue Pfälzer night, and so on." Reetz nevertheless affirmed the existence of Pfälzerness, reachable not through repetition of the adjective but through penetration of the spirit. He suggested a contest for the best piece of Heimat writing in which the word *Pfälzer* would never appear: "Essence is the thing," he concluded, "not stereotype."[42]

The ambivalence and yet the desire to believe were both reflected in post-war discussions about the place of local dialect, in particular dialect literature, in German culture. On the one hand were the countless products of the wine-soaked imagination, banal and inauthentic; on the other hand was the vision of what dialect could be, as well as a few outstanding poets who had realized it. In 1948, Oskar Bischoff lamented the fact that "outside our province, the common image of the Pfälzer, his essence and his distinctiveness, his interior and his exterior, is often one-sided, if not completely distorted." Bad dialect poetry had contributed substantially to this distortion, he thought, and unfortunately good dialect poetry was increasingly rare because "few of our dialect poets have recognized that inherent in Pfälzer dialect is an authentic power of speech suited to image making . . . indeed to genuinely poetic pictures and lyrical expressions."[43] In the opening issue of *Pfalz und Pfälzer*, Ernst Christmann, a distinguished scholar of Pfälzer dialect, took up the argument with "an earnest word" on the failures of contemporary dialect writing. Most dialect poets, he thought, had failed to exercise the proper "self-criticism," creating hopelessly bad doggerel out of inauthentic bits of dialect with inappropriate pieces of high German thrown in to make the piece scan or rhyme. Contemporary writing, "exactly like the good or kitschy buildings that are being built on our public streets," either "honored or dis-

41. Bischoff, Reetz, et al., "Wir protestieren," p. 16.

42. The Nietzschean reference in the title clues us in to the audience (educated Germans) and to the subject (cultural standards) that he is addressing: "Pfälzisch—überpfälzisch—allzu pfälzisch," *PP* 2 (October 1951): 21.

43. Bischoff, "Pfälzer Mundartdichtung, Ein Wort zuvor!" *Pfälzer Bote: Volks- und Heimat-kalender* (Neustadt/Pfalz, 1948): 93.

figured and disgraced the Heimat itself"; restraint and taste were the order of the day, but neither was much in evidence.[44]

Predictably, Christmann provoked several strong defenses of dialect. As one writer asserted, it was the only means to express what was "felt as a Pfälzer"; similarly for Albert Becker, "each province must preserve its dialect, for it is indeed the element in which the soul can breathe."[45] And some miscellaneous efforts were subsequently made to elevate the medium—through competitions, through scholarly recordings of dialect, and through the reprinting of the so-called classic works of Pfälzer dialect, mostly products of the nineteenth century.[46] Nevertheless, the battle against literary, visual, and musical kitsch that Oskar Bischoff had declared in 1950 was probably doomed to failure. In 1955, *Pfalz und Pfälzer* had to close (for financial reasons, significantly, unable to compete in a market of mass production), and no journal took up its task of promoting the poetry inherent in the Pfälzer soul. But that the battle had taken place at all attested to the importance of regional particularity to German identity. Heimat was not peripheral to the cultural heritage in which Meinecke placed his hopes for Germany's regeneration, but instead was part of it. For Bischoff and others, there could be no revival of German culture as a whole without first recovering the local self.

The capacity of the community of the Pfalz to survive may have been the real issue in the fate of Bischoff's literary journal, as reactions to its closing in 1955 made clear. For Willi Gutting, a writer and teacher in the Pfälzer village of Sondernheim, the journal had been "more than the organ of a literary circle, more than the mouthpiece of creative people in our region"; rather, it had been "the manifestation of a community, whose capital lay outside the material sphere in the timeless landscape above the clouds." In Berlin, Theodor Bohner, honorary president of the Vereinigung Deutscher Schriftstellerverbände (Union of German Writers' Leagues), declared himself "shocked" at the inability of the Pfalz to sustain the journal: "The Rheinpfalz has always been a decapitated land, . . . and precisely because the Pfälzer, despite all the hymns to wine, is nowhere at home, I, a Pfälzer who lives out his life in partial infidelity to his land, felt the existence of the journal as a kind of protection over my own life. It affects me deeply to witness such a display of Pfälzer impotence." According to the Schutzverband Deutscher Schriftsteller Rheinland-Pfalz (League for the Protection of German Writers in Rhineland-Pfalz), "the consciousness of a landscape is de-

---

44. Ernst Christmann, "Von pfälzischer Auch-Mundartdichtung," *PP* 1 (April 1950): 3–4.

45. Heinz Lorenz, "Offener Brief an Dr. E. Christmann," *PP* 1 (June 1950): 16; Albert Becker, "Von Pfälzer Mundart, Mundartdichtung und Mundartforschung," *PP* 2 (January 1950): 6.

46. *PP* 5 (November 1954); *PH* 8 (1957): 72; Peter Luginsland, "In Memoriam Paul Münch," *PP* 2 (February 1951): 1.

pendent on the intensity with which the poets, writers, and artistically active people of all kinds experience its incorporeal existence."[47] From these perspectives, the inability of the Pfalz to sustain the journal seemed damaging testimony to the tenuousness of its existence as a real community, something more than a mere political arrangement. The journal's own concern for authenticity in a world filled with kitsch had expressed a deeper insecurity of Pfälzers themselves about the truth of their identity. As long as the journal existed—an experiment (as Bischoff characterized it, after Albert Schweitzer) in "sober idealism"—the vitality of the Pfälzer as such seemed amply demonstrated; when it failed, it took a piece of that illusion with it.

The hopes invested in *Pfalz und Pfälzer* were, however, only one manifestation of many that revealed the insecurities of postwar Germans about the survival—and truth—of the community, as it was traditionally constituted and understood. The Nazis' representation of Volksgemeinschaft could be easily abandoned, for it had found its only realization in a war that made all Germans vulnerable to hardship, displacement, and death. Whether pre-Nazi images of the community offered comfort was certainly not clear to the clear-sighted, though to the traumatized and the weary the temptation of "normality" was enormous. The immediate resurgence of Heimat in the first decade after the war attested to the weariness rather than the wisdom of Germans; certainly for some, Heimat endeavors represented a high calling, a challenge, but for most they were simply the easiest path to recovery, as well as the least objectionable expression of togetherness. Even the standard of authenticity could be too strenuous. Heimat was attractive for representing not something truer than the Nazis' "community of blood," but something essentially peaceful, noneventful. The notion of Heimat also expressed the immortality of the community to which one belonged, and that illusion, above all, had been destroyed in Hitler's final mad attempt to take the German nation down with him.[48]

The humble almanac was one of the first forms of Heimat consciousness to revive after the war, preceding the more sophisticated historical and literary ones and providing at least as revealing a glimpse into the mood of the period. Describing his product as a "tender sprout," the editor of the *Pfälzerland* wrote in 1946 that "after the apocalyptic catastrophe of the so-called Third Reich, we must start again from the beginning. . . . Let us not fail . . . to take up the task of directing thoughts of the Heimat again into healthy

47. Gutting, Bohner, and the Schutzverband Deutscher Schriftsteller were all quoted in Bischoff, "Wir heißen Euch hoffen," *RPM* 6 (September 1955): 1.

48. See the chapter entitled "Betrayal" in Sebastian Haffner, *The Meaning of Hitler*, trans. Ewald Osers (New York, 1979), pp. 149–65. Note also the enthusiasm of the so-called *Heimatvertriebene* (Heimat exiles) for association building and Heimat activities in their new homes. To recreate a "Heimat" for oneself was to begin to heal from the traumas of postwar displacement.

channels. The Pfälzer must again learn to feel himself as a Pfälzer."[49] To this end, the almanac dispensed advice on survival and regeneration disguised as jokes, folk sayings, and paeans to the Pfälzer character—its stoicism, its aversion to war from long historical experience, its openness to change and diversity, its friendliness, and its capacity for humor even in the grimmest of times.[50] An article in the newspaper *Rheinpfalz* attempted to be similarly inspiring when it lamented, "What remains now of our justly famous Rheinpfälzer temperament, where are our light hearts and our busy hands, working together to rebuild the Heimat?"[51] The existence of the Pfälzer character affirmed—or perhaps assumed—the existence of a community based on collectively held traits and values.

That community was the implicit concern of a Heimat-celebratory tendency among postwar educators also. In an article recommending the use of Heimatgeschichte for teaching children about the past, Gustav Knapp concluded that "Heimat knowledge can translate into the feeling of belonging together and of closeness, as well as into the inclination toward community. Herein lie the strongest intellectual and emotional roots for everything that would grow and prosper."[52] To some extent, Heimat was a community understood without reference to political or moral obligations, and Heimat instruction in the schools made a similar retreat from the Weimar agendas of civic instruction, settling into a relentlessly factual attention to geography, geology, and local history. The new Heimatkunde texts approved for use in the schools often consisted simply of slightly rewritten versions of discredited Nazi schoolbooks, stripped of references not just to Adolf Hitler and Horst Wessel, but to political citizenship and political entities of any kind, bad or good.[53]

Yet the community of Pfälzers, specifically its embodiment of common needs and common rights, was at the same time the implicit subject of a postwar political rhetoric concerned with the reanimation of public life.

49. "Zum Geleit," *Pfälzerland: Illustrierter Familien-Kalender 1947*, p. 9.

50. See, e.g., "Ihr lieben Pfälzer!" *Pfälzer Bote* (Neustadt/Pfalz, 1947), p. 1; E. Johann, "Pfälzer Land und Leute" and "Stimmen der Meister gegen den Krieg," in *Pfälzerland 1947*, pp. 12–13. For the same interpretations of character in more serious form, see Karl Kollnig, *Wandlungen im Bevölkerungsbild des pfälzischen Oberrheingebietes*, p. 35; and Albert Pfeiffer, "Die Pfalz" (8 June 1947), fragment of manuscript in PLAS, C1382.

51. "Fröhliche Pfalz—Gott erhälts!" *Rheinpfalz* (18 May 1946): 2.

52. "Die Heimat im Geschichtsunterricht," *Westdeutsche Schulzeitung* (formerly *Pfälzische Lehrerzeitung*) 62 (28 July 1953): 175.

53. See, e.g., the series "Von Heimatkreis zur weiten Welt" by Hans Mann and Alfred Stoffel, esp. the Pfalz volume *Pfälzer Land. Eine kleine Heimat- und Landeskunde der Rheinpfalz und des benachbarten Saarlandes* (Bonn, 1956), which relied to some extent on writings published in *Die Westmark*; or Albert Zink, *Die Pfalz mein Heimatland. Eine Heimatkunde für die Pfälzer Jugend* (Neustadt/Pfalz, 1950), a revision of his *Die Pfalz: Heimatkunde des Gaues Westmark*.

Here, Heimat and Pfalztum were invoked at least as often as in the speeches of the antioccupation politicians of the early 1920s, but this time to secure forgiveness and to emphasize commonalities across party divisions, not to inflame nationalist emotions. In early 1946, for instance, district president Eichenlaub, speaking at a civic gathering in Neustadt, blamed the Prussians (implicitly interpreting Nazism as a form of Prussianism) for the hatred that had theretofore existed between France and Germany. The new *Landrat*, Hanns Haberer, who followed Eichenlaub at the podium, pledged himself "to restor[ing] the well-being and future of the Heimat" in a spirit of forgiveness, repeating the word *Heimat* twelve times in a speech of five minutes. He concluded with a plea for "all of us to put our work at the service of the higher ideals of the people and the Heimat." The final speech of the evening was an emotional affirmation of Heimat as the basis of German collective life:

> Out of destruction and want and disgrace and guilt we have saved one thing: our glowing heart for our Heimat! . . . It lies here before us: wineland and tilled land, mountain and valley and stream, cities and villages, all bleeding from many wounds, torn apart by thousands of scars. . . . Hatred, injustice, revenge, force, terror, sycophancy, and knavery have all passed over us, but of one thing we can be sure, we did not betray our Heimat—in our hearts we resisted. And our Heimat will expiate our sins. . . . Heart, soul, Heimat, your best sons stand before you, caught up in your distress, laboring and creating with you, suffering and sacrificing with you, rising with you out of destruction to the rights of humanity. People of my Heimat, I call to you, hand to hand, heart to heart, victim to victim, hope to hope, love to love, with belief in the highest good: democracy and freedom for our Pfälzer Heimat.[54]

The idiom of Heimat allowed Germans to speak indirectly of the unspeakable, extinguishing their guilt in the process. Thus Heimat came to embody the political and social community that could be salvaged from the Nazi ruins.

Moreover, in seeking that "democracy and freedom" to which the speaker in Neustadt had referred, the heimatlich past could still inspire and instruct—as a new community association in Landstuhl, dedicated to the restoration of Franz von Sickingen's castle of Ebernburg, proved. At least from 1520 to 1523, the Ebernburg had been "a shelter to justice, a place of humanistic and religious renewal." One of the leaders of the Verein expressed the hope that "we in our work on the Ebernburg also encounter the freedom and justice and living faith that the young reformer [Franz von Sickingen] also sought and understood." The so-called Ebernburg tradition should be regarded "by people of our times as particularly necessary and healing to their distresses, dangers, and fears."[55] Needless to say, the postwar years in

54. Speeches reprinted in *Rheinpfalz* (9 January 1946): 3.
55. Plümacher, "Die Ebernburg, Geschichte und Bedeutung," pp. 111–14.

the Pfalz and in all of western Germany saw an enthusiastic revival of interest in the Hambach Festival, with its potentially powerful symbolism for a renewed republic.[56] More generally, the democratic and popular movement in nineteenth-century Pfalz, "so long ridiculed or ignored," enjoyed a popularity unparalleled even in the Weimar period, as representative of "our good democratic tradition": "The past of our own small Heimat," declared one local official, Günter Söfsky, "is rich in examples of the history-building powers of this landscape. And the German southwest, the old land of kings, . . . is also the land of origin of German dmocracy."[57] If democracy could not be rooted in Germany as a whole, it could still be rooted in the German locality, the Heimat; from such small beginnings would grow national traditions.

Looking at activities and speeches like these, H. W. Jung has rightly pointed out that politicians and public figures of the immediate postwar years, specifically in the Rhineland, did not address the difficult questions about their political culture that the local success of fascism had raised, but relied instead on the specter of Prussianism on the one hand and communism on the other to escape real responsibility. What he characterizes as "southwest German *ressentiment*" manifested itself in a renewed nostalgia for the old Reich, the first and only true Reich, of Karl der Große—Charlemagne to the French, and thus a symbol too of Franco-Rhenish friendship.[58] Yet political particularism was perhaps not the most striking feature of this tendency. Certainly, small communities and larger regions alike sought to define a past and a present "unburdened" by the heavy weights of *Machtstaat* and *Militarismus*, with one practical consequence being a marked resistance to any form of "denazification" of individuals. But though the process had Rhenish peculiarities, it was not peculiar to the Rhineland, nor was it simply the expression of a renewed small-statism.[59]

Rather, the rhetoric of Heimat, predicated as it was on the integrity of the

56. On the local level, see the account of restorations undertaken by the Rheinland-Pfalz Kultusministerium and a summary of the symbolic importance of Hambach in *PH* 8 (1957): 69, 150–57; on popular enthusiasm for Hambach at the time, see Lorenz Wingerter, "'Klingt noch ein höher Lied als Vaterland?': Fritz Eckerle zum Gedächtnis," *PP* 3 (May 1952): 3 (the answer in Eckerle's words was "Ja, Freiheit!"). More recently, Chancellor Helmut Kohl (a Pfälzer) tried to make Hambach the rhetorical centerpiece of Ronald Reagan's German tour of 1985. Reagan's speech there to a carefully selected group of German high school students was, of course, overshadowed by Bitburg—appropriately, to be sure, and, from the perspective of those beleaguered German democrats of the Pfalz, typically.

57. Söfsky, introduction to *Veröffentlichungen der PGFW* 69, p. 9; Trautz, *Die Pfalz am Rhein*, p. 30. See also Kurt Baumann, "Pfälzer kämpfen um die Freiheit Amerikas," *PP* 1 (August 1950): 9–10; Hans Fessmeyer, "Der Grünstadter Revolutionär August Mosbach," *PH* 4 (1953): 43–46; District President Keller, introduction to Karl Heinz, *150 Jahre Bezirksverband Pfalz* (Neustadt/Pfalz, 1966), pp. 5–7.

58. Jung, *Rheinland-Pfalz zwischen Antifaschismus und Autikommunismus*, pp. 1, 9, 14–17.

59. On the failure of *Entnazifizierung*, see ibid., p. 33.

locality within a national state, represented the recovery of that distinctively German, locally rooted patriotism that Nazism had discouraged. Whether in schoolbooks, almanacs, poetry collections, films, or political speeches, Heimat promised healing and health through the peculiar virtues of authentically local experience. The solution to the German problem, thought a writer in Saxony, was to follow the rule "Outwardly as unified as necessary, inwardly as diversified as possible."[60] The cultivation of Heimat embodied this rule in the purest form, for it gave the state its due without ceding all local claims to autonomy and distinctiveness. Best of all, Heimat gave the Germans as a whole something all their own: "How happy we are compared to totally uniform states, for the colorful diversity that the German Volkstum inherited from the old Stämme and the individualized landscape finds its expression in the diversity of our federal states. . . . All these particularities in the colorful picture of the German state are rooted in the Heimat."[61]

In 1951, the author of a tribute to Paul Münch, one of the great Pfälzer dialect poets, described the genre as "the last refuge of Heimat bliss and Heimat ties in our cultureless and godless world." Münch's masterwork in the local dialect was a comic celebration of Pfälzer self-regard called *Die pälzisch Weltgeschicht*, or World History According to the Pfälzer. Writing in 1909 at the height of the prewar Heimat movement, Münch found the sense as well as the place of world events firmly in the Pfalz itself. His death in the first days of 1951, his memorialist thought, may well have marked the end of Mundart and with it the end of the Heimat feeling it had engendered: "perhaps in the atomic age and in the age of the ubiquitous 'pidgin English' they will soon disappear forever."[62]

Certainly, as the shape of a postwar German nation began to emerge, much seemed to militate against the survival of local identities and locally referential views of the nation. At the level of popular culture, the once-flourishing Heimat organizations and activities have been almost entirely displaced by the postwar rage for American film, food and drink, television, and music. Although a European-wide phenomenon that has only become more marked over time, the process of "Americanization" was accelerated in the Pfalz by the terms of the NATO alliance. Since 1955 large numbers of American military and civilian personnel, air bases, training grounds, and PXs have covered the infertile landscape of the western Pfalz, and since the 1960s the U.S. government has been the largest employer in the region. American culture and American troops together have symbolized the eclipse

60. Georg Schnath, *Heimat und Staat. Betrachtungen eines Niedersachsen* (Hannover, 1958), p. 20.
61. Ibid., p. 21.
62. Peter Luginsland, "In Memoriam Paul Münch," *PP* 2 (1951): 1.

of European power and influence. Since 1945, the national character of popular cultures in Europe has been increasingly attenuated.

Yet, the charge of cultural imperialism notwithstanding, the choice to consume American popular culture is no more a matter of coercion than is any other choice involving consumable goods. Indeed, is there anything more intrinsically "real" about the invented Pfälzer folk dress than about a pair of Levi jeans? Maybe at the turn of the century there was, but even then the cultural force of the folk dress had as much to do with the contemporary desire for it as with any qualities all its own. As a critic of artificial attempts to promote "German folk customs" through Heimatkunde in the schools has written, "What cannot be lived and experienced outside the school cannot be conserved inside it."[63] That lesson was there to be learned in the experience of the Nazi years; and despite entirely sincere efforts since the war to restore integrity and vitality to local customs, the lesson has remained valid in the cities of a reconstructed Germany.

What is at stake here is a more ineffable product of culture: the way we identify ourselves and the terms by which we do so. From such a perspective, the historically grounded inclination of Germans to seek the key to their national identity in the multiplicity of their provincial origins has not proven completely susceptible to the scourge of "Americanization." Much evidence suggests that Germans, including German youth, are not ashamed of their dialects and are capable of switching back and forth between them and high German at will.[64] Dialect writing enjoyed a revival in the new genre of antinuclear poetry and prose, where its essential localness expresses a protest against the alien forces responsible for the nuclear power plant, the bomb emplacements, and the like.[65] That Germans as a whole continue to regard Heimat, however defined, as an essential part of their social identity is attested to not just by political scientists and contemporary anthropologists but by the phenomenal success on West German television in 1984 of a long treatment of life in the locality called, simply, *Heimat*.[66] Perhaps most telling

63. Kopp in 1961, cited by Greverus, *Auf der Suche nach Heimat*, p. 11.

64. See, e.g., Jürgen Macha and Thomas Weger, "Mundart im Bewußtsein ihrer Sprecher: Eine explorative Studie am Beispiel des Bonner Raumes," *Rheinische Vierteljahresblätter* 47 (1983): 265–301.

65. For perspectives on Heimat and contemporary German literature, see H. W. Seliger, ed., *Der Begriff "Heimat" in der deutschen Gegenwartsliteratur* (Munich, 1987).

66. See Chapter 1, p. 18, above. The film, by Edgar Reitz, is the subject of a special issue of *New German Critique* (no. 36 [Fall 1985]); see also Timothy Garten Ash, "The Life of Death," *New York Review of Books* 32 (19 December 1985), pp. 26–29. In Germany, see esp. "Sehnsucht nach Heimat," *Spiegel* (1 October 1984) (cover story); Christian Graf von Krockow, "Heimat," *Die Zeit* (5 October 1984); Anna Mikula, "Edgar Reitz, ein Deutscher," *Die Zeit Magazine* (26 October 1984). On Heimat in general, see the representative pieces in Weigelt, *Heimat und Nation*; and Bausinger and Köstlin, *Heimat und Identität*.

of all, German provincial identities and "Heimat consciousness" have been unobtrusively but steadily reasserting themselves in East Germany since the opening of the Berlin Wall in November 1989.

The concept of Heimat has also come to speak to the persistent concern of industrial societies for something more than mere physical survival—as well as the fear that this something has not been achieved. Ever since Karl Marx first characterized the state of alienation in the worker as the inability to regard his surroundings "as his Heimat," the term has expressed a concern for a community that transcends a political world divided along the parliamentary concepts of left and right.[67] Ernst Bloch regarded Heimat as the very essence of his "principle of hope." It has the last word in his enormously long philosophical attempt to bring together Marxism and world religions in a synthetic vision of man's capacity to overcome alienation (*Entfremdung*) and voicelessness (*Entäußerung*): "At such a time there will arise in the world something that appears to all in their childhood and yet in which none have dwelt: Heimat."[68] Bloch's current popularity in Germany, moreover, reflects the same sense of cultural angst that finds expression in the Green movement and in the peace movement, both of which, significantly, have found political support and ideological inspiration on the local level of German experience and have spread from there into the political mainstream.

For Heimat, despite all its misadventures over the years, has become essential to the German conception of community. Since its first tentative revival in the period of an emergent, German-wide public culture, it has come today to have more legitimacy and more power of evocation than such terms as *Fatherland* or even *nation*. The provincialness of Germans, a state responsible for their sense of inferiority and for their pride, has similarly survived many rises and falls in the political fortunes of their late-achieved nation. And as Germans, more than any other people in Europe, continue to question the sources of their national identity, in newspapers and public speeches, in films and literature, and now in renewed discussions of the future of East and West, the problem of local diversity and the promise of Heimat will continue to shape their answers.

67. In the 1844 manuscripts, he spoke of the "Kellerwohnung des Armen, die eine fremde Macht spiegelt, die er nicht als seine Heimat . . . betrachten darf, wo er sich vielmehr in dem Hause eines andern, in einem fremden Hause, befindet" (cited in Greverus, *Auf der Suche nach Heimat*, p. 14).

68. "So entsteht in der Welt etwas, das allen in die Kindheit scheint und worin noch niemand war: Heimat" (Ernst Bloch, *Das Prinzip Hoffnung* [Frankfurt, 1959], 3:1628).

Bibliography

PRIMARY MATERIAL

Archival Sources

Munich, Bayerische Hauptstaatsarchiv. Staatsministerium des Äussern (BHStAM, MA): MA 106018, 106019, 106032–36, 107709–13, 107736, 107737, 107772, 107785, 107806, 107814, 107816, 107924, 107927, 107932, 107935, 107937, 108042, 108046–48, 108071, 108074, 108076, 108078, 108326, 108363, 108372, 108454.

————. Staatsministerium des Unterricht und Kultus (BHStAM, MK): MK 11834, 15530–36, 15541, 15543, 155549–53, 15555, 15557–58, 15566–68, 15575, 15584, 15586, 15590–92.

Speyer, Pfälzisches Landesarchiv (PLAS). Historischer Verein der Pfalz. Tl (1848–1927); Albert Pfeiffer, "Die Pfalz," MSS, 8 June 1947, C 1382.

Speyer, Pfälzische Landesbibliothek (PLBS). Historischer Verein der Pfalz. Misc. papers; papers of Albert Becker (1879–1957), August Becker (1828–91), Daniel Häberle (1864–1934), Friedrich Hildenbrand (1853–1924), Christian Mehlis; Georg Reismüller, "Die Pfälzische Landesbibliothek in der Separatistenzeit: Ein Erinnerungsblatt," 1930, Rara Hs. 290.

Stanford, California, Hoover Institution Archives. Abel Collection.

Stanford, California, Hoover War Library. Homefront periodicals from Germany, 1914–18, 1940–44. NSDAP Hauptarchiv (Microfilm Collection). Pamphlets on the Rhineland Question (Arbeitsausschuß Deutscher Verbände).

Wiesbaden, Hessische Landesbibliothek. Papers of Wilhelm Heinrich Riehl, Hs. 140.

Contemporary Printed Sources and Published Documentary Sources

Anaker, Heinrich. *Heimat und Front. Gedichte aus dem Herbst.* Munich, 1940.

Aretin, Erwein Freiherr von. "Leidensjahre der Pfalz, auf Grund der Akten der bayerischen Regierung." *Süddeutsche Monatshefte* 22 (1925): 1–54.

Auswärtiges Amt. *Notenwechsel zwischen der Deutschen und der Französischen Regierung über die separatistischen Umtriebe in den besetzten Gebiete.* Berlin, 1924.

Baer, Georg. *Heil Wittelsbach! Heil Bayern!* Zweibrücken, 1905.

————. *Die Pfalz am Rhein: Pfälzische Heimatkunde.* Nuremberg, 1915.

Bassermann-Jordan, Friedrich von. *Geschichte des Weinbaus unter besonderer Berücksichtigung der bayerischen Rheinpfalz.* Frankfurt, 1907.

Bayerisches Kriegsarchiv, ed. *Die Bayern im Großen Kriege 1914–1918. Auf Grund der Kriegsakten dargestellt.* Munich, 1923.

Becker, Albert. *Deutschlands Wiedergeburt. Stimmen der Zeit und Bilder aus der Heimat des Hambacher Festes.* Beiträge zur Heimatkunde der Pfalz, 13. Kaiserslautern, 1932.

————. *Frauenrechtliches in Brauch und Sitte.* Beiträge zur Heimatkunde der Pfalz, 4. Kaiserslautern, 1913.

————. *Der "Garten Deutschlands." Ein Beitrag zur Entdeckungsgeschichte der bayerischen Pfalz am Rhein.* Beiträge zur Heimatkunde der Pfalz, 9. Kaiserslautern, 1928.

————. *Goethe und Zweibrücken.* Beiträge zur Heimatkunde der Pfalz, 6. Kaiserslautern, 1923.

————. *Hambach und Pirmasens. Ein Beitrag zur Geschichte des Hambacher Festes.* Beiträge zur Heimatkunde der Pfalz, 8. Pirmasens, 1928.

————. *Heimatkündliches aus der Westmark.* Beiträge zur Heimatkunde der Pfalz, 23. Frankenthal, 1941.

————. *Hundert Jahre Pfälzer Geschichtsforschung, 1827–1927.* Speyer, 1927.

————. *Hutten-Sickingen im Zeitenwandel. Ein Beitrag zur Pfälzer Geistesgeschichte.* Beiträge zur Heimatkunde der Pfalz, 16. Heidelberg, 1936.

————. *Karl Joseph Schuler.* Beiträge zur Heimatkunde der Pfalz, 3. Kaiserslautern, 1909.

————. *Pfälzer Frühlingsfeiern.* Beiträge zur Heimatkunde der Pfalz, 2. Kaiserslautern, 1908.

————. *Pfälzische Volkskunde.* Bonn, 1925.

————. "Politik und Volkstum. Volkskundliches um ein altes Volksfest, Hambach, 1832." *Giessener Beiträge zur deutschen Philologie* 60 (1939).

————. *Schiller und die Pfalz.* Beiträge zur Heimatkunde der Pfalz, 1. Ludwigshafen, 1907.

————. *Die Wiedererstehung der Pfalz. Zur Erinnerung an die Begründung der bayerischen Herrschaft auf dem linken Rheinufer. . . .* Beiträge zur Heimatkunde der Pfalz, 5. Kaiserslautern, 1916.

————. *Wilhelm Bauer, der Erfinder des Unterseebootes, und seine Beziehungen zur Pfalz.* Kaiserslautern, 1916.

————. *Ziele und Aufgaben eines Heimatmuseums.* Kaiserslautern, 1914.

Becker, August. *Die Pfalz und die Pfälzer,* 1858. Reprint edited by Oskar Bischoff. Landau/Pfalz, 1983.

Die befreite Pfalz im Spiegel der Münchener Zeitung. Munich, 1930.

Beltz, Julius. *Beltz' Bogenlesebuch der Pfalz.* Langensalza, 1926.

Betsch, Roland, and Lorenz Wingerter. *Rheinpfalz. Ein Heimatbuch.* Leipzig, 1928.

Binz, Gerhard. *Pfälzer im Krieg, 1914–1918.* Munich, 1928.

Böhmer, E. *Sprach- und Gründungsgeschichte der pfälzischen Colonie am Niederrhein.* Marburg, 1909.

Böshenz, Jakob. *Heil Luitpold, Dir! Schülerfestspiel.* Grünstadt/Pfalz, 1911.

——. *Heimat-Lebenskunde und Stoffverteilung für die Volksfortbildungsschulen Bayerns.* 3 vols. Grünstadt/Pfalz, 1921–22.

Bossert, Gustav. *Die Historische Vereine vor dem Tribunal der Wissenschaft.* Berlin, 1883.

Buchheit, Gert. "Nur engere Heimatforschung wie bisher? Zur Diskussion um die Arbeit im Historischen Verein der Pfalz," *Ludwigshafener General Anzeiger,* 10 March 1955, p. 6.

Bühler, Johannes. *Das Hambacher Fest. Deutsche Sehnsucht vor hundert Jahren.* Ludwigshafen, 1932.

Christmann, Ernst. *Wie wurde ich Mundartforscher und wie erforschte ich Mundart. Erinnerungen und Erlebnisse.* Kaiserslautern, 1965.

——. *Wir Saarpfälzer.* Vol. 20 of *Deutsches Volk.* Berlin, *1939.*

"Die deutsche Pfalz." Special edition of *Heimat-Aufbau: Mitteilungsblatt der Reichszentrale für Heimatdienst, Landesabteilung Bayern* 1 (1921).

Deutschland Berichte der Sozialdemokratischen Partei Deutschlands. 7 vols (1934–40). Frankfurt, 1980.

Dokumente aus dem Befreiungskampf der Pfalz. Special Edition of the *Pfälzische Rundschau.* Ludwigshafen, 1930.

Doll, Anton, ed. *Nationalsozialismus im Alltag. Quellen zur Geschichte der NS-Herrschaft im Gebiet des Landes Rheinland-Pfalz.* Speyer, 1983.

Eid, Ludwig. "Die gelehrten Gesellschaften der Pfalz." *Palatina,* nos. 38–42 (1926): 301, 307, 316, 324, 332, 345, 351, 360, 366.

——. *Heimatliches Volkstum und der Lehrer in der Pfalz.* Ludwigshafen, 1925.

——. *Pfälzer Volk. Vortrag im Ferienkurs der bayerischen Lehrerbildner zu Speyer.* Bayreuth, 1926.

Ewig. Eugen. *Die geschichtliche Grundlagen des Landes Rheinland-Pfalz.* Koblenz, 1954.

Fitz, Hermann. "Zur Gründung des Pfälzischen Verbandes für freie Volksbildung und zum 1. pfälzischen Volksbildungstag am 10. und 11. Juli 1920 zu Neustadt." *Pfälzische Lehrerzeitung* (1920): 163–64.

Fontane, Theodore. *Gedichte.* 17th ed. Stuttgart, 1912.

Franz, Günther, Ernst Christmann, and Hermann Emrich, eds. *Abhandlungen zur Saarpfälzischen Landes- und Volksforschung.* Kaiserslautern, 1937.

Franzosenzeit. 10 Aufsätze und 30 Bilder zur Räumung der Pfalz von den Franzosen. Special edition of the *Landauer Anzeiger.* Landau/Pfalz, 1930.

Gedächtnisschrift für Albert Pfeiffer. Edited by the Freudeskreis der Stuhlbrüder in Speyer. Speyer, 1949.

Gellert, Georg, ed. *Das eiserne Buch. Die Führenden Männer und Frauen zum Weltkrieg 1914/15.* Hamburg, 1915.

Germann, Georg (pseud.). *Im Gefängnis der Separatisten. Wahre Begebenheit aus den Leidensjahren der Pfalz.* Nuremberg, 1927.

Gesellschaft der Freunde des deutschen Heimatschutzes. *Der Deutsche Heimatschutz. Ein Rückblick und Ausblick.* Munich, 1930.

Grimm, Jakob and Wilhelm Grimm. *Deutsches Wörterbuch*. Vol. 4, pt. 2. Leipzig, 1877.
Häberle, Daniel. *Auswanderung und Koloniegründung der Pfälzer im 18. Jahrhundert*. Kaiserslautern, 1909.
———. *Die natürlichen Landschaften der Pfalz*. Kaiserslautern, 1913.
———. *Der Pfälzerwald. Entstehung seines Namens, seine geographische Abgrenzung und die Geologie seines Gebietes*. Kaiserslautern, 1911.
Häberle, Daniel, Albert Becker, and Theodor Zink. *Die Pfalz am Rhein. Ein Heimatbuch*. Berlin, 1924.
Haenisch, Konrad. *Sozialdemokratische Kulturpolitik*. Berlin, 1918.
Halm, P. M. "Volkskunde, Volkskunst, Heimatschutz." In *Dem bayerischen Volke. Der Weg der Bayern durch die Jahrhunderte*, edited by Georg Jacob Wolf. Munich, 1930.
Hardt, Tino. "Die Bedeutung der Heimatschutzbewegung." *Palatina*, 3 April 1930, 106–7.
Hartmann, Peter. *Französische Kulturarbeit am Rhein*. Leipzig, 1921.
Haupthilfstelle für die Pfalz. *Dokumentensammlung zur Geschichte des pfälzischen Separatismus (auf amtlichen Unterlagen beruhend)*. 3 vols. Heidelberg, 1924.
Häusser, Ludwig. *Geschichte des Rheinischen Pfalz*. 2 vols. 1856; reprint Pirmasens, 1970.
Heeger, Georg, and Wilhelm Wüst. *Volkslieder aus der Rheinpfalz, mit Singweisen*, Kaiserslautern, 1908.
Herzberg, Wilhelm. *Das Hambacher Fest*. 1908, reprint Darmstadt, 1982.
Heuser, Emil. *Pfälzerland in der Vergangenheit*. Neustadt, 1922.
Hild, Hermann. *Das Saarland*. Heimatkunde des Gaues Westmark, 1. Saarbrücken, 1941.
Historischer Verein der Pfalz. *Einladung zur Betheiligung an einem historischen Vereine der Pfalz*. Speyer, 1869.
———. *Erster Jahresbericht des historischen Vereines der Pfalz*. Speyer, 1842.
———. *Hundert-Jahrfeier der Gründung des Historischen Vereins der Pfalz 1827–1927*. Kaiserslautern, 1927.
———. *Satzungen des Historischen Vereines der Pfalz*. Speyer, 1869, 1880, 1890.
———. *Verzeichnis der Mitglieder des Historischen Vereins der Pfalz, nach dem Stande von 1 Oktober 1918*. Speyer, 1918.
———. *Zweiter Bericht des Historischen Vereins der Pfalz*. Speyer, 1847.
Historisches Museum der Pfalz. *Bericht des Historischen Museums der Pfalz in Speier, 1914–1917*. Speyer, 1918.
———. *Satzungen des Vereins Historisches Museum der Pfalz, e.V. (Historischer Verein der Pfalz)*. Speyer, 1923.
Horlacher, Michael. *Der Wert der Pfalz Für Bayern und das Reich*. Diessen vor München, 1920.
Hundertjahrfeier der Gründung des Historischen Vereins der Pfalz, Speyer, 1827–1927. Festgabe der "Speierer Zeitung." Speyer, 1927.
Jacquot, Paul. *Général Gérard et le Palatinat*. Translated into German as *Enthüllungen aus dem französischen Generalstabs*, edited by Dr. Ritter [von Eberlein]. Berlin, 1920.
Jahraus, Johannes, ed. *Des pfälzers Heimat in Wort und Bild*. Speyer, 1910.
Knebel, Hajo. *Pfälzer unter sich über sich*. Frankfurt, 1977.
Kohl, Hermann. *Pfälzer Land und Volk in der Schule erlebt. Die neue Heimatkunde für die Westmark, auf nationalsozialistischer Grundlage*. Pirmasens, 1935.

Köhrer, Erich, and Franz Hartmann, eds. *Die Pfalz, Ihre Entwicklung und ihre Zukunft. Ein Sammelwerk unter Mitwirkung führender Persönlichkeiten der Pfalz und mit besonderer Förderung der Staatsbehörden.* Berlin, 1926.

Kölsch, Kurt. "Die 'Westmark' in Front: Von der Arbeit unserer Kulturpolitischen Monatschrift." *NSZ-Rheinfront*, no. 219 (19 September 1935).

Krämer, Wolfgang. *Saarpfälzische Heimattage und Heimatpflege während der Trennungszeit.* Saarbrücken, 1935.

Kranz, Fritz. *Das nordpfälzische Bergland. Landschaft und Mensch in Nordpfalz und Westrich.* Diss., Universität München, 1935.

Lehmann, Johann Georg. *Urkundliche Geschichte der Burgen und Bergschlößer in den ehemaligen Gauen, Grafschaften und Herrschafte in der bayerischen Pfalz.* Kaiserslautern, 1859.

Lintz, Karl-Heinz. *Großkampftage aus der Separatistenzeit in der Pfalz.* Edenkoben/Pfalz, 1930.

Liste der von der Interalliierten Rheinlandkommission in Coblenz für das besetzte Gebiet verbotenen Bücher, Lichtbildstreifen und Zeitungen. Berlin, 1925.

Literarischer Verein der Pfalz, ed. *Heimatgrüße aus der Pfalz fürs Feld.* Speyer, 1917.

————. *Heimatgrüße den Pfälzer Landsleuten ins Feld.* Speyer, 1916.

Löffler, Eugenie. *Landschaft und Stadt in Pfalz und Saar. Geographische Charakterbilder.* Saarbrücken, 1936.

Mann, Hans, and Alfred Stoffel. *Pfälzer Land. Eine kleine Heimat- und Landeskunde der Rheinpfalz und des benachbarten Saarlandes.* Bonn, 1956.

Mann, Thomas. *The German Catastrophe: Reflections and Recollections.* Translated by Sidney B. Fay. Cambridge, Mass., 1950.

————. *Reflections of a Nonpolitical Man.* Translated by Walter D. Morris. New York, 1983. (Originally published as *Betrachtungen eines Unpolitischen.* Berlin, 1918.)

Manz, Karl von, Alois Mitterweiser, and Hans Zeiss, eds. *Heimatarbeit und Heimatforschung. Festgabe für Christian Frank zum 60. Geburtstag.* Munich, 1927.

Mehlis, Christian. *Bilder aus der Pfalz.* Neustadt/Pfalz, 1895.

————. *Fahrten durch die Pfalz. Historische Landschaftsbilder.* Augsburg, 1877.

————. *Touristische Erfahrungen in Rheinlande.* Mannheim, 1900.

————. *Von den Burgen der Pfalz.* Freiburg, 1902.

Morgenthau, Henry, Jr. *Germany Is Our Problem: A Plan for Germany.* New York, 1945.

Müller-Meiningen, Ernst. *Aus Bayerns schwersten Tagen. Erinnerungen und Betrachtungen aus der Revolutionszeit.* Berlin, 1923.

Münch, Paul. *Die pälzisch Weltgeschicht.* Kaiserslautern, 1910.

Nadler, K. G. *Fröhlich Palz, Gott erhalt's!* Frankfurt, 1847.

Nationalsozialistische Karte Rheinfront. Neustadt/Pfalz, 1934.

Nebenius, Carl Friedrich. *Geschichte der Pfalz.* Mannheim, 1873.

Oberhauser, Robert. *Der Kampf um die Rheinpfalz. Frankreich, Separatismus und Abwehrbewegung, 1918–1924.* Diss., Universität Leipzig, 1932.

————. *Kampf der Westmark. Frankreich, Separatismus und Abwehrbewegungen 1918–1922.* Neustadt, 1934.

Oncken, Hermann. *Nation und Geschichte. Reden und Aufsätze 1919–1935.* Berlin, 1935.

————. *The Historical Rhine Policy of the French.* New York, 1923.

Organizations, Verkehrs und Statistische Karte Gau Westmark, unter Mitwirkung der Landesplanungsgemeinschaft Westmark. Kaiserslautern, 1941.

Petto, Alfred, ed. *Westmärkische Heimat. Eine Heimatgabe für unsere Soldaten.* Saarbrücken, 1941.

Die Pfalz—Ein adlig Land. Zensuren zeitgenössischer deutscher Schriftsteller. Neustadt/Pfalz, 1963.

"Die Pfalz am Rhein." *Merian* 6 (1953).

"Pfalz-Ausstellung: Berlin 1934." Sondernummer der *NSZ Rheinfront* (1934).

Pfalz-Bayerischer Heimgarten 1919–1920. Edited by the Bayerische Landesverein für Heimatschutz. Munich, 1919.

Pfälzische Gesellschaft zur Förderung der Wissenschaften. *Arbeitsbericht 1958–1959.* Speyer, 1959.

―――. *Pfälzische Gesellschaft zur Förderung der Wissenschaften.* Speyer, 1926.

―――. *Satzungen der PGFW.* Speyer, 1926.

Pfälzische Rundschau, ed. *25 Jahre "Pfälzische Rundschau," bedeutendste Zeitung der Pfalz.* Ludwigshafen, 1924.

Pfeiffer, Albert. *August Becker zum Gedächtnis.* Landau/Pfalz, 1930.

―――. "Die kulturelle Bedeutung der Pfalz." In *Dem bayerischen Volke. Der Weg der Bayern durch die Jahrhunderte,* edited by Georg Jacob Wolf. Munich, 1930.

―――. *Pfälzer Land—Deutsches Land.* Berlin, 1926.

―――. "Die Pfalz unter französischer Besatzung, 1918–1930." *Zeitschrift für bayerische Landesgeschichte* 5 (1932): 89–128.

Pfeiffer, Anton. *Pfeiffer-Chronik.* Munich, 1927.

Pfeiffer, Maximilian. *Hochzeitsschrift für Albert Pfeiffer, 26 Nov. 1921. Archivalisches Lustwäldlein.* Neustadt/Pfalz, 1921.

―――. *Kyrie Eleison.* Speyer, 1925.

―――. "Die Pfalz." In *Der Kampf um die deutschen Grenzen. Sieben historisch-politische Abhandlungen.* Berlin, 1925.

―――. *Die Pfalz ein deutsches Land! Rede vor den Pfälzern in Berlin und Mannheim am 15 Dec. 1918 und 1 Feb. 1919.* Wirmelsdorf/Berlin, 1918.

―――. *Rede des Ministers Dr. Pfeiffer, Deutschen Gesandten in Wien, bei der Pfalzkundgebung im Sitzungssaale des Reichstages zu Berlin.* Berlin, 1924.

Raumer, Kurt von. "Das Hambacher Fest." In *Staat und Volkstum: Neue Studien aus baierischen und deutschen Geschichte und Volkskunde. Festgabe für Karl Alexander von Müller,* edited by W. Andreas et al. Diessen vor München, 1933.

―――. *Der politische Sinn der Landesgeschichte.* Kaiserslautern, 1938.

―――. *Der Rhein im deutschen Schicksal. Reden und Aufsätze zur Westfrage.* Berlin, 1936.

Raumer, Kurt von, and Kurt Baumann. *Deutscher Westen—Deutsches Reich. Saarpfälzische Lebensbilder.* Kaiserslautern, 1938.

Reetz, Hans, ed. *Pfälzerland: Illustrierter Familien-Kalender.* Landau/Pfalz, 1946.

Reichskarte: Gau Saarpfalz. Berlin, 1936.

Reismüller, Georg. "Der Pfälzische Gesellschaft zur Förderung der Wissenschaften zum Geleit! Der Stand der wissenschaftlichen Pfalzkunde." *Pfälzer Zeitung* 76 (24 October 1925): 3.

Renard, Rudolf. *Rheinland-Pfalz. Heimatkunde in Bild und Karte.* Frankfurt, 1953.

"Die Rheinpfalz." *Europäische Staats- und Wirtschaftszeitung* 7 (15 January 1922).

Riehl, Wilhelm Heinrich. *Kulturstudien aus drei Jahrhunderten.* Stuttgart, 1903.

―――. *Die Naturgeschichte des deutschen Volkes.* 3 vols. Stuttgart, 1851–55.

―――. *Die Pfälzer. Ein rheinisches Volksbild.* 1857; rev. ed. Neustadt/Pfalz, 1973.

Rotteck, Carl von, and Carl Welcker. *Staats-Lexikon oder Enzyklopadie der Staatswissenschaften*, vol. 7. Altona, 1839.

Schandein, Ludwig, et al. *Rheinpfalz.* In *Bavaria. Landes und Volkskunde des Königreichs Bayern*, edited by Wilhelm Heinrich Riehl. Munich, 1860–68.

Schnath, Georg. *Heimat und Staat. Betrachtungen eines Niedersachsen.* Hannover, 1958.

Schönhöffer, Hanns. "Besprechungen zur Jahrhundertfeier des Historischen Vereins der Pfalz." *Zeitschrift für bayerische Landesgeschichte* 1 (1928): 96–101.

Schreibmüller, Hermann. "Ein bayerischer Geschichtsforscher: Hermann Schreibmüller berichtet über sich selbst." *Heimatglocken: Beilage für heimatliche Belehrung und Unterhaltung* 2 (1950): 3.

———. *Bayern und Pfalz.* Kaiserslautern, 1916.

———. "Bayern und Pfalz in Geschichte und Gegenwart." *Volk und Reich: Politische Monatshefte* 4 (1928): 286–99.

———. "Der Begriff Pfalz im Wandel der Jahrhunderte." *Mannheimer Generalanzeiger*, 13 November 1920.

———. *Frei ist die Pfalz! Ansprache gehalten bei der Pfalzbefreiungsfeier des Pfälzer Treubundes.* Ansbach, 1930.

———. "Der geplante Pfälzische Heimatatlas." *Zeitschrift für bayerische Landesgeschichte* 1 (1928): 81–95.

———. *100 Jahre pfälzischer Geschichtsforschung.* Gotha, 1916.

———. "Die linksrheinischen Gebiete: Eine deutsche Denkschrift vor dem Diktatfrieden." *Pfälzische Rundschau*, 9 September 1930.

Schurz, Carl. *Vormärz in Deutschland.* Reprint edited by Herbert Pönicke. Munich, 1948.

Sprater, Friedrich, "Aus der Urzeit der Pfälzer Heimat." *Heimatkundliche Vorträge des Pfälzischen Verbandes für freie Volksbildung.* Speyer, 1921.

Springer, Max. *Die Franzosenherrschaft in der Pfalz 1792–1814.* Stuttgart, 1926.

———. *Loslösungsbestrebungen am Rhein, 1918–1924.* Berlin, 1924.

———. *Der politische Charakter der französischen Kulturpropaganda am Rhein.* Berlin, 1923.

Stein, Thomas. *Französische Pressestimmen über die Rheinlandpolitik.* Mannheim, 1921.

Tuckermann, Walter. *Das Altpfälzische Oberrheingebiet von der Vergangenheit bis zur Gegenwart.* Cologne, 1936.

Verein der Rheinpfälzer, Stuttgart. *Einladung zur Feier unseres 50-jährigen Jubiläums 1911–1961.* Stuttgart, 1961.

Volksbildung in der Pfalz. 30 Jahre Kulturarbeit im Dienste unserer Heimat. Edited by the Pfälzische Verband für freie Volksbildung. Neustadt/Pfalz, 1952.

Walter, Michael. *Kleiner Führer für Heimatforscher. Winke, Stoffe und Hilfsmittel.* Karlsruhe, 1924.

Wappes, Lorenz, ed. *Die Pfalz unter französischer Besatzung. Kalendarische Darstellung der Ereignisse vom Einmarsch 1918 bis November 1924.* Munich, 1925.

Weiss, Franz. *Die malerische und romantische Pfalz.* 1840; reprint Hildesheim, N.Y., 1975.

Wenz, Richard, ed. *Des rheinischen Volkes geistige Heimat. Tausend Jahre rheinischer Dichtung.* Leipzig, 1925.

Das Westmarkbuch: Bildbuch eines deutschen Gaues. Neustadt/Pfalz, 1944.

Das Westmark Buch: Ehrengabe des Winterhilfswerkes. Neustadt/Pfalz, 1934.

Wingerter, Lorenz. *Geschichte der "Palatina."* Speyer, 1926.

————. *Heimat, öffne deine Quellen.* Speyer, 1923.

Wünschel, Hans-Jürgen, ed. *Schicksalsjahre der Pfalz. Dokumente zur Geschichte von Rheinland-Pfalz.* Neustadt/Pfalz, 1979.

Zimmer, Ludwig. *Heimatkunde für die Schulen der Rheinpfalz.* Pirmasens, 1905.

Zink, Albert. *Die Pfalz am Rhein. Eine Heimatkunde.* Speyer, 1952.

————. *Die Pfalz am Rhein. Heimatkunde des Gaues Westmark.* Saarbrücken, 1943.

————. *Die Pfalz mein Heimatland. Eine Heimatkunde für die Pfälzer Jugend.* Neustadt/Pfalz, 1950, 1954.

Zink, Theodor. *Deutsche Geschichte auf heimatlicher Grundlage.* 2 vols. Kaiserslautern, 1907, 1921.

————. *Die Pfalz.* Vol. 12 of *Deutsche Volkskunst,* edited by Edwin Redslob. Munich, 1934.

Zink, Theodor, and Ludwig Mang. *Das Wirtschaftsleben der Pfalz in Vergangenheit und Gegenwart.* Munich, 1913.

Die Zukunft der Pfalz. Bericht über die Versammlung zu Zweibrücken. Zweibrücken, 1919.

Zur Hundertjahrfeier des Historischen Vereins der Pfalz. Speyer, 1927.

Periodical Literature

Arbeitshefte: Verband für Volkstum und Heimat in Rheinland-Pfalz (1959–63).

Die Ausschau: Neupfälzische Landeszeitung Kulturelle Beilage (1926).

Das Bayerland: Illustrierte Zeitschrift für Bayerns Volk und Land (1921, 1930).

Bei uns daheim: Aus Vergangenheit und Gegenwart der Pfalz, Beilage zur "Pfälzischen Post" (1925–32).

Blätter für Geschichte und Heimatkunde der Glan und Lautergegend (1894–95).

Frankenthal einst und jetzt.

Heimatblätter für Ludwigshafen (1912, 1934).

Die Heimath: Pfälzisches Sonntagsblatt (1886).

Hoch die Pfalz! Illustriertes Monatsblatt des Pfalzbundes (1919).

Korrespondenzblatt des Gesamtvereins der Deutschen Geschichts- und Altertümsverein.

Die Kurpfalz: Mitteilungsblatt der Verein "Kurpfalz" (1950–55).

Mitteilungen des Historischen Vereins der Pfalz (1870–1932, 1947–present).

Mitteilungen des Literarischen Vereins der Pfalz (1913–21).

Nordpfälzer Geschichtsblätter des Nordpfälzer Geschichtsvereins (1904–10).

Palatina: Belletristisches Beiblatt zur "Pfälzer Zeitung" (1859–1913, 1922–33).

Die Pfalz am Rhein: Mitteilungen des Bezirksverbandes Pfalz (1926–30, 1933–38, 1950–62, 1963–67).

Die Pfalz am Rhein: Pfälzische Verkehrs- und Heimatzeitschrift; formerly, *Verkehrs-Zeitung für die Pfalz, Pfälzische Verkehrszeitung,* and *Die Pfalz am Rhein: Touristen-Zeitung* (1898–1926, 1927–present).

Pfalz, Bayern und Reich: Nationale Wochenschrift zur Pflege des deutschen Gedankens gegen alle Separationsbestrebungen (1923–24).

Pfalz und Pfälzer: Monatshefte für Kultur, Heimatpflege und Unterhaltung; later, *Rheinisch-pfälzische Monatshefte* (1950–55).

Die Pfälzer: Ein Taschenbuch für die Pfalz vom Pfalz-Verband der Bayerischen Volkspartei (1928–32).

Pfälzer am Niederrhein: Heimatblätter für Geschichte, Brauchtum und Mundartpflege (1968–77).

Pfälzer Bote: Volks- und Heimatkalender (1947–49).

Pfälzer Familien-Kalender (1920).

Pfälzer Heimat (1950–present).

Pfälzer Herold: Halbmonatschrift für die kurpfälzische Heimat (1924).

Der Pfälzer in Amerika: Wochenschrift den Interessen der Rhein-Pfälzer in den Vereinigten Staaten gewidmet (1915, 1916).

Der Pfälzer in Berlin: Mitteilungen des Pfälzerwald-Vereins, e.V. Ortsgruppe Berlin (1921–41).

Pfälzer in der weiten Welt: Veröffentlichungen der Heimatstelle Pfalz (1957–61).

Pfälzer Land: Beilage der unabhängigen Pfälzer Heimatpresse (1953–55).

Pfälzerland: Monatsschrift des Bunds Bayern-Pfalz (1956).

Des Pfälzers Heimat in Wort und Bild: Ein Heimatblatt für Ausland (1910).

Pfälzer Volkskalender (1922).

Pfälzerwald: Mitteilungsblatt des Pfälzerwald Vereins, e.V. (1906–19, 1959–present).

Pfälzerwald: Wochenschrift für den Touristik, Radfahren, und Fremdenverkehr in der Pfalz (1900–1906).

Pfälzische Heimatblätter (1952–71).

Der Pfälzische Heimatkalender; after 1922, *Der Jäger aus Kurpfalz: Pfälzischer Heimatkalender* (1922–42, 1944, 1951–72).

Pfälzische Heimatkunde: Illustrierte Monatsschrift zur Förderung von Natur- und Landeskunde in der Rheinpfalz (1904–20).

Pfälzische Lehrerzeitung; later, *Westdeutsche Schulzeitung* (1921–33, 1950–55).

Pfälzisches Museum: Monatsschrift für heimatliche Literatur und Kunst, Geschichte und Volkskunde (1884–1920).

Pfälzisches Museum—Pfälzische Heimatkunde (1921–33).

Stimme der Pfalz (1951–65).

Der Trifels: Heimatbeilage der Pfälzischen Rundschau (1928).

Unsere Heimat: Blätter für saarländisch-pfälzisches Volkstum (1935–39).

Unsere Heimat: Heimatbriefe aus der Gau Saarpfalz (1938–40).

Unsere Pfalz: Blätter in zwangloser Folge für Heimat-, Wirtschafts-, Kultur- und Literaturgeschichte der Pfalz (1922–26).

Veröffentlichungen der Pfälzischen Gesellschaft zur Förderung der Wissenschaften (1926–present).

Völkische Wissenschaft: Periodische Beilage zur Monatsschrift "Die Westmark" (1934–37).

Volk und Heimat: Zeitschrift der Liga zum Schutze der Deutschen Kultur (1920).

Wald-Heil! Mitteilungen des Pfälzerwald-Vereins der Ortsgruppe Ludwigshafen-Mannheim (1917–26).

Wanderbuch des Pfälzerwald Vereins (1907–14, 1928–39).

Die Welt der Kleinen (1924–33).

Die Westmark: Monatsschrift des Volksbildungsverbandes Pfalz-Saar/Kampfbund für Deutsche Kultur in der Westmark (1933–42).

Westpfälzische Geschichtsblätter (1897).

SECONDARY MATERIAL

Abel, Theodore. *Why Hitler Came into Power.* 1938. Reprint edited by Thomas Childers. Cambridge, Mass., 1986.

Abelein, Manfred. *Die Kulturpolitik des Deutschen Reiches und der Bundesrepublik Deutschland.* Cologne, 1968.

Albisetti, James C. *Secondary School Reform in Imperial Germany.* Princeton, 1983.

Albrecht, Willy. *Landtag und Regierung in Bayern am Vorabend der Revolution von 1918.* Berlin, 1968.

Alexander, Thomas, and Beryl Parker. *The New Education in the German Republic.* New York, 1929.

Allen, Henry T. *My Rhineland Journal.* Boston, 1923.

———. *The Rhineland Occupation.* Indianapolis, 1927.

Allmann, Ludwig. "Die Wahlbewegung zum Ersten Deutschen Zollparlament in der Rheinpfalz." Diss., Universität Strassburg, 1913.

Alter, Willi, ed. *Pfalzatlas.* 2 vols. Speyer, 1964–71.

Anderson, Benedict. *Imagined Communities: Reflections on the Origin and Spread of Nationalism.* London, 1983.

Andreas, Willy. "Ludwig Häusser und Karl Hillebrand: Eine geistesgeschichtliche Studie." *Zeitschrift für die Geschichte des Oberrheins* 65 (1956): 489–507.

Arnold, Hermann. *Von den Juden in der Pfalz.* Speyer, 1967.

Ay, Karl Ludwig. *Die Entstehung einer Revolution. Die Volksstimmung in Bayern während des Ersten Weltkrieges.* Berlin, 1968.

Barkin, Kenneth D. *The Controversy over German Industrialization, 1890–1902.* Chicago, 1970.

———. "Modern Germany: A Twisted Vision." *Dissent* (Spring 1987): 252–55.

Bason, Cecilia Hatrick. *Study of the Homeland and Civilization in the Elementary Schools of Germany.* New York, 1937.

Baumann, Kurt. "Bayern und die oberrheinischen Territorialfragen vom Wiener Kongress bis zum Ausgang des Ersten Weltkrieges." In *Die Raumbeziehungen der Pfalz in Geschichte und Gegenwart. Niederschrift über die Verhandlungen der Arbeitsgemeinschaft für westdeutsche Landes- und Volksforschung in Kaiserslautern 6–9.X.1954.* Bonn, 1954.

———. "Kronprinz Ludwig von Bayern, und die Oberrheinlande, 1809–1819." *Abhandlungen zur saarpfälzischen Landes- und Volksforschung* 1 (1937).

———. "Ludwig I." In *Deutscher Westen—Deutsches Reich. Saarpfälzische Lebensbilder,* edited by Karl von Raumer and Kurt Baumann. Kaiserslautern, 1938.

———. "Ludwig Roediger aus Neunkirchen am Potzberg, ein Vorkämpfer der Burschenschaft, 1798–1866." *Pfälzer Heimat* 2 (1951).

———. "Probleme der pfälzischen Geschichte im 19. Jahrhundert." *Mitteilungen des Historischen Vereins der Pfalz* 51 (1953).

———. *Von Geschichte und Menschen der Pfalz. Ausgewählte Aufsätze.* Edited by Kurt Andermann. Speyer, 1984.

———, ed. *Pfälzer Lebensbilder.* 2 vols. Speyer, 1964–70.

Bausinger, Hermann. *Volkskunde. Von der Altertumsforschung zur Kulturanalyse.* Berlin, n.d.

Bausinger, Hermann, and Konrad Köstlin, eds. *Heimat und Identität. Probleme regionaler Kultur*. Neumünster, 1980.

Bensusan, S. L. *Some German Spas: A Holiday Record*. London, 1925.

Benz, Wolfgang. *Süddeutschland in der Weimarer Republik. Ein Beitrag zur deutschen Innenpolitik 1923–1928*. Berlin, 1970.

Berdahl, Robert. "New Thoughts on German Nationalism." *American Historical Review* 77 (1972): 65–80.

Bergmann, Klaus. *Agrarromantik und Großstadtfeindschaft*. Meisenheim am Glan, 1970.

Bischof, Erwin. *Rheinischer Separatismus, 1918–1924*. Bern, 1969.

Bischoff, Oskar, Karl Heinz, and Alf Rapp, eds. *Das große Pfalzbuch*. Neustadt/Pfalz, 1980.

Black, Antony. *Guilds and Civil Society in European Political Thought from the Twelfth Century to the Present*. Ithaca, N.Y., 1984.

Blackbourn, David. *Class, Religion, and Local Politics in Wilhelmine Germany: The Centre Party in Württemberg Before 1914*. New Haven, 1980.

———. "The German Petite Bourgeoisie Between Resignation and Volatility." In *Shopkeepers and Master Artisans in Nineteenth-Century Europe*, edited by Geoffrey Crossick and Gerhard Haupt. London, 1984.

———. "The Mittelstand in German Society and Politics, 1871–1914." *Social History* 2 (1977): 410–33.

Blackbourn, David, and Geoff Eley. *The Peculiarities of German History*. New York, 1984.

Blackburn, Gilmer W. *Education in the Third Reich: A Study of Race and History in Nazi Textbooks*. Albany, N.Y., 1985.

Blanning, T.C.W. *The French Revolution in Germany: Occupation and Resistance in the Rhineland, 1792–1802*. Oxford, 1983.

———. *Reform and Revolution in Mainz, 1743–1803*. Cambridge, 1974.

Blessing, Werner K. "The Cult of the Monarchy, Political Loyalty, and the Workers' Movement in Imperial Germany." *Journal of Contemporary History* 13 (1978): 357–75.

———. *Staat und Kirche in der Gesellschaft. Institutionelle Autorität und mentaler Wandel*. Göttingen, 1982.

Bloch, Ernst. *Das Prinzip Hoffnung*. 3 vols. Frankfurt, 1959.

Bois, Jean-Pierre. "L'opinion catholique rhénane devant le séparatisme en 1923." *Revue d'Histoire Moderne et Contemporaine* 21 (1974): 221–51.

Bosl, Karl. *Die Geschichte der Repräsentation in Bayern*. Munich, 1974.

———. "Die historische Staatlichkeit der bayerischen Lande." *Zeitschrift für bayerische Landesgeschichte* 25 (1962): 3–19.

Braatz, Thea. *Das Kleinbürgertum in München und seine Öffentlichkeit von 1830–1870. Ein Beitrag zur Mentalitätsforschung*. Munich, 1977.

Braubach, Max. *Landesgeschichtliche Bestrebungen und historische Vereine im Rheinland*. Düsseldorf, 1954.

———. "Vom Westfälischen Frieden bis zum Wiener Kongress (1648–1815)." In *Rheinische Geschichte*, edited by Franz Petri and Georg Droege, vol 2. Düsseldorf, 1976.

Braun, Rudolf. *Sozialer und kultureller Wandel in einem ländlichen Industriegebiet im 19. und 20. Jahrhundert*. Erlenbach/Zürich, 1965.

Bräunche, Ernst Otto. *Parteien und Reichstagswahlen in der Rheinpfalz von der Reichsgründung 1871 bis zum Ausbruch des Ersten Weltkrieges 1914.* Speyer, 1982.

Brecht, Arnold. *Federalism and Regionalism in Germany.* New York, 1945.

Brepohl, Wilhelm. "Die Heimat als Beziehungsfeld: Entwurf einer soziologischen Theorie der Heimat." *Soziale Welt* 4 (1952–53): 12–22.

———. "Heimat und Heimatgesinnung als soziologische Begriffe und Wirklichkeiten." In *Das Recht auf die Heimat. Vorträge, Thesen, Kritik,* edited by Kurt Rabl. Munich, 1965.

———. *Industrievolk im Wandel von der agraren zur industriellen Daseinsform dargestellt am Ruhrgebiet.* Tübingen, 1957.

Brunner, Otto, Werner Conze, and Reinhart Koselleck, eds. *Geschichtliche Grundbegriffe. Historische Lexikon zur politisch-sozialen Sprache in Deutschland.* Stuttgart, 1972.

Burmeister, Helmut, and Dieter Kramer, eds. *Volkskultur und Regionalplanung.* Giessen, 1977.

Bytwerk, Randall L. "Rhetorical Aspects of Nazi Holidays." *Journal of Popular Culture* 13 (1979): 239–47.

Cahnmann, W. J., ed. *Ferdinand Tönnies: A New Evaluation.* Leiden, 1973.

Carsten, F. L. *War Against War: British and German Radical Movements in the First World War.* Berkeley and Los Angeles, 1982.

Chickering, Roger. *We Men Who Feel Most German.* Boston, 1984.

Childers, Thomas. *The Nazi Voter: The Social Foundations of Fascism in Germany, 1919–1933.* Chapel Hill, N.C., 1933.

———, ed. *The Formation of the Nazi Constituency 1919–1933.* Totowa, N. J., 1986.

Christiansen, Jörn. *"Die Heimat": Analyse einer regionalen Zeitschrift und ihres Umfeldes.* Neumünster, 1980.

Clapham, J. H. *The Economic Development of France and Germany, 1815–1914.* Cambridge, 1921.

Clasen, Claus-Peter. *The Palatinate in European History, 1559–1660.* Oxford, 1963.

Cohn, Henry J. *The Government of the Rhine Palatinate in the Fifteenth Century.* Oxford, 1965.

Cole, John W., and Eric Wolf. *The Hidden Frontier: Geology and Ethnicity in an Alpine Valley.* New York, 1974.

Conze, Werner. "Der Verein als Lebensform des 19. Jahrhunderts." *Die Innere Mission: Zeitschrift des Werkes Innere Mission und Hilfswerk der Evangelischen Kirche in Deutschland* 50 (1960): 266–84.

Craig, Gordon. *Germany: 1866–1945.* New York, 1978.

Dann, Otto. "Die Anfänge politischer Vereinsbildung in Deutschland." In *Soziale Bewegung und politische Verfassung,* edited by U. Engelhardt, Volker Sellin, and Horst Stuke. Stuttgart, 1976.

Dawson, William Harbutt. *German Life in Town and Country.* New York, 1901.

Debus, Karl-Heinz. "Christen und Juden in der Pfalz zur Zeit des Nationalsozialismus." In *Pfälzische Landeskunde. Beiträge zu Geographie, Biologie, Volkskunde und Geschichte,* vol. 3, edited by Michael Geiger, Günter Preuß, and Karl-Heinz Rothenberger. Landau/Pfalz, 1981.

Demel, Walter. *Der Bayerische Staatsabsolutismus 1806/08–1817. Staats- und gesellschaftspolitische Motivationen und Hintergründe der Reformära in der ersten Phase des Königreichs Bayern.* Munich, 1983.

Deneke, Bernward, and Rainer Kahsnitz, eds. *Das Germanische Nationalmuseum Nürnberg 1852–1977*. Munich, 1978.

Denger, Martin, ed. *125 Jahre Industrie- und Handelskammer für die Pfalz. Beiträge zur pfälzischen Wirtschaftsgeschichte*. Speyer, 1968.

Dennewitz, Bodo. *Föderalismus: Sein Wesen und seine Geschichte*. Hamburg, 1947.

Deuerlein, Ernst. *Bayern und die deutsche Einheit, 1848–1948*. Altötting, 1948.

Deutsch, Karl. *Nationalism and Social Communication*. Cambridge, Mass., 1966.

Dieck, Leonore. "Die literargeschichtliche Stellung der Heimatkunst." Diss., Universität München, 1938.

Doeberl, Michael. *Bayern und die Bismarkische Reichsgründung*. Munich, 1925.

Domröse, Ortwin. *Der NS-Staat in Bayern von der Machtergreifung bis zum Röhm-Putsch*. Munich, 1974.

Donohoe, James. *Hitler's Conservative Opponents in Bavaria, 1930–1945*. Leiden, 1961.

Dotzauer, Winfried. "Kontinuität und Wandel in den Führungsschichten des pfälzischen Raumes." In *Strukturwandel im pfälzischen Raum von Ancien Régime bis zum Vormärz*, edited by Friedrich Ludwig Wagner. Speyer, 1982.

———. "Lesegesellschaft und Loge: 'Trois flammes vivifiantes' in Neustadt." *Blätter für pfälzische Kirchengeschichte und religiöse Volkskunde* 42 (1975): 59–70.

Düwell, Kurt. "Staat und Wissenschaft in der Weimarer Republik: Zur Kulturpolitik des Ministers C. H. Becker." *Historische Zeitschrift*, Beiheft 1 (1971): 31–74.

Eley, Geoff. "Nationalism and Social History." *Social History* 6 (1981): 83–107.

———. "Nationalist Pressure Groups in Germany." In *Nationalist and Racialist Movements in Britain and Germany before 1914*, edited by Paul Kennedy and Antony Nicholls. London, 1981.

———. *Reshaping the German Right: Radical Nationalism and Political Change After Bismarck*. New Haven, 1980.

———. "State Formation, Nationalism, and Political Culture: Some Thoughts on the Unification of Germany." In *Culture, Ideology, and Politics: Essays in Honour of Eric Hobsbawm*, edited by R. Samuel and G. Stedman Jones. London, 1983.

———. "What Produces Fascism—Preindustrial Traditions or a Crisis of a Capitalist State?" *Politics and Society* 12 (1983): 53–82.

———. "The Wilhelmine Right: How It Changed." In *Society and Politics in Wilhelmine Germany*, edited by Richard Evans. London, 1978.

Eliot, George. "The Natural History of German Life: Wilhelm Heinrich Riehl." In *The Essays of George Eliot*, edited by Nathan Sheppard. New York, 1883.

Elkar, Rainer S. *Junges Deutschland in polemischen Zeitalter. Das schleswig-holsteinische Bildungsbürgertum in der ersten Hälfte des 19. Jahrhunderts*. Düsseldorf, 1979.

———, ed. *Europas unruhige Regionen: Geschichtsbewußtsein und europäischer Regionalismus*. Stuttgart, 1981.

Emmerich, Wolfgang. *Germanische Volkstumsideologie*. Tübingen, 1968.

Faber, Karl-Georg. "Neuzeitlicher Wandel der Stadt-Land-Beziehungen in der Pfalz." In *Institut für Landeskunde: 25 Jahre Amtliche Landeskunde*, edited by E. Meynen. Bad Godesberg, 1967.

———. "Die rheinischen Institutionen." In *Hambacher Gespräche 1962*. Wiesbaden, 1964.

———. "Die südlichen Rheinlande." In *Rheinische Geschichte*, edited by Franz Petri and Georg Droege, vol. 2. Düsseldorf, 1976.

———. "Überlegungen zu einer Geschichte der Pfälzischen Landeskirche unter dem Nationalsozialismus." *Blätter für pfälzische Kirchengeschichte und religiöse Volkskunde* 41 (1974): 29–58.

———. "Was ist eine Geschichtslandschaft?" In *Geschichtliche Landeskunde: Festschrift für Ludwig Petry.* Wiesbaden, 1968.

Fehrenbach, Elisabeth. "Die Einführung des französischen Rechts in der Pfalz und in Baden." In *Strukturwandel im pfälzischen Raum von Ancien Régime bis zum Vormärz,* edited by Friedrich Ludwig Wagner. Speyer, 1982.

Fendler, Rudolf. "Die Pfalz in der Weimarer Zeit." In *Pfälzische Landeskunde. Beiträge zu Geographie, Biologie, Volkskunde und Geschichte,* vol. 3, edited by Michael Geiger, Günter Preuß, and Karl-Heinz Rothenberger. Landau/Pfalz, 1981.

Fenske, Hans. "Der Konflikt zwischen Bayern und dem Reich im Herbst 1923 und die pfälzische Sozialdemokratie." *Mitteilungen des Historischen Vereins der Pfalz* 71 (1973): 203–15.

———. *Konservatismus und Rechtsradikalismus in Bayern nach 1918.* Bad Homburg, 1969.

Flory, Günter Reiner. "Die kirchenpolitischen Gruppierung in der Pfalz und ihr Schicksalsjahr 1933." *Blätter für pfälzische Kirchengeschichte und religiöse Volkskunde* 50 (1983): 77–92.

Fraenkel, Ernst. *Military Occupation and the Rule of Law: Occupation Government in the Rhineland, 1918–1924.* London, 1944.

Friedel, Heinz. *Die Machtergreifung 1933 in Kaiserslautern. Ein Beitrag zum Werden des Nationalsozialismus in der Westpfalz.* Otterbach/Kaiserslautern, 1983.

Fussell, Paul. *The Great War and Modern Memory.* New York, 1975.

Gedye, G.E.R. *The Revolver Republic: France's Bid for the Rhine.* London, 1930.

Geisler, Michael. "'Heimat' and the German Left: The Anamnesis of a Trauma," *New German Critique,* no. 36 (Fall 1985): 25–66.

Geramb, Victor von. *Wilhelm Heinrich Riehl. Leben und Wirken 1823–1897.* Salzburg, 1954.

Gerdes, D., ed. *Aufstand der Provinz. Regionalismus in Westeuropa.* Frankfurt, 1980.

Gerhard, Dietrich. "Regionalismus und ständisches Wesen als ein Grundthema europäischer Geschichte." *Historische Zeitschrift* 174 (1952): 307–37.

Gierke, Otto von. *Das deutsche Genossenschaftsrecht.* Vol. 1. Berlin, 1868.

Ginzel, Hannes. "Der Raumgedanke in der Volkskunde unter Berücksichtigung Wilhelm Heinrich Riehls," Diss., Universität Würzburg, 1971.

Glaser, Hermann. *The Cultural Roots of National Socialism (Spiesser-Ideologie).* Translated by Ernest Menze. Austin, Tex., 1978.

———. *Die Kultur der wilhelminischen Zeit. Topographie einer Epoche.* Frankfurt, 1984.

Gockerell, Nina. *Das Bayernbild in der literarischen und "wissenschaftlichen" Wertung durch fünf Jahrhunderte.* Munich, 1974.

Goebbel, Erwin. *Die pfälzische Presse im Abwehrkampf der Pfalz gegen Franzosen und Separatisten, 1918–1924.* Ludwigshafen, 1931.

Gollwitzer, Heinz. "Die politische Landschaft in der deutschen Geschichte des 19./20. Jahrhunderts: Eine Skizze zum deutschen Regionalismus." *Zeitschrift für bayerische Landesgeschichte* 27 (1964): 523–52.

Gordon, Harold J., Jr. *Hitler and the Beer Hall Putsch.* Princeton, 1972.

Greiner, Martin. "Heimatkunst." In *Real-Lexikon der deutschen Literaturgeschichte*, edited by Klaus Kanzog et al., vol 1. Berlin, 1958.

Greverus, Ina-Maria. *Auf der Suche nach Heimat*. Munich, 1979.

———. *Der territoriale Mensch. Ein literatur-antropologisches Versuch zum Heimatphänomen*. Frankfurt, 1972.

Gropper, Wolf von. "Wilhelm Heinrich Riehl: Ein Gedenkblatt zum 50. Todestag." In *Pfalzer Bote: Volks- und Heimatkalender 1948*. Neustadt/Pfalz, 1947.

Gruber, Karl. "W. H. Riehl und August Becker schreiben über die Pfalz." *Kurpfalz* (April 1953).

Haan, Heiner. "Bayern und die Pfalz von 1816 bis 1870: Eine historische Fallunter-suchung zum Problem der Gebietsintegration." Habilitationschrift, University of Regensburg, 1972.

———. "Die Stellung der Pfalz in der bayerischen Verfassung von 1818." In *Land und Reich, Stamm und Nation. Probleme und Perspektiven bayerischer Geschichte*, edited by Andreas Kraus, vol. 2. Munich, 1984.

———, ed. *Hauptstaat–Nebenstaat. Briefe und Akten zum Anschluß der Pfalz an Bayern, 1815/17*. Koblenz, 1977.

Haas, Rudolf. *Die Pfalz am Rhein. 2000 Jahre Landes-, Kultur- und Wirtschaftsgeschichte*. Mannheim, 1968.

Habermas, Jürgen. *Strukturwandel der Öffentlichkeit*. Neuwied, 1962.

———, ed. *Observations on the "Spiritual Situation of the Age."* Translated by Andrew Buchwalter. Cambridge, Mass., 1984.

Haffner, Sebastian. *The Meaning of Hitler*. Translated by Ewald Osers. New York, 1979.

Hamilton, Richard. *Who Voted for Hitler?* Princeton, 1982.

Hansen, Miriam. "Dossier on *Heimat*." *New German Critique*, no. 36 (Fall 1985): 3–24.

Hartmann, Wolfgang. *Der historische Festzug. Seine Entstehung und Entwicklung im 19. und 20. Jahrhundert*. Munich, 1976.

Heberle, Rudolf. *Landbevölkerung und Nationalsozialismus. Eine soziologische Untersuchung der politischen Willensbildung in Schleswig-Holstein 1918 bis 1932*. Stuttgart, 1963.

Heffter, Heinrich. *Die deutsche Selbstverwaltung im 19. Jahrhundert. Geschichte der Ideen und Institutionen*. Stuttgart, 1950.

Hehr, Erich. *Albert Decker und Klingenmünster*. Speyer, 1983.

Heiden, Konrad. *Der Fuehrer: Hitler's Rise to Power*. Translated by Ralph Manheim. Boston, 1944.

Heimpel, Hermann. "Über Organisationsformen historischer Forschung in Deutsch-land." *Historische Zeitschrift* 189 (1959): 139–222.

———. ed, *Geschichtswissenschaft und Vereinswesen im 19. Jahrhundert*. Göttingen, 1972.

Heinz, Karl. *150 Jahre Bezirksverband Pfalz*. Neustadt/Pfalz, 1966.

Heinz, Volker. "Soziologische Aspekte der Denkmalpflege . . . mit besonderer Be-rücksichtigung der Verhältnisse in Rheinland-Pfalz und Hambacher Schloß." Diss., Universität Heidelberg, 1968.

Heupel, Carl, ed. *Die Pfalz auf der Suche nach sich selbst. Über bedeutsame Pfalzbe-schreibungen der letzten 150 Jahre*. Landau/Pfalz, 1983.

Heyen, Franz-Josef, ed. *Geschichte des Landes Rheinland-Pfalz*. Freiburg, 1981.

———, ed. *Rheinland-Pfalz entsteht. Beiträge zu den Anfängen des Landes Rheinland-Pfalz in Koblenz 1945–1951*. Boppard am Rhein, 1984.

Hobsbawm, Eric. "Some Reflections on Nationalism." In *Imagination and Precision in the Social Sciences*, edited by T. J. Nossiter, S. Rokkan, and A. H. Hanson. London, 1972.

———. "What Are Nations?" Lecture, Stanford University, 10 October 1985.

Hobsbawm, Eric, and Terence Ranger, eds. *The Invention of Tradition*. Cambridge, 1983.

Höfig, Willi. *Der deutsche Heimatfilm 1947–1960*. Stuttgart, 1973.

Hornig, Antonie. "Wilhelm Heinrich Riehl und König Max II von Bayern." Diss., Universität München, 1938.

Hroch, Miroslav. *Social Preconditions of National Revival in Europe*. Translated by Ben Fowkes. Cambridge, 1985.

Huch, Gerhard, ed. *Sozialgeschichte der Freizeit: Untersuchungen zum Wandel der Alltagskultur in Deutschland*. Wuppertal, 1980.

Hüttenberger, Peter. *Die Gauleiter. Studie zum Wandel des Machtgefüges in der NSDAP*. Stuttgart, 1969.

Janssen, Karl-Heinz. *Macht und Verblendung. Kriegszielpolitik der deutschen Bundesstaaten, 1914/18*. Göttingen, 1963.

Jasper, Gotthard. *Der Schutz der Republik. Studien zur staatlichen Sicherung dur Demokratie in der Weimarer Republik*. Tübingen, 1963.

Jenny, Erika. "Die Heimatkunstbewegung." Diss., Universität Basel, 1934.

Joeckle, Rudolf. "Die Geschichte der 'Pfälzer Zeitung' unter besonderer Berücksichtigung ihrer politischen Berichterstattung in den Jahren 1849–1870." Diss., Universität München, 1954.

Johann, Ernst. *Deutschland deine Pfälzer. Wo Witz wie Wein wächst*. Hamburg, 1971.

Jung, Horst-W. *Rheinland-Pfalz zwischen Antifaschismus und Antikommunismus. Zur Geschichte des Landesparlaments 1946–1948*. Meisenheim am Glan, 1976.

Kaes, Anton. *From Hitler to Heimat: The Return of History as Film*. Cambridge, Mass., 1989.

Kellogg, Vernon. *Germany in the War and After*. New York, 1919.

Kermann, Joachim. "Die Industrialisierung der Pfalz im 19. Jahrhundert." In *Pfälzische Landeskunde. Beiträge zu Geographie, Biologie, Volkskunde und Geschichte*, vol. 2, edited by Michael Geiger, Günter Preuß, and Karl-Heinz Rothenberger. Landau/Pfalz, 1981.

Kershaw, Ian. *Popular Opinion and Political Dissent in the Third Reich: Bavaria 1933–1945*. Oxford, 1983.

Kettenacker, Lothar. *Nationalsozialistische Volkstumspolitik im Elsaß*. Stuttgart, 1973.

Klein, Walther. *Der Napoleonkult in der Pfalz*. Munich, 1934.

Kleinschmidt, Wolfgang. "Zum Wandel der Interessendominanz bei pfälzischen Vereinen." *Rheinisch-westfälische Zeitschrift für Volkskunde* 25 (1979/80): 198–222.

Kock, Peter Jakob. *Bayerns Weg in die Bundesrepublik*. Stuttgart, 1983.

Kocka, Jürgen. *Facing Total War: German Society 1914–1918*. Translated by Barbara Weinberger. Cambridge, Mass., 1984.

Kollnig, Karl. *Wandlungen im Bevölkerungsbild des pfälzischen Oberrheingebietes*. Heidelberg, 1952

Koshar, Rudy. *Social Life, Local Politics, and Nazism: Marburg, 1880–1935*. Chapel Hill, N.C., 1986.

Kritzer, Peter. *Die bayerische Sozialdemokratie und die bayerische Politik in den Jahren 1918 bis 1923.* Munich, 1969.

Künkele, Theodor, et al., eds. *Festschrift zum 90. Geburtstag von Lorenz Wappes.* Munich, 1950.

Lacqueur, Walter. *German Today: A Personal Report.* Boston, 1985.

Lange, Günther. *Heimat—Realität und Aufgabe. Zur marxistischen Auffassung des Heimatbegriffs.* Berlin, 1973.

Lebovics, Hermann. *Social Conservatism and the Middle Classes in Germany, 1914–1933.* Princeton, 1969.

Leed, Eric J. *No Man's Land: Combat and Identity in World War I.* Cambridge, 1979.

Lenz, Siegfried. *Heimatmuseum.* Hamburg, 1978.

Lidtke, Vernon. *The Alternative Culture.* New York, 1986.

McCort, Dennis. *Perspectives on Music in German Fiction: The Music Fiction of Riehl.* Frankfurt and Bern, 1974.

McDougall, Walter. *France's Rhineland Diplomacy, 1914–1924: The Last Bid for a Balance of Power in Europe.* Princeton, 1978.

Macha, Jürgen, and Thomas Weger. "Mundart im Bewußtsein ihrer Sprecher: Eine explorative Studie am Beispiel des Bonner Raumes." *Rheinische Vierteljahresblätter* 47 (1983): 265–301.

Magin, Theodor. "Die Lage der rheinpfälzischen Landwirtschaft im Jahre 1926, als Ergebnis der Kriegs- und Nachkriegszeit." Diss., Universität Heidelberg, 1928.

Mason, Tim. "Women in Germany, 1925–1940: Family, Welfare, and Work." *History Workshop Journal,* nos. 1 and 2 (1976).

Maurer, Friedrich, and Friedrich Stroh. *Deutsche Wortgeschichte.* Vol. 2. Berlin, 1959.

Mayer, Eugen. *Pfälzische Kirchengeschichte.* Kaiserslautern, 1939.

Mecklenburg, Norbert. *Erzählte Provinz. Regionalismus und Moderne im Roman.* Königstein/Taunus, 1982.

Meinecke, Friedrich. *The German Catastrophe: Reflections and Recollections.* Translated by Sidney B. Fay. Cambridge, Mass., 1950.

Merkl, Peter. *Political Violence Under the Swastika: 581 Early Nazis.* Princeton, 1975.

Meyer, Wolfgang. "Das Vereinswesen der Stadt Nürnberg im 19. Jahrhundert." Diss., Universität Würzburg, 1970.

Mitchell, Allan. *Revolution in Bavaria, 1918–1919: The Eisner Regime and the Soviet Republic.* Princeton, 1965.

Mitscherlich, Alexander, and Gert Kalow, eds. *Hauptworte—Hauptsachen. Zwei Gespräche: Heimat, Nation.* Munich, 1971.

Möckl, Karl. "Föderalismus und Regionalismus im Europa des 19. und 20. Jahrhunderts." In *Von der freien Gemeinde zum föderalistischen Europa.* Berlin, 1983.

———. *Die Prinzregentenzeit: Gesellschaft und Politik während der Ära des Prinzregenten Luitpold in Bayern.* Munich, 1972.

Mosse, George. "Caesarism, Circuses, and Movements." *Journal of Contemporary History* 6 (1971): 167–82.

———. *The Crisis of German Ideology: Intellectual Origins of the Third Reich.* New York, 1964.

———. *The Nationalization of the Masses: Political Symbolism and Mass Movements in Germany from the Napoleonic Wars Through the Third Reich.* New York, 1975.

Nelson, Keith. *Victors Divided: America and the Allies in Germany, 1918–1923*. Berkeley and Los Angeles, 1975.

Nipperdey, Thomas. "Der deutsche Föderalismus zwischen 1815 und 1866 im Rückblick." In *Land und Reich, Stamm und Nation. Probleme und Perspektiven bayerischer Geschichte*, edited by Andreas Kraus. Munich, 1984.

———. *Deutsche Geschichte 1800–1866. Bürgerwelt und starker Staat*. Munich, 1983.

———. *Gesellschaft, Kultur, Theorie. Gesammelte Aufsätze zur neueren Geschichte*. Göttingen, 1976.

———. "Nationalidee und Nationaldenkmal in Deutschland im 19. Jahrhundert." *Historische Zeitschrift* 206 (1968): 529–85.

———. *Die Organisation der deutschen Parteien vor 1918*. Düsseldorf, 1961.

Nösbusch, Johannes, and Karl-Heinz Rothenberger. "Die Pfalz im Zweiten Weltkrieg." In *Pfälzische Landeskunde*, vol. 3. Landau/Pfalz, 1983.

Osmond, Jonathan. "German Peasant Farmers in War and Inflation, 1914–1924: Stability or Stagnation?" In *Die deutsche Inflation—Eine Zwischenbilanz/The German Inflation Reconsidered—A Preliminary Balance*, edited by Gerald Feldman et al. Berlin, 1982.

Oswald, Josef. "Bayerische Heimatbewegung und -forschung zwischen den zwei Weltkriegen." *Historisches Jahrbuch* 72 (1953): 604–14.

Paul, Wolfgang. *Der Heimatkrieg 1939 bis 1945*. Esslingen am Neckar, 1980.

Petry, Ludwig. "Das Rhein-Main Gebiet als active und passive Geschichtslandschaft." In *Landschaft und Geschichte. Festschrift für Franz Petri*, edited by Georg Droege et al. Bonn, 1970.

Peukert, Detlev. *Inside Nazi Germany: Conformity, Opposition, and Racism in Everyday Life*. Translated by Richard Deveson. New Haven, 1987.

Plum, Günther. *Gesellschaftsstruktur und politisches Bewußtsein in einer katholischen Region, 1928–1933*. Stuttgart, 1972.

Plümacher, Walter. "Der große Wanderer durch unsere Heimat: W. H. Riehl und die Pfälzer." *Pfälzische Heimatblätter* 1 (15 October 1952).

Prantl, Helmut. "Zur Geschichte der katholischen Kirche in der Pfalz unter nationalsozialistischer Herrschaft." *Blätter für pfälzische Kirchengeschichte und religiöse Volkskunde* 42 (1975): 79–117.

Pridham, Geoffrey. *Hitler's Rise to Power: The Nazi Movement in Bavaria, 1923–1933*. London, 1973.

Reh, Kurt. "Christian Grünewald. *Beschreibung von Rheinbaiern*." In *Die Pfalz auf der Suche nach sich selbst. Über bedeutsame Pfalzbeschreibungen der letzten 150 Jahre*, edited by Carl Heupel. Landau/Pfalz, 1983.

Reimer, Klaus. *Rheinlandfrage und Rheinlandbewegung, 1918–1933. Ein Beitrag zur Geschichte der regionalistischen Bestrebungen in Deutschland*. Frankfurt, 1979.

Ringer, Fritz K. *The Decline of the German Mandarins: The German Academic Community 1890–1933*. Cambridge, Mass., 1969.

Ritter, Ernst. *Das Deutsche Auslands-Institut in Stuttgart 1917–1945. Ein Beispiel deutscher Volkstumsarbeit zwischen den Weltkriegen*. Wiesbaden, 1976.

Rossbacher, Karlheinz. *Heimatkunstbewegung und Heimatroman: Zu einer Literatur-Soziologie der Jahrhundertwende*. Stuttgart, 1975.

Rothenberger, Karl-Heinz. "Aus der Nationalsozialistischen Zeit der Pfalz." In *Pfälzische Landeskunde*, vol. 3. Landau/Pfalz, 1983.

Sahrmann, Adam. *Pfalz oder Salzburg? Geschichte des territorialen Ausgleiches zwischen Bayern und Österreich von 1813 bis 1819.* Munich, 1921.

Samuel, R. H., and R. Hinton Thomas. *Education and Society in Modern Germany.* London, 1949.

Scharfe, Martin. "Towards a Cultural History: Notes on Contemporary *Volkskunde* in German-speaking Countries." *Social History* 4 (1979): 333–44.

Schelsky, Helmut. "Heimat und Fremde: Die Flüchtlingsfamilie." *Kölner Zeitschrift für Soziologie und Sozialpsychologie* 3 (1950–51): 159–77.

———. *Wandlungen der deutschen Familie in der Gegenwart.* Stuttgart, 1953.

Scherer, Karl, ed. *Pfälzer-Palatines. Beiträge zur pfälzischen Ein- und Auswanderung.* Kaiserslautern, 1981.

Schieder, Theodor. *Das deutsche Kaiserreich von 1871 als Nationalstaat.* Cologne, 1961.

———. *Die kleindeutsche Partei in Bayern in den Kämpfen um die nationale Einheit 1863–1871.* Munich, 1936.

———. "Partikularismus und Nationalbewußtsein im Denken des deutschen Vormärz." In *Staat und Gesellschaft im deutschen Vormärz, 1815–1848,* edited by W. Conze. Stuttgart, 1962.

Schieder, Wolfgang. "Der rheinpfälzische Liberalismus von 1832 als politische Protestbewegung." In *Vom Staat des Ancien Régimes zum modernen Parteienstaat. Festschrift für Theodor Schieder,* edited by Helmut Berding et al. Munich, 1978.

Schineller, Werner. *Die Regierungs-Präsidenten der Pfalz.* Neustadt/Pfalz, 1980.

Schivelbusch, Wolfgang. *The Railway Journey: The Industrialization of Time and Space in the 19th Century.* Berkeley and Los Angeles, 1986.

Schlegel, Wolfgang. "Die Pfalz und die deutsche Einigung von 1870/71." In *Pfälzische Landeskunde. Beiträge zu Geographie, Biologie, Volkskunde und Geschichte,* vol. 3, edited by Michael Geiger, Günter Preuß, and Karl-Heinz Rothenberger. Landau/Pfalz, 1981.

Schmid, Wolfgang Maria. *Anleitung zur Denkmalpflege im Königreich Bayern.* Munich, 1897.

Schmidt, Bernhard. "W. H. Riehl: Seine geistige Entwicklung bis zur Übernahme seiner Professur in München." Diss., Universität Strassburg, 1913.

Schmidt, Walter. "Heimatschutz und Denkmalpflege im deutschen und bayerischen Recht." Diss., Universität Erlangen, 1929.

Schmitt, A. "August Beckers Leben und Werke." *Pfälzisches Museum. Monatsschrift für heimatliche Literatur und Kunst, Geschichte und Volkskunde* 19 (1902).

Schmitt, Hans A. "From Sovereign States to Prussian Provinces: Hanover and Hesse-Nassau, 1866–1871." *Journal of Modern History* 57 (March 1985): 24–56.

Schmitt, Heinz. *Das Vereinsleben der Stadt Weinheim an der Bergstraße.* Weinheim, 1963.

Schmitz, Kurt Thomas. *Opposition in Landtag. Merkmale oppositionellen Verhaltens in Länderparlamenten am Beispiel der SPD in Rheinland-Pfalz.* Hannover, 1971.

Schneider, Erich. "Die Anfänge der sozialistischen Arbeiterbewegung in der Rheinpfalz 1864–1899: Ein Beitrag zur süddeutschen Parteiengeschichte." Diss., Universität Mainz, 1956.

Schoenbaum, David. *Hitler's Social Revolution.* Garden City, N.Y., 1966.

Schönhoven, Klaus. *Die Bayerische Volkspartei, 1924–1932.* Düsseldorf, 1972.

Schreiber, Georg. *Deutsche Weingeschichte.* Cologne, 1980.

Schreiber, Rudolf. "Grundlagen der Entstehung eines Gemeinschaftsbewußtseins der Pfälzer im 19. Jahrhundert." In *Die Raumbeziehungen der Pfalz in Geschichte und*

Gegenwart. Niederschrift über die Verhandlungen der Arbeitsgemeinschaft für westdeutsche Landes- und Volksforschung in Kaiserslautern 6–9.X.1954. Bonn, 1954.

Schuhmann, Günther. "Zur Erinnerung an Dr. h.c. Hermann Schreibmüller." *Jahrbuch des Historischen Vereins für Mittelfranken* 76 (1956): 2–5.

Schulz, Gerhard. *Zwischen Demokratie und Diktatur. Verfassungspolitik und Reichsreform in der Weimarer Republik.* Berlin, 1963.

Schwend, Karl. *Bayern zwischen Monarchie und Diktatur. Beiträge zur bayerischen Frage in der Zeit von 1918 bis 1933.* Munich, 1954.

Seliger, H. W., ed. *Der Begriff "Heimat" in der deutschen Gegenwartsliteratur.* Munich, 1987.

Sheehan, James J. *German Liberalism in the Nineteenth Century.* Chicago, 1978.

———. "What Is German History? Reflections on the Role of the Nation in German History and Historiography." *Journal of Modern History* 53 (1981): 1–23.

Speer, Albert. *Inside the Third Reich: Memoirs.* Translated by Richard Winston and Clara Winston. New York, 1970.

Spindler, Max, ed. *Handbuch der bayerischen Geschichte.* Vol. 4. Munich, 1975.

———. "Die Pfalz in ihrem Verhältnis zum bayerischen Staat in der ersten Hälfte des 19. Jahrhunderts." In *Festgabe für seine königliche Hoheit Kronprinz Rupprecht von Bayern.* Munich, 1953.

———. "Zur Lage der bayerischen Geschichtsvereine." *Zeitschrift für bayerische Landesgeschichte* 15 (1949): 262–68.

Stache, Christa. *Bürgerlicher Liberalismus und katholischer Konservatismus in Bayern, 1867–1871.* Frankfurt, 1981.

Stachura, Peter D., ed. *The Nazi Machtergreifung.* London, 1983.

Stamer, Ludwig. *Kirchengeschichte der Pfalz.* Vol. 4. Speyer, 1964.

Steigner, Georg. *Presse zwischen Rhein und Saar. Angriff und Abwehr der Sonderbündler im Spiegel der Publizistik.* Zweibrücken, 1962.

Stein, Wolfgang Hans. *Untertan-Citoyen-Staatsbürger. Die Auswirkungen der Französischen Revolution auf den rheinisch-pfälzischen Raum.* Koblenz, 1981.

Steinert, Marlis G. *Hitler's War and the Germans: Public Mood and Attitude During the Second World War.* Translated by Thomas E. J. DeWitt. Athens, Ohio, 1977.

Stern, Fritz. *The Politics of Cultural Despair.* Berkeley and Los Angeles, 1961.

Stockhorst, Erich. *Fünftausend Köpfe: Wer war was im Dritten Reich.* Bruchsal/Baden, 1967.

Sturm, Heinz. *Die pfälzischen Eisenbahnen.* Speyer, 1967.

Suval, Stanley. *Electoral Politics in Wilhelmine Germany.* Chapel Hill, N.C., 1985.

Thränhardt, Dietrich. *Wahlen und politische Strukturen in Bayern.* Düsseldorf, 1973.

Tipton, Frank B. *Regional Variations in the Economic Development of Germany During the Nineteenth Century.* Middletown, Conn., 1976.

Trautz, Fritz. *Die Pfalz am Rhein in der deutschen Geschichte.* Neustadt, 1959.

Treinen, Heiner. "Symbolische Ortsbezogenheit: Eine soziologische Untersuchung zum Heimatproblem." *Kölner Zeitschrift für Soziologie und Sozialpsychologie* 17 (1965): 73–97, 254–97.

Turner, Victor. *Dramas, Fields, and Metaphors: Symbolic Action in Human Society.* Ithaca, N.Y., 1974.

Valentin, Veit. *Geschichte der deutschen Revolution von 1848–1849.* Vol. 2. Berlin, 1931.
———. *Das Hambacher Nationalfest.* Berlin, 1932.
Vincent, C. Paul. *The Politics of Hunger: The Allied Blockade of Germany, 1915–1919.* Athens, Ohio, 1985.
Vondung, Klaus. "Zur Lage der Gebildeten in der wilhelminischen Zeit." In *Das wilhelminische Bildungsbürgertum,* edited by Klaus Vondung. Göttingen, 1976.
Wagner, Friedrich Ludwig, ed. *Ministerialität im pfälzischen Raum.* Speyer, 1975.
Wagner, Georg. "Heißt es 'Pfälzerwald' oder 'Pfälzer Wald'? Ursprung, Bedeutung und Schreibung dieses geographischen Sammmelnamens." *Pälzer Feierowend* 5 (1953).
Walker, Mack. *German Home Towns: Community, State, and General Estate, 1648–1871.* Ithaca, N.Y., 1971.
———. *Germany and the Emigration.* Cambridge, Mass., 1964.
Weber, Eugen. *Peasants into Frenchmen: The Modernization of Rural France, 1870–1914.* Stanford, 1976.
Weidenfeld, Werner. *Die Identität der Deutschen.* Munich, 1984.
Weigelt, Klaus, ed. *Heimat und Nation: Zur Geschichte und Identität der Deutschen.* Mainz, 1984.
White, Dan S. *The Splintered Party: National Liberalism in Hessen and the Reich, 1867–1918.* Cambridge, Mass., 1976.
———. "Tönnies Revisited: Community in Imperial Germany." Paper delivered at the Conference of the New York State Association of European Historians, Niagara University, September 1989.
Wiegelmann, Günter, ed. *Kultureller Wandel im 19. Jahrhundert.* Göttingen, 1973.
Wiesemann, Falk. *Die Vorgeschichte der nationalsozialistischen Machtübernahme in Bayern, 1932/1933.* Berlin, 1975.
Williams, Raymond. *Culture and Society: 1780–1950.* New York, 1966.
———. *Keywords.* Rev. ed. Oxford, 1983.
Willis, F. Roy. *The French in Germany 1945–1949.* Stanford, 1962.
Winkler, Heinrich August. "Vom linken zum rechten Nationalismus: Der deutsche Liberalismus in der Krise von 1878/89." *Geschichte und Gesellschaft* 4 (1978): 5–28.
A Woman's Life in the Court of the Sun King: Letters of Liselotte von der Pfalz. Translated by Elborg Forster. Baltimore, 1984.
Wünschel, Hans-Jürgen. "Die Entwicklung der Presse in der Pfalz in den ersten Nachkriegsmonaten 1945." *Publizistik: Vierteljahreshefte für Kommunikationsforschung,* Heft 2 (1976).
———. "Der Separatismus in der Pfalz nach dem Zweiten Weltkrieg." Diss., Universität Heidelberg, 1975.
Wysocki, Josef. "Zwischen zwei Weltkriegen: Wirtschaftliche Probleme der Pfalz 1918–1939." In *125 Jahre Industrie- und Handelskammer für die Pfalz. Beiträge zur pfälzischen Wirtschaftsgeschichte,* edited by Martin Denger. Speyer, 1968.
Zang, Gert, ed. *Provinzialisierung einer Region: Regionale Unterentwicklung und liberale Politik in der Stadt und im Kreis Konstanz im 19. Jahrhundert.* Frankfurt, 1978.
Zentner, Christian, and Fridemann Bedürftig, eds. *Das Große Lexikon des Dritten Reiches.* Munich, 1985.

Zimmermann, Werner Gabriel. *Bayern und das Reich 1918–1923. Der bayerische Föderalismus zwischen Revolution und Reaktion.* Munich, 1953.

Zink, Albert. "Die pfälzische Auswanderung des 19. Jahrhunderts im Lichte des pfälzischen Wirtschaftslebens." *Pfälzer Heimat* 5 (1954): 56–60.

Zorn, W. *Kleine Wirtschafts- und Sozialgeschichte Bayerns, 1806–1933.* Munich/Pasing, 1962.

INDEX

Compositor: Asco Trade Typesetting Ltd.
Text: 10/12 Baskerville
Display: Baskerville
Printer: Thomson-Shore, Inc.
Binder: Thomson-Shore, Inc.